P9-CET-540

Contents

This *Handbook*, along with the National Trust's website at **www.nationaltrust.org.uk**, provides the complete guide for members and visitors to 420 places to visit in England, Wales and Northern Ireland in 2013.

Cover: **Sheffield Park and Garden, East Sussex**
This page: **The Leas, Tyne & Wear**

What's new in
2013

The great outdoors

This year, have an outdoors adventure and discover the many exciting experiences the Trust offers.

From cycling, surfing and climbing to riding, hiking and geocaching, there is an activity to suit every taste.

Why not head off on one of our new walking trails? As well as downloadable and guided walks, we offer many themed walks – ancient trees or butterflies being just two – as well as ones designed with little legs in mind. Visit **www.nationaltrust.org.uk/visit/activities/walking**

If you really want to get close to nature, we have a fabulous range of campsites. Set in beautiful locations, they are ideally placed for exploring the countryside. And, if canvas isn't quite your thing, then try comfy camping. We have yurts, pods and even bothies and bunkhouses – all perfect for escaping from modern life. Visit **www.nationaltrust.org.uk/visit/activities/camping**

Above: **a group of adventurers prepare to get active on a 'Family Safari', organised by the award-winning Stackpole Outdoor Learning Centre in Pembrokeshire, Wales**

In the *Handbook* for the first time

In the South West
Market Hall, Gloucestershire (page 70). Outstanding 400-year-old timber-framed hall.

In London
575 Wandsworth Road, Lambeth (page 166). Modest terraced house with breathtaking hand-carved fretwork interior.

London partners (pages 168 to 170). Groundbreaking new venture between the National Trust and ten small, independent heritage attractions and museums.

In the North West
Allan Bank and Grasmere, Cumbria (page 264). Partially restored house, once home to William Wordsworth and a National Trust founder, Canon Rawnsley.

Ambleside and Windermere, Cumbria (page 265). Towns on England's longest lake, with fells, woodland, lakeshore parks and Roman fort.

Arnside and Silverdale, Cumbria (page 265). Outstanding coastal landscape, with exceptional views across Morecambe Bay to the Lake District. Wildlife-rich limestone grasslands, woodlands, pavements and screes.

Sandscale Haws National Nature Reserve, Cumbria (page 282). High, grass-covered sand dunes, home to very rare flora and fauna.

Wray Castle, Cumbria (page 292). Mock-gothic castle set in beautiful grounds on Lake Windermere's western shore.

In Wales
Stackpole Outdoor Learning Centre, Pembrokeshire (page 348). Award-winning activity centre on the beautiful Stackpole Estate.

In Northern Ireland
Minnowburn, County Down (page 366). Tranquil riverbank trails and woodland, just a few miles from Belfast city centre.

Buy prints of images in this *Handbook* from www.ntprints.com

Top ten places for family fun

Arlington Court, Devon (page 16).
Take a horse-drawn ride in a wagon from the National Trust Carriage Museum, with its working horses and elegant carriages straight out of *Downton Abbey*!

Bodiam Castle, East Sussex (page 105).
Imagine the life of a knight in shining armour as you explore the spiral staircases and battlements of this most romantic of castles.

Osterley Park and House, Middlesex (page 163). The large park is perfect for family cycling, and the house offers dressing-up and lots of hands-on activities for children.

Wimpole Estate, Cambridgeshire (page 201). Discover the rare breeds among the Home Farm animals and sign up for a bat or wildlife walk to learn more about unfamiliar species.

Sudbury Hall and the Museum of Childhood, Derbyshire (page 249). The main challenge may be prising children away from experiencing (and adults from remembering) what it was like to be young in times past.

Quarry Bank Mill and Styal Estate, Cheshire (page 280). Marvel at Europe's most powerful working waterwheel and thrill to the sound and smell of the steam engine driving the mill's clattering machinery.

Cragside, Northumberland (page 302).
Nelly's Labyrinth among the rhododendrons and the adventure playground are a child's delight, and the house is full of ingenious surprises!

Ormesby Hall, Redcar & Cleveland (page 317).
Admire the beautifully kept horses in the Cleveland Mounted Police stables and enjoy the meticulous detail in the model railways.

Chirk Castle, Wrexham (page 333).
Stand guard in armour in this 700-year-old castle, and imagine what it must have been like to be thrown into its dungeon!

Castle Ward, County Down (page 360).
Hire a bike for 21 miles of woodland trails, try the 'mega slide' in the adventure playground and go back in time in the Victorian indoor play centre.

Using your Handbook

Your 2013 *Handbook* covers the period from January to December inclusive.

Entries for individual places to visit are grouped geographically into areas and then ordered alphabetically. Each area opens with a look at its coast and countryside, and then the alphabetical entries.

Maps are grouped together at the back of this *Handbook* (see pages 381 to 394) and show the places mentioned in the text, including the London Partner Museums and Historic House Hotels.

For detailed routes and admission prices visit **www.nationaltrust.org.uk** (or call supporter services on 0844 800 1895).

At the few places where there is a charge for members, this is indicated in the entry as a special note, which appears at the end of the description.

Black type indicates that the place or facility is **open** on these days.

A grey dot indicates that the place or facility is **closed** on these days.

Hinton Ampner		M	T	W	T	F	S	S
House								
11 Feb–4 Nov	11–5	M	T	W	T	F	S	S
5 Nov–28 Nov	11–5	M	T	W	·	·	S	S
1 Dec–9 Dec	10:30–4:30	M	T	W	T	F	S	S
Garden, shop and tea-room								
11 Feb–30 Mar	10–5	M	T	W	T	F	S	S
31 Mar–30 Sep	10–6	M	T	W	T	F	S	S
1 Oct–4 Nov	10–5	M	T	W	T	F	S	S
5 Nov–28 Nov	10–5	M	T	W	·	·	S	S
1 Dec–9 Dec	10–4:30	M	T	W	T	F	S	S

Last entry to house and tea-room 20 minutes before closing. 7 December: open to 7.

Special notes or important information relating to opening arrangements.

Please note the following points about this year's *Handbook*:

Getting there
Each alphabetical entry includes address and contact details, a grid reference to help locate it on the numbered maps at the back and Sat Nav details, where these differ from the address postcode. We recommend consulting the Trust's website for up-to-date details of how to reach each place without using a car, as many places are easily accessible on foot or by bicycle, train, bus or ferry.

Facilities
You can assume that all the places mentioned have car parking onsite or nearby; on the rare occasions where this isn't the case, this is indicated. The same is true for toilets, which are only mentioned when there aren't any or they're more than about 300 yards away.

Measurements
Where mentioned, areas are shown in hectares (1 hectare = 2.47 acres) with acres in brackets. Short distances are in yards (1 yard = 0.91 metre); longer distances are in miles. Heights are shown in metres.

Opening arrangements
These are shown in tables (please see the example above) in date order, with special notes underneath. Occasionally opening arrangements may be changed at short notice and/or facilities withdrawn (reasons include special events or dangerous weather conditions).

Please be aware that, unless otherwise indicated, last admission is 30 minutes before the stated closing time, to allow a minimal time for the visit.

Extra copies of the National Trust *Handbook* are available to buy, while stocks last.

Access

Symbols (see inside front cover) indicate access provisions at each place.

The usual membership fee or admission price applies to the disabled person. Carers or essential companions of a disabled visitor enjoy free entry on request.

An Admit One card can be issued to make this easier, call 01793 817634 or email enquiries@nationaltrust.org.uk

To obtain a copy of the *Access Guide* contact the Supporter Service Centre. Telephone 0844 800 1895, email enquiries@nationaltrust.org.uk or write to PO Box 574, Manvers, Rotherham S63 3FH.

The *Access Guide* is also available on CD, as is *The National Trust Magazine*; contact Sound Talking by calling 01435 862737 or email admin@soundtalking.co.uk

Before you visit

Here are the 'need to know' essentials before your visit – see also page 375 for Q and As.

What you pay
National Trust members enjoy free entry virtually everywhere for an unlimited number of visits – see page 379 for more information for members.

There may be a charge for everyone, including members, on special event days. For accurate up-to-date admission prices visit www.nationaltrust.org.uk or call supporter services on 0844 800 1895.

Prices may vary during off-peak and busy periods – check the website, which is definitive. Admission prices include VAT and may change if VAT rates change. Most prices include a voluntary 10 per cent donation under the Gift Aid on Entry scheme, see page 377.

Children
Under-fives are free, and five to 16 year olds enjoy a reduced admission price (typically 50 per cent). Seventeens and over pay the adult price. Children not accompanied by an adult are admitted at the Trust's discretion. Discounted prices apply to families in most cases and we offer a range of family-friendly facilities (see 'Making the most of your day' in each entry).

Concessions
As a registered charity, which has to raise all its own funds, we cannot afford to offer concessions on admission prices. Free entry is offered on Heritage Open Days and occasionally at other times.

Group visits
All group visits should be booked in advance with your destination. Discounts are usually available for groups of 15 plus. Travel trade information is at **www.nationaltrust.org.uk/groups**, telephone 0844 800 2329 or email traveltrade@nationaltrust.org.uk

Guided tours
Many tours are available at a range of Trust places; check website for details.

Eating and shopping
We offer the best of local and seasonal food and fine gift shops at most places, and in some tourist centres such as York.

Dogs
Assistance dogs always welcome. See 'Dogs' at the end of the 'Making the most of your day' section in each entry for more information and page 372.

Events
Our website has full details of a great range of events. Sometimes places have to close for bigger events and many are chargeable, including members.

Booking in advance
At some smaller places such as Mr Straw's House, advance booking is essential. Timed tickets are sometimes issued to all visitors – including members – on busy days.

Safety
We take your safety very seriously and strive to provide a safe and healthy environment for your visit. But this is a shared responsibility between us and you. As the landscape becomes more rugged and remote, the balance shifts towards you.

Please ensure that you are properly prepared, see our website for practical suggestions and observe onsite notices and instructions.

Getting there

Each entry gives its address, map location and Sat Nav details where necessary. Up-to-date details of how to get there without a car are given on our website and other helpful resources are below.

Further information to help plan your journey

Transport Direct: plan how to get there by public transport or car from any UK location or postcode using **www.transportdirect.info**

Sustrans: for NCN routes and cycling maps visit **www.sustrans.org.uk** or telephone 0117 929 0888.

National Rail Enquiries: for train times visit **www.nationalrail.co.uk** or telephone 08457 48 49 50.

Traveline: for bus routes and times for England, Wales and Scotland visit **www. traveline.info** or telephone 0871 200 2233.

Taxis from railway stations: **www.traintaxi.co.uk**

Public transport in Northern Ireland (train and bus): www.translink.co.uk or telephone 028 9066 6630.

Transport for London: for all travel information visit **www.tfl.gov.uk** or telephone 0843 222 1234.

National Trust online

See **www.nationaltrust.org.uk** for a vast range of information, news and events. You can sign up for regular e-newsletters at **www.nationaltrust.org.uk/email**

All the information relating to places featured in the *Handbook* can be downloaded for free as an app for your iPhone, iPad, Nokia or Android device.

 Find us on Facebook at facebook.com/nationaltrust

 Follow us on Twitter at twitter.com/nationaltrust

South West

Rock pools never lose their power
to fascinate – whatever your age.
South Milton Sands, Devon

Outdoors in the South West

Many of the natural features in the South West would be a highlight on their own; when you take into account the sheer number and scale of these places, it's easy to see why this region is such a popular destination. There are few places where, within the space of a few hours, you can be on the beach, pass through deep wooded valleys and then step out onto a spectacular high moor.

There is nothing quite like the 'Great British Outdoors' to recharge and cheer: Thomas Hardy, Robert Stephen Hawker and D. H. Lawrence all broke into prose and poetry at the sight of places we now care for.
Let us inspire you too.

Right: **power kiting on the cliffs above Lantic Bay, Cornwall**

So much to do, so much to see

Getting a breath of fresh air can be all things to all men, and you can do it all with us. If you want to run the South West Coast Path – you can; if you'd rather find a quiet car park with a great view – we've got loads. No matter what your idea of a great day out might be, we've probably got the key components: butterflies at Brean Down, 'barrels' at Godrevy or blossoms at Trelissick.

If you prefer the active life, we've got brilliant biking, coasteering, kiting and walking. In fact pretty much any outdoor activity you can think of, you can do on Trust land.

We also care for some of the most beautiful and sensitive sites. Our rangers have a huge depth of conservation knowledge and all you need to do is pick their brains if you want to know more about the amazing wildlife which surrounds us.

Some facts and figures

The Trust protects more than 50,000 hectares (123,500 acres) of countryside in the counties of Cornwall, Devon, Dorset, Somerset, Wiltshire and Gloucestershire, including nearly 6,000 hectares (14,826 acres) of woodland and 420 miles of coast (36 per cent of the Devon and Cornwall coast alone).

It's YOUR membership that helps us to protect and manage these precious landscapes for everyone to enjoy in their own way, and with all the accompanying health benefits – mental, spiritual and physical – that can come from something as simple as going for a walk in a beautiful place.

Many of the South West's most iconic and wildlife-rich landscapes are partly owned and protected by the Trust: great swathes of Exmoor and Dartmoor, for example; the Jurassic Coast of Dorset and East Devon and the old mining areas of Cornwall and West Devon (both World Heritage Sites); the famous cliffs of Cheddar Gorge in Somerset; the historic chalk downs of Wiltshire and Dorset; and the upland woods, meadows and commons of the northern Cotswolds; along with nature reserves, heathlands and ancient woodlands scattered across the six counties.

Around the peninsula from Minehead in Somerset to Poole in Dorset runs the 630-mile South West Coast Path – the longest national trail in the country – 290 miles of which runs through Trust land.

Above: **hunting for bugs at Studland, Dorset**

Below: **fly fishing in the East Lyn River at Watersmeet on Exmoor**

How can you find out about all of this open country, and the many things you can do once you get there? Some of the best-known places have their own entries in this *Handbook* – see pages 14 to 92 – but there are hundreds more. To discover them, visit **www.nationaltrust.org.uk/southwest**

Where to start

Car parks are often the first step into Trust countryside. There are simply too many to include them all here, but some key ones are listed on page 13. The website is the best place to find complete coverage of all our coast and countryside, along with details of access, activities and events.

If you're down in the far west of Cornwall, drop in and see us at our new Welcome Centre, between the railway and bus stations in Penzance: it's a great starting point for discovering all you can do in the amazing landscapes of west Cornwall.

Above right:
coasteering at Mullion Cove, Cornwall
Below: **Arlington, North Devon**

Why not try…?

Walking to each compass point
For a truly uplifting walk, the path along the high west-facing coast between Lizard Point and Mullion Cove in Cornwall cannot be beaten. Afterwards just catch the bus back to your starting point. Look out for the Cornish choughs on your way, as they breed on the cliffs here. Choughs are easily identified by their red bills and legs, tumbling flight and 'cheow' calls. You can stop off at dramatic Kynance Cove for some essential refreshment in the café, and enjoy the pioneering eco-loos!

Up on the north coast of Devon, spot seals and wonder at the sheer power of nature as the waves crash against rocks at Baggy Point and Morte Point. Further east, a sheltered wooded walk down lovely Heddon Valley from the Trust's shop and car park leads you to the drama of Heddon's Mouth, where a rushing river meets the sea across a wild pebble beach.

If you like hidden combes and mighty beech hedgebanks, in inland Somerset you can follow ancient trackways to discover the spectacular views and quiet beauty of the Quantock Hills. As a good starting point, why not download the 'Drove Road, Great and Marrow Hills' walk from the downloadable walks pages on our website?

The spectacular Jurassic Coast in Dorset and East Devon is a richly rewarding place to go walking. It's fun to combine a breezy walk with fossil hunting and rock-pooling, fascinating for children of all ages. Golden Cap, with its panoramic clifftop views and miles of wide-open space, is particularly striking.

Further east, in Wiltshire, you can explore a less well-known part of the famed prehistoric Stonehenge landscape on a gentle four-mile circuit that takes in Woodhenge, Durrington Walls and New King Barrows. Again, you will find details of this walk on our website.

In Gloucestershire, discover the glorious limestone grasslands of Minchinhampton and Rodborough Commons. A summer stroll here takes you through wildflower meadows bursting with butterflies, combined with an archaeological landscape and far-reaching views – well worth a good walk and a picnic!

For downloadable walks visit
www.nationaltrust.org.uk/walks

Above right: **cycling in Plymbridge Woods, Devon**
Below: **walkers in the Teign Gorge near Castle Drogo, Devon**

An adventure by bike

The Trust's founders had a clear mission: 'To improve the quality of life for people living in cities, and to satisfy the common human need for fresh air and open space.'

These are the 'radical roots' that we are returning to, with a focus on our outdoor spaces. Yet again we find ourselves facing this disconnect between city living and our need for green space and fresh air; with rising fuel prices and the threat of climate change, there has never been a better time to think about using a bike to visit your favourite places.

Your local ride may well go past or through Trust land, as there are more than 200 Trust places within a mile of the National Cycle Network. Many of these are in the South West, and we are working with Sustrans to ensure that the last mile is as good as it can be.

Significant time and resources are being put into developing and improving the Trust's offer to all cyclists. We're not only focusing on cycling as recreation, but as an important means of transport for getting from A to B, and as a way of visiting several of our amazing sites without having to get in a car. You can take in Barrington and Montacute via a stunning rural cycle ride, for instance.

So go on, give it a go. If you need to build your confidence, come and have a ride along the disused railway line at Plymbridge, near Plymouth; bring the family to enjoy the cycle tracks at Killerton, near Exeter; or visit A la Ronde on the Exe Estuary Trail. On the other hand, if you're a seasoned veteran the bridleways of Dartmoor, Exmoor and the Quantock Hills await you.

A night under canvas

From Golden Cap through Dartmoor to the Lizard, there are many ways you can come camping with us in the South West. At Chyvarloe Campsite, between Loe Pool and Gunwalloe Beach on the Lizard, you are right on the South West Coast Path. There are simple, basic facilities for tents and small campervans, and you can walk to the beaches or saunter to the pub in the evening.

Highertown Farm has a small campsite in a hallowed spot in the churchtown of Lansallos between Fowey and Polperro on Cornwall's south coast. Popular with families and couples, this eco-friendly site is a pleasant three-quarters of a mile walk from a secluded beach, on the unspoilt sweep of Lantivet Bay. You can truly get away from it all here, and spend days walking, rock-pooling or lazing on Lantic Beach.

In Devon, Prattshayes Campsite is popular with families, sun lovers, beachcombers, birdwatchers and walkers. A short stroll away lies Exmouth Beach, well known for its fine sand and sea quality. A small and friendly place to stay – with special facilities for barbecues, food preparation and recycling – the campsite is down a quiet country lane among fields.

Find out about all of our campsites at **www.nationaltrust.org.uk/camping**

Wild swimming

We have so many secret spots and favourite places where you can go for a dip around the South West. Look out for Cornwall's guided 'wild swimming' events down Frenchman's Creek and off Tremayne Quay on the Helford Estuary. Or take yourself off for a splash at Knoll Beach at Studland in Dorset, safe in the knowledge that it will just be you and your fellow crazy dippers in the zoned-off area – with not a lifeguard in sight to blow a whistle at you.

Taking to the water

There can be few things in life better than finding yourself up a creek with a paddle! Well, here's your chance. Why not spend a day with the Trust exploring the creeks and harbour of the Fowey Estuary in Cornwall by canoe? Keep your eyes open for fleeting glimpses of kingfishers and little egrets and, if you're really lucky, dormice. You can hire a kayak from one of our tenant businesses in Studland in Dorset, or at the watersports playground that is South Milton Sands in Devon.

Or get up close and personal with the riverbanks and wildlife of the Helford, guided by a Trust ranger. You could get buzzed by a heron or come nose-to-nose with a seal. We also have full-day expeditions in Canadian canoes up the creeks of the Salcombe-Kingsbridge Estuary in South Devon, where you'll discover the wildlife and archaeology on Trust land, with a well-earned lunch on the shore.

For more details, visit the downloadable canoe and kayak trails on our website.

Catching a wave

We have an ace up our sleeves: some of the best surfing beaches in the UK! Head down to Crantock Beach on the North Cornwall coast, Godrevy Beach further west on St Ives Bay, or Poldhu and Gunwalloe on the Lizard, and you'll be greeted by one of our ambassador surf schools. You'll be kitted out with all the gear and shown all the tricks… it'll be like living in an endless summer.

Above: **camping at Lansallos in Cornwall**
Below: **one of the UK's top surfers, and a National Trust Ambassador, at Sandymouth in North Cornwall**

Coastal and countryside car parks

The Trust provides hundreds of places to park throughout the South West: your thresholds to all that the outdoors has to offer. They range from inconspicuous parking spots leading to remote coves, cliffs, hills and undisturbed wildlife havens, to busy car parks for popular destinations, often manned in season, where you can buy walks guides and find facilities such as cafés and toilets. Listed below are the Ordnance Survey grid references of some of the busy ones (excluding those with main *Handbook* entries) and some of the quieter spots. There are too many to include them all, but you can find complete details on the South West pages of our website.

Right: **building a traditional stone wall on Crickley Hill, Gloucestershire**

Cornwall

Morwenstow	SS	205 154
Duckpool	SS	202 117
Sandymouth	SS	203 100
Northcott Mouth	SS	204 084
Strangles Beach	SX	134 952
Glebe Cliff, Tintagel	SX	050 884
Port Quin	SW	972 805
Lundy Bay	SW	953 796
Pentireglaze	SW	942 799
Park Head	SW	853 707
Crantock	SW	789 607
Treago Mill (Polly Joke)	SW	778 601
Holywell Bay	SW	767 586
St Agnes Beacon	SW	704 503
Wheal Coates	SW	703 500
Chapel Porth	SW	697 495
Reskajeage Downs	SW	623 430
Derrick Cove	SW	620 429
Fishing Cove	SW	599 427
Trencrom	SW	517 359
Carn Galver	SW	422 364
Botallack	SW	366 334
Cape Cornwall	SW	353 318
Cot Valley	SW	358 308
Penrose	SW	639 259
Chyvarloe	SW	653 235
Gunwalloe	SW	660 207
Predannack	SW	669 162
Poltesco	SW	725 157
Bosveal (Durgan)	SW	775 276
St Anthony Head	SW	847 313

Porth Farm		
(Towan Beach)	SW	867 329
Pendower Beach	SW	897 384
Carne Beach	SW	905 384
Nare Head	SW	922 379
Penare (Dodman)	SW	998 404
Lamledra (Vault Beach)	SW	011 411
Coombe Farm	SX	110 512
Pencarrow Head	SX	150 513
Frogmore	SX	157 517
Lansallos	SX	174 518
Hendersick	SX	236 520

Devon

Countisbury	SS	747 497
Combe Park	SS	740 477
Woody Bay	SS	676 486
Trentishoe Down	SS	635 480
Torrs Walk, Ilfracombe	SS	512 476
Hartland:		
Brownsham	SS	285 259
Exmansworthy	SS	271 266
and East Titchberry	SS	244 270
Stoke	SX	558 466
Ringmore	SX	649 457
East Soar	SX	713 376
Snapes Point	SX	739 404
Prawle Point	SX	775 354
Little Dartmouth	SX	874 492
Higher Brownstone	SX	905 510
Coleton Camp	SX	909 513

Scabbacombe	SX	912 523
Man Sands	SX	913 531
Salcombe Hill	SY	148 889
Branscombe	SY	197 887
Plymbridge Woods	SX	524 585
Cadover Bridge	SX	533 636
Shaugh Prior	SX	554 645

Dorset

Cogden, West Dorset	SY	503 883
Stonebarrow Hill	SY	383 933
Langdon Hill	SY	413 931
Burton Bradstock	SY	491 888
Ringstead Bay	SY	760 822
Spyway	SY	996 785
Studland: Shell Bay	SZ	035 864
Knoll Beach	SZ	035 836
Middle Beach	SZ	037 828
South Beach	SZ	038 825

Gloucestershire

Haresfield: Cripplegate	SO	832 086
and Ash Lane	SO	824 066
Rodborough Common:		
Hill Fort	SO	852 035
Minchinhampton:		
Reservoir	SO	855 013
Mayhill	SO	691 221

Somerset

Sand Point	ST	330 660

A la Ronde

Summer Lane, Exmouth, Devon EX8 5BD

Map G7 🏠♿🍵

This unique 16-sided house, described by Lucinda Lambton as having 'a magical strangeness that one might dream of only as a child', was built for two spinster cousins, Jane and Mary Parminter, on their return from a European grand tour in the late 18th century. It contains many objects and mementoes of their travels, and the extraordinary interior decoration includes a feather frieze from many species of birds, including game birds, fowl, jays and parrots, laboriously stuck down with isinglass. The fragile shell-encrusted gallery, said to contain nearly 25,000 shells, is viewed via a 360-degree touchscreen virtual tour. **Note**: small, fragile rooms. Allow at least an hour to visit. Non-flash photography welcome.

Eating and shopping: shop selling gifts, local produce, plants, drinks and ice-cream. Award-winning licensed tea-room with open-air seating and sea views (Trust-approved concession) – morning coffee, homemade lunches and cream teas. Orchard picnic area. Second-hand book sales.

Diamond-shaped window at A la Ronde

Making the most of your day: events, new fortnightly art exhibition, rural skills, nature walks, school holiday craft workshops. Self-guided themed tours, house family trail. Views over Exe Estuary. **Dogs**: welcome on leads throughout the garden and grounds. Complimentary dog biscuits in shop.

Access for all: 🅿️♿🚻♿♿📷🚻♿ :: Ⓐ
House ♿♿ Grounds ♿➡️

Getting here: 192:SY004834. 2 miles north of Exmouth. **Foot**: East Devon Way alongside. South West Coast Path 2 miles. **Cycle**: £1 shop or tea-room voucher for visitors arriving by green transport. **Bus**: Exeter to Exmouth and Budleigh Salterton, stops within ½ mile. **Train**: Lympstone village 1¼ miles; Exmouth 2 miles. **Road**: off A376. **Parking**: free. Caravans and trailers telephone in advance.

Finding out more: 01395 265514 (office). 01395 255918 (shop). 01395 278552 (tea-room) or alaronde@nationaltrust.org.uk

A la Ronde		M	T	W	T	F	S	S
5 Jan–3 Feb*	12–4						S	S
9 Feb–24 Feb	11–5	M	T	W	T	F	S	S
2 Mar–3 Nov	11–5	M	T	W	T	F	S	S
9 Nov–15 Dec*	12–4						S	S

Grounds and shop open 30 minutes earlier and close 30 minutes later. Tea-room opens 30 minutes earlier; last orders at 5 and closes as shop and grounds. *5 January to 3 February and 9 November to 15 December house shown 'put to bed' by guided tours only (last tour 3:15). Main season: last admission to house 4.

A la Ronde, Devon: quirky shell chimneypiece

Antony

Torpoint, Cornwall PL11 2QA

Map (1) E8

Still the home of the Carew Pole family after hundreds of years, this beautiful early 18th-century house contains fine collections of paintings, furniture and textiles. The grounds, landscaped by Repton, sweep down towards the Lynher Estuary and include a formal garden with topiary, a knot garden, modern sculptures and the National Collection of Daylilies. The Woodland Garden has outstanding rhododendrons, azaleas, magnolias and camellias. The magic of Antony was recognised by Walt Disney when it was chosen as the set for the film *Alice in Wonderland*, directed by Tim Burton. **Note**: members admitted free to Woodland Garden (not National Trust) only when house is open.

Eating and shopping: self-service tea-room offering light lunch or afternoon tea. Gift shop with souvenirs, plants and local produce.

Making the most of your day: garden and family events. Modern sculpture throughout gardens. Croquet on lawn. Quizzes and trails.

Dogs: assistance dogs only.

Access for all:
House **Grounds**

Getting here: 201:SX418564. 2 miles north-west of Torpoint. **Cycle**: NCN27, 2 miles. **Ferry**: 6 miles west of Plymouth via Torpoint car ferry. **Bus**: from Plymouth, alight Trevithick Avenue ¾ mile. **Train**: Plymouth 6 miles. **Road**: north of A374, 16 miles south-east of Liskeard. **Parking**: free, 250 yards.

Finding out more: 01752 812191 or antony@nationaltrust.org.uk

Antony		M	T	W	T	F	S	S
House								
2 Apr–30 May	1–5	·	**T**	**W**	**T**	·	·	·
2 Jun–29 Aug	1–5	·	**T**	**W**	**T**	·	·	**S**
3 Sep–31 Oct	1–5	·	**T**	**W**	**T**	·	·	·
Garden, shop and tea-room								
2 Apr–30 May	12–5	·	**T**	**W**	**T**	·	·	·
2 Jun–29 Aug	12–5	·	**T**	**W**	**T**	·	·	**S**
3 Sep–31 Oct	12–5	·	**T**	**W**	**T**	·	·	·
Woodland Garden (not National Trust)								
2 Mar–31 Oct	11–5:30	·	**T**	**W**	**T**	·	**S**	**S**

Also open Good Friday, Easter Sunday, Sunday 5 and Sunday 26 May and Bank Holiday Mondays. Timed ticket entry to house. Bath Pond House interior can only be seen by written application to the Property Manager, on days house is open.

Exploring the magical gardens at Antony in Cornwall

Arlington Court and the National Trust Carriage Museum

Arlington, near Barnstaple, Devon EX31 4LP

Map (1) F5 🏛 ✝ 🐴 ✿ 🎪 🛏 🔔

An unexpected jewel, Arlington incorporates history, beauty and nature in a remarkable setting. From the elegantly engineered carriages in the museum, where you can try our carriage comfort test, to the Aladdin's Cave of collections in the house, including treasures from around the world spanning centuries, there's plenty to keep everyone busy in all weathers. Our kitchen garden, where we grow produce for our tea-room, is a particular delight, and there are numerous walks to be had on the wider estate, where there is wildlife in abundance – you can even spy on our bat colony with the bat-cam.

Eating and shopping: chutneys and preserves made from Arlington-grown produce. Tea-room serving estate produce. Arlington veg boxes (August to September).

Making the most of your day: daily family activities (main school holidays). Handle historic objects in our Explorer Room. Bird hide for viewing wildlife, plus heronry. Costumed interpretation second Saturday of month. Holiday cottages. **Dogs**: welcome on leads in garden, Carriage Museum and wider estate.

A day out for all the family at Arlington Court

Access for all: 🅿 ♿ ♿ 🚾 🚻 ♿ 📷 🎧 VT ♿
👓 Ⓐ House 🏛♿ 🏛♿ ♿ Museum 🏛 ♿ ♿
Grounds ➡ ♿ ♿

Getting here: 180:SS611405. 8 miles north of Barnstaple. **Bus**: infrequent service Barnstaple to Lynton. **Train**: Barnstaple, 8 miles. **Road**: A39 from Barnstaple; from east – A399 from South Molton. **Sat Nav**: from South Molton, don't turn left into unmarked lane (deliveries' entrance only). **Parking**: free, 150 yards.

Finding out more: 01271 850296 or arlingtoncourt@nationaltrust.org.uk

Arlington Court		M	T	W	T	F	S	S
House, Carriage Museum and bat-cam								
16 Feb–24 Feb	11–4	M	T	W	T	F	S	S
16 Mar–3 Nov	11–5	M	T	W	T	F	S	S
9 Nov–22 Dec	11–4	·	·	·	·	·	S	S
Shop, tea-room and garden								
1 Jan–6 Jan	11–3	·	T	W	T	F	S	S
16 Feb–24 Feb	11–4	M	T	W	T	F	S	S
16 Mar–3 Nov	10:30–5	M	T	W	T	F	S	S
9 Nov–22 Dec	11–4	·	·	·	·	·	S	S
23 Dec–31 Dec*	11–4	M	T	·	T	F	S	S

Limited access to house and Carriage Museum in February, November and December. *Property closed 24 and 25 December. Grounds open dawn till dusk, all year.

Arlington Court, Devon: making an equine friend

Ashleworth Tithe Barn

Ashleworth, Gloucestershire GL19 4JA

Map ① J2 🏠

Barn, with immense stone-tiled roof, picturesquely situated close to the River Severn. **Note**: no toilet.

Finding out more: 01452 814213 or www.nationaltrust.org.uk

Avebury

near Marlborough, Wiltshire

Map ① K4 🏠✚🍴🏛✳🦪🛏

In the 1930s the pretty village of Avebury, partially encompassed by the stone circle of this World Heritage Site, witnessed archaeologist Alexander Keiller's excavations. In re-erecting many of the stones which make up the largest stone circle in the world, Keiller uncovered the true wonder of one of Europe's most important megalithic monuments. His fascinating finds are on display in the Alexander Keiller Museum, housed in the 17th-century threshing barn and stables, where interactive displays and children's activities bring the landscape to life. In 2011 the manor house was transformed by a unique collaboration between the National Trust and BBC. **Note**: English Heritage holds guardianship of Avebury Stone Circle, owned and managed by the National Trust.

Eating and shopping: Circle Café and Manor tea-room. Shop selling local gifts, including Avebury honey, and books.

Making the most of your day: museum and world-renowned archaeology experts. Events, from archaeology workshops to wildlife walks. Newly transformed Victorian kitchen garden.

Avebury, Wiltshire: the Billiard Room in the manor

Dogs: assistance dogs only in house, garden and café. Elsewhere dogs on leads welcome.

Access for all: 🅿♿♿🚻♿♿📷💻♿♿🅰
Buildings 🏢🅿 Grounds 🅿🏢➡

Getting here: 173:SU102699. 6 miles west of Marlborough. **Foot**: Ridgeway National Trail. **Cycle**: NCN4 and 45. **Bus**: frequent buses pass nearby. **Train**: Pewsey; Swindon.

Road: on A4361. **Sat Nav**: use SN8 1RD.
Parking: pay and display. National Trust
and English Heritage members free.
Overnight parking prohibited. Please
respect the community and do not park
on the village streets.

Finding out more: 01672 539250 or
avebury@nationaltrust.org.uk.
National Trust Estate Office, High Street,
Avebury, Wiltshire SN8 1RF

Avebury		M	T	W	T	F	S	S
Stone circle								
Open all year	Dawn–dusk	M	T	W	T	F	S	S
Manor house and garden*								
9 Feb–22 Mar	11–4	M	T	·	T	F	S	S
23 Mar–18 Jun	11–5	M	T	·	T	F	S	S
23 Jun–31 Oct	11–5	M	T	·	T	F	S	S
1 Nov–22 Dec	11–4	M	T	·	T	F	S	S
Museum*								
1 Jan–22 Mar	10–4	M	T	W	T	F	S	S
23 Mar–31 Oct	10–6	M	T	W	T	F	S	S
1 Nov–31 Dec	10–4	M	T	W	T	F	S	S
Shop and Circle Café*								
1 Jan–22 Mar	10–4	M	T	W	T	F	S	S
23 Mar–31 Oct	10–5:30	M	T	W	T	F	S	S
1 Nov–31 Dec	10–4	M	T	W	T	F	S	S

Timed entry tickets to manor available on arrival and
online. During winter only part of the garden may open.
Manor closed 20 to 22 June. *Close dusk if earlier.
All except stone circle closed 24 to 26 December.
Barn Gallery may close in cold weather.

Ancient stones in the stone circle at Avebury, Wiltshire

Baggy Point

Moor Lane, Croyde, Devon EX33 1PA

Map ① E5

Baggy Point is the impressive headland at Croyde,
one of the best surfing beaches in North Devon.
With stunning coastal views, great walks along
the South West Coast Path and opportunities
to climb, surf and coasteer, it's a must-do
destination for anyone visiting North Devon.
Note: toilets (not National Trust) on main beach
slipway, 500 yards from Trust car park.

Eating and shopping: Sandleigh Tea-room and
Garden (tenant-run) serving local and seasonal
produce grown onsite in their market garden
(at end of car park, close to beach slipway).

Making the most of your day: free family
activity pack (available to borrow) on
local wildlife and history. Walks leaflet.
Dogs: welcome on leads.

Access for all:

Getting here: SS433397. Outside Croyde
village. **Foot**: on Moor Lane. Walk through
Croyde village, and follow brown signs to
Baggy Point car park. **Bus**: regular service from
Barnstaple to Croyde, then follow brown signs.
Train: Barnstaple. **Road**: A361 to Braunton,
take Saunton Road B3231 to Croyde, then
follow brown signs. **Parking**: free (manned
from late March to October).

Finding out more: 01271 870555 or
baggypoint@nationaltrust.org.uk

Baggy Point		M	T	W	T	F	S	S
Open every day all year	Dawn–dusk							

Car park is usually manned between March and November.

We welcome dogs assisting visitors with disabilities

Barrington Court

Barrington, near Ilminster, Somerset TA19 0NQ

Map ① l6

This beautiful manor house, owned by the Trust since 1907, is a hidden gem. Set amid apple orchards and surrounded by rolling parkland, it was restored in the 1920s by Colonel Lyle, whose family firm became Tate & Lyle. His idea of a medieval estate remains: a testament to his vision and the skills of craftsmen from a bygone age. The delightful flower garden, designed in consultation with Gertrude Jekyll, adjoins the kitchen garden, producing fruit and vegetables for the restaurant.

Eating and shopping: Orchard Café and Strode House Restaurant. Shop selling souvenirs and award-winning Barrington cider and apple juice. Plant sales and second-hand books. Craft workshops.

Walking among apple trees at Barrington Court, Somerset, below, and the west and south front, above

Making the most of your day: daily activities and annual events, including Jazz on the Lawn and Chutfest. Family trails and downloadable walks. New outdoors guide (available from shop). Restored Chestnut Avenue. **Dogs**: assistance dogs only in garden. Shaded parking available.

Access for all: 🅿️ 🄳 ♿ ♿ 🄻 🔲 🔲 🄹 🄰
Building 🄻   Grounds 🄰 ➡️ 🄰 🄱

Getting here: 193:ST396182. In Barrington village, 5 miles north-east of Ilminster.
Foot: numerous public footpaths.
Cycle: NCN30. Cycle hire in Langport (01458 250350). **Bus**: service from Ilminster to Martock, with connections from Taunton.
Train: Crewkerne, 7 miles. **Road**: on B3168. Signposted from A358 (Ilminster to Taunton) or off A303 (London to Exeter).
Sat Nav: incorrectly directs visitors to rear entrance – please follow brown tourist signs. **Parking**: free.

Finding out more: 01460 241938 or barringtoncourt@nationaltrust.org.uk

Barrington Court		M	T	W	T	F	S	S
House								
5 Jan–24 Feb	12–3	·	·	·	·	·	S	S
1 Mar–3 Nov	11–5	M	T	W	T	F	S	S
9 Nov–29 Dec	12–3	·	·	·	·	·	S	S
Garden, parkland, café, restaurant and shop								
1 Mar–3 Nov	10–5	M	T	W	T	F	S	S
Garden, parkland, restaurant and shop								
5 Jan–24 Feb	11–4	·	·	·	·	·	S	S
9 Nov–29 Dec	11–4	·	·	·	·	·	S	S

Whole place closed 24 and 25 December.

Bath Assembly Rooms

Bennett Street, Bath, Somerset BA1 2QH

Map (1) J4

The Assembly Rooms were at the heart of fashionable Georgian society. When completed in 1771, they were described as 'the most noble and elegant of any in the kingdom'. The Fashion Museum (Bath and North East Somerset Council) is on the lower ground floor. **Note**: limited visitor access during functions. Entry charge for The Fashion Museum (including members).

Eating and shopping: café, gift shop and renowned fashion bookshop.

Making the most of your day: holiday activities for families. New museum displays and exhibitions. Concerts and music festivals.

Access for all: [icons]
Building [icons] Grounds [icons]

Getting here: 156:ST749653. In centre of Bath. **Cycle**: NCN4, ¼ mile. **Bus**: from Bath Spa ≊ and surrounding areas. **Train**: Bath Spa ¾ mile. **Road**: north of Milsom Street, east of the Circus. **Parking**: pay and display car parks (not National Trust), nearest Charlotte Street. Virtually no onstreet parking, park and ride recommended.

Finding out more: 01225 477789 or bathassemblyrooms@nationaltrust.org.uk

Bath Assembly Rooms		M	T	W	T	F	S	S
1 Jan–28 Feb	10:30–5	M	T	W	T	F	S	S
1 Mar–31 Oct	10:30–6	M	T	W	T	F	S	S
1 Nov–31 Dec	10:30–5	M	T	W	T	F	S	S

Last admission one hour before closing. Closed when in use for booked functions and on 25 and 26 December. Access to all rooms guaranteed in August until 4:30, at other times some rooms may be closed. Visitors should telephone in advance.

The elegant ball room at Bath Assembly Rooms, Somerset

Blaise Hamlet

Henbury, Bristol BS10 7QY

Map (1) I3

Delightful hamlet of nine picturesque cottages, designed by John Nash in 1809 for Blaise Estate pensioners. **Note**: access to green only; cottages not open. No toilet.

Finding out more: 01275 461900 or www.nationaltrust.org.uk

Bolberry Down

near Salcombe, Devon

Map (1) F9   [icons]

Dramatic clifftop with far-reaching views. Bolberry Down has levelled circular trails through a breathtaking coastal landscape. **Note**: no toilet.

Finding out more: 01752 346585 or www.nationaltrust.org.uk

The unusual harbour at Boscastle in Cornwall lies at the end of a sheltered natural inlet

Boscastle

Cornwall PL35 0HD

Map ① D7

Much of the land in and around Boscastle is owned by the National Trust. This includes the cliffs of Penally Point and Willapark, which guard the sinuous harbour entrance, Forrabury Stitches, high above the village and divided into ancient 'stitchmeal' cultivation plots, as well as the lovely Valency Valley. **Note:** toilet by main car park (not National Trust).

Eating and shopping: café, shop and visitor centre.

Making the most of your day: children's quiz/ trail. Family events in school holidays. Holiday cottages. **Dogs:** welcome in café courtyard.

Access for all: Grounds

Getting here: 190:SX097914. 5 miles north of Camelford, 3 miles north-east of Tintagel. **Bus:** services from Bude and Wadebridge (connections at Wadebridge for Bodmin Parkway). **Train:** Bodmin Parkway. **Road:** on B3263. **Parking:** pay and display, 100 yards (not National Trust).

Finding out more: 01840 250010 or boscastle@nationaltrust.org.uk

Boscastle	M	T	W	T	F	S	S
Open all year	M	T	W	T	F	S	S
Shop, café and visitor centre							
1 Jan–1 Mar	10:30–4	M	T	W	T	F	S	S
2 Mar–3 Nov	10–5	M	T	W	T	F	S	S
4 Nov–24 Dec	10:30–4	M	T	W	T	F	S	S
27 Dec–31 Dec	10:30–4	M	T			F	S	S

Shop and visitor centre sometimes open later than 5 in high season. Last café orders 30 minutes before closing.

Bradley

Newton Abbot, Devon TQ12 1LX

Map ① G8

Unspoilt medieval manor house, still a relaxed family home, set among riverside meadows and woodland. **Note:** no toilet. Parking from 10:30 on open days.

Finding out more: 01803 661907 or www.nationaltrust.org.uk

Branscombe: the Old Bakery, Manor Mill and Forge

Branscombe, Seaton, Devon EX12 3DB

Map ① H7

Nestling in a valley that reaches down to the sea, these thatched buildings date back more than 200 years. As well as the Old Bakery, there is a working forge, complete with blacksmith, and a restored water-powered mill. Miles of paths run through the woodlands and down to the beach. **Note**: nearest toilets at bakery and village hall.

Eating and shopping: quality ironwork on sale. Old Bakery serving homemade soups, ploughman's, sandwiches and cream teas.

Making the most of your day: extensive network of paths. **Dogs**: on leads in garden, Old Bakery information room and wider countryside.

Access for all: 🚻 **Building** 🖐️🦽
Mill 🖐️🧍 **Grounds** 🦽

Getting here: 192:SY198887. 8 miles from Honiton. **Foot**: South West Coast Path within ¾ mile. **Cycle**: public bridleway from Great Seaside to Beer. **Bus**: services from Sidmouth and Seaton. **Train**: Honiton, 8 miles. **Road**: off A3052, signposted Branscombe. **Parking**: small car park next to Old Forge (donations welcome); car park next to village hall (not National Trust: donation).

Finding out more: 01752 346585 (South and East Devon Countryside Office). 01297 680333/680481 (Old Bakery Tea-room/ Old Forge) or branscombe@nationaltrust.org.uk. South and East Devon Countryside Office, The Stables, Saltram House, Plymouth, Devon PL7 1UH •

Branscombe		M	T	W	T	F	S	S
Open all year		M	T	W	T	F	S	S
Old Bakery								
27 Mar–28 Jul	10:30–5	·	·	W	T	F	S	S
29 Jul–1 Sep	10:30–5	M	T	W	T	F	S	S
4 Sep–3 Nov	10:30–5	·	·	W	T	F	S	S
Manor Mill								
24 Mar–30 Jun	2–5	·	·	·	·	·	·	S
3 Jul–28 Aug	2–5	·	·	W	·	·	·	S
1 Sep–27 Oct	2–5	·	·	·	·	·	·	S
Old Forge*								
Open all year	10–5	M	T	W	T	F	S	S

*Old Forge: telephone 01297 680481 to confirm opening times.

Blacksmith at work in the Old Forge at Branscombe, Devon

Brean Down

Brean, North Somerset

Map ① H4

One of the most striking landmarks of the Somerset coastline, Brean Down projects dramatically into the Bristol Channel and offers magnificent views for miles around. It is rich in wildlife and history, with a fascinating ruined fort. **Note**: steep climbs and cliffs. Tide comes in quickly.

Eating and shopping: Cove Café serving cooked breakfasts and burger and chips. Shop selling ice-cream and beach games.

Making the most of your day: events. Circular walks available from website. Kite-flying.

Dogs: welcome on leads.

Access for all: 🚾♿ **Building** 🏠♿

Getting here: 182:ST290590. Between Weston-super-Mare and Burnham-on-Sea.
Bus: Highbridge to Weston-super-Mare, alight Brean, 1¾ miles. **Train**: Highbridge 8½ miles.
Road: 8 miles from M5 exit 22. **Sat Nav**: use TA8 2RS. **Parking**: 200 yards, at Cove Café at the bottom of Brean Down.

Finding out more: 01643 862452 or breandown@nationaltrust.org.uk

Brean Down		M	T	W	T	F	S	S
Café and shop								
1 Jan–6 Jan	10–4		T	W	T	F	S	S
9 Feb–17 Feb	10–4	M	T	W	T	F	S	S
9 Mar–3 Nov	10–5	M	T	W	T	F	S	S
21 Dec–31 Dec	10–4	M	T	W	T	F	S	S
Countryside								
Open all year		M	T	W	T	F	S	S

Café and shop opening hours vary according to weather. Closed 24 and 25 December.

Making the most of the beach on Brownsea Island, which is wonderfully located in Poole Harbour, Dorset

Brownsea Island

Poole Harbour, Poole, Dorset BH13 7EE

Map ① K7

Brownsea Island, an SSSI, is dramatically located in Poole Harbour, with spectacular views across to the Purbeck Hills. Thriving natural habitats – including woodland, heathland and a lagoon – create a haven for wildlife. There are rare red squirrels and a wide variety of birds to spot, and the island also has a rich history, for as well as boasting daffodil farming and pottery works, it was the birthplace of the Scouting and Guiding movement. **Note**: no public access to castle. Small entry fee to Dorset Wildlife Trust Nature Reserve (including members).

Eating and shopping: coffee bar and Villano Café. Gift and souvenir shop, also selling Brownsea Island outdoors range and old-fashioned sweets and ice-cream.

Deer grazing on Brownsea Island, Dorset

Making the most of your day: seasonal family activities and trails. Tracker Packs. Events. Wildlife walks and talks. Open-air theatre. Outdoor and Visitor centres. Introductory walks and guided electric buggy tours for less mobile visitors (bookable). **Dogs**: assistance dogs only.

Access for all: 🚻 ♿ 👁 📋 🅿

Building ♿ Grounds ♿ ➡

Getting here: 195:SZ032878. In Poole Harbour via ferry. **Foot**: close to South West Coast Path at Shell Bay. **Ferry**: half-hourly boat service from 10 (not National Trust). Poole Quay (01202 631828/01929 462383), Sandbanks (01929 462383). Wheelchair users: contact ferry operators. **Bus**: for Sandbanks: services from Bournemouth, Swanage and Poole. For Poole Quay: alight Poole Bridge. **Train**: Poole ½ mile to Poole Quay; Branksome or Parkstone 3½ miles to Sandbanks.

Finding out more: 01202 707744 or brownseaisland@nationaltrust.org.uk

Brownsea Island		M	T	W	T	F	S	S
Boats from Sandbanks Jetty only								
9 Feb–10 Mar	10–4	·	·	·	·	·	S	S
Full boat service from Poole Quay and Sandbanks								
16 Mar–3 Nov	10–5	M	T	W	T	F	S	S
Limited opening for booked groups only								
3 Nov–22 Dec	10–4	M	T	W	T	F	S	S

Gift shop and Villano Café open until 5 when island is open.

Buckland Abbey, Garden and Estate

Yelverton, Devon PL20 6EY

Map ① E8 🏛 ✝ 🌸 ⚓ 🛏 🍴

Hundreds of years ago, Cistercian monks chose this tranquil valley as the perfect spot in which to worship, farm their estate and trade. The abbey, later converted into a house by Sir Richard Grenville and then lived in by Sir Francis Drake, is now part-museum and part-home. Outdoors, our new gem, the Cider House Garden, includes a walled kitchen garden and wild garden, and was opened just last year. There are community growing areas, orchards and the impressive Great Barn, as well as woodland walks with far-reaching views and late spring bluebells. **Note**: abbey interior presented in association with Plymouth City Museum.

Enjoying the garden at Buckland Abbey, Devon

Eating and shopping: refurbished restaurant (available to hire) serving freshly cooked local produce. Picnics welcome in grounds. Shop selling gifts and plants. Ox Yard Bookshop and Ox Yard Gallery. New holiday cottage.

Making the most of your day: new Willow Patch family area. Events. Estate walks and letterbox trail. Family pack and information sheets available. **Dogs**: welcome on leads on designated walk only (conservation and wildlife reasons).

Access for all: ⓟⓖ♨♿ⓦⓒ♿ⓗⓖⓒ🅿🖼♿🔌☷🅰
Abbey ♿♨ⓖ Reception ♨ⓖ
Grounds ♿♨ⓖ➡ⓖ

Getting here: 201:SX487667. 6 miles south of Tavistock, 11 miles north of Plymouth.
Cycle: Drake's Trail, NCN27, 2 miles. **Bus**: from Yelverton (with connections from Plymouth ♒), Monday to Saturday. **Train**: Plymouth 11 miles.

Buckland Abbey, including the monastic Great Barn on the left

Road: turn off A386, ¼ mile south of Yelverton. **Parking**: free, 150 yards.

Finding out more: 01822 853607 or bucklandabbey@nationaltrust.org.uk

Buckland Abbey		M	T	W	T	F	S	S
Abbey								
16 Feb–8 Mar	12–4	M	T	W	T	F	S	S
9 Mar–3 Nov	11:30–4:30	M	T	W	T	F	S	S
8 Nov–1 Dec	12–4	·	·	·	·	F	S	S
6 Dec–22 Dec	12–4	M	T	W	T	F	S	S
Estate, garden, restaurant, shop and gallery								
16 Feb–3 Nov	10:30–5:30	M	T	W	T	F	S	S
8 Nov–1 Dec	10:30–5:30	·	·	·	·	F	S	S
6 Dec–22 Dec	10:30–5:30	M	T	W	T	F	S	S

Ox Yard Gallery opening times may vary, telephone to check. Entire place closed from 23 December to mid-February.

Road: just off B3276 from Newquay to Padstow.
Parking: seasonal charge for non-members.

Finding out more: 01637 860563 or carnewas@nationaltrust.org.uk. Bedruthan, St Eval, Wadebridge, Cornwall PL27 7UW

Carnewas and Bedruthan Steps		M	T	W	T	F	S	S
Clifftop walks								
Open all year		M	T	W	T	F	S	S
Shop								
16 Feb–24 Feb	11–4	M	T	W	T	F	S	S
2 Mar–3 Mar	11–4	·	·	·	·	·	S	S
9 Mar–24 Mar	11–4	M	T	W	T	F	S	S
25 Mar–3 Nov	10:30–5	M	T	W	T	F	S	S
Café								
16 Feb–24 Mar	11–4	M	T	W	T	F	S	S
25 Mar–3 Nov	10:30–5	M	T	W	T	F	S	S
9 Nov–15 Dec	11–4	·	·	·	·	·	S	S
26 Dec–31 Dec	11–4	M	T	·	T	F	S	S

Cliff staircase closed 4 November to mid-February. Telephone 01637 860701 to confirm café opening times in winter.

View along the cliffs towards Bedruthan Steps, Cornwall

Carnewas and Bedruthan Steps

Bedruthan, near Padstow, Cornwall PL27 7UW

Map ① C8

This is one of the most popular destinations on the Cornish coast. Spectacular clifftop views stretch across Bedruthan beach (not National Trust). The Trust has rebuilt the steep cliff staircase to the beach, but visitors need to be aware of the risk of being cut off by the tide. **Note**: unsafe to bathe at any time. Toilet not always available.

Eating and shopping: National Trust shop and café (National Trust-approved concession) with adjoining clifftop tea garden.

Making the most of your day: children's quiz/trail, walks leaflet and information panel. Play area beside perfect picnic spot. Bunkhouse and holiday cottages. **Dogs**: allowed.

Access for all: ⯑⯑⯑⯑⯑
Car park and clifftop ⯑⯑

Getting here: 200:SW849692. 6 miles south-west of Padstow. **Foot**: ¾ mile of South West Coast Path runs through this site. **Bus**: Newquay to Padstow. **Train**: Newquay 7 miles.

Castle Drogo

Drewsteignton, near Exeter, Devon EX6 6PB

Map ① F7

As the battle begins to save Castle Drogo, there is an opportunity to take a 'once in a lifetime' peep behind the scenes and explore newly opened areas. You can find out about the people who created the castle, see its contents displayed in new ways, walk through storerooms and even get up close to the building work. The terraced garden, which was designed for the Drewe family, who lived in the castle, contains borders of roses, rhododendrons and herbaceous plants. Trees and high yew hedges shelter the garden from the harsh Dartmoor weather.

Eating and shopping: café with indoor and open-air seating, public Wi-fi and play area (available for functions and parties). Shop selling local products and plants inspired by Castle Drogo's garden.

Making the most of your day: waymarked walks through garden and countryside. Family quizzes, trails and events. Croquet.

Dogs: welcome on leads throughout countryside and informal garden.

Access for all: 🅿️♿🏢🚻🔦🎧📖🎫🅰️
Building 🔦♿♿ Grounds 🔦♿♿➡️

Getting here: 191:SX721900. On Dartmoor. **Foot**: Two Moors Way. **Bus**: Exeter to Moretonhampstead (passing Exeter Central ➡️) Monday to Saturday. **Train**: Yeoford 8 miles. **Road**: 5 miles south of A30. Take A382 Whiddon Down to Moretonhampstead road; turn off at Sandy Park. Approach lanes narrow with tight corners. **Parking**: free, 400 yards.

Far-reaching views over Dartmoor from Castle Drogo

Finding out more: 01647 433306 or castledrogo@nationaltrust.org.uk

Castle Drogo		M	T	W	T	F	S	S
Castle								
16 Feb–24 Feb*	11–4	M	T	W	T	F	S	S
2 Mar–3 Mar*	11–4	·	·	·	·	·	S	S
9 Mar–3 Nov	11–5	M	T	W	T	F	S	S
9 Nov–22 Dec*	11–4	·	·	·	·	·	S	S
Garden, shop, visitor centre								
1 Jan–8 Mar	11–4	M	T	W	T	F	S	S
9 Mar–3 Nov	10–5:30	M	T	W	T	F	S	S
4 Nov–31 Dec	11–4	M	T	W	T	F	S	S
Café								
1 Jan–8 Mar	11–4	M	T	W	T	F	S	S
9 Mar–3 Nov	9–5:30	M	T	W	T	F	S	S
4 Nov–31 Dec**	11–4	M	T	W	T	F	S	S

Over the next five years we are embarking on a major project to stop the castle from leaking. New areas of the castle will be accessible and presented in different ways including the roof. *Castle access by guided tour only. **Café: weekends open until 5. Garden: closes dusk if earlier. Property closed 24 to 26 December. Café and shop closed 14 to 20 January for stock taking and redecorating.

Castle Drogo, Devon: footbridge over the River Teign

Cheddar Gorge

The Cliffs, Cheddar, Somerset

Map ① I4

One of England's most iconic landscapes, with dramatic views and National Trust information centre/shop. **Note**: terrain can be adverse. Caves and car parks privately owned (charge including members).

Finding out more: 01643 862452 or www.nationaltrust.org.uk

Chedworth Roman Villa

Yanworth, near Cheltenham,
Gloucestershire GL54 3LJ

Map ① K2 🏛

The extraordinary relics of one of the country's largest Roman villas were unveiled anew in 2012 following a major project to bring to life the golden age of Roman Britain. Our striking new building provides all-weather access to the distinctive mosaics, while the wider site offers a tranquil setting and the opportunity to wander among the Roman ruins and enjoy the idyllic rural views. There are also stories about how the Victorians shaped the site and artefacts from past excavations in our historic museum.

Eating and shopping: café serving light lunches, cakes, hot drinks and ice-creams from award-winning local suppliers, with indoor and open-air seating. Shop offering Roman-themed gifts and books, seasonal plants and gifts.

Making the most of your day: new guidebook and free audio guides. Roman dressing-up box for children, costumed interpreters and living history events throughout season. Children's mosaic-making sessions, trails and quizzes during school holidays. **Dogs**: assistance dogs only.

Access for all: 🅿️ 💺 🚾 ⛛ 📷 👶
Reception 🚻♿🦽 Museum ♿🦽♿
Grounds 🚻♿

Getting here: 163:SP053135. 3 miles north-west of Fossebridge. **Foot**: on Monarch's Way. **Train**: Cheltenham Spa 14 miles. **Road**: on Cirencester to Northleach road (A429); approach from A429 via Yanworth, or from A436 via Withington. **Parking**: on lane at entrance, plus woodland (overflow). Limited, particularly during and after rain (when the woodland car park may close).

Finding out more: 01242 890256 or chedworth@nationaltrust.org.uk

Uncovering a mosaic, above, and dressing up, top, at Chedworth Roman Villa, Gloucestershire

Chedworth Roman Villa		M	T	W	T	F	S	S
9 Feb–22 Mar	10–4	M	T	W	T	F	S	S
23 Mar–27 Oct	10–5	M	T	W	T	F	S	S
28 Oct–1 Dec	10–4	M	T	W	T	F	S	S

The Church House

Widecombe-in-the-Moor, Newton Abbot,
Devon TQ13 7TA

Map ① F7

Fine example of a 16th-century Church House,
originally used for parish festivities or 'ales'.
Note: used by local community. Please check
with National Trust shop next door to see if
you can visit. No toilet.

Finding out more: 01364 621321
or www.nationaltrust.org.uk

Clevedon Court

Tickenham Road, Clevedon,
North Somerset BS21 6QU

Map ① I4 🏛🌼

Home to the lords of the manor of Clevedon
for centuries, the core of the house is a
remarkable survival from the medieval period.
The house was bought by Abraham Elton in
1709 and it is still the much-loved family home
of his descendants today. **Note**: the Elton
family opens and manages Clevedon Court
for the National Trust.

Clevedon Court, North Somerset: the chapel, below,
and Great Hall with family portraits, above

Eating and shopping: National Trust tea kiosk
serving cream teas and soft drinks.

Making the most of your day: family guide and
children's quiz/trail. **Dogs**: assistance dogs only.

Access for all: 🅿♿🚾📷📹📷📷
Building 🅱 Grounds 🅱

Getting here: 172:ST423716. 1½ miles east
of Clevedon. **Bus**: services from Clevedon to
Bristol, and Yatton to Clevedon. **Train**: Yatton
3 miles. **Road**: on Bristol road (B3130),
signposted from M5 exit 20. **Parking**: free,
50 yards. Unsuitable for trailer caravans or
motor caravans. Alternative parking 100 yards
east of entrance in cul-de-sac.

Finding out more: 01275 872257 or
clevedoncourt@nationaltrust.org.uk

Clevedon Court		M	T	W	T	F	S	S
31 Mar–29 Sep	2–5			**W**	**T**			**S**

Car park open 1:15. House entry by timed ticket, not
bookable. Open Bank Holiday Mondays.

Clouds Hill

Wareham, Dorset BH20 7NQ

Map ① J7

This tiny isolated brick and tile cottage in the heart of Dorset was the peaceful retreat of T. E. Lawrence ('Lawrence of Arabia'). The austere rooms are much as he left them and reflect his complex personality and close links with the Middle East, as detailed in a fascinating exhibition. **Note**: no toilet.

Eating and shopping: shop selling books, gifts and Lawrence memorabilia.

Making the most of your day: events. 'Lawrence Trail' – three-mile circular walk. **Dogs**: welcome on leads in grounds only.

Access for all: 👓 Building 🏠 Grounds 🏠

Getting here: 194:SY824909. 9 miles east of Dorchester. **Train**: Wool 3½ miles; Moreton 3½ miles. **Road**: 1 mile north of Bovington Tank Museum, 9 miles east of Dorchester, 1½ miles east of Waddock crossroads (B3390), 4 miles south of A35 Poole to Dorchester. **Parking**: free.

Finding out more: 01929 405616 or cloudshill@nationaltrust.org.uk

Clouds Hill		M	T	W	T	F	S	S
13 Mar–3 Nov	11–5			·	·	W	T	F	S	S

Open Bank Holiday Mondays. Closes at dusk if earlier (no electric light).

T. E. Lawrence's music room at Clouds Hill, Dorset

Coleridge Cottage

35 Lime Street, Nether Stowey, Bridgwater, Somerset TA5 1NQ

Map ① H5

Discover the former home of Romantic poet Samuel Taylor Coleridge (below). This is where he wrote *The Rime of the Ancient Mariner*, and his work while in Somerset is considered to have launched the Romantic poetry movement. The rooms are dressed as they might have looked when Coleridge lived here.

Eating and shopping: tea-room and shop selling gifts reflecting Coleridge's life and work.

Making the most of your day: children's trail for cottage. Displays and poetry books in reading room. New information panels.

Access for all: 🚻 📖 ♿ 👓 🅿
Building 🏠 Garden 🏠

Getting here: 181:ST191399. 8 miles west of Bridgwater. **Bus**: Bridgwater to Williton (passing close Bridgwater ≋). **Train**: Bridgwater 8 miles. **Road**: Lime Street, opposite Ancient Mariner pub. **Parking**: pub car park opposite, or village car park, 500 yards (neither National Trust).

Finding out more: 01278 732662 (Infoline). 01643 821314 or coleridgecottage@nationaltrust.org.uk

Coleridge Cottage		M	T	W	T	F	S	S
9 Mar–3 Nov	11–5	M	·	·	T	F	S	S
7 Dec–22 Dec	11–3	·	·	·	·	·	S	S

Coleton Fishacre

Brownstone Road, Kingswear, Devon TQ6 0EQ

Map ① G9 🏠♣️🎋🏎️🛏️🍽️

This evocative 1920s Arts and Crafts-style country house, with its elegant Art Deco interior, perfectly encapsulates the spirit of the Jazz Age. The home of the D'Oyly Carte family, there is a light, joyful atmosphere and inspiring views. Newly opened rooms, such as the servants' dining room, laundry and guest bedrooms, allow a glimpse of life 'upstairs and downstairs'. In the garden, paths weave through glades and past tranquil ponds and rare tender plants from New Zealand and South Africa. **Note**: narrow approach lane requires some reversing at busy times (especially between 1 and 2:30).

Eating and shopping: Café Coleton, licensed jazz tea-room, serving light lunches, cakes and cream teas. Art Deco-inspired shop selling china, music, gifts and plants seen in this RHS-accredited garden.

Making the most of your day: daily guided walk, led by member of the garden team. 'Upstairs, downstairs' tours. Monthly jazz club. Theatre in the garden. **Dogs**: welcome on leads around garden perimeter (map from reception).

Access for all: 🅿️♿🚾👪🧎🖼️📷📱♿️
Building 🏠♿ Grounds 🏠➡️♿

Getting here: 202:SX910508. 3 miles from Kingswear. **Foot**: South West Coast Path within ¾ mile. **Bus**: services from Paignton or Brixham to Kingswear: alight ¾ mile south-west of Hillhead, 1½-mile walk to garden. **Train**: Paignton 8 miles; Kingswear (Dartmouth Steam Railway and Riverboat Company) 2¼ miles by footpath, 2¾ miles by road. **Road**: 3 miles from Kingswear: take Lower Ferry road, turn right at toll house. 6 miles from Brixham, take A3022 to Kingswear, turn left at toll house. **Parking**: for visitors to house and garden only.

Finding out more: 01803 842382 or coletonfishacre@nationaltrust.org.uk

Coleton Fishacre		M	T	W	T	F	S	S
16 Feb–31 Oct	10:30–5	M	T	W	T	·	S	S
2 Nov–23 Dec	11–4	M	·	·	·	·	S	S
27 Dec–31 Dec	11–4	M	T	·	·	F	S	S

Open Good Friday.

Coleton Fishacre, Devon: the exterior of the D'Oyly Carte's country home, left, and Art Deco elegance, above

Compton Castle

Marldon, Paignton, Devon TQ3 1TA

Map (1) G8

A rare survivor, this medieval fortress with high curtain walls, towers and two portcullis gates, set in a landscape of rolling hills and orchards, is a bewitching mixture of romance and history. Home for nearly 600 years to the Gilbert family, including Sir Humphrey Gilbert, half-brother to Sir Walter Ralegh. **Note**: hall, sub-solar, solar, medieval kitchen, scullery, guard room and chapel open. Credit cards not accepted.

Eating and shopping: Castle Barton restaurant (not National Trust). Table-top shop selling souvenirs, gifts and postcards. Guidebooks and seasonal plants for sale.

Making the most of your day: history and squirrel trails for children. Drop-in garden workshops during season. **Dogs**: assistance dogs only.

Access for all: 🖐🦮📖♿👁
Building 🦽🦼 Grounds 🦽🦼

Getting here: 202:SX865648. At Compton, 5 miles west of Torquay. **Bus**: Marldon to Paignton ≋; Dartmouth to Torquay (passing Totnes ≋), on both alight Marldon, 1½ miles. **Train**: Torquay 3 miles. Newton Abbot 6 miles. **Road**: 1½ miles north of Marldon. Signposted off A380 to Marldon or turn south from A381 Totnes road at Ipplepen – 2 miles to Compton. **Parking**: free, 30 yards. Additional parking at Castle Barton opposite entrance, 100 yards.

Finding out more: 01803 661906 or comptoncastle@nationaltrust.org.uk

Compton Castle		M	T	W	T	F	S	S
2 Apr–31 Oct	10:30–4:30	·	**T**	**W**	**T**	·	·	·

Open Bank Holiday Mondays: 1 April, 6 May, 27 May and 26 August.

Corfe Castle

The Square, Corfe Castle, Wareham, Dorset BH20 5EZ

Map (1) K7

One of Britain's most iconic and evocative survivors of the English Civil War, the castle was partially demolished in 1646 by the Parliamentarians. A favourite haunt for adults and children alike, the romantic ruins, with their breathtaking views across Purbeck, are totally captivating. There are 1,000 years of history as a royal palace and fortress to discover and, with fallen walls and secret places, 'murder holes' and arrow loops, every corner has a tale to tell of treachery and treason. More recently, a wide variety of wildlife has made its home here.

Note: steep, uneven slopes; steps; sudden drops. All/parts of castle may close in high winds.

Eating and shopping: 18th-century tea-room serving cream teas. National Trust shop in village square, offering products ranging from pocket-money treats to luxury locally made gifts.

Making the most of your day: daily family trail. Events, including living history, festivals, open-air theatre and cinema. **Dogs**: welcome on short leads.

Access for all:
Grounds

Getting here: 195:SY959824. In Corfe. **Bus**: Poole to Swanage (passing Wareham). **Train**: Wareham 4½ miles. Corfe Castle (Swanage Steam Railway) nearby (park and ride from Norden). **Road**: on A351 Wareham to Swanage road.

Parking: pay and display at foot of castle, off A351 (800 yards walk uphill). Norden park and ride (all-day parking, ½ mile walk) and West Street in village (pay and display), neither National Trust.

Finding out more: 01929 481294 (ticket office). 01929 480921 (shop). 01929 481332 (tea-room) or corfecastle@nationaltrust.org.uk

Corfe Castle		M	T	W	T	F	S	S
Castle, shop and tea-room								
1 Jan–28 Feb	10–4	**M**	**T**	**W**	**T**	**F**	**S**	**S**
1 Mar–31 Mar	10–5	**M**	**T**	**W**	**T**	**F**	**S**	**S**
1 Apr–30 Sep	10–6	**M**	**T**	**W**	**T**	**F**	**S**	**S**
1 Oct–31 Oct	10–5	**M**	**T**	**W**	**T**	**F**	**S**	**S**
1 Nov–31 Dec	10–4	**M**	**T**	**W**	**T**	**F**	**S**	**S**

Shop and tea-room: close at 5:30 April to September. Tea-room: closed for refurbishment 2 to 11 January. Castle, shop and tea-room: closed 5 March and 25 to 26 December.

The breathtaking ruins of Corfe Castle in Dorset: one of the South West's most evocative places

Cotehele

St Dominick, near Saltash, Cornwall PL12 6TA

Map (1) E8 　🏠✝🏛⚓🌸🏊🛏🍸

Cotehele's medieval origins provided a perfect setting for the Edgcumbes to show off their ancestral home to guests, such as King George III in 1789. The interior tour has changed little, although the furnishings were titivated as Cotehele continued to inspire its adoring owners. From early spring flowers to herbaceous borders in high season, to the orchards in the autumn, there is something for everyone all year round in the garden. The sailing barge *Shamrock* is moored at the quay, where the Discovery Centre tells the gripping story of the Tamar Valley, offering a gateway to the wider estate. **Note**: from Tavistock, follow brown signs and ignore Sat Nav.

Eating and shopping: Barn Restaurant and The Edgcumbe on Cotehele Quay. Shop selling Cornish food, gifts and local plants. Art and craft available at Cotehele Gallery. Nine holiday cottages.

Restored Tamar sailing barge at Cotehele Quay

Making the most of your day: activities, including family activities and 'Behind the Scenes'. Camping weekends. Exhibitions. Tours and walks (on request). **Dogs**: welcome on estate, assistance dogs only in formal garden.

Access for all: 🅿♿🚾🦽♿🐕📷📖♿🔎📷
Building 🔎🏠🔽　Grounds 🔎🏠➡

Getting here: 201:SX422685. 1 mile west of Calstock, on west bank of Tamar. **Foot**: 1½-mile riverside walk from Calstock. **Bus**: local service (01822 834571 for details). **Train**: Calstock 1½ miles. **Road**: 8 miles from Tavistock, 14 miles from Plymouth. **Sat Nav**: ignore from Tavistock, follow brown signs. **Parking**: free.

Playing croquet in a magnificent setting, on the lawn in front of Cotehele, Cornwall

Finding out more: 01579 351346 (office). 01579 352711 (Barn Restaurant). 01579 352717 (Edgcumbe) or cotehele@nationaltrust.org.uk

Cotehele		M	T	W	T	F	S	S
House								
16 Mar–3 Nov	11–4	M	T	W	T	.	S	S
Hall of house and garland								
4 Nov–31 Dec	11–4	M	T	W	T	F	S	S
Garden and estate								
Open all year	Dawn–dusk	M	T	W	T	F	S	S
Barn Restaurant, shop, plant sales and gallery								
16 Feb–15 Mar	11–4	M	T	W	T	F	S	S
16 Mar–3 Nov	11–5	M	T	W	T	F	S	S
4 Nov–31 Dec	11–4	M	T	W	T	F	S	S
The Edgcumbe								
5 Jan–15 Mar	11–4	M	T	W	T	F	S	S
16 Mar–3 Nov	11–5	M	T	W	T	F	S	S
4 Nov–31 Dec	11–4	M	T	W	T	F	S	S

House open Good Friday and special CSI-Friday openings in August (bring a torch). Barn Restaurant opens 10:30, 16 March to 3 November. Hall of house, The Edgcumbe, Barn Restaurant, shop and gallery closed on 25 and 26 December.

The waterwheel in action at Cotehele Mill

Cotehele Mill

St Dominick, near Saltash, Cornwall PL12 6TA

Map (1) E8

This working mill is an atmospheric reminder of the recent past when corn was ground here for the local community. A range of outbuildings includes a traditional chairmaker and a pottery, along with re-creations of wheelwrights', saddlers' and blacksmiths' workshops. **Note**: no toilets or parking (park at Cotehele Quay).

The working mill at Cotehele, Cornwall

Eating and shopping: Cotehele flour, apple juice and gifts for sale. Cornish pasties or ice-cream available at nearby Cotehele Quay.

Making the most of your day: daily tours at 3. Family trails and bakery demonstrations. Two holiday cottages. **Dogs**: welcome, but assistance dogs only in workshops.

Access for all: 🄳🄹 🚾 🖥 🎵
Building 🔊 Grounds 🔊

Getting here: 201:SX417682. On west bank of the Tamar. **Bus**: local service to Cotehele reception (01822 834571 for details). **Train**: Calstock, 2 miles. 1½-mile riverside walk to Cotehele. **Road**: 8 miles from Tavistock, 14 miles from Plymouth. **Parking**: by arrangement only. Shuttle bus from Cotehele house.

Finding out more: 01579 350606. 01579 351346 (property office) or cotehele@nationaltrust.org.uk

Cotehele Mill		M	T	W	T	F	S	S
16 Mar–30 Sep	11–5	M	T	W	T	F	S	S
1 Oct–3 Nov	11–4:30	M	T	W	T	F	S	S

The terrace in The Courts Garden, Wiltshire

The Courts Garden

Holt, near Bradford on Avon, Wiltshire BA14 6RR

Map ① J4

Full of variety, this charming garden shows the English country style at its best. Peaceful water gardens and herbaceous borders, with unusual shaped topiary, demonstrate an imaginative use of colour and planting, creating unexpected vistas. There is also an arboretum, with wonderful species of trees and naturally planted spring bulbs.

Eating and shopping: tea-room serving coffee, lunches and afternoon tea (not National Trust). Guidebook, gifts and plants for sale, some grown here. Second-hand bookshop. New 'trust' gallery shop in nearby Glove Factory Studios (not National Trust).

Making the most of your day: events and exhibitions, guided tours (booking essential) and children's trail. Cross-country walk map (available from reception) to Great Chalfield Manor and Garden. **Dogs**: assistance dogs only.

Access for all: ⬚⬚⬚⬚⬚⬚⬚⬚
Garden ⬚⬚⬚

Getting here: 173:ST861618. In centre Holt. **Cycle**: NCN254, 1¼ miles. **Bus**: Trowbridge to Melksham (passing close Trowbridge ≋). **Train**: Bradford on Avon 2½ miles; Trowbridge 3 miles. **Road**: 3 miles south-west of Melksham, 2½ miles east of Bradford on Avon, on south side of B3107.

Follow signs to Holt. **Parking**: free (not National Trust), 80 yards, in village hall car park opposite, on B3107. Additional overflow parking: follow signs. Please respect the community and don't park on the village streets.

Finding out more: 01225 782875 or courtsgarden@nationaltrust.org.uk

The Courts Garden		M	T	W	T	F	S	S
Garden and tea-room								
2 Feb–3 Mar	11–5:30	·	·	·	·	·	S	S
4 Mar–3 Nov	11–5:30	M	T	·	T	F	S	S
Shop: 'trust' at the Glove Factory Studios*								
5 Jan–3 Mar	11–4	·	·	W	T	F	S	S
4 Mar–3 Nov	11–5	M	T	W	T	F	S	S
6 Nov–22 Dec	11–4	·	·	W	T	F	S	S

Tea-room last orders 4:45. Garden access out of season by appointment only. *Shop off site, approximately 150 yards from garden entrance.

Dinton Park and Philipps House

Dinton, Salisbury, Wiltshire SP3 5HH

Map ① K5

Neo-Grecian house in a tranquil park, designed by Jeffry Wyatville for William Wyndham in 1820. **Note**: no toilet. For opening arrangements see website or call 01672 538014.

Finding out more: 01722 716663 or www.nationaltrust.org.uk

Dunster Castle

Dunster, near Minehead, Somerset TA24 6SL

Map ① G5

Dramatically sited on top of a wooded hill, a castle has existed here since at least Norman times, with an impressive medieval gatehouse and ruined tower giving a reminder of its turbulent history. The castle that you see today became a lavish country home during the 19th century, remodelled in 1868–72 by Antony Salvin. The fine oak staircase and plasterwork ceiling he adapted can still be seen. The sunny south terrace is home to a variety of subtropical plants, and there are stunning panoramic views over the surrounding countryside and moorland.

Eating and shopping: 17th-century stables shop selling unusual local and regional gifts and guidebook. Selection of places to eat at Dunster village or Dunster Working Watermill.

Making the most of your day: family trails around castle and garden. Events and behind-the-scenes tours and re-enactments, many costumed, throughout season. New Crypt exhibition. **Dogs**: welcome in parkland and garden on leads.

Access for all: ⓟ 🏚 ⓦⓒ 🖥 💻 🚻 🔎 ◎
Castle 🏚🏚 Stables 🏚 Grounds 🏚➡🚶

Getting here: 181:SS995435. 3 miles south-east of Minehead. **Cycle**: cycle lane from Minehead along A39. **Bus**: services from Tiverton and Taunton to Minehead; alight Dunster Steep, ½ mile. **Road**: 3 miles south-east of Minehead, off A39. **Parking**: 300 yards, shuttle to entrance available. Enter from A39.

Finding out more: 01643 823004 (Infoline). 01643 821314 or dunstercastle@nationaltrust.org.uk

Dunster Castle		M	T	W	T	F	S	S
Castle								
9 Mar–3 Nov	11–5	M	T	W	T	F	S	S
7 Dec–22 Dec	11–3	·	·	·	·	·	S	S
Shop, garden and park*								
1 Jan–8 Mar	11–4	M	T	W	T	F	S	S
9 Mar–3 Nov	10–5	M	T	W	T	F	S	S
4 Nov–31 Dec	11–4	M	T	W	T	F	S	S

Last entry to castle one hour before closing (except 19 July to 1 September). 'Dunster by Candlelight': castle open 5 to 9 Friday 6 and Saturday 7 December. *Shop: open January 1 and then weekends only in January; closed 25 and 26 December.

Dunster Castle, Somerset, seen from the village

Dunster Working Watermill

Mill Lane, Dunster, near Minehead, Somerset TA24 6SW

Map ① G5 🏚🏚

Working 18th-century watermill built on the site of a mill mentioned in the Domesday survey of 1086. **Note**: the mill is a private business. Admission charge (including members).

Finding out more: 01643 821759 (mill). 01643 821314 (Dunster Castle) or www.nationaltrust.org.uk

Dyrham Park

Dyrham, near Bath,
South Gloucestershire SN14 8ER

Map (1) J4 🏛️➕❄️🍽️

There are more than 110 hectares (270 acres) of ancient parkland at Dyrham Park, where a historic herd of 200 fallow deer roams freely and magnificent trees and breathtaking views abound. At the beautiful late 17th-century home, which once belonged to hard-working civil servant William Blathwayt, visitors can discover how fashions changed over the centuries – from the original 17th-century Dutch-inspired interiors and formal garden, to the very different style of Victorian country squire Colonel Blathwayt. The elegant West Garden is perfect for a quiet, relaxing stroll, and there are splendid borders, ancient ponds and a perry pear orchard.

Dyrham Park, South Gloucestershire: the east front, below, and Samuel van Hoogstraten painting, above. Right: there is so much to see and do for families

Eating and shopping: garden kiosk (with outdoor seating) and courtyard kiosk offering drinks and snacks; tea-room serving hot lunches. Shop selling plants, garden products and locally made gifts.

Making the most of your day: events and activities all year, including Saxon living history camps, guided tours of park and garden, dry-stone walling courses, croquet, jazz on lawn and open-air theatre (summer). For families, there are trails for toddlers, children's nature walks, family fun in the Old Lodge play and picnic area, plus park and garden Tracker Packs. **Dogs**: welcome in car park only (exercise area at far end of car park).

Access for all: 👶♿♿🚻♿♿📷
Building 🏠♿ Grounds 🏛️▶️

Getting here: 172:ST743757. 8 miles north of Bath, 12 miles east of Bristol. **Foot**: Cotswold Way passes by. **Cycle**: Avon and Wiltshire cycleways. **Train**: Bath Spa 8 miles. **Road**: on Bath to Stroud road (A46), 2 miles south of Tormarton interchange with M4, exit 18. **Sat Nav**: use SN14 8HY. **Parking**: free, 500 yards.

Finding out more: 0117 937 2501 or dyrhampark@nationaltrust.org.uk

Dyrham Park		M	T	W	T	F	S	S
Garden, shop and tea-room								
16 Feb–28 Jun	10–5	M	T	·	·	F	S	S
29 Jun–1 Sep	10–5	M	T	W	T	F	S	S
2 Sep–27 Oct	10–5	M	T	·	·	F	S	S
2 Nov–15 Dec	10–4	·	·	·	·	·	S	S
House								
9 Mar–28 Jun	11–5	M	T	·	·	F	S	S
29 Jun–1 Sep	11–5	M	T	W	T	F	S	S
2 Sep–27 Oct	11–5	M	T	·	·	F	S	S
Basement and kitchen only								
16 Feb–8 Mar	11–4	M	T	·	·	F	S	S
2 Nov–15 Dec	11–4	·	·	·	·	·	S	S
Park								
Open all year	10–5	M	T	W	T	F	S	S

Last admission one hour before closing. Closes dusk if earlier than 5. Property open every day during Easter holidays (25 March to 7 April) and May half-term (27 May to 2 June). 4 and 18 September, 6, 13, 20 November and 4 December: whole property closed until 1. Closed 25 December.

East Pool Mine

Pool, near Redruth, Cornwall

Map (1) C9

East Pool Mine celebrates the extraordinary lives of the people who lived and worked at the very heart of the Cornish Mining World Heritage Site. There are many reminders of the mine's innovative past, including two great beam engines, preserved in their towering engine houses. The pumping engine is the third largest surviving Cornish beam engine in the world. Each day, the restored winding engine springs into life as if beckoning you to work. A great place for all the family to discover the dramatic story of Cornish mining. **Note**: Trevithick Cottage at nearby Penponds open Wednesdays, April to October (2 to 5). For Sat Nav use TR15 3NH.

Eating and shopping: small shop selling gifts, including local minerals, mining and Cornish history books, plus hot drinks and snacks.

Above: looking inside the boiler in the winding engine house at East Pool Mine, Cornwall. Top: the winding engine house

Why not visit us on foot or by public transport? See pages 6 and 374

Making the most of your day: family activities and trails. Free guided tours. Hands-on exhibits and working models. **Dogs**: welcome in outdoor areas.

Access for all: 🚻♿🏠📷🎫👁️📱

Taylor's engine house 🏠

Michell's engine house 🏠♿ Grounds ➡️

Getting here: 203:SW672415. At Pool, on either side of A3047 midway between Redruth and Camborne. **Cycle**: NCN3, ½ mile. **Bus**: frequent services from Penzance, St Ives and Truro (passing Camborne and Redruth 🚌). **Train**: Redruth 2 miles; Camborne 2 miles. **Road**: leave A30 at Camborne East or Redruth junctions. Site signposted on A3047. **Sat Nav**: use TR15 3NH. **Parking**: free parking in Morrisons' superstore (far end). Parking also at Michell's engine house off A3047.

Finding out more: 01209 315027 or eastpool@nationaltrust.org.uk. Trevithick Road, Pool, Cornwall TR15 3NP

East Pool Mine			M	T	W	T	F	S	S
16 Feb–2 Nov	10:30–5		·	T	W	T	F	S	·

Open Bank Holiday Mondays and Sundays (February to October). Last entry one hour before closing.

The waterwheel in action at Finch Foundry, Devon

Finch Foundry

Sticklepath, Okehampton, Devon EX20 2NW

Map ① F7

Last remaining water-powered forge in England. Set amid beautiful Dartmoor countryside, the foundry gives a unique insight into 19th-century village life. At its peak, it made 400 tools a day, including sickles, scythes and shovels for farmers and miners. **Note**: narrow entrance to car park – height restrictions.

Eating and shopping: local food, gifts and plants on sale in shop.

Making the most of your day: family activities. Stories, demonstrations and tours of machinery. St Clement's Day in November. Great starting point for moorland walks.

Dogs: welcome in all areas except tea-room, shop and foundry during demonstrations.

Access for all: 🚻♿🏠📷👁️

Foundry 🏠🚹 Grounds 🏠

Getting here: 191:SX641940. In the centre of Sticklepath village. **Foot**: on 180-mile Tarka Trail. **Cycle**: on West Devon Cycle Route. **Bus**: regular services from Okehampton and Exeter. **Train**: Okehampton (Sunday, June to September only) 4½ miles. **Road**: 4 miles east of Okehampton off A30. **Parking**: free. Not suitable for high vehicles.

Finding out more: 01837 840046 or finchfoundry@nationaltrust.org.uk

Finch Foundry		M	T	W	T	F	S	S
16 Mar–3 Nov	11–5	M	T	W	T	F	S	S

Foundry and shop open for St Clement's Day, 23 November (patron saint of blacksmiths).

The old boathouse at Fyne Court, Somerset

Fyne Court

Broomfield, Bridgwater, Somerset TA5 2EQ

Map (1) H5 🏠✿🏊🧍🍴

A real hidden Somerset gem. Although the house is no longer standing, Fyne Court is a wonderful place to spend a magical time walking through the estate's woodland garden and delightful meadows. A great place for families to explore.

Eating and shopping: tea-room serving homemade lunches, cream teas and cakes.

Making the most of your day: events, including bush crafts and open-air theatre. Outdoor play trail. Wild Wednesdays in school holidays. **Dogs**: welcome on leads.

Access for all: 🅳🎫♿ Grounds ♿➡️

Getting here: ST222321. 5 miles north of Taunton; 6 miles south-west of Bridgwater in Broomfield. **Train**: Taunton 5 miles, Bridgwater 6 miles. **Road**: follow signs to Broomfield. **Parking**: 150 yards.

Finding out more: 01643 862452 or fynecourt@nationaltrust.org.uk

Fyne Court		M	T	W	T	F	S	S
Tea-room								
9 Mar–3 Nov	10:30–4:30	M			T	F	S	S
Estate								
Open all year		M	T	W	T	F	S	S

Tea-room has extended opening hours at various times of year. Opening times may vary according to weather.

Magical Glastonbury Tor, Somerset

Glastonbury Tor

near Glastonbury, Somerset

Map (1) I5 ✝️

Iconic tor, topped by a 15th-century tower, with spectacular views. **Note**: no toilet.

Finding out more: 01643 862452 or www.nationaltrust.org.uk

Glendurgan Garden

Mawnan Smith, near Falmouth,
Cornwall TR11 5JZ

Map (1) C9 ▢▢▢▢▢

Glendurgan Garden was described by its
creators, the Quakers Alfred and Sarah Fox, as
a 'small peace [sic] of heaven on earth'. Visitors
can find out why it proved to be just this for
the Foxes and their 12 children by exploring
Glendurgan's three valleys, which run down to
the Helford River. On the way to the re-created
schoolroom, you can learn about education
for such a large family. There is a wonderfully
puzzling maze, created by Alfred and Sarah
to entertain the family, exotic plants, carpets
of wild flowers and a variety of wildlife, which
changes throughout the year.

Eating and shopping: tea-house
(Trust-approved concession) serving
breakfast, light lunches and afternoon tea.
Shop and plant centre.

Making the most of your day: Durgan
beach on Helford River. Durgan Fish Cellar:
local information and children's activities.
Dogs: assistance dogs only in garden.

Access for all: ▢▢▢▢▢▢
Visitor reception ▢▢

Getting here: 204:SW772277. ½ mile
south-west of Mawnan Smith, 4 miles
south-west of Falmouth. **Foot**: South West
Coast Path within ¾ mile. **Ferry**: link between
Helford Passage (1½-mile walk from Durgan)
and Helford village on south side of river.
Bus: services from Helston to Falmouth pass
entrance. **Train**: Penmere 4 miles. **Road**: on
road to Helford Passage. **Parking**: free.
Gates locked at 5:30.

Finding out more: 01326 252020 or
glendurgan@nationaltrust.org.uk

Glendurgan Garden	M	T	W	T	F	S	S
16 Feb–2 Nov	10:30–5:30	·	**T**	**W**	**T**	**F**	·

Garden closes dusk if earlier. Open Bank Holiday Mondays
and all Mondays in August.

Glendurgan Garden, Cornwall: challenging laurel maze

Godolphin

Godolphin Cross, Helston, Cornwall TR13 9RE

Map ① B9 🏠 🏚 ⬆ 🐾 ✿ ♿ 🚻

A beautiful and romantic place, with a long and fascinating history. Time has stood still here, giving the garden, house and surrounding estate buildings a haunting air of antiquity and peace. The garden is largely unchanged since the 16th century. The estate walks are rich in prehistoric and mining archaeology. **Note**: the house is open to visit between holiday cottage bookings: check house opening dates.

Eating and shopping: Piggery serving tea, coffee, biscuits, sandwiches and cakes. Souvenirs and postcards available.

Making the most of your day: trails, tours and guided walks. Blankets available to borrow from the Piggery for picnics in the orchard, garden or estate. **Dogs**: welcome in the garden on short leads and under control throughout the estate.

Access for all: 🅿 🔌 ♿ 🚻 ♿ 📷 Garden ♿

Getting here: 203:SW599321. 9 miles to Camborne. **Bus**: Camborne to Helston. **Road**: from Helston take A394 to Sithney Common, turn right B3302 to Leedstown, turn left, follow signs. From Hayle B3302 Leedstown, turn right, follow signs. From west, B3280 through Goldsithney, right at Townshend. **Parking**: free.

Finding out more: 01736 763194 or godolphin@nationaltrust.org.uk

Godolphin		M	T	W	T	F	S	S
Estate								
Open all year		M	T	W	T	F	S	S
Garden								
2 Feb–3 Nov	10–5	M	T	W	T	F	S	S
4 Nov–23 Dec	10–4	M	T	W	T	F	S	S
26 Dec–31 Dec	10–4	M	T		T	F	S	S
House								
2 Feb–7 Feb	10–4	M	T	W	T		S	S
2 Mar–7 Mar	10–4	M	T	W	T		S	S
6 Apr–11 Apr	10–4	M	T	W	T		S	S
4 May–9 May	10–4	M	T	W	T		S	S
1 Jun–6 Jun	10–4	M	T	W	T		S	S
6 Jul–11 Jul	10–4	M	T	W	T		S	S
7 Sep–12 Sep	10–4	M	T	W	T		S	S
5 Oct–10 Oct	10–4	M	T	W	T		S	S
30 Nov–15 Dec	10–4	M	T	W	T	F	S	S

Atmospheric corner at Godolphin, Cornwall

Godrevy

Gwithian, near Hayle, Cornwall TR27 5ED

Map ① B9 🏚 ♿ 🚗

Expanse of sandy beaches on St Ives Bay, with wildlife-rich cliffs and popular café. **Note**: unstable cliffs and incoming tides. Toilet not always available; car park closes at dusk.

Finding out more: 01208 265212 or www.nationaltrust.org.uk

Great Chalfield Manor and Garden

near Melksham, Wiltshire SN12 8NH

Map (1) J4

This medieval manor, with its fine oriel windows and rooftop adorned with soldiers, griffins and monkeys, sits in peaceful countryside. Visitors crossing the upper moat, pass barns, gatehouse and parish church before reaching the house. The romantic garden offers terraces, topiary houses, gazebo, lily pond, roses and a spring-fed fishpond. **Note**: home to donor family tenants, who manage it for the National Trust.

Eating and shopping: tea/coffee available in Motor House (not National Trust). Plant sales. Guidebook and postcards available.

Making the most of your day: history posters and slide show of garden in Edwardian Motor House. Nearby Courts Garden, offering lunch or tea.

Access for all: P♿ D♿ 🅦 📷 ♪ ∴ ⌨
Manor ♿ ♿ ♿   Garden ♿ ➡

Getting here: 173:ST860631. 3 miles south-west of Melksham. **Foot**: 1-mile walk by public footpath from The Courts Garden (National Trust), Holt. **Cycle**: NCN254. On the Wiltshire Cycleway. **Bus**: Bradford-on-Avon to Holt. **Train**: Bradford-on-Avon, 3 miles. **Road**: off B3107 via Broughton Gifford Common, follow sign for Broughton Gifford (warning, narrow lane). Coaches must approach from Broughton Gifford (lanes from south too narrow). **Parking**: free, 100 yards, on grass verge outside manor gates.

Finding out more: 01225 782239 or greatchalfieldmanor@nationaltrust.org.uk

Great Chalfield		M	T	W	T	F	S	S
Manor*								
31 Mar–31 Oct	See note	·	**T**	**W**	**T**	·	·	**S**
Garden								
31 Mar–27 Oct	2–5	·	·	·	·	·	·	**S**
2 Apr–31 Oct	11–5	·	**T**	**W**	**T**	·	·	·

*Admission to manor house by 45-minute guided tour only (places limited, not bookable). Tuesday, Wednesday and Thursday: at 11, 12, 2, 3 and 4. Sunday: at 2, 3 and 4. Additional timed manor tickets may be available on Sundays and other busy days.

Colourful blue border at the fine medieval Great Chalfield Manor and Garden in Wiltshire

Greenway

Greenway Road, Galmpton, near Brixham,
Devon TQ5 0ES

Map ① G8

Greenway offers an extraordinary glimpse
into the holiday home of the famous author
Agatha Christie and her family. The relaxed
and atmospheric house is set in the 1950s
and contains many of the family's collections,
including archaeology, Tunbridge ware, silver,
botanical porcelain and books. Outside there
is a large and romantic woodland garden, with
restored vinery and peach house, wild edges
and rare plantings, which drift down the
hillside towards the sparkling Dart estuary.
Please consider 'green ways' to get here:
for example, ferry (shuttle service available
up from the quay), bus, cycling or walking.
Note: Greenway operates a traffic
management system to reduce traffic
impact on the local village.

Eating and shopping: licensed Barn Café or
Greenway kitchen serving light lunches, pasties,
cakes and cream teas. Agatha Christie-inspired
shop selling books, DVDs, music, local food,
gifts and plants.

Making the most of your day: afternoon
guided garden tours. Events, including art
exhibitions, artists in residence, twilight tours
and garden workshops. Theatre in the garden.
Family croquet, clock golf, trails and quizzes.
1950s vintage bus. **Dogs**: welcome in garden on
leads (tethering rings available in courtyard).

Greenway, Devon, sits on its own private promontory

The 1950s vintage bus outside Greenway

Access for all: 🅿 ♿ ♿ 🚻 ♿ ✍ 🆅🆃 👓 🔍

Buildings 🏛️   Garden ♿

Getting here: 202:SX876548. **Foot**: Dart Valley
Trail, Kingswear 3 miles, Dartmouth 6 miles.
Greenway walk from Broadsands or Churston
station 3½ miles. **Ferry**: from Dartmouth
(use park and ride), Totnes (tidal, Steamer
Quay), Brixham or Torquay (details from
Greenway Ferry Service, 01803 882811 or
website). Tickets from National Trust shop
and Dartmouth ticket office opposite Trust
shop. Six hours minimum parking required.
Bus: vintage bus daily from Torquay, Paignton
and Brixham park and ride (01803 882811).
Train: Paignton 4½ miles, Churston 2 miles
(Dartmouth Steam Railway and River Boat
Company 01803 555872). **Parking**: spaces
must be booked (telephone 01803 842382 or
visit website) – same-day booking possible.
No parking on Greenway road or in village.

Finding out more: 01803 842382 or
greenway@nationaltrust.org.uk

Greenway		M	T	W	T	F	S	S
16 Feb–31 Mar	10:30–5	·	·	W	T	F	S	S
2 Apr–14 Apr	10:30–5	·	T	W	T	F	S	S
17 Apr–21 Jul	10:30–5	·	·	W	T	F	S	S
23 Jul–15 Sep	10:30–5	·	T	W	T	F	S	S
18 Sep–3 Nov	10:30–5	·	·	W	T	F	S	S
27 Dec–31 Dec	11–4	M	T	·	·	F	S	S

Also open Tuesdays 28 May and 29 October.

Hailes Abbey, Gloucestershire: once a Cistercian abbey, it was founded in 1246 and dissolved in 1539

Hailes Abbey

near Winchcombe, Cheltenham,
Gloucestershire GL54 5PB

Map ① K1

Once a Cistercian abbey, founded in 1246 by
Richard of Cornwall and dissolved Christmas
Eve 1539, Hailes never housed large numbers
of monks but had extensive and elaborate
buildings. It was financed by pilgrims visiting
its renowned relic, 'the Holy Blood of
Hailes' – allegedly a phial of Christ's blood.
Note: financed, managed and maintained by
English Heritage (0117 975 0700).

Eating and shopping: shop and refreshments.

Making the most of your day: interpretation
panels. Picnics welcome in grounds.
Dogs: on leads in grounds only.

Access for all: **Building**

Getting here: 150:SP050300. 2 miles
north-east of Winchcombe. **Foot**: Cotswold
Way within ¾ mile. **Bus**: Cheltenham to
Willersey, alight Greet, 1¾ miles by footpath.
Train: Cheltenham 10 miles. **Road**: 1 mile east
of Broadway road (B4632, originally A46).
Parking: free (not National Trust).

Finding out more: 01242 602398 or
hailesabbey@nationaltrust.org.uk

Hailes Abbey		M	T	W	T	F	S	S
1 Apr–30 Jun	10–5	M	T	W	T	F	S	S
1 Jul–31 Aug	10–6	M	T	W	T	F	S	S
1 Sep–30 Sep	10–5	M	T	W	T	F	S	S
1 Oct–31 Oct	10–4	M	T	W	T	F	S	S

Opening times subject to change.

Hardy Monument

Black Down, Portesham, Dorset DT2 9HY

For opening arrangements, please contact
West Dorset Office on 01297 489481.

Hardy's Birthplace

Higher Bockhampton, near Dorchester,
Dorset DT2 8QJ

Map ① J7

Thomas Hardy was born in 1840 in this small cob and thatch cottage, which was built by his great-grandfather and is little altered since the family left. His early novels *Under the Greenwood Tree* and *Far from the Madding Crowd* were written here. **Note**: no toilet.

Eating and shopping: Thomas Hardy's books for sale, postcards and small gifts.

Making the most of your day: guided tours of house available on request. Events for all ages during open season, including poetry readings, storytelling, children's trail and performances. **Dogs**: welcome on leads in garden only.

Access for all: ⬚⬚⬚⬚⬚
Building ⬚ Grounds ⬚⬚

Getting here: 194:SY728925. 3 miles north-east of Dorchester. **Train**: Dorchester South 4 miles; Dorchester West 4 miles. **Road**: from A35 Dorchester bypass, follow signs to Higher Bockhampton and Kingston Maurward College from roundabout. Follow signs to Hardy's Cottage once past college. **Parking**: free (not National Trust), 600 yards. Telephone to arrange drop-off at cottage.

Finding out more: 01305 262366 or hardysbirthplace@nationaltrust.org.uk

Hardy's Birthplace		M	T	W	T	F	S	S
13 Mar–3 Nov	11–5	·	·	W	T	F	S	S
Open Bank Holiday Mondays.								

Heddon Valley

Parracombe, Barnstaple, Devon EX31 4PY

Map ① F5

The West Exmoor coast, favourite landscape of the Romantic poets, offers not only the Heddon Valley, but also Woody Bay and the Hangman Hills to explore. There are spectacular coastal and woodland walks, as well as a car park, shop and information centre in Heddon Valley itself.

Eating and shopping: shop selling outdoor wear, Exmoor products and gifts. Local ice-cream available.

Making the most of your day: two all-terrain children's buggies available for families to borrow at Heddon Valley shop. Car park barbecues. **Dogs**: welcome.

Access for all: ⬚⬚⬚⬚⬚⬚
Countryside ⬚⬚

Getting here: 180:SS655481. Halfway between Combe Martin and Lynton. **Foot**: South West Coast Path within ¾ mile. **Bus**: regular service from Barnstaple to Lynton (passing close Barnstaple ≋), alight just north of Parracombe, then 2 miles. **Road**: off A39 at Hunter's Inn. **Parking**: 50 yards.

Hardy's Birthplace, Dorset, remains little altered

Walkers enjoying the Heddon Valley in Devon, above, and below, the hillside above Heddon's Mouth

Finding out more: 01598 763402 or heddonvalley@nationaltrust.org.uk

Heddon Valley		M	T	W	T	F	S	S
Coast and countryside								
Open all year		**M**	**T**	**W**	**T**	**F**	**S**	**S**
Shop								
9 Mar–28 Mar	10:30–4:30	**M**	**T**	**W**	**T**	**F**	**S**	**S**
29 Mar–29 Sep	10:30–5	**M**	**T**	**W**	**T**	**F**	**S**	**S**
30 Sep–3 Nov	10:30–4:30	**M**	**T**	**W**	**T**	**F**	**S**	**S**

Heelis

Kemble Drive, Swindon, Wiltshire SN2 2NA

Map (1) K3

The National Trust's award-winning central office is a remarkable example of an innovative and sustainable building. Timber from our woodlands and wool from Herdwick sheep grazed on Trust farmlands have been used in its construction, making Heelis a unique working environment.

Eating and shopping: café serving local food. Spacious shop.

Making the most of your day: virtual tour available at reception daily during normal opening hours. Guided tours every Friday.

Access for all:
Building

Getting here: 173:SU141850. On historic railway site, next door to Designer Outlet Centre. **Bus**: alight Rodbourne Road (200 yards). **Train**: Swindon, ¾ mile. **Road**: from M4 junction 16, follow signs for Outlet Centre North car park. **Parking**: 100 yards, not National Trust (charge including members).

Finding out more: 01793 817575 or heelis@nationaltrust.org.uk

Heelis
Admission to offices by booked guided tour only. Shop and café open daily throughout year, apart from 1 January, Easter Sunday, 25 and 26 December.

Hidcote

Hidcote Bartrim, near Chipping Campden, Gloucestershire GL55 6LR

Map (1) L1 ✤ ♨ ⊤

Memories don't get any better than this. At Hidcote, one of the country's great gardens, you can experience for yourself the fulfilment of a quiet American's English fantasy. There are exquisite garden rooms, each with its own unique character, with rare shrubs and trees, herbaceous borders and unusual plants from around the world. The garden changes in harmony with the seasons, from vibrant spring bulbs to autumn's spectacular Red Border. Nestled in the Cotswolds with sweeping views across the Vale of Evesham, a visit to Hidcote is inspirational at any time of year.

Eating and shopping: Barn Café, plus Winthrop's Café and conservatory. Largest Trust plant centre. Shop selling exclusive Hidcote souvenirs.

Making the most of your day: daily introductory talks. Exclusive evening Head Gardener tours. Open-air theatre. Themed family activities and workshops. **Dogs**: assistance dogs only.

Access for all: 🅿♿ 🄳♿ 🚾 🅱 🛗 💻 🔘 ⓐ
Visitor reception 🌡♿ **Grounds** 🌡➡♿

Getting here: 151:SP176429. 4 miles north-east of Chipping Campden.
Foot: 1½ miles by steep uphill footpath from Mickleton. **Cycle**: NCN5, 1¼ miles.
Train: Honeybourne 4½ miles. **Road**: close to Mickleton village, 1 mile east of B4632 (originally A46), off B4081. **Parking**: free, 100 yards.

Finding out more: 01386 438333 or hidcote@nationaltrust.org.uk

Hidcote		M	T	W	T	F	S	S
16 Feb–10 Mar	11–4	.	.	.	.	.	S	S
16 Mar–28 Apr	10–6	M	T	W	.	.	S	S
29 Apr–1 Sep	9–7	M	T	W	T	F	S	S
2 Sep–29 Sep	10–6	M	T	W	.	.	S	S
30 Sep–3 Nov	10–5	M	T	W	.	.	S	S
9 Nov–22 Dec	11–4	.	.	.	.	.	S	S

Open Good Friday. Last admission to garden one hour before closing. Barn Café closed during November and December.

The Bathing Pool Garden at Hidcote, Gloucestershire, above, and below, the Old Garden

The south and west façades of High Cross House, Devon, a gem of the Modern Movement, showing the servants' block (blue)

High Cross House

Dartington, near Totnes, Devon TQ9 6ED

Map ① G8 🏠 ✳ 🍵

Built as a 'machine for living in' for William Curry, headmaster of Dartington Hall School, commissioned by Leonard Elmhirst and designed by William Lescaze in 1932. A contemporary arts programme of installations, exhibitions and artists' residencies adorn this modernist gem. **Note**: owned by Dartington Hall but managed by the National Trust. Limited disabled access.

Eating and shopping: first-floor shop and café (balcony seating and views) serving cakes, light snacks, wine and nibbles in the evening. Art sales, art and architectural books, stationery, gifts and cards.

Making the most of your day: family and community events, talks and demonstrations and musical evenings. **Dogs**: welcome on leads in garden.

Access for all: 🅿️♿🚾 Grounds 🦽👶➡️♿

Getting here: 202:SX796627. 2½ miles north-west of Totnes. **Foot**: walk along the River Dart to Dartington Hall. **Cycle**: Sustrans cycle path from Totnes to Dartington Hall estate. **Bus**: services from Buckfastleigh and Totnes to Dartington Hall. Buses stop outside door.

Train: Totnes 1½ miles. **Road**: from Plymouth A38 take the A384 exit signposted Dartington 4 miles. **Parking**: limited parking at house; overflow parking at shops at Dartington and Dartington Hall (not National Trust), charges with refunds may apply.

Finding out more: 01803 842382 or highcrosshouse@nationaltrust.org.uk

High Cross House	M	T	W	T	F	S	S
2 Jan–29 Dec	10:30–5	·	·	W	T	F	S	S

Closed 25 December. Late night opening on Thursday evenings until 8:30.

Holnicote Estate

Near Minehead, Somerset

Map ① G5 ✝🏠🏊🏛️🐦🛶

Dunkery Beacon on the Holnicote Estate is Europe's only Dark Sky Reserve and is the highest point on Exmoor, as well as Somerset, so is ideal for star gazing. Rugged paths, invigorating views, unique wildlife and orienteering are just a few of the delights available at the Holnicote Estate. **Note**: toilets at Bossington and Horner car parks; also at Selworthy (not National Trust).

Holnicote Estate, Somerset: view from Dunkery Hill

Eating and shopping: shop and visitor centre. Periwinkle tea-room serving cream teas (on Selworthy Green).

Making the most of your day: orienteering trails (Selworthy and Horner woods). Mountain bikes welcome. Downloadable walks. Events. Visitor centre, with new estate map mural for information on exploring the estate. **Dogs**: welcome on leads.

Access for all: 🚻 Grounds 🦽🏞️

Getting here: SS920469. Selworthy Village. **Foot**: 3¾ miles of South West Coast Path; Coleridge Way; Macmillan Way. **Bus**: services from Minehead to Porlock, and Taunton to Lynmouth. **Road**: off A39, Minehead. **Sat Nav**: use TA24 8TP (Selworthy). **Parking**: Bossington, Dunkery, North Hill, Selworthy, Webbers Post. Allerford and Horner, pay and display (charge, including members).

Finding out more: 01643 862452 or holnicote@nationaltrust.org.uk

Holnicote Estate		M	T	W	T	F	S	S
Tea-room								
9 Mar–7 Apr	10:30–5	M	T	W	T	F	S	S
9 Apr–21 Jul	10:30–5	·	T	W	T	F	S	S
22 Jul–1 Sep	10:30–5	M	T	W	T	F	S	S
3 Sep–3 Nov	10:30–5	·	T	W	T	F	S	S
Shop								
9 Mar–7 Apr	12–5	M	T	W	T	F	S	S
9 Apr–21 Jul	12–5	·	T	W	T	F	S	S
22 Jul–1 Sep	12–5	M	T	W	T	F	S	S
3 Sep–3 Nov	12–5	·	T	W	T	F	S	S
Countryside								
Open all year		M	T	W	T	F	S	S

Tea-room and shop open Bank Holidays; opening hours vary according to weather conditions. Estate office open Monday to Friday, 8:30 to 5.

Horton Court

Horton, near Chipping Sodbury, South Gloucestershire BS37 6QR

Map ① J3   🏠❖

These fascinating remains of a 12th-century rectory include a Norman hall and early Renaissance decoration.

Finding out more: 01225 833977 or www.nationaltrust.org.uk

Jurassic Coast

Dorset

Map ① H-J7   🏛️📷🎣🚗🛏️▲

England's only natural World Heritage Site, this spectacular swathe of Jurassic coastline – with its 95 miles of unspoilt cliffs and beaches – traces almost 185 million years of the Earth's history, creating a unique 'walk through time'.

Eating and shopping: National Trust shop on Marine Parade, Lyme Regis.

Getting here: visit www.nationaltrust.org.uk for transport details. **Parking**: pay and display car parks at various points.

Finding out more: 01297 489481 or jurassiccoast@nationaltrust.org.uk

Jurassic Coast	Open every day all year

Killerton

Broadclyst, Exeter, Devon EX5 3LE

Map ① G6   🏠➕🏛✳♣♥🛏🍽

Would you give away your family home for your political beliefs? Sir Richard Acland did just this with his estate, at 2,590 hectares (6,400 acres), one of the largest the Trust has acquired (20 farms and 250 cottages). Killerton House, built in 1778–9, brings to life generations of Aclands, one of Devon's oldest families. The family bedrooms now house this year's historic fashion exhibition 'Objects of Desire', fashion to die for. The garden, created by John Veitch, is Killerton's highlight. Beautiful year-round, it features ancient rhododendrons, magnolias, rare trees and views of the surrounding rolling Devon countryside.

Eating and shopping: gift shop selling award-winning Killerton cider, chutney, flour and honey. Plant centre. Orchard tea-room or Killerton Kitchen restaurant serving morning coffee, lunch or afternoon tea. Second-hand bookshop.

Making the most of your day: replica costumes to try on, even for men. Events. Activities for families and children, including Tracker Packs, a play trail, Discovery Centre (school holidays) and various trails – little ones will love the house mouse trail. Waymarked walks, cycle track and orienteering routes. 'Killerton's Characters'. **Dogs**: welcome on leads in park and estate walks only. Dog bowls and posts available.

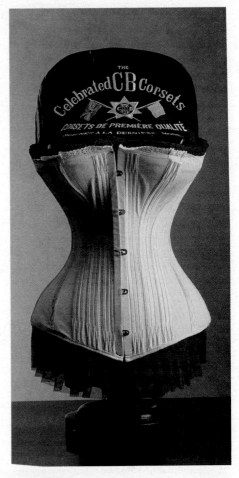

Corset from the costume collection at Killerton, Devon, above, and the elegant house itself, below

Access for all: ▢▢▢▢▢▢▢▢▢▢▢
▢▢ House ▢▢▢▢ Grounds ▢▢▢

Getting here: 192:SS973001. 7 miles north-east of Exeter. **Cycle**: NCN52. **Bus**: services from Exeter to Tiverton, alight Killerton Turn ¾ mile. **Train**: Pinhoe (not Sunday), 4½ miles; Whimple, 6 miles; Exeter Central and St David's, both 7 miles. **Road**: off Exeter to Cullompton road (B3181); from M5 northbound, exit 30 via Pinhoe and Broadclyst; from M5 southbound, exit 28. **Parking**: free, 280 yards. Follow signs (do not go up drive to house).

Finding out more: 01392 881345 or killerton@nationaltrust.org.uk

Killerton		M	T	W	T	F	S	S
Park and garden								
Open all year	10–7	M	T	W	T	F	S	S
House and Killerton Kitchen								
16 Feb–8 Mar	11–3	M	T	W	T	F	S	S
9 Mar–3 Nov	11–5	M	T	W	T	F	S	S
23 Nov–31 Dec	11–4	M	T	W	T	F	S	S
Stables Café								
5 Jan–10 Feb	11–4	·	·	·	·	·	S	S
16 Feb–31 Dec	11–5	M	T	W	T	F	S	S
Shop and plant sales								
5 Jan–10 Feb	11–5	·	·	·	·	·	S	S
16 Feb–3 Nov	11–5:30	M	T	W	T	F	S	S
4 Nov–31 Dec	11–5	M	T	W	T	F	S	S

Stables Café and shop close at 3 on 24 December and all day Christmas Day and Boxing Day. House and Killerton Kitchen closed 24, 25 and 26 December. House, Killerton Kitchen, Stables Café and shop open daily 1 January to 31 December. Late night opening on Wednesday 4, 11 and 18 December.

Killerton: Budlake Old Post Office

Broadclyst, Killerton, Exeter, Devon EX5 3LW

Map ① G7   ▣▣

Close to Killerton, this small thatched cottage was the village post office, serving Killerton House and the local community until the 1950s. The cottage has a delightful cottage garden including rose borders, herb and vegetable plots. **Note**: nearest toilets at Killerton.

Eating and shopping: tea-rooms, shop and plants at nearby Killerton.

Making the most of your day: footpath to Killerton along old carriage drive. **Dogs**: on leads in garden only.

Access for all: ▢ Building ▢ Grounds ▢

Getting here: 192:SS973001. **Cycle**: NCN52. Cycle path between Clyston Mill and Killerton via Budlake Old Post Office. **Bus**: services from Exeter to Tiverton Parkway ▣ (passing close Exeter Central ▣), alight Killerton Turn ¾ mile. **Train**: Pinhoe, not Sunday, 4½ miles; Whimple, 6 miles; Exeter Central and St David's, both 7 miles.

Relaxing in Killerton's glorious hillside garden, where there are beautiful views of the surrounding countryside

Killerton: Budlake Old Post Office, Devon. Its delightful cottage garden includes rose borders, herb and vegetable plots

Road: off Exeter to Cullompton road (B3181); from M5 northbound, exit 30 via Pinhoe and Broadclyst; from M5 southbound, exit 28. **Parking**: limited. Ample parking at Killerton, 800 yards.

Finding out more: 01392 881690 or budlakepostoffice@nationaltrust.org.uk

Budlake Old Post Office		M	T	W	T	F	S	S
30 Mar–3 Nov	1–5	M	T	W	·	·	S	S

Last admission 10 minutes before closing.

Killerton: Clyston Mill

Broadclyst, Exeter, Devon EX5 3EW

Map (1) G7

Historic water-powered mill in a picturesque setting by the River Clyst, surrounded by farmland and orchards. Grain is still ground here to make flour, keeping alive traditional skills. **Note**: nearest parking and toilets in Broadclyst.

Eating and shopping: flour for sale. Produce made from Clyston Mill flour for sale at Killerton.

Making the most of your day: children's trail. Hands-on activities and interpretation. New cycle track from Broadclyst, via Clyston, to Killerton. **Dogs**: welcome on a lead.

Access for all: Building 🏛 Grounds 🏛

Getting here: 192:SX981973. In Broadclyst village. **Foot**: from village car park, walk towards church and follow signs through churchyard. **Cycle**: NCN52. **Bus**: Exeter to Tiverton, alight Broadclyst village. **Train**: Pinhoe, not Sunday, 4½ miles; Whimple, 6 miles; Exeter Central and St David's, both 7 miles. **Road**: off Exeter to Cullompton Road (B3181). **Parking**: free (not National Trust), 450 yards.

Finding out more: 01392 462425 or clystonmill@nationaltrust.org.uk

Clyston Mill		M	T	W	T	F	S	S
30 Mar–3 Nov	1–5	M	T	W	·	·	S	S

Telephone Killerton 01392 881345/462425 for further information.

Killerton: Marker's Cottage

Townend, Broadclyst, Exeter, Devon EX5 3HS

Map ① G7

An intriguing thatched medieval cob cottage with a fascinating history, smoke-blackened timbers and unusual painted decorative screen showing St Andrew. A cross passage opens out onto a garden with a contemporary cob summerhouse and blacksmith's workshop. **Note**: nearest parking and toilets in Broadclyst.

Eating and shopping: tea-rooms, shop and plant centre at nearby Killerton.

Making the most of your day: handling collection and trail (including village trail). Clyston Mill nearby.

Access for all: 🅳♿ Building 🔥 Grounds 🔥

Getting here: 192:SX985973. In Broadclyst village. **Cycle**: NCN52. Cycle track from Broadclyst to Killerton. **Bus**: Exeter to Tiverton, alight Broadclyst village.

Train: Pinhoe, not Sunday, 2½ miles; Whimple, 4½ miles; Exeter Central and St David's, both 6 miles. **Road**: from village car park turn left, then right and right again onto Townend. Marker's Cottage is second cottage on left. **Parking**: free (not National Trust), 250 yards.

Finding out more: 01392 461546 or markerscottage@nationaltrust.org.uk

Marker's Cottage		M	T	W	T	F	S	S
30 Mar–3 Nov	1–5	M	T	W	.	.	S	S

King John's Hunting Lodge

The Square, Axbridge, Somerset BS26 2AP

Map ① I4

This early Tudor timber-framed wool merchant's house (*circa* 1500) provides a fascinating insight into local history. **Note**: run as local history museum by Axbridge and District Museum Trust. Small entry charge (including members).

Eating and shopping: shop in museum (not National Trust).

Making the most of your day: occasional tours of historic Axbridge start from museum.

Access for all: 🚽 Building 🔥

Getting here: 182:ST431545. In the Square, Axbridge, on corner of High Street. **Bus**: Weston-super-Mare to Wells (passing close Weston-super-Mare ➤). **Train**: Worle 8 miles. **Parking**: 100 yards (not National Trust).

Finding out more: 01643 862452 or kingjohns@nationaltrust.org.uk

King John's Hunting Lodge		M	T	W	T	F	S	S
1 Apr–1 Sep	1–4	M	T	W	T	F	S	S

Open at 11, first Saturday of every month.

Killerton: Marker's Cottage, Devon. The simple hall with plank screen decorated with 15th-century paintings

The magnificent 17th-century Kingston Lacy in Dorset: a house noted for its lavish interiors and outstanding art collection

Kingston Lacy

Wimborne Minster, Dorset BH21 4EA

Map (1) K7

Home of the Bankes family for more than 300 years, this striking 17th-century house is noted for its lavish interiors. The outstanding art collection includes paintings by Rubens, Van Dyck, Titian and Tintoretto, as well as the largest private collection of Egyptian artefacts in the UK. Outside, there are beautiful lawns, a restored Japanese tea garden and several waymarked walks through the surrounding parkland, with its fine herd of North Devon cattle. The 3,443-hectare (8,500-acre) estate is dominated by the Iron Age hill fort of Badbury Rings, home to 14 varieties of orchid.

Eating and shopping: prize-winning scones, beef from the Kingston Lacy North Devon herd, regional and local foods and wines, plants, high-quality gifts and souvenirs for sale.

Making the most of your day: events and activities, including farmers' markets, open-air theatre, tractor-trailer tours, children's crafts, Hallowe'en event, 'Above and Below Stairs' days and 'Putting the House to Bed' tours and lecture lunches in November (booking essential). Art collection, with works by Rubens, Titian and Tintoretto. Outside there is an Edwardian Japanese Garden, a Winter Garden, Egyptian obelisk and sarcophagus, plus Eyebridge riverside walk and Badbury Rings. **Dogs**: on leads in restaurant courtyard, park and woodlands only.

Fun and games in the garden at Kingston Lacy, Devon

Access for all: 🅿️ 🏭 🚾 ♿ 🅿️ 📷 🖼️ 📹 🎵 ⏸️ 📷 **Building** 🏠 **Grounds** 🏛️ ➡️ ♿ ♿

Getting here: 195:ST980019. 1½ miles west of Wimborne Minster. **Bus**: services from Bournemouth and Poole, alight Wimborne Square. **Train**: Poole 8½ miles. **Road**: on B3082 Blandford to Wimborne road. **Sat Nav**: data unreliable, follow B3082. **Parking**: free. Charge at Badbury Rings on point-to-point race days.

Finding out more: 01202 883402 or kingstonlacy@nationaltrust.org.uk

Kingston Lacy		M	T	W	T	F	S	S
House								
2 Mar–3 Nov	11–5	·	·	**W**	**T**	**F**	**S**	**S**
Garden, park, shop and restaurant								
1 Jan–1 Mar	10:30–4	**M**	**T**	**W**	**T**	**F**	**S**	**S**
2 Mar–3 Nov	10:30–6	**M**	**T**	**W**	**T**	**F**	**S**	**S**
4 Nov–22 Dec	10:30–4	**M**	**T**	**W**	**T**	**F**	**S**	**S**
27 Dec–31 Dec	10:30–4	**M**	**T**	·	·	**F**	**S**	**S**

Open Bank Holiday Mondays. Timed tickets may operate on Bank Holiday Sundays and Mondays. Last admission to house one hour before closing. Shop and restaurant close 30 minutes earlier than main closing time. House Entrance Hall and Servants' Hall decorated for Christmas during December weekends (6 to 22 December). Property may close in poor weather.

Tintoretto painting: part of the fabulous collection

Knightshayes

Bolham, Tiverton, Devon EX16 7RQ

Map ① G6

Built for the grandson of pioneer lace-maker John Heathcoat, Knightshayes is a country estate on a grand scale. The house, a rare survival of the work of eccentric designer William Burges, dating from 1869, is an extraordinary Gothic delight, with rich Victorian interiors and far-reaching views of Tiverton and the Exe Valley. The garden is one of the finest in Devon, with formal terraces, unique topiary, rare shrubs, many fine specimen trees, glorious spring flowers and summer borders and a fully productive walled kitchen garden, providing the restaurant with fresh seasonal fruit and vegetables all year round.

The imposing south front of Knightshayes

Eating and shopping: Stables restaurant serving organic kitchen garden produce. Plant centre and gift shop selling local wares. Fresh kitchen garden produce available.

Making the most of your day: waymarked trails and leaflets. Free introductory garden walks. Seasonal family events and activities. Children's parties and pizza-making workshops at Stables. **Dogs**: welcome on leads in parkland (off leads in woods). Assistance dogs only in house and gardens.

Access for all: ⬛⬛⬛⬛⬛⬛⬛⬛⬛⬛⬛
House ⬛⬛⬛ Visitor reception ⬛⬛⬛
Gardens ⬛➡⬛

Getting here: 181:SS960151. 1½ miles north of Tiverton. **Cycle**: NCN3. **Bus**: Tiverton to Minehead, alight Bolham ¾ mile. Exeter to Tiverton (passing close Exeter Central ≋) alight Tiverton 1¾ miles. **Train**: Tiverton Parkway 8 miles. **Road**: 7 miles from M5 exit 27 (A361, North Devon link road); turn off Tiverton to Bampton road (A396) at Bolham. **Sat Nav**: on nearing Tiverton/Bolham follow signs. **Parking**: free.

Finding out more: 01884 254665 or knightshayes@nationaltrust.org.uk

Knightshayes		M	T	W	T	F	S	S
House and shop								
9 Feb–3 Nov	11–5	M	T	W	T	F	S	S
6 Nov–22 Dec	11–4	·	·	W	T	F	S	S
23 Dec–31 Dec	11–4	M	T	·	T	F	S	S
Garden, plant centre and restaurant								
9 Feb–3 Nov	10–5	M	T	W	T	F	S	S
6 Nov–22 Dec	10–4	·	·	W	T	F	S	S
23 Dec–31 Dec	10–4	M	T	·	T	F	S	S

'Discovery Fridays': themed access to house on Fridays during main season and throughout winter. Knightshayes open until 5 January 2014.

Knightshayes, Devon: the atmospheric Great Hall

Lacock Abbey, Fox Talbot Museum and Village

Lacock, near Chippenham, Wiltshire SN15 2LG

Map ① K4

Picturesque Lacock village, by the banks of the River Avon, is often seen in films. At its heart is Lacock Abbey, with its tranquil, golden cloisters and medieval nunnery rooms. Now a quirky country home with 800 years of history and architectural changes, the Abbey has a relaxed, lived-in feel. Above the cloisters entrance is the famous window where photographic pioneer William Henry Fox Talbot created the first negative. The Fox Talbot Museum celebrates the invention of photography and offers unique topical exhibitions set within the timber-framed gallery.

Eating and shopping: Stables tea-rooms. High Street gift shop. Museum shop for photography and plant sales. Abbey courtyard second-hand bookshop. Village shops (not National Trust).

Making the most of your day: events (many themed) and activities, including open-air theatre, music and musical picnics, photographic exhibitions and interactive presentation of Abbey life. Behind-the-scenes tours, Abbey trails, walks with our Head Gardener and winter dog walking. New interactive garden sculptures and colourful summer borders. Family and children's events and activities, including picnics, trails, fun days, dressing-up clothes, willow play structure, play leaflet and children's guide. Lacock is a living film set, where you can walk in the footsteps of the stars (*Cranford, Pride and Prejudice, Harry Potter*). **Dogs**: welcome in Abbey grounds from 1 November to 31 March (Easter if earlier).

Access for all: 🅿️ 🚹 ♿ 🚻 🏨 📷 🖼️ 📖 ♿ 🎦

Abbey 🔼🔽 Museum ♿🐕♿

Grounds ♿♿➡️♿

The golden cloisters at Lacock Abbey in Wiltshire

Photograph of William Henry Fox Talbot, taken in 1866

Getting here: 173:ST919684. 3 miles south of Chippenham. **Foot**: beside Wilts/Berks Canal. **Cycle**: NCN4, 1 mile. **Bus**: Chippenham to Frome (passing Melksham, close to Chippenham and Trowbridge ≷). **Train**: Melksham 3 miles; Chippenham 3½ miles. **Road**: M4 exit 17, signposted Chippenham, Poole, Warminster, then Lacock (A350). **Parking**: 220 yards (pay and display). No visitor parking on village streets.

Finding out more: 01249 730459 or lacockabbey@nationaltrust.org.uk

Lacock Abbey		M	T	W	T	F	S	S
Village*								
Open all year		M	T	W	T	F	S	S
Cloisters, grounds, museum, exhibition and shop								
2 Jan–8 Feb	11–4	M	T	W	T	F	S	S
9 Feb–3 Nov	10:30–5:30	M	T	W	T	F	S	S
4 Nov–24 Dec	11–4	M	T	W	T	F	S	S
27 Dec–31 Dec	11–4	M	T	·	·	F	S	S
Abbey rooms								
5 Jan–3 Feb	12–4	·	·	·	·	·	S	S
9 Feb–3 Nov	11–5	M	·	W	T	F	S	S
9 Nov–15 Dec	12–4	·	·	·	·	·	S	S
Abbey rooms (Great Hall only for Christmas)								
21 Dec–29 Dec	11–4	·	·	·	·	·	S	S
Tea-room and High Street shop								
2 Jan–8 Feb	11–4	M	T	W	T	F	S	S
9 Feb–3 Nov	10–5:30	M	T	W	T	F	S	S
4 Nov–24 Dec	11–4	M	T	W	T	F	S	S
27 Dec–31 Dec	11–4	M	T	·	·	F	S	S

Last admission 45 minutes before closing (218 yards from reception to Abbey). *Village businesses open at various times.

Lanhydrock, Cornwall: the rooftops, above, gatehouse, opposite top, and barrel-vaulted drawing room, opposite bottom

Lanhydrock

Bodmin, Cornwall PL30 5AD

Map ① D8

The home of the Victorian Agar-Robartes family appears as if they have just popped out for tea. After a devastating fire in 1881, the 17th-century house was refurbished in high-Victorian style, with all the latest mod cons. There are more than 50 rooms to explore and it is easy to see the contrasts between the servants' life 'downstairs' and the elegant family rooms. The extensive garden is full of colour all year. The roses, herbaceous borders and dazzling parterre brighten any summer, and in spring the camellias, magnolias and rhododendrons are breathtaking. **Note**: car park expansion works may cause some disruption.

Eating and shopping: Victorian Servants' Halls restaurants. Shop selling local food and gifts. Plant centre. Second-hand bookshop.

Making the most of your day: indoors there is a remarkable ceiling in the Long Gallery, and Victorian servants' quarters and extensive kitchens to explore. Outside there are garden tours, walks through the network of woodland, park and riverside paths, as well as a magnificent collection of magnolias flowering through spring. There is also a family museum. **Dogs**: assistance dogs only in garden (dog-friendly walks throughout estate).

Access for all: ♿ 🅿️ 🚗 🏠 🚾 🍴 💺 🎧 📷 🎪
House 🚶 🚶 ⬆️ 🚻 ♿
Grounds 🏛️ ➡️ ♿ ♿

Getting here: 200:SX088636. 2½ miles south-east of Bodmin. **Foot**: 1¾ miles from Bodmin Parkway via original carriage-drive to house, signposted in station car park. **Cycle**: NCN3 runs past entrance. **Train**: Bodmin Parkway 1¾ miles by cycle or foot; 3 miles by road. **Road**: signed from A30, A38 Bodmin to Liskeard, and B3268 off A390 at Lostwithiel. **Parking**: free, 600 yards.

We welcome dogs assisting visitors with disabilities

Finding out more: 01208 265950 or
lanhydrock@nationaltrust.org.uk

Lanhydrock		M	T	W	T	F	S	S
House									
1 Mar–31 Mar	11–5	·	T	W	T	F	S	S
2 Apr–29 Sep	11–5:30	·	T	W	T	F	S	S
1 Oct–3 Nov	11–5	·	T	W	T	F	S	S
Garden									
16 Feb–3 Nov	10–6	M	T	W	T	F	S	S
Estate									
Open all year	Dawn–dusk	M	T	W	T	F	S	S
Shop and refreshments*									
5 Jan–10 Feb	11–4	·	·	·	·	·	S	S
16 Feb–28 Feb	11–4	M	T	W	T	F	S	S
1 Mar–31 Mar	11–5	M	T	W	T	F	S	S
1 Apr–30 Sep	11–5:30	M	T	W	T	F	S	S
1 Oct–3 Nov	11–5	M	T	W	T	F	S	S
4 Nov–31 Dec	11–4	M	T	W	T	F	S	S

House: also open Mondays 1 and 8 April, 6 and 27 May,
22 and 29 July, plus all Mondays in August and 28 October;
entry is controlled (queueing at busy times). Plant centre
and second-hand bookshop: open daily 1 March to
3 November. *Refreshments: open 10:30, 16 February to
3 November. Shop and refreshments are inside tariff area.
Closed 25 and 26 December.

Lawrence House

9 Castle Street, Launceston, Cornwall PL15 8BA

Map (1) E7

Georgian town house built in 1753 – now a museum and civic centre. **Note:** leased to Launceston Town Council.

Finding out more: 01566 773277 or www.nationaltrust.org.uk

Leigh Woods

near Bristol, Avon

Map (1) I4

Beautiful haven on Bristol's doorstep, with diverse woodland and wonderful views of Avon Gorge and suspension bridge. Excellent network of paths, including a 1¾-mile easy-access trail, links to the National Cycle Network and new 'Yer Tiz' off-road cycle trail. **Note:** no toilets.

Making the most of your day: natural play area. Permanent orienteering course (map available from the office). Ideal for picnics. **Dogs:** welcome (but be aware of cattle).

An enticing path through Leigh Woods, Avon

Getting here: 172:ST555730. 2 miles south-west of Bristol. **Foot:** River Avon Trail (Pill to Bristol) links with footpath up Nightingale Valley. **Cycle:** blue trail through woods connects with NCN41. **Bus:** Bristol to Portishead (alight Beggar Bush Lane and follow Valley Road). **Train:** Clifton Down 🚆 2½ miles, Bristol Temple Meads 3 miles. **Road:** off A369 Bristol to Portishead road: from Bristol via Clifton Suspension Bridge; from M5 junction 19 take A369. **Parking:** roadside parking on North Road off A369, or Forestry Commission car park.

Finding out more: 0117 973 1645 or leighwoods@nationaltrust.org.uk. Reserve Office, Valley Road, Leigh Woods, Bristol, Avon BS8 3PZ

Leigh Woods	Open every day all year

Levant Mine and Beam Engine

Trewellard, Pendeen, near St Just, Cornwall TR19 7SX

Map (1) A9

In its dramatic clifftop setting on the edge of the Atlantic Ocean, Levant was, for 110 years, 'the queen of Cornwall's submarine mines', with undersea levels stretching more than a mile out under the Atlantic. Today, as part of the Cornwall and West Devon Mining World Heritage Site, Levant embodies an atmospheric and awe-inspiring landscape that has made the local mining district famous worldwide. The surviving buildings and ruins offer a moving glimpse into the lives and stories of the men and women who toiled to extract the riches of the earth from beneath the crashing waves.

Eating and shopping: light refreshments available. Small shop selling mining-related goods and books.

Making the most of your day: daily steam engine and guided tours. Children's activities in school holidays. Downloadable walks to Geevor and Botallack. **Dogs:** welcome on leads.

Levant Mine and Beam Engine, Cornwall, in its dramatic clifftop setting on the Atlantic Ocean coast

Access for all:
Building

Getting here: 203:SW368346. 1 mile west of Pendeen. **Foot**: South West Coast Path passes entrance. **Bus**: hourly service from Penzance to Trewellard (1 mile from site). **Train**: Penzance, 7 miles. **Road**: on B3306 St Just to St Ives road. **Parking**: free, 100 yards.

Finding out more: 01736 786156 or levant@nationaltrust.org.uk

Levant Beam Engine		M	T	W	T	F	S	S
Steaming								
17 Feb–1 Nov	11–5		M	T	W	T	F	S

Little Clarendon

Dinton, Salisbury, Wiltshire SP3 5DZ

Map (1) K5

Late 15th-century stone house with curious 20th-century chapel. **Note**: no toilet.

Finding out more: 01985 843600 or www.nationaltrust.org.uk

Lizard Point and Kynance Cove

The Lizard, near Helston, Cornwall TR12 7NT

Map (1) C10

Lizard Point, Britain's most southerly mainland point, offers dramatic cliff walks, wild flowers and geological features. Two miles north lies Kynance Cove, considered one of the most beautiful beaches in the world. Marconi's historic wireless experiments are celebrated at the Lizard Wireless Station at Bass Point. **Note**: Kynance car park toilets closed in winter.

Eating and shopping: café at Kynance Cove (March to October), café at Lizard Point (open all year) – both Trust-approved concessions. Café open all year at Poldhu (not National Trust).

Making the most of your day: surfing lessons at Poldhu. Kayak events on the Helford. **Dogs**: seasonal day-time dog bans on some beaches, including Kynance and Poldhu.

Access for all:
Kynance and Lizard

Getting here: 203:SW688133. 11 miles south-east of Helston. **Foot**: South West Coast Path around peninsula. **Cycle**: visit website for trails. **Bus**: Helston to Lizard (Kynance Cove 1 mile, Lizard Point 1.5 miles). **Road**: A3083 from Helston to Lizard. Kynance signposted. **Parking**: at Lizard and Kynance.

Finding out more: 01326 561407 or lizard@nationaltrust.org.uk. The Stables, Penrose, Helston, Cornwall TR13 0RD

The Lizard	Open every day all year

Telephone for opening times of the Lizard Wireless Station at Bass Point and the Marconi Centre at Poldhu.

The east front of Lodge Park, Gloucestershire

Lodge Park and Sherborne Estate

Lodge Park, Aldsworth, near Cheltenham, Gloucestershire GL54 3PP

Map ① K/L2 🏛️🏊🛏️🔔🍴

England's only surviving 17th-century deer course and grandstand, created in 1634 by John 'Crump' Dutton, inspired by his passion for gambling, banqueting and entertaining. The National Trust's first restoration project relying on archaeological evidence. Impressive views of the deer course and park (designed by Charles Bridgeman in the 1720s). **Note**: toilet at Lodge Park only.

Eating and shopping: small shop and courtyard café.

Making the most of your day: open-air theatre and opera. Outdoor events and living history. Walks through the surrounding Sherborne Estate. **Dogs**: welcome under close control.

Access for all: 🅿️♿🚻📷👓 Building 🏠♿

Getting here: 163:SP146123. 3 miles east of Northleach. **Road**: approach from A40 only.

Kynance Cove, Cornwall, just north of Lizard Point

Parking: free for Lodge Park. For Sherborne Estate: Ewe Pen Barn car park 163:SP158143, Water Meadows 163:SP175154 (off A40 towards Sherborne).

Finding out more: 01451 844130 or lodgepark@nationaltrust.org.uk

Lodge Park and Sherborne Estate	M	T	W	T	F	S	S
Lodge Park							
1 Mar–27 Oct	11–4	·	·	·	**F**	**S**	**S**
Sherborne Estate							
Open all year		**M**	**T**	**W**	**T**	**F**	**S**	**S**

Lodge Park opens Bank Holiday Mondays. Access to Sherborne Estate from Ewe Pen car park. Occasionally closes for weddings (telephone to confirm opening times).

Loughwood Meeting House

Dalwood, Axminster, Devon EX13 7DU

Map ① H7

Atmospheric 17th-century thatched Baptist meeting house dug into the hillside; open daily all year. **Note**: no toilet.

Finding out more: 01752 346585 or www.nationaltrust.org.uk

Lundy

Bristol Channel, Devon EX39 2LY

Map ① D5

Undisturbed by cars, this wildlife-rich island, designated the first Marine Conservation Area, encompasses a small village with an inn, Victorian church and the 13th-century Marisco Castle. **Note**: financed, administered and maintained by the Landmark Trust. MS *Oldenburg* fares (including members), discounts available.

Eating and shopping: tavern serving hot and cold food and drinks. Shop selling souvenirs, Lundy stamps, snacks and ice-creams.

Making the most of your day: diving, walking, letterboxing, bird and wildlife-watching. Holiday cottages (not National Trust). **Dogs**: assistance dogs only.

Access for all: [icons]
Building [icon]   Grounds [icon]

Getting here: 180:SS130450. In Bristol Channel; 11 miles from Hartland Point, 25 miles from Ilfracombe. **Ferry**: Bideford or Ilfracombe (tide dependent) up to four days a week, end March to end October. **Bus**: regular services from Barnstaple, Ilfracombe, Bideford. **Train**: Barnstaple. **Sat Nav**: Ilfracombe: EX34 9EQ. Bideford: EX39 2EY. **Parking**: Bideford, Ilfracombe (pay and display).

Finding out more: 01271 863636 or lundy@nationaltrust.org.uk.
The Lundy Shore Office, The Quay, Bideford, Devon EX39 2LY

Lundy

MS *Oldenburg* sails from Bideford or Ilfracombe up to four times a week from the end of March until the end of October carrying both day and staying passengers. A helicopter service operates from Hartland Point from November to mid-March, Mondays and Fridays only, for staying visitors.

Wildlife-rich Lundy, in the Bristol Channel, Devon

Lydford Gorge

Lydford, near Tavistock, Devon EX20 4BH

Map ① F7 🖼

Legend-rich river gorge (the deepest in the South West) offering a variety of exhilarating walks. Around every corner the River Lyd plunges, tumbles, swirls and gently meanders as it travels through the steep-sided, oak-wooded gorge. Throughout the seasons there is an abundance of wildlife and plants to see, from woodland birds to wild garlic in the spring and fungi in the autumn. **Note**: rugged terrain, vertical drops.

Eating and shopping: shop selling plants, outdoor clothing and footwear. Two tea-rooms serving cream teas, pasties and local ice-cream. Takeaway drinks and food.

Making the most of your day: family events, wildlife-themed and bushcraft activities, wild food area, children's play area, bird hide. **Dogs**: welcome on leads.

Access for all: 🅿️♿️🚻🔤📷🎨♨️👓🖼
Buildings ♿️ Gorge 🦽

Getting here: 191/201:SX509845. At the end of Lydford village.

Lydford Gorge, Devon: Whitelady Waterfall, bottom, and the Devil's Cauldron, above

Foot: as road directions or via Blackdown Moor from Mary Tavy. **Cycle**: NCN27 and 31. **Bus**: regular service from Tavistock. **Road**: 7 miles south of A30. Halfway between Okehampton and Tavistock, 1 mile west off A386 opposite Dartmoor Inn: Devil's Cauldron entrance at west end of Lydford village; waterfall entrance near Manor Farm. **Parking**: free.

Finding out more: 01822 820320 or lydfordgorge@nationaltrust.org.uk

Lydford Gorge		M	T	W	T	F	S	S
Gorge and Devil's Cauldron tea-room								
9 Mar–6 Oct	10–5	M	T	W	T	F	S	S
7 Oct–3 Nov	10–4	M	T	W	T	F	S	S
Waterfall tea-room and shop								
16 Feb–8 Mar	11–3:30	·	·	W	T	F	S	S
9 Mar–6 Oct	11–5*	M	T	W	T	F	S	S
7 Oct–3 Nov	11–4*	M	T	W	T	F	S	S
Shop**								
6 Nov–22 Dec	11–3:30	·	·	W	T	F	S	S

*Shop opens at 10. **6 November to 22 December: opening dependent on weather. Majority of gorge closed January, February, November and December due to weather conditions, higher river levels, reduced daylight hours and maintenance work (there is still access to Whitelady Waterfall from the waterfall entrance). 16 to 24 February: top path also open to the Whitelady Waterfall, 11 to 4.

Lytes Cary Manor

near Somerton, Somerset TA11 7HU

Map ① I5　

Intimate medieval manor house with beautiful Arts and Crafts garden. Originally the family home of Henry Lyte, Lytes Cary was lovingly restored in the 20th century by Sir Walter Jenner. The garden rooms contain a magical collection of topiary and herbaceous borders, while tranquil walks on the estate take you alongside the River Cary. Our community allotments are bursting with creative and colourful designs.

Eating and shopping: food kiosk serving light snacks and afternoon teas. Rustic shop selling garden accessories and plants.

Making the most of your day: daily talks and activities. Family activities and trails. **Dogs**: welcome on leads on estate walks only.

Access for all: ⏏⏏⏏⏏⏏⏏⏏ ⏏⏏
Building ⏏⏏　Grounds ⏏⏏

Getting here: 183:ST529269. Near Somerton. **Bus**: Wells to Yeovil; Taunton to Yeovil (passing close Taunton ☒). Both pass within ¾ mile Yeovil Pen Mill ☒. Alight Kingsdon, 1 mile. **Train**: Yeovil Pen Mill 8 miles; Castle Cary 9 miles; Yeovil Junction 10 miles. **Road**: off A372. Signposted, 1 mile from A303 (London to Exeter). **Parking**: free, 40 yards.

Finding out more: 01458 224471 or lytescarymanor@nationaltrust.org.uk

Lytes Cary Manor		M	T	W	T	F	S	S
16 Mar–3 Nov	10:30–5	M	T	W	.	F	S	S

House opens at 11.

The fountain in the Pond Garden at Lytes Cary Manor in Somerset: one of many garden rooms

Market Hall

High Street, Chipping Campden,
Gloucestershire GL55 6AJ

Map (1) K1

Outstanding building, constructed nearly 400
years ago to give shelter to market traders.
Note: no toilet, nearest in town centre.

Finding out more: 01386 438333
or www.nationaltrust.org.uk

Max Gate, Dorset, was designed by Thomas Hardy

Max Gate

Alington Avenue, Dorchester, Dorset DT1 2AB

Map (1) J7

Max Gate, home to Dorset's most famous
author and poet Thomas Hardy, was designed
by the writer himself in 1885. This atmospheric
Victorian home is where Hardy wrote some of
his most famous novels including *Tess of the
d'Urbervilles* and *Jude the Obscure*, as well as
most of his poetry.

Eating and shopping: Hardy books,
souvenirs and small gifts on sale.
Light refreshments available.

Making the most of your day: guided tours
available on request. Events, including poetry
readings, storytelling, children's trail and
performances. **Dogs**: welcome on leads
in garden only.

Access for all: ☐ ⣿ ⓐ Building ⌲

Getting here: 194:SY704899. 1 mile east
of Dorchester. **Bus**: regular services from
Dorchester. **Train**: Dorchester South/West
1 mile. **Road**: from A35 Dorchester Bypass, turn
off onto A352 Wareham Road to Max Gate
roundabout. Go straight over roundabout
and turn left into cul-de-sac outside the house.
Signposted from roundabout if approaching
from other directions.

Sat Nav: directions can be unreliable.
Look for signs from A352. **Parking**: free
(not National Trust), 50 yards.

Finding out more: 01305 262538 or
maxgate@nationaltrust.org.uk

Max Gate		M	T	W	T	F	S	S
13 Mar–3 Nov	11–5			·	·	W	T	F	S	S

Open Bank Holiday Mondays.

Mompesson House

The Close, Salisbury, Wiltshire SP1 2EL

Map (1) K5   🏠 ❀ ⊤

When walking into the celebrated Cathedral
Close in Salisbury, visitors step back into
a past world, and on entering Mompesson
House, featured in the award-winning film
Sense and Sensibility, the feeling of leaving the
modern world behind deepens. The tranquil
atmosphere is enhanced by the magnificent
plasterwork, fine period furniture and graceful
oak staircase, which are the main features
of this perfectly proportioned Queen Anne
house. In addition, the Turnbull collection of
18th-century drinking glasses is of national
importance. The delightful walled garden
has a pergola and traditionally planted
herbaceous borders.

Mompesson House, Wiltshire: Queen Anne perfection

Montacute House

Montacute, Somerset TA15 6XP

Map ① l6 🏠✿♟️🛏️🔔🍽️

A magnificent golden mansion surrounded by formal lawns, famous wobbly hedges, grand trees and garden pavilions. This Elizabethan house is full of oak-panelled rooms with period furniture and tapestries. It has the longest gallery in England, and, as part of a partnership with the National Portrait Gallery, shows more than 50 Tudor and Jacobean portraits (including Henry VIII and Elizabeth I) from the national collection. There is spring colour and vivid flower and rose borders in summer. In winter, follow the crisp lines of the lawns and hedges and enjoy stunning views of the house.

Eating and shopping: tea-room serving locally baked scones and cakes, light lunches and teas. National Trust shop only 60 yards away. Turnbull Glass Collection catalogue for sale.

Making the most of your day: regular croquet sessions on lawn. Music, including pianists playing our 1790s Broadwood square piano and Northumbrian Pipers' sessions. New this year: Barbara Townsend's 19th-century painting room re-created. **Dogs**: assistance dogs only.

Access for all: 🅿️♿🚻♿🔄📷💻♿👓📷
Building 🔼♿ Grounds 🔼♿

Getting here: 184:SU142297. On north side of Choristers' Green in the Cathedral Close, near High Street Gate. **Foot**: from city centre follow signs to the Cathedral. **Bus**: buses from surrounding area. **Train**: Salisbury ½ mile. **Road**: park and ride on all main routes into city. **Parking**: 260 yards in city centre (not National Trust, pay and display).

Finding out more: 01722 420980 (Infoline). 01722 335659 or mompessonhouse@nationaltrust.org.uk

Eating and shopping: Courtyard Café. Shop selling gifts and souvenirs. Plant sales.

Making the most of your day: daily talks and activities. Events, including farmers' markets, open-air theatre. Family trails. Tudor visits for schools. Combine with a visit to Tintinhull Garden. **Dogs**: welcome under control in parkland. On leads in garden during the winter season.

The grand drive up to Montacute House, Somerset

Mompesson House		M	T	W	T	F	S	S
16 Mar–3 Nov	11–5	M	T	W	·	·	S	S
Open Good Friday.								

Croquet on the lawn at Montacute House, Somerset

Access for all: ⬛⬛⬛⬛⬛⬛⬛
Building ⬛⬛⬛ Grounds ⬛⬛⬛

Getting here: 183/193:ST499172. In Montacute village, 4 miles west of Yeovil. **Bus**: Yeovil bus station to South Petherton. **Train**: Yeovil Pen Mill 5 miles; Yeovil Junction 7 miles. **Road**: 3 miles south of, and signed from, A303. Take A3088 towards Yeovil. **Parking**: free.

Finding out more: 01935 823289 or montacute@nationaltrust.org.uk

Montacute House		M	T	W	T	F	S	S
House								
5 Jan–10 Mar*	12–3						S	S
16 Mar–3 Nov	11–5	M		W	T	F	S	S
9 Nov–29 Dec*	12–3						S	S
Garden, parkland, café and shop								
2 Jan–15 Mar	11–4			W	T	F	S	S
16 Mar–3 Nov	10–5	M	T	W	T	F	S	S
6 Nov–29 Dec	11–4			W	T	F	S	S

Property closed 24 and 25 December. *House open by guided tour only (last tour 2:30).

Newark Park

Ozleworth, Wotton-under-Edge, Gloucestershire GL12 7PZ

Map (1) J3   ⬛⬛⬛⬛⬛

Overlooking the splendid Ozleworth Valley, Newark Park commands breathtaking, unspoilt views to the Mendips. The house and grounds are steeped in history, from Tudor beginnings to their dramatic rescue by a Texan architect in the 20th century.

Eating and shopping: light refreshments.

Making the most of your day: waymarked countryside walks and footpath link to Cotswold Way. Family events and children's quiz. Garden games for hire. Picnics welcome in garden. **Dogs**: on leads in grounds only.

Newark Park, Gloucestershire, originally a hunting lodge

Overbeck's

Sharpitor, Salcombe, Devon TQ8 8LW

Map ① F9

Perched high on the cliffs above Salcombe, Overbeck's boasts an exotic, hidden garden with banana and palm trees, woodland, and a spectacular panorama across miles of beautiful coastline and estuary. The Edwardian house was once the seaside home of inventor Otto Overbeck, and you can see his amazing 'rejuvenator', the intriguing and eclectic collections of natural and maritime history, as well as hearing the polyphon, a giant Victorian music box. The perfect day out for families who enjoy exploring, or the keen gardener who wants to be inspired and excited. **Note**: entrance path and grounds are very steep in places.

Eating and shopping: tea-room (book a takeaway picnic hamper) and shop. Plant sales.

Access for all: 🖪🖼🚶♿📷
Building 👣♿ Grounds ♿

Getting here: 172:ST786934. 1½ miles north-east of Wotton-under-Edge.
Foot: Cotswold Way passes. **Bus**: Bristol to Thornbury, connecting Thornbury to Dursley, alight Wotton-under-Edge, 1¾ mile.
Train: Stroud 10 miles. **Road**: 1¾ miles south of junction of A4135 and B4058, follow signs for Ozleworth. House signposted from main road.
Parking: free, 100 yards.

Finding out more: 01793 817666 (Infoline). 01453 842644 or newarkpark@nationaltrust.org.uk

Newark Park		M	T	W	T	F	S	S
9 Feb–17 Feb	11–4	·	·	**W**	**T**	**F**	**S**	**S**
2 Mar–1 Nov	11–5	·	·	**W**	**T**	**F**	**S**	**S**
7 Dec–8 Dec	11–4	·	·	·	·	·	**S**	**S**

Open Bank Holidays. Closes dusk if earlier.

Overbeck's, Devon, with the estuary beyond

Making the most of your day: self-guided garden trails, including 'Japanese', 'Cooks' and 'Non-Gardeners'. Events, including regular tours. Museum. Coastal walks.
Dogs: assistance dogs only.

Access for all: 🅿🖪🖼🔔🖼📖🖼📷
Building 👣 Grounds 👣➡

Exotic planting at Overbeck's, Devon

Getting here: 202:SX728374. Above Salcombe. **Foot**: South West Coast Path. **Ferry**: Salcombe to South Sands, then ½-mile uphill walk. **Bus**: Totnes or Kingsbridge, alight Salcombe. **Road**: narrow and unsuitable for large vehicles. **Sat Nav**: ignore in Malborough; pick up brown signs towards Salcombe. **Parking**: small car park. Alternative, East Soar, one mile.

Finding out more: 01548 842893 or overbecks@nationaltrust.org.uk

Overbeck's		M	T	W	T	F	S	S
16 Feb–3 Nov	11–5	M	T	W	T	F	S	S

Tea-room closes 4:15.

Parke

near Bovey Tracey, Devon TQ13 9JQ

Map ① G7

Set on the south-eastern edge of Dartmoor, this tranquil country park contains numerous delights. Riverside paths follow the course of the Bovey, as it meanders through woodlands and meadows rich in plant and wildlife. There is also a medieval weir, walled garden and orchard with historic apple trees.

Eating and shopping: café serving light lunches and afternoon tea. Local products for sale.

Making the most of your day: orienteering trails and geocaching. Wildlife events and apple days. Self-guided garden, woodland trails and quizzes. Outdoor Tracker Packs. **Dogs**: on leads where stock grazing.

Access for all: 🖼🚻♿🅰 Countryside 🖼

Getting here: 191:SX805786. In Bovey Tracey. **Cycle**: Newton Abbot to Bovey Tracey cycleway. **Bus**: Exeter bus station to Newton Abbot, alight at Bovey Tracey (1 mile). Also Widecombe to Bovey Tracey, May to October Saturdays only. **Train**: Newton Abbot 6 miles. **Road**: 2 miles north of A38, Exeter to Plymouth. Take the A382 towards Bovey Tracey. **Parking**: free.

Finding out more: 01626 834748 or parke@nationaltrust.org.uk. Home Farm, Parke, Bovey Tracey, Devon TQ13 9JQ

Parke		M	T	W	T	F	S	S
Parkland, woodland and walks								
Open all year	Dawn–dusk	M	T	W	T	F	S	S
Home Farm Café								
7 Jan–28 Mar	10–4	M	T	W	T	F	S	S
29 Mar–3 Nov	10–5	M	T	W	T	F	S	S
4 Nov–23 Dec	10–4	M	T	W	T	F	S	S

Café opening and closing times in winter are dependent on weather.

Tranquil Parke on the edge of Dartmoor, Devon

Visitors enjoy the graceful Palladian Bridge at Prior Park Landscape Garden in Bath, Somerset

Penrose

Penrose, Helston, Cornwall TR13 0RD

Map (1) B10

Loe Bar separates Cornwall's largest freshwater lake, Loe Pool, from the sea; at Gunwalloe, beautiful beaches frame a medieval church.

Finding out more: 01326 561407
or www.nationaltrust.org.uk. The Stables, Penrose, Helston, Cornwall TR13 0RD

Priest's House, Muchelney

Muchelney, Langport, Somerset TA10 0DQ

Map (1) I6

Medieval hall-house, built in 1308, and little altered since the early 17th century.
Note: tenanted. No toilet.

Finding out more: 01458 253771
or www.nationaltrust.org.uk

Prior Park Landscape Garden

Ralph Allen Drive, Bath, Somerset BA2 5AH

Map (1) J4

One of only four Palladian bridges of this design in the world can be crossed at Prior Park, which was created in the 18th century by local entrepreneur Ralph Allen, with advice from 'Capability' Brown and the poet Alexander Pope. The garden is set in a sweeping valley where visitors can enjoy magnificent views of Bath. Restoration of the 'Wilderness' has reinstated the Serpentine Lake, Cascade and Cabinet. A five-minute walk leads to the Bath Skyline, a six-mile circular route encompassing beautiful woodlands and meadows, an Iron Age hill fort, Roman settlements, 18th-century follies and spectacular views.
Note: mansion not accessible. Steep slopes, steps and uneven paths.

Eating and shopping: tea kiosk by lake.

Making the most of your day: free family activity packs. Open-air events. Guided tours of the Wilderness.
Dogs: on short leads only.

Access for all:
Grounds

Getting here: 172:ST760633. **Foot:** 1 mile uphill (very steep) walk from rear of railway station: cross river, pass Widcombe shopping parade, turn right onto Prior Park Road at White Hart pub, proceed uphill, garden on left. Kennet & Avon Canal path ¾ mile. **Cycle:** NCN4, ¾ mile. **Bus:** frequent services from Bath Spa ⬛, Abbey and Dorchester Street by the bus station. **Train:** Bath Spa 1 mile. **Road:** no brown signs. **Parking:** for disabled visitors only.

Finding out more: 01225 833422 or priorpark@nationaltrust.org.uk

Prior Park Landscape Garden		M	T	W	T	F	S	S
Garden								
5 Jan–27 Jan	10–5	·	·	·	·	·	S	S
1 Feb–3 Nov	10–5:30	M	T	W	T	F	S	S
9 Nov–29 Dec	10–5	·	·	·	·	·	S	S
Tea kiosk								
2 Feb–17 Mar	11–5	·	·	·	·	·	S	S
23 Mar–3 Nov	11–5	M	T	W	T	F	S	S
9 Nov–29 Dec	11–5	·	·	·	·	·	S	S

Last admission one hour before closing. Closes dusk if earlier than 5:30. Tea kiosk also open 9 to 17 February, events and Bank Holidays.

Prior Park Landscape Garden with Bath beyond

Purbeck Countryside, Dorset: the Agglestone

Purbeck Countryside

Purbeck, near Corfe Castle, Dorset

Map ① K7

From dinosaur-era Purbeck limestones to recent sand dunes of Studland, nowhere else packs such a variety of habitats into such a small area. This is the richest place for plant life in Britain – there are more than 54 miles of paths and bridleways on which you can explore these landscapes.

Eating and shopping: shops and cafés at Studland beach and Corfe Castle village.

Making the most of your day: walking, horse riding, cycling, geocaching and water sports. Bird hides at Studland and Hartland. **Dogs:** welcome under close control, some restrictions may apply (see signs).

Getting here: OL15:SY9615. **Foot:** South West Coast Path begins at Shell Bay, Studland; many other footpaths. **Cycle:** NCN2 between Hartland and Studland, plus 23 miles of bridleways. **Ferry:** Sandbanks car ferry for access to Studland. **Bus:** Wareham to Swanage bus serves Hartland Moor, Corfe Castle and Spyway. Bournemouth to Swanage bus for Studland Heath and Dunes, plus Ballard Down. **Parking:** free at Durnford Drove, Langton and Slepe road verges. Pay and display at Castle View by Corfe Castle and Studland.

Finding out more: 01929 450002 or purbeck@nationaltrust.org.uk. Purbeck Office, Currendon Farm, Ulwell Road, Swanage, Dorset BH19 3AA

Purbeck Countryside	Open every day all year

Free parking sites open all year.

St Michael's Mount

Marazion, Cornwall TR17 0HT

Map ① B9 [icons]

This iconic rocky island, crowned by a medieval church and castle, is home to the St Aubyn family and a 30-strong community of islanders. Visitors can immerse themselves in history at the Mount, where the architecture dates back to the 12th century and legends – such as that of Jack the Giant Killer – abound. There is a subtropical terraced garden and spectacular views of Mount's Bay and the Lizard from the castle battlements. If the tide is in, you can take an evocative boat trip to the island or, at low tide, walk across the ancient causeway from Marazion. **Note**: steep climb to castle up uneven, cobbled pathway. St Aubyn family/National Trust partnership.

Eating and shopping: Island Café (licensed), not National Trust, serving cream teas, pasties and light bites. Sail Loft Restaurant (licensed) serving hearty dishes and homemade cakes. Island shop and National Trust shop selling local gifts and art.

Making the most of your day: children's quiz. Tours (by arrangement). Events. Live music most Sundays; Sunday church services Whitsun to end September.

Dogs: assistance dogs only in castle and garden.

Access for all: [icons] Castle [icon] Village [icons]

Getting here: 203:SW515298. Off coast at Marazion. **Foot**: South West Coast Path within ¾ mile. **Ferry**: small boats cross at high tide (may not run in bad weather). **Bus**: Penzance to Helston or St Ives. All pass Penzance ⊠. **Train**: Penzance 3 miles. **Road**: ½ mile south of A394 at Marazion. **Parking**: ample parking in Marazion opposite St Michael's Mount (not National Trust, charge including members).

Finding out more: 01736 710265/710507 or stmichaelsmount@nationaltrust.org.uk. Estate Office, King's Road, Marazion, Cornwall TR17 0EL

St Michael's Mount		M	T	W	T	F	S	S
Castle								
18 Mar–30 Jun	10:30–5	M	T	W	T	F	·	S
1 Jul–30 Aug	10:30–5:30	M	T	W	T	F	·	S
1 Sep–3 Nov	10:30–5	M	T	W	T	F	·	S
Garden								
15 Apr–28 Jun	10:30–5	M	T	W	T	F	·	·
4 Jul–30 Aug	10:30–5:30	·	·	·	T	F	·	·
5 Sep–27 Sep	10:30–5	·	·	·	T	F	·	·

Last admission 45 minutes before castle closes (enough time should be allowed for travel from the mainland). Castle winter opening: call for details.

Saltram

Plympton, Plymouth, Devon PL7 1UH

Map ① F8 🏛️✳️♿🍴

The rolling lawn by the west front of Saltram

Saltram stands high above the River Plym in a rolling and wooded landscape park that now provides precious green space on the outskirts of Plymouth. The house, with its magnificent decoration and original contents, was home to three generations of the Parker family. Highlights include Robert Adam's Neo-classical Saloon, exquisite plasterwork ceilings, original Chinese wallpapers and ceramics and an exceptional collection of paintings including several by Sir Joshua Reynolds and Angelica Kauffman. The garden is predominantly 19th-century and contains an 18th-century Orangery and follies, as well as beautiful shrubberies and imposing specimen trees offering year-round interest and delight.

Eating and shopping: Park Café serving meals and snacks. Shops selling plants, gifts and local arts and crafts.

Making the most of your day: family, costumed and seasonal events. Open-air theatre. Craft fairs. Family trails. Themed guided tours on certain days. **Dogs**: welcome in woods and parkland.

Access for all: 🅿️♿🚻♿♿🔲👶
House ♿🅖 Grounds ♿➡️♿🅖

Getting here: 201:SX520557. 3½ miles east of Plymouth city centre. **Foot**: South West Coast Path within 4 miles. **Cycle**: NCN27. **Bus**: service from city centre drops off within one mile. **Train**: Plymouth 3½ miles. **Road**: 3½ miles east of Plymouth city centre. Travelling south (from Exeter): exit from A38 is signed Plymouth City Centre/Plympton/Kingsbridge. At roundabout take centre lane, then third exit for Plympton. Take right-hand lane and follow brown signs. Travelling north (from Liskeard): leave A38 at Plympton exit. From roundabout as before. **Sat Nav**: enter Merafield Road. **Parking**: members free, 50 yards.

Finding out more: 01752 333500 or saltram@nationaltrust.org.uk

Saltram		M	T	W	T	F	S	S
Park								
Open all year	Dawn–dusk	M	T	W	T	F	S	S
House								
9 Mar–3 Nov	12–4:30	M	T	W	T	·	S	S
House*								
16 Feb–3 Mar	11–4	·	·	·	·	·	S	S
7 Dec–15 Dec	11–4	·	·	·	·	·	S	S
Garden and shop								
2 Jan–8 Mar	11–4	M	T	W	T	F	S	S
9 Mar–3 Nov	11–5	M	T	W	T	F	S	S
4 Nov–31 Dec	11–4	M	T	W	T	F	S	S
Park Café								
1 Jan–8 Mar	10–4	M	T	W	T	F	S	S
9 Mar–3 Nov	10–5	M	T	W	T	F	S	S
4 Nov–31 Dec	10–4	M	T	W	T	F	S	S
Chapel arts and crafts**								
2 Feb–23 Dec	11–4:30	M	T	W	T	F	S	S

Last admission to house 45 minutes before closing. House open Good Friday and first Friday of the month, April to October for special tours. *House partially open for special events. Garden and shop closed 24 to 26 December. Park Café closed 25 and 26 December. **Chapel arts and crafts limited opening until 9 March, closes 4 in winter.

Saltram, Devon: setting off on a cycle ride

Shute Barton

Shute, near Axminster, Devon EX13 7PT

Map ① H7 🏠 ❄ 💺 🏠

Medieval manor house, with later Tudor gatehouse and battlemented turrets – now a holiday cottage. **Note**: open four weekends a year only.

Finding out more: 01752 346585 or www.nationaltrust.org.uk

Snowshill Manor and Garden

Snowshill, near Broadway, Gloucestershire WR12 7JU

Map ① K1 🏠 ❄ 🏠

Charles Paget Wade's passion for craftsmanship, colour and design began when he was just seven years old. His motto was 'Let nothing perish', and his life was dedicated to finding, restoring and enjoying objects of beauty, both everyday and extraordinary. He packed his treasures into the Cotswold manor house which he bought and renovated for the purpose. From tiny toys to Samurai armour, musical instruments to fine clocks, thousands of treasures are laid out just as Mr Wade intended. The Manor nestles in an intimate Arts and Crafts-style terraced garden with hidden vistas and quiet corners.

Eating and shopping: restaurant serving lunches, cream teas and homemade cakes. Shop selling gifts, plants and local produce. Second-hand bookshop.

Making the most of your day: Tracker Packs, indoor and outdoor children's trails. Introductory and garden talks. Events. **Dogs**: assistance dogs only.

Dovecote in the garden at Snowshill, Gloucestershire

Access for all: 🅿️🚻♿🚻🚻🏠🏠 📷 VT •• 🅰️
Manor 🏠 Garden 🏠🏠

Getting here: 150:SP095341. 2½ miles south-west of Broadway. **Foot**: Cotswold Way within ¾ mile. **Bus**: Evesham to Broadway, then 2½ miles uphill. **Train**: Moreton-in-Marsh 7 miles, Evesham 8 miles. **Road**: turn off A44 Broadway bypass into Broadway village; at green turn right uphill to Snowshill. **Parking**: free, 500 yards. Transfer available.

Finding out more: 01386 852410 or
snowshillmanor@nationaltrust.org.uk

Snowshill Manor and Garden		M	T	W	T	F	S	S
Manor								
29 Mar–30 Jun	12–5	·	·	W	T	F	S	S
1 Jul–26 Aug	11:30–4:30	M	·	W	T	F	S	S
28 Aug–3 Nov	12–5	·	·	W	T	F	S	S
Garden, shop and restaurant								
29 Mar–30 Jun	11–5:30	·	·	W	T	F	S	S
1 Jul–26 Aug	11–5	M	·	W	T	F	S	S
28 Aug–3 Nov	11–5:30	·	·	W	T	F	S	S
9 Nov–1 Dec	12–4	·	·	·	·	·	S	S
Priest's House								
29 Mar–30 Jun	11–5	·	·	W	T	F	S	S
1 Jul–26 Aug	11–4:30	M	·	W	T	F	S	S
28 Aug–3 Nov	11–5	·	·	W	T	F	S	S
Manor by guided tour only (additional charge)								
9 Nov–1 Dec	12–4	·	·	·	·	·	S	S

Manor admission is by limited timed tickets, issued on a
first-come, first-served basis. Tickets run out on peak days.
Last admission to Manor one hour before it closes.
Open all Bank Holidays between March and October.

Zodiac clock in the Well Court at Snowshill

South Milton Sands

Thurlestone, near Kingsbridge, Devon TQ7 3JY

Map (1) F9

Long sandy beach and dunes, with rock-pooling,
kayaking, snorkelling and beach café.

Finding out more: 01548 561144 (Beach House
café) or www.nationaltrust.org.uk

Stembridge Tower Mill

High Ham, Somerset TA10 9DJ

Map (1) I5

Built in 1822, this is the last remaining thatched
windmill in England – the last survivor of five
in the area. **Note**: holiday cottage on site,
please respect the tenants' privacy. No toilet.
Parking limited.

Finding out more: 01935 823289
or www.nationaltrust.org.uk

Stoke-sub-Hamdon Priory

North Street, Stoke-sub-Hamdon,
Somerset TA14 6QP

Map (1) I6

Fascinating small complex of buildings, home
to priests serving the Chapel of St Nicholas
(now destroyed). **Note**: no toilet.

Finding out more: 01935 823289
or www.nationaltrust.org.uk

The Great Hall of Stoke-sub-Hamdon Priory, Somerset

Stonehenge Landscape

near Amesbury, Wiltshire

Map ① K5

Within the Stonehenge World Heritage Site, the Trust manages 827 hectares (2,100 acres) of downland surrounding the famous stone circle. On the ridges all around Stonehenge are fine Bronze Age round barrows, the resting places of the privileged. The shallow banks of Stonehenge's Great Cursus enclosure are 5,500 years old, pre-dating the stone circle. The massive henge of Durrington Walls, 4,500 years ago the site of feasting and huge gatherings, encloses a natural valley. Large areas of arable land are being restored as chalk grassland, habitat for a diverse range of insects, birds and wild flowers. **Note**: stone circle managed by English Heritage (admission free to Trust members).

Eating and shopping: catering kiosk at the stone circle (not National Trust).

Making the most of your day: walks and workshops throughout year. **Dogs**: welcome under close control (assistance dogs only at stone circle).

Access for all: 🅿♿ 🚻♿

Getting here: 184:SU120420. 2 miles west of Amesbury. **Bus**: Stonehenge Tour bus Salisbury ➡ to Stonehenge. **Train**: Salisbury 9½ miles. **Road**: on A344, off A303. **Parking**: 50 yards (not National Trust). Charge may apply June to October (National Trust members free).

Finding out more: 01980 664780 or stonehenge@nationaltrust.org.uk. 3 Stonehenge Cottages, King Barrows, Amesbury, Wiltshire SP4 7DD

Stonehenge Landscape	M	T	W	T	F	S	S
Open every day all year	Dawn–dusk						

King Barrow, part of Stonehenge Landscape in Wiltshire, a site steeped in ancient history

Stourhead

near Mere, Wiltshire BA12 6QD

Map ① J5

'A living work of art' is how a magazine described Stourhead when it first opened in the 1740s. The world-famous landscape garden has as its centrepiece a magnificent lake reflecting classical temples, mystical grottoes and rare and exotic trees. Stourhead House, set amid 'picnic perfect' lawns and parkland, contains a unique Regency library, Chippendale furniture and inspirational paintings, and offers an Italian 'Grand Tour' adventure. The garden and house are at the heart of a 1,072-hectare (2,650-acre) estate, where chalk downs, ancient woods and farmland are managed for wildlife.

Eating and shopping: extended shop and plant centre. Farm shop. Award-winning restaurant. Spread Eagle Inn. Ice-cream parlour. Art gallery. Picnics welcome.

Making the most of your day: events and activities for all, including climbing trees, hands-on conservation, behind-the-scenes glimpses and fresh-air workouts. Spring blooms and autumn colour spectacular. Free garden and countryside tours. Family Tracker Packs and trails. Italian adventures at Stourhead House. Private hire and special experiences. Visit our website and download our seasonal newsletter. **Dogs**: welcome in countryside all year; and on short fixed leads in landscape garden December to February, and after 4, March to November.

Access for all: 🅿️🚻♿🚹♿🅿️👓📷
Building 🪜♿♿ Grounds ♿➡️🚃♿

Getting here: 183:ST780340. Stourton, 3 miles north-west of Mere, 8 miles south of Frome. **Cycle**: Wiltshire Cycle Way. **Bus**: from Warminster and Shaftesbury, alight Zeals, 1¼ miles. **Train**: Gillingham 6½ miles; Bruton 7 miles. **Road**: brown signs off A303. B3092 from Frome. **Parking**: 400 yards. King Alfred's Tower 50 yards.

The Temple of Apollo at Stourhead in Wiltshire

Finding out more: 01747 841152 or stourhead@nationaltrust.org.uk.
Stourhead Estate Office, Stourton, Warminster, Wiltshire BA12 6QD

Stourhead		M	T	W	T	F	S	S
Garden and restaurant								
1 Jan–31 Mar	9–5	M	T	W	T	F	S	S
1 Apr–30 Sep	9–7	M	T	W	T	F	S	S
1 Oct–31 Dec	9–5	M	T	W	T	F	S	S
House								
5 Jan–10 Mar	11–3	·	·	·	·	·	S	S
16 Mar–3 Nov	11–4:30	M	T	W	T	F	S	S
9 Nov–24 Nov	11–3	·	·	·	·	·	S	S
30 Nov–22 Dec	11–3	M	T	W	T	F	S	S
Shop								
1 Jan–31 Mar	10–5	M	T	W	T	F	S	S
1 Apr–30 Sep	10–6	M	T	W	T	F	S	S
1 Oct–31 Dec	10–5	M	T	W	T	F	S	S
King Alfred's Tower								
2 Mar–27 Oct	12–4	·	·	·	·	·	S	S

House winter openings: 5 January to 10 February and
9 to 24 November (weekends), 'Winter Warmers' fire lit
and board games in the Entrance Hall. 16 February to
10 March (weekends): 'Conservation in Action', selected
rooms only. 30 November to 22 December (daily):
'The Christmas House', selected rooms decorated.
King Alfred's Tower: also open Bank Holidays and selected
special periods, please call for details. Stourhead closed
25 December.

Stourhead, Wiltshire: the west front of the house

Studland Beach

Studland, near Swanage, Dorset

Map ① K7

Off for a day on the beach at Studland, Dorset

Glorious slice of Purbeck coastline with a
four-mile stretch of golden, sandy beach,
gently shelving bathing waters and views of
Old Harry Rocks and the Isle of Wight. Includes
the most popular naturist beach in Britain.
The heathland behind the beach is a haven
for native wildlife and features all six British
reptiles. Designated trails through the sand
dunes and woodlands allow for exploration and
spotting of deer, insects and bird life as well
as numerous wild flowers. Studland was the
inspiration for Toytown in Enid Blyton's *Noddy*.
Note: Shell Bay toilets are low-water flush, only
other toilets at Knoll Beach and Middle Beach.

Eating and shopping: shop selling
seaside-themed goods and local gifts.
Knoll Beach with spectacular sea views.

Making the most of your day: year-
round events, including children's trails,
wildlife guided walks, food events and
Discovery Centre. Watersports. Coastal
change interpretation hut open all year.
Dogs: restrictions 1 May to 30 September.

Sandcastle fun at Studland Beach, Dorset

Access for all: 🄿♿🚾♿🍴♿ Grounds ♿🚽

Getting here: 195:SZ035835. 5 miles south of Poole and north of Swanage.
Foot: 5 miles of South West Coast Path. **Ferry**: car ferry from Sandbanks, Poole, to Shell Bay. **Bus**: Bournemouth to Swanage. **Train**: Branksome or Parkstone, both 3½ miles to Shell Bay (via vehicle ferry) or Wareham 12 miles. **Parking**: Shell Bay and South Beach, 9 to 11; Knoll Beach and Middle Beach, 9 to 8 or dusk if earlier. Car parks mainly pay and display.

Finding out more: 01929 450500 or studlandbeach@nationaltrust.org.uk. Purbeck Office, Currendon Farm, Currendon Hill, Swanage, Dorset BH19 3AA

Studland Beach		M	T	W	T	F	S	S
Shop and café								
1 Jan–23 Mar	10–4	M	T	W	T	F	S	S
24 Mar–30 Jun*	9:30–5	M	T	W	T	F	S	S
1 Jul–8 Sep	9–6	M	T	W	T	F	S	S
9 Sep–27 Oct*	9:30–5	M	T	W	T	F	S	S
28 Oct–31 Dec	10–4	M	T	W	T	F	S	S
Beach								
Open all year		M	T	W	T	F	S	S

*Shop and café open one hour later at weekends. Shop and café opening hours may be longer in fine weather and shorter in poor. Visitor centre, shop and café closed 25 December. Car parks can be very full in peak season.

Tintagel Old Post Office

Fore Street, Tintagel, Cornwall PL34 0DB

Map ① D7 🏠❄️

Built around 1380 as a farmhouse, this building never actually sold stamps but has had various uses across the centuries. The homely rooms are mostly furnished with 16th-century oak furniture, while the cottage garden provides a peaceful retreat from the bustling high street. **Note**: nearest toilet, 54 yards.

Eating and shopping: shop in Post Room.

Making the most of your day: family trail and garden games. Rag rug making. **Dogs**: assistance dogs only.

Access for all: 🏠📷♿••🏠
Building ♿🚽 Grounds ♿🚽

Getting here: 200:SX056884. On high street, opposite King Arthur's car park. **Foot**: South West Coast Path within ¾ mile. **Bus**: services from Wadebridge to Boscastle. **Road**: follow signs off A39 for Tintagel. **Parking**: no onsite parking. Pay and display (not National Trust).

Finding out more: 01840 770024 or tintageloldpo@nationaltrust.org.uk

Tintagel Old Post Office		M	T	W	T	F	S	S
16 Feb–24 Feb	11–4	M	T	W	T	F	S	S
2 Mar–24 Mar	11–4	M	T	W	T	F	S	S
25 Mar–29 Sep	10:30–5:30	M	T	W	T	F	S	S
30 Sep–3 Nov	11–4	M	T	W	T	F	S	S

The 14th-century Tintagel Old Post Office in Cornwall

Tintinhull Garden

Farm Street, Tintinhull, Yeovil,
Somerset BA22 8PZ

Map (1) I6

The vision of the amateur gardener Phyllis
Reiss lives on today in this delightful garden.
Described as one of the most harmonious small
gardens in Britain, it surrounds a charming
manor house that you can rent as a holiday
cottage. The garden rooms have secluded
lawns, pools and colourful mixed borders, and
the lovely kitchen garden provides vegetables
for the restaurant at nearby Montacute House.

Eating and shopping: tea-room serving cakes
and cream teas. Plant sales and small shop.

Making the most of your day: village explorer
sheet available. Montacute House nearby.
Dogs: assistance dogs only in garden.

Access for all: [symbols]
Building [symbols]   Gardens [symbols]

Getting here: 183:ST503198. In Tintinhull
village, 4 miles west of Yeovil. **Bus**: Yeovil bus
station to South Petherton. **Train**: Yeovil Pen
Mill 5 miles; Yeovil Junction 7 miles. **Road**: 1 mile
south of A303 (London to Exeter). Follow signs
to Tintinhull village. **Parking**: free, 150 yards.

Finding out more: 01935 823289 or
tintinhull@nationaltrust.org.uk

Tintinhull Garden		M	T	W	T	F	S	S
27 Mar–31 May	11–5			W	T	F	S	S
1 Jun–31 Jul	11–5		T	W	T	F	S	S
1 Aug–3 Nov	11–5			W	T	F	S	S

Open Bank Holiday Mondays. House closes at 4.

Tintinhull Garden, Somerset: west front of the house

The still waters of the Pool Garden at Tintinhull

Treasurer's House, Martock

Martock, Somerset TA12 6JL

Map (1) I6   [symbol]

Medieval house including Great Hall,
completed 1293, with 15th-century kitchen
and unusual wall-painting in upstairs room.
Note: tenanted house. No toilet or
onsite parking.

Finding out more: 01935 825015
or www.nationaltrust.org.uk

Trelissick Garden

Feock, near Truro, Cornwall TR3 6QL

Map ① C9 🎨🏛️♣️🖼️🚻☕

Starting in a complex of former farm buildings and garden walls, explore this elevated garden with its views of deep-wooded valleys and flashes of blue water. Trelissick sits on its own peninsula in an unspoiled stretch of the River Fal. Picturesque planting is heightened by the folding contours and the informal wooded setting. There are places in both sun and shade to discover a wide range of plants and to sit and recharge the batteries. All of Trelissick's many owners have made their mark and built on the framework that their predecessors laid out before them.

Eating and shopping: self-service café. Barn restaurant serving Sunday lunches. Shop, Cornish art and craft gallery, second-hand bookshop. Six holiday cottages.

Trelissick Garden, Cornwall, with the River Fal beyond

Making the most of your day: walks in the parkland and woodland, open-air theatre in summer, exhibitions and shows held in the stables by local groups, illuminated garden walks in the run-up to Christmas. **Dogs**: welcome on woodland walks surrounding garden. Assistance dogs only in garden.

Access for all: 🅿️♿️♿️🔆🅿️🄰
Visitor reception ♿️ Garden ♿️♿️➡️♿️♿️

Getting here: 204:SW837396. 5 miles south of Truro. **Cycle**: NCN3. **Ferry**: from Falmouth, Truro and St Mawes (www.falriver.co.uk). **Bus**: Truro to Trelissick and Feock. **Train**: Truro 5 miles; Perranwell 4 miles. **Road**: on B3289 above King Harry ferry. **Parking**: 50 yards.

Finding out more: 01872 862090 or trelissick@nationaltrust.org.uk

Trelissick Garden		M	T	W	T	F	S	S
1 Jan–15 Feb	11–4	M	T	W	T	F	S	S
16 Feb–3 Nov	10:30–5:30	M	T	W	T	F	S	S
4 Nov–23 Dec	11–4	M	T	W	T	F	S	S
26 Dec–31 Dec	11–4	M	T	·	T	F	S	S

Garden closes dusk if earlier. Parts of garden lit up at night in run-up to Christmas.

Trengwainton Garden

Madron, near Penzance, Cornwall TR20 8RZ

Map ① B9 ⚅ 🛏

The spirit of the plant hunters lives on in this 10-hectare (25-acre) garden, which invites you to explore – then come back for more. There are breathtaking spring displays of magnolias, rhododendrons and camellias, and a walled kitchen garden full of ideas for your own growing space. The wide-open views across Mount's Bay will inspire every budding photographer, and the winding, wooded paths, picnic spots by the stream and quiet corners allow visitors to breathe in the peace of this special place.

Eating and shopping: award-winning tea-room in its own lovely walled garden (Trust-approved concession). National Trust shop including locally sourced gifts and plants.

Making the most of your day: events, activities and family trails. Nearby Godolphin can be visited in the same day. **Dogs**: welcome on leads.

Access for all: 🅿️ 🅓 📶 🚾 ⛪ 🅹 🔽 📷 🅐
Reception 🏔 Grounds 🏔 ➡ 🔽

Getting here: 203:SW445315. 2 miles north-west of Penzance. **Foot**: from Penzance via Heamoor. **Cycle**: NCN3, 2½ miles. **Bus**: frequent service (from Penzance ➷), stops at garden entrance. **Train**: Penzance 2 miles. **Road**: follow signs from A30 or A3071 St Just to Penzance road. **Parking**: free, 150 yards.

Finding out more: 01736 363148 or trengwainton@nationaltrust.org.uk

Trengwainton Garden		M	T	W	T	F	S	S
17 Feb–3 Nov	10:30–5	M	T	W	T	·	·	S
6 Dec–15 Dec	11–4	·	·	·	·	F	·	S

Open Good Friday. Tea-room opens 10. Last admission 15 minutes before closing.

The walled garden, below, and bridge, above, at Trengwainton Garden, Cornwall

The garden above Trerice, Cornwall, with the east front of the Tudor manor house in the background

Trerice

Kestle Mill, near Newquay, Cornwall TR8 4PG

Map ① C8 🏠 🏛 ❀ 🚻 🍴

Intimate Tudor manor house and garden re-imagined by successive owners and tenants. Behind 576 panes of glass is the magnificent Great Hall with its refined plasterwork ceiling. Upstairs the Great Chamber has an even finer ceiling and views out to lands once part of the extensive estate. The story of the Trust's tenants in the 1950s – who rebuilt a fallen part of the house and devoted themselves to the restoration of Trerice – unfolds in the North Wing. Tudor defence and entertainment are brought to life by visitors trying on armour and playing traditional games. **Note**: from 25 February to 29 March there may be disruptive conservation work taking place in the house, resulting in its partial or total closure.

Eating and shopping: self-service Barn tea-room serving morning coffee, light lunches and afternoon tea. Shop.

Making the most of your day: Tudor-themed workshops, costume days, behind-the-scenes days and atmospheric evening openings. **Dogs**: welcome in car park only.

Access for all: 🅿️♿ 🚽♿ 🛗♿ 🏠♿ 📷 ⛱ ⚲ ♿
House ♿♿ Garden ♿♿♿➡️♿

Getting here: 200:SW841585. 3 miles southeast of Newquay. **Cycle**: NCN32. **Bus**: Newquay ➡ to St Austell ➡, alight Kestle Mill, ¾ mile. **Train**: Quintrell Downs, 1½ miles. **Road**: southeast of Newquay via A392 and A3058, signed from Quintrell Downs (turn right at Kestle Mill), or signed from A30 at Summercourt via A3058. **Parking**: free, 300 yards.

Finding out more: 01637 875404 or trerice@nationaltrust.org.uk

Trerice		M	T	W	T	F	S	S
House								
16 Feb–3 Nov	11–5	M	T	W	T	F	S	S
Garden, shop and tea-room								
16 Feb–3 Nov	10:30–5	M	T	W	T	F	S	S
9 Nov–22 Dec	11–4	.	.	.	.	.	S	S
Great Hall only								
9 Nov–22 Dec	11–4	.	.	.	.	.	S	S

Atmospheric evening opening every Friday in March and October.

Tyntesfield

Wraxall, Bristol, North Somerset BS48 1NX

Map (1) I4   🏛➕🔷🦮🛏️🍴

Lived in by four generations of the Gibbs family, all making their mark and never throwing anything away, Tyntesfield – the Trust's largest conservation project – offers a fascinating day out whatever the weather. There are Gothic towers and flower-filled terraces, an enchanting rose garden and productive kitchen garden, while the wider estate, with its wonderful views, is breathtaking.

Eating and shopping: Cow Barn kitchen serving dishes made with estate-grown ingredients. Courtyard coffee bar, Pavilion café and P&J's pit stop. Gift shop selling locally made gifts. Garden and second-hand book shops.

Making the most of your day: events all year, including open-air theatre, living history, hands-on family activities, plus workshops, walks and talks with specialists. Free daily garden tours. Two summer estate walks and winter 'walkies' (two legs and four). Children's play area and family trails. Local food and craft market (first Sunday of month, April to October). Christmas festivities, including concerts, food, shopping, decorations and Father Christmas. 'Unpacked in 2013' – more objects from the collection and stories, some from the carpenters' workshop, forge and Orangery. **Dogs**: welcome on woodland estate walks. Assistance dogs only in house and garden.

Access for all: 🅿️♿🚻♿♿🎨📺♿👓
House ♿♿♿ Grounds ♿♿♿♿

Getting here: ST502724. 7 miles south-west of Bristol. **Bus**: frequent services from Bristol bus station. **Train**: Nailsea & Backwell station 2 miles. **Road**: on B3128. M5 southbound exit 19 via A369 (towards Bristol), B3129, B3128. M5 northbound exit 20, B3130 (towards Bristol), B3128. **Parking**: 50 yards from ticket office.

An aerial view of Tyntesfield, North Somerset, below, and the Stuart Room, above

Finding out more: 0844 800 4966 (Infoline). 01275 461900 or tyntesfield@nationaltrust.org.uk

Tyntesfield		M	T	W	T	F	S	S
House and chapel								
9 Feb–17 Feb	11–3	M	T	W	·	·	S	S
18 Feb–3 Mar	11–3	M	T	W	·	·	S	S
9 Mar–3 Nov	11–5	M	T	W	·	·	S	S
5 Jul–1 Nov	11–5	M	T	W	·	F	S	S
2 Dec–20 Dec	11–3	M	T	W	·	F	·	·
Garden, estate, restaurant and shop*								
1 Jan–8 Mar	10–5	M	T	W	T	F	S	S
9 Mar–3 Nov	10–6	M	T	W	T	F	S	S
4 Nov–31 Dec	10–5	M	T	W	T	F	S	S
Refreshments								
9 Mar–3 Nov	10–5:30	M	T	W	T	F	S	S

*Restaurant and shop open 10:30 and close 30 minutes earlier than garden and estate. Last admission to house one hour before closing. Timed tickets to house (limited numbers). Friday: booking available. 18 February to 3 March: access to house by tour only. *Garden and estate: close 5 or dusk if earlier. House: open Good Friday. Garden and estate: closed 25 December. 24 and 31 December: closes 3.

Discussing tactics at Tyntesfield, North Somerset

Watersmeet

Watersmeet Road, Lynmouth, Devon EX35 6NT

Map F5

This area, where the lush valleys of the East Lyn and Hoar Oak Water tumble together, is a haven for wildlife and offers excellent walking. At the heart sits Watersmeet House, a 19th-century fishing lodge, which is now a tea garden, shop and information point. **Note**: deep gorge with steep walk down to house.

Eating and shopping: tea garden serving local seasonal food. Shop selling Exmoor produce and gifts, walking gear and maps.

Making the most of your day: Exmoor Spotter chart for families and *Exmoor Coast of Devon* walks leaflet available. **Dogs**: allowed on leads in tea garden.

Access for all: ⬛⬛⬛ Building ⬛ Grounds ⬛

Getting here: 180:SS744487. 1½ miles east of Lynmouth. **Foot**: South West Coast Path within ¾ mile. 1½ miles from Lynmouth. **Bus**: regular services from Barnstaple (passing close Barnstaple ≋), and Minehead, alight Lynmouth. **Road**: on east side of Lynmouth to Barnstaple road (A39). **Parking**: pay and display (not National Trust), steep walk to house. Free at Combe Park and Countisbury.

Finding out more: 01598 753348 or watersmeet@nationaltrust.org.uk

Watersmeet		M	T	W	T	F	S	S
Countryside								
Open all year		M	T	W	T	F	S	S
Tea-room and tea garden								
16 Feb–24 Feb	11–3	M	T	W	T	F	S	S
9 Mar–28 Mar	10:30–4:30	M	T	W	T	F	S	S
29 Mar–29 Sep	10:30–5	M	T	W	T	F	S	S
30 Sep–3 Nov	10:30–4:30	M	T	W	T	F	S	S

Watersmeet House shop opens 30 minutes after tea-room and tea garden, except for 16 to 24 February, when shop is closed.

Wembury

Wembury Beach, Wembury, Devon PL9 0HP

Map F9

A coastal village, near the Yealm estuary, with a small, pretty beach and a charming 19th-century mill (now a tea-room). Beautiful views, excellent rock-pooling and a great starting point for coastal and inland walks.

Eating and shopping: coffee, cakes, soups, pasties and ice-creams. Local arts and crafts. Beach shop selling everything from spades and wetsuits to windbreaks. Deckchairs for hire (weekends and school holidays).

Making the most of your day: activities, including rock-pooling (01752 862538), sailing, surfing, kayaking, walking and horse riding.

Dogs: welcome on coast path. Banned on beach 1 May to 30 September.

Access for all: Café 🦽
Marine Centre 🧑‍🦽 **Beach** 🦽

Getting here: 201:SX517484. On edge Wembury village. **Foot**: South West Coast Path. **Ferry**: seasonal ferries to Noss Mayo and Bantham. **Bus**: Plymouth to Wembury daily (limited on Sunday). For Wembury Point: Plymouth to Heybrook Bay. **Train**: Plymouth 10 miles. **Road**: Wembury Point and beach follow the A379 from Plymouth, turn right at Elburton, follow signs to Wembury. At Wembury follow the road until you see Wembury primary school, turn left where you see a brown sign for café. **Parking**: free (charge for non-members). Manned during busy times.

Finding out more: 01752 346585 (South Devon Coast and Countryside Office). 01752 862314 (Old Mill Café) or wembury@nationaltrust.org.uk. South and East Devon Countryside Office, The Stables, Saltram House, Plymouth, Devon PL7 1UH

Wembury	M	T	W	T	F	S	S
Beach and coast							
Open all year	M	T	W	T	F	S	S
Old Mill Café							
1 Jan–6 Jan	11–3	·	T	W	T	F	S	S
16 Feb–24 Feb	10:30–4	M	T	W	T	F	S	S
30 Mar–3 Nov	10:30–5	M	T	W	T	F	S	S
26 Dec–31 Dec	11–3	M	T	·	T	F	S	S

Café opening hours may vary depending on weather.

Westbury College Gatehouse

College Road, Westbury-on-Trym, Bristol BS9 3EH

Map ① I3   🏠

15th-century gatehouse to 13th-century College of Priests – former home of theological reformer John Wyclif. **Note**: access by key. No toilet.

Finding out more: 01275 461900 or www.nationaltrust.org.uk

Westbury Court Garden

Westbury-on-Severn, Gloucestershire GL14 1PD

Map ① J2   ❖

Originally laid out between 1696 and 1705, this is the only restored Dutch water garden in the country. There are canals, clipped hedges, working 17th-century vegetable plots and many old varieties of fruit trees.

Making the most of your day: evening garden tours, Easter Egg trails, Apple Day. **Dogs**: welcome on short leads at all times.

Access for all: 🅿♿🚽📷 **Grounds** 🏛🧑‍🦽♿

Getting here: 162:SO718138. 9 miles south-west of Gloucester. **Foot**: River Severn footpath runs from garden to river. **Bus**: Gloucester 🚆 to Chepstow or Coleford. **Train**: Gloucester 9 miles. **Road**: on A48. **Parking**: free, 300 yards.

Finding out more: 01452 760461 or westburycourt@nationaltrust.org.uk

Westbury Court Garden		M	T	W	T	F	S	S
13 Mar–30 Jun	10–5	·	·	W	T	F	S	S
1 Jul–1 Sep	10–5	M	T	W	T	F	S	S
4 Sep–27 Oct	10–5	·	·	W	T	F	S	S

Open Bank Holiday Mondays, other times by appointment.

Westbury Court Garden, Gloucestershire: the parterre

Westwood Manor

Westwood, near Bradford-on-Avon,
Wiltshire BA15 2AF

Map (1) J4

This beautiful small manor house (below),
built over three centuries, has late Gothic and
Jacobean windows, decorative plasterwork and
two important keyboard instruments. There
is also some fine period furniture, as well as
17th- and 18th-century tapestries and a modern
topiary garden. **Note**: administered by the tenant.
No toilet. House unsuitable for under-fives.

Eating and shopping: CD of atmospheric
musical recordings of the recently restored
virginal and spinet for sale.

Making the most of your day: children's quizzes.

Access for all: Manor   Garden

Getting here: 173:ST812590. 1½ miles south-
west of Bradford-on-Avon, in Westwood
village, beside church. **Cycle**: NCN254,
¾ mile. **Bus**: Bath to Trowbridge (passing
close Trowbridge). **Train**: Avoncliff 1 mile;
Bradford-on-Avon 1½ miles. **Road**: Westwood
village signed off B3109 Bradford-on-Avon to
Rode. Turn left opposite the New Inn towards
the church. **Parking**: free, 90 yards.

Finding out more: 01225 863374 or
westwoodmanor@nationaltrust.org.uk

Westwood Manor	M	T	W	T	F	S	S
31 Mar–29 Sep 2–5		T	W				S

Small groups at other times by written arrangement.

White Mill

Sturminster Marshall, near Wimborne Minster,
Dorset BH21 4BX

Map (1) K6

Corn mill with original wooden machinery in a
peaceful riverside setting.

Finding out more: 01258 858051
or www.nationaltrust.org.uk

Woodchester Park

Nympsfield, near Stonehouse,
Gloucestershire GL10 3TS

Map (1) J3

The tranquil wooded valley contains a 'lost
landscape': remains of an 18th- and 19th-century
park with a chain of five lakes. Its restoration is
an ongoing project. Trails (steep in places) pass
an unfinished Victorian mansion (not National
Trust). **Note**: toilet not always available.

Making the most of your day: waymarked
trails through valley. **Dogs**: under close control,
on leads where requested.

Access for all: Grounds

Getting here: 162:SO797012. 4 miles south-
west of Stroud. **Foot**: Cotswold Way within
¾ mile. **Bus**: Stroud to Nympsfield (passing
close Stroud). **Train**: Stroud 5 miles.
Road: off B4066 Stroud to Dursley road.
Parking: £2 (pay and display). Accessible from
Nympsfield road, 300 yards from junction with
B4066. Last admission one hour before dusk.

Finding out more: 01452 814213 or
woodchesterpark@nationaltrust.org.uk.
The Ebworth Centre, The Camp, Stroud,
Gloucestershire GL6 7ES

Woodchester Park	M	T	W	T	F	S	S
Open every day all year	Dawn–dusk						

South East

Ghostly ensemble: dressmakers'
dummies intrigue young visitors at
Chastleton House, Oxfordshire

Outdoors in the South East

The South East of England is one of the country's most densely populated areas; however, thanks to the National Trust and similar organisations, it still boasts extensive and beautiful green spaces, waterways and miles of dramatic coastline – perfect places to enjoy some fun outdoors.

Above:
sweeping views
at Devil's Dyke,
South Downs,
West Sussex

South Downs – Britain's newest national park

The South Downs, stretching for more than 70 miles across Sussex, is a destination valued for its internationally rare habitats, stunning wildlife, ancient history and outdoor activities. There is something for everyone: from bracing coastal walks or gentle strolls, to exciting activities, including zorbing (rolling down a hill in a giant blow-up hamster ball), mountain boarding, cycling, kayaking and power kiting. Or, for a more leisurely time, just take a picnic and admire the views.

Escape London for a day and head to the Surrey Hills

The rolling hills of Surrey are only a stone's throw from London, but seem a million miles away from city living. Get away from it all with challenging cycling, tranquil boating or walks with some of the region's best views. Follow the footpaths up Leith Hill and climb to the top of the Gothic tower and you may be able to see St Paul's Cathedral away to the north, while to the south you can enjoy panoramic views all the way to the English Channel.

New Forest Northern Commons

The beauty of the New Forest's isolated wilderness and wonderful colours – from heather hues to autumn blazes – is completely captivating. Climb to the top of a hill or stroll through wild open landscapes at Rockford, then be inspired by the regeneration of wildlife-rich landscapes at Bramshaw, shaped by historic rural practices that still thrive today.

Explore the Chiltern Hills

We look after a group of popular beauty spots in the picturesque Chiltern Hills, where there are many fabulous walking opportunities. There can be few more pleasant ways of spending a day than exploring this attractive landscape of woods, farms and hamlets, stopping for a spot of lunch at a pub. Popular places include Watlington Hill, West Wycombe Hill, Coombe Hill and Ivinghoe Beacon along the Chiltern escarpment. For an action-packed day, the Ashridge Estate, covering more than 2,000 hectares (5,000 acres), offers fine walks, picnic areas and family-friendly cycle routes.

Above:
a rider on Rockford Common, Hampshire, looks out towards Ibsley Common, in the same county

Below:
Aston Wood, Oxfordshire

Above:
chilling out
at East Head,
West Wittering,
West Sussex
Below: taking
the long view
at Needles
Old Battery,
Isle of Wight

Kent: England's garden

Kent is a hidden gem. Blow away the cobwebs at the iconic White Cliffs of Dover or enjoy a woodland walk at Toys Hill, Petts Wood and Hawkwood. You can take a number of trails through Knole Park, spotting the resident deer along the way, or visit Old Soar Manor, following the trail to Ightham Mote, where you can refuel with a cream tea.

Coast and countryside on the Isle of Wight

The most southerly point of the region is the Isle of Wight. Here much of the finest countryside and coastline is owned by the National Trust, including the magnificent chalk downs of Ventnor, Tennyson Down and the Needles Headland. This is the place to head for an outdoor adventure, complete with walking, surfing and wildlife spotting. Alternatively just relax on a beach and listen to the crashing of the waves.

Take in the pretty villages

If you feel like stepping back in time, why not visit one of our historic villages? Walk through Chiddingstone in Kent to see a beautiful example of a Tudor village, or wander among the 16th-century cottages and inns of West Wycombe Village or the scenic cottages of Bradenham Village.

Why not try…?

Taking to the water

We look after some of the magnificent coastline of East Sussex and the Isle of Wight – places where wildlife is abundant. From the birds that make their home on the cliffs of the Seven Sisters, to the creatures that hide in the pools left by the sea at Birling Gap and St Helen's Beach, there's a new world waiting to be explored.

The adventurous will love the surf at Compton Bay, one of the Isle of Wight's favourite beaches, or at Birling Gap, a top spot to ride the waves in the South East; or try kayaking or canoeing in the Cuckmere Valley. For sea lovers, a bracing swim in the sea at East Head, West Wittering, can't be beaten.

For a more relaxing water experience, hire a boat to take in the delights of the River Wey, the largest stretch of waterway we care for. Escape the hustle and bustle by boating down this river as it meanders through the stunning Surrey countryside.

Walking, camping, kite flying or a picnic

We are spoilt for choice with the number of stunning walks in our region, and new walking trails and routes are being developed all the time, such as the Octavia Hill trail around Toys Hill. A well-known route in Oxfordshire not to be missed is to the famous White Horse at Uffington, while the nearby villages and agricultural estates of Buscot and Coleshill have many pleasant circular walks.

While out and about, enjoy a play trail at Coombe Hill, a picnic at Watlington Hill or fly a kite at Devil's Dyke. The more adventurous will be excited to hear that we are working with the British Mountaineering Council to offer experienced climbers the amazing opportunity to climb the famous White Cliffs of Dover (on restricted routes).

Right: **mountain biking at Black Down, West Sussex**

After all this activity, you'll need somewhere to rest your weary head. Stay outdoors and spend a night at Gumber Bothy on the South Downs, or under canvas at Etherley Farm in Surrey.

Sightseeing by bike

Cycling is a great way to stay fit and enjoy the outdoors. Why not retrace the Olympic 2012 cycling route at Box Hill – the hairpin bends of the famous zigzag road are a real challenge. With the visitor centre and servery at the top, you can always stop for a well-deserved break. Or head to Stowe, where there is a new cycling route running around the outside of the landscape gardens. You could also enjoy lunch in the New Inn café.

For more information on all our countryside and coastal places, visit **www.nationaltrust.org.uk/southeast**

The colourful cottage-style garden at Alfriston Clergy House, East Sussex: the first building the Trust acquired

Alfriston Clergy House

The Tye, Alfriston, Polegate,
East Sussex BN26 5TL

Map ② H8

This rare 14th-century Wealden 'hall-house' was the first building to be acquired by the National Trust, in 1896. The thatched, timber-framed house is in an idyllic setting, with views across the River Cuckmere, and is surrounded by a tranquil cottage garden full of wildlife. **Note**: nearest toilet in village car park.

Eating and shopping: shop selling souvenirs.

Making the most of your day: children's quizzes and trails. Varied events all year. Short circular walks and longer distance hikes over South Downs.

Access for all: ⬛⬛⬛⬛⬛⬛
Building ⬛⬛ Grounds ⬛⬛

Getting here: 189:TQ521029. In Alfriston village. **Foot**: South Downs Way within ¾ mile. **Cycle**: NCN2. **Bus**: services from Lewes, Eastbourne and Seaford (pass close Lewes ≋ and Seaford ≋). **Train**: Berwick 2½ miles. **Road**: 4 miles north-east of Seaford, east of B2108, in Alfriston, adjoining The Tye and St Andrew's church. **Parking**: 500 yards across village (not National Trust).

Finding out more: 01323 871961 or alfriston@nationaltrust.org.uk

Alfriston Clergy House		M	T	W	T	F	S	S
23 Feb–10 Mar	11–4	.	.	.	.	.	**S**	**S**
16 Mar–28 Jul	10:30–5	**M**	**T**	**W**	.	.	**S**	**S**
29 Jul–30 Aug	10:30–5	**M**	**T**	**W**	.	**F**	**S**	**S**
31 Aug–3 Nov	10:30–5	**M**	**T**	**W**	.	.	**S**	**S**
4 Nov–22 Dec	11–4	**M**	**T**	**W**	.	.	**S**	**S**

Open Good Friday. Special Friday openings in August.

Members may have to pay on special events days

Ascott

Wing, near Leighton Buzzard,
Buckinghamshire LU7 0PR

Map ② E3

This half-timbered Jacobean farmhouse,
transformed by the de Rothschilds towards
the end of the 19th century, now houses
an exceptional collection of paintings,
fine furniture and superb oriental porcelain.
The extensive gardens are an attractive mix of
formal and natural, with specimen trees and
shrubs and some unusual features.

Making the most of your day: unusual
features to spot in the gardens.
Dogs: assistance dogs only.

Access for all: ⬚⬚⬚⬚⬚⬚
Building ⬚⬚⬚⬚ Grounds ⬚⬚⬚➡

Getting here: 165:SP891230. ½ mile east of
Wing, 2 miles south-west of Leighton Buzzard.
Bus: from Aylesbury to Milton Keynes (passing
close Aylesbury ⬛ and Leighton Buzzard ⬛).
Train: Leighton Buzzard 2 miles. **Road**: on
south side of A418. **Parking**: free, 220 yards.

Finding out more: 01296 688242 or
ascott@nationaltrust.org.uk

Ascott		M	T	W	T	F	S	S
12 Mar–28 Apr	2–6	·	T	W	T	F	S	S
30 Apr–25 Jul	2–6	·	T	W	T	·	·	·
30 Jul–6 Sep	2–6	·	T	W	T	F	S	S

Open Bank Holiday Mondays and Good Friday.
Last admission one hour before closing. Gardens open in
aid of National Gardens Scheme on 6 May and 26 August
(charges including members). Some areas of the gardens
may be roped off when conditions are bad.

Ashdown House

Lambourn, Newbury, Berkshire RG17 8RE

Map ② C5 ⬚⬚⬚⬚

Extraordinary 17th-century chalk-block house,
with doll's-house appearance and fine portrait
collection, built for the Queen of Bohemia.
Note: access via staircase of 100 steps up to
roof viewing area. Property is tenanted, so
please check opening times before travelling.

Finding out more: 01494 755569 (Infoline).
01793 762209
or www.nationaltrust.org.uk

A unique sundial, created from box hedge topiary, in the gardens at Ascott in Buckinghamshire

Ashridge Estate

Visitor Centre, Moneybury Hill, Ringshall,
Berkhamsted, Hertfordshire HP4 1LT

Map ② E3 ☒🏛♿♨

Countryside estate covering 2,000 hectares
(5,000 acres) and running along the main ridge
of the Chiltern Hills. Its breathtaking scenery
ranges from ancient oak and beech woodland
to rolling chalk grassland at Ivinghoe Beacon.
There is a huge network of paths, with the
chance to spot wildlife – including wild fallow
deer and red kites. Every season brings its own
delights, with carpets of bluebells in spring,
beautiful orchids and butterflies in summer,
spectacular leaf colour in autumn and
frost-covered trees in winter. Our Visitor
Centre, near the Bridgewater Monument,
offers ideas for walks and family days out.
Note: toilets only available when café open.

Eating and shopping: shop selling
gifts, books, local maps and self-guided
walk leaflets. Brownlow Café (National
Trust-approved concession).

An ancient beech tree on the Ashridge Estate

Making the most of your day: events, including
wildlife walks, talks and countryside festival.
Children's activities in Discovery Room.
Dogs: allowed under close control
(deer roam freely).

Access for all: 🅿♿🚹♿🔧
Visitor centre ♿🚻 Grounds ♿➡🚲

Getting here: 181:SP970131. Between
Berkhamsted and Dagnall. **Foot**: Visitor Centre
short detour from Ridgeway footpath at
Ivinghoe Beacon. **Bus**: to Monument Drive,
Aldbury (½-mile uphill walk) and Tring
(1¾-mile walk). **Train**: Tring ≋ 1¾ miles.
Ivinghoe Beacon: Cheddington ≋ 3½ miles.
Road: off B4506 between Berkhamsted and
Dagnall. **Parking**: free.

Finding out more: 01494 755557 (Infoline).
01442 851227 or ashridge@nationaltrust.org.uk

Ashridge Estate		M	T	W	T	F	S	S
Estate								
Open all year		M	T	W	T	F	S	S
Visitor centre and shop								
11 Feb–20 Dec	10–5	M	T	W	T	F	S	S
Bridgewater Monument (weather dependent)								
30 Mar–27 Oct	12–4:30	·	·	·	·	·	S	S
Brownlow Café								
1 Jan–22 Mar	8–4	M	T	W	T	F	S	S
23 Mar–3 Nov	8–6	M	T	W	T	F	S	S
4 Nov–31 Dec	8–4	M	T	W	T	F	S	S

Visitor Centre, shop and café may close at dusk if earlier.
Last entry to monument 4:15. Monument open
Bank Holiday Mondays. Café closed 25 December.

Ashridge Estate, Hertfordshire: Bridgewater Memorial

Basildon Park, Berkshire: 18th-century house, 1950s home

Basildon Park

Lower Basildon, Reading, Berkshire RG8 9NR

Map ② D5 🏠 ❄ ♨ ♠ ☂

The Basildon Park you see today is a re-creation and restoration of the 18th-century mansion, brought back to life in the 1950s as the country home of Lord and Lady Iliffe. Inspired by the original designs of the architect John Carr, the Iliffes collected important 18th- and 19th-century paintings and antiques especially for the interiors of Basildon Park. There are weekly guided walks through the historic parkland and you can explore the gardens and our newly opened Old Kitchen and enjoy family activities. **Note**: main show rooms on first floor – 21 steps.

Eating and shopping: tea-room serving traditional English fare, cakes and scones. New 'Pit-Stop' in stableyard offering snacks, and wide range of local products available in shop.

Making the most of your day: guided house tours and parkland walks. Events. Woodland 'Scramble' for children. Piano for visitors to play. Greys Court, Nuffield Place and The Vyne nearby. **Dogs**: welcome on leads.

Access for all: 🅿️ ♿ 🏢 🅦🅒 🕶 🔈 ♿ 📷 🖼 🆚 ♿
⬛🅰 Mansion ♿♿🅱
Grounds 🏢♿➡🅱

Getting here: 175:SU611782. 7 miles north-west of Reading. **Bus**: from Reading. **Train**: Pangbourne 2½ miles; Goring 3 miles. **Road**: on west side of A329. Leave M4 at exit 12 and follow signs for Beale Park and Pangbourne, then for Basildon Park. **Sat Nav**: use RG8 9NU for main entrance. **Parking**: free, 400 yards from mansion (buggy available).

Finding out more: 0118 984 3040 or basildonpark@nationaltrust.org.uk

Basildon Park		M	T	W	T	F	S	S
House								
9 Mar–3 Nov	12–5	M	T	W	T	F	S	S
30 Nov–22 Dec	11–4	M	T	W	T	F	S	S
House tours								
9 Feb–3 Mar	12–3	·	·	·	·	·	S	S
9 Mar–3 Nov	11–12	M	T	W	T	F	S	S
4 Nov–29 Nov	12–3	M	T	W	T	F	S	S
Grounds, shop and tea-room								
2 Feb–8 Mar	10–4	M	T	W	T	F	S	S
9 Mar–3 Nov	10–5	M	T	W	T	F	S	S
4 Nov–22 Dec	10–4	M	T	W	T	F	S	S

On Tuesdays, entry by guided tour only.

There is plenty of room for everyone to have fun at Bateman's in East Sussex

Bateman's

Bateman's Lane, Burwash,
East Sussex TN19 7DS

Map ② H7

'That's She! The Only She! Make an honest woman of her – quick!' was how Rudyard Kipling and his wife, Carrie, felt the first time they saw Bateman's. Surrounded by the wooded landscape of the Sussex Weald, this 17th-century house, with its secluded garden and acres of countryside, provided a much-needed sanctuary for this world-famous writer. Don't miss Kipling's 1928 Rolls-Royce Phantom I or the working watermill near the river that runs through the garden. **Note:** free entry to garden, shop and restaurant in November.

Eating and shopping: shop selling Kipling books and souvenirs. Restaurant.

Making the most of your day: family fun days, storytelling, re-enactment weekends, garden and countryside walks. Children's quizzes and trails. Scotney Castle and Bodiam Castle nearby. **Dogs:** on leads in car park and countryside paths only. Dog crèche available.

Access for all: ♿🅿♿♿♿♿♿♿♿♿♿♿
Building ♿♿♿ Grounds ♿➡♿

Getting here: 199:TQ671238. ½ mile south of Burwash. **Bus:** hourly service from Uckfield to Etchingham (weekdays) – less frequent at weekends. **Train:** Etchingham 3 miles. **Road:** ½ mile south of Burwash. A265 west from Burwash, first turning on left. **Parking:** free, 30 yards.

Finding out more: 01435 882302 or batemans@nationaltrust.org.uk

Bateman's		M	T	W	T	F	S	S
House								
2 Mar–3 Nov	11–5	M	T	W	T	F	S	S
30 Nov–23 Dec	11:30–3:30	M	T	W	T	F	S	S
Garden, shop and tea-room								
2 Mar–3 Nov	10–5	M	T	W	T	F	S	S
4 Nov–23 Dec	11–4	M	T	W	T	F	S	S
26 Dec–31 Dec	11–4	M	T		T	F	S	S

Shop and garden close 5:30, 2 March to 3 November.
Mill grinds corn most Wednesdays and Saturdays at 2.
House: downstairs rooms decorated for traditional Edwardian Christmas 30 November to 23 December.

Places may occasionally close for conservation, safety or events

Bembridge Fort

Bembridge Down, near Bembridge,
Isle of Wight PO36 8QY

Map (2) D9

In a commanding position on top of
Bembridge Down, this derelict Victorian fort
is open for volunteer-run guided tours.
Note: no toilets or other facilities. Access by
guided tour, booking essential, £3.50 charge
(including members).

Finding out more: 01983 741020
or www.nationaltrust.org.uk.
c/o Longstone Farmhouse, Strawberry Lane,
Mottistone, Isle of Wight PO30 4EA

Bembridge Windmill

High Street, Bembridge,
Isle of Wight PO35 5SQ

Map (2) D9

This little gem, the only surviving windmill
on the Isle of Wight, is one of its most iconic
images. Built around 1700 and last operated in
1913, it still has most of its original machinery
intact. Climb to the top and follow the milling
process back down its four floors.

Bembridge Windmill on the Isle of Wight

Eating and shopping: ice-cream kiosk, hot and
cold drinks, including tea, hot chocolate and
various coffees. Postcards, sweets, gifts and
souvenirs. Picnic table in grounds.

Making the most of your day: walks, including
the start of Culver Trail. Nature trails (school
holidays). Bembridge Fort (booking essential)
nearby. **Dogs**: on leads welcome in grounds.
Assistance dogs only in windmill.

Access for all:

Building

Getting here: 196:SZ639874. On outskirts of
village where High Street becomes Mill Road.

Cycle: NCN67, ½ mile. **Ferry**: Ryde (Wightlink)
6 miles (0871 376 1000); East Cowes (Red
Funnel) 13 miles (0844 844 9988). **Bus**: from
Ryde Esplanade ☒ to within ½ mile; Newport
and Sandown to within ¼ mile. **Train**: Brading
2 miles by footpath. **Road**: ½ mile south of
Bembridge on B3395. **Sat Nav**: do not use
postcode, look for brown signs. **Parking**: free
(not National Trust), 100 yards in lay-by.

Finding out more: 01983 873945 or
bembridgemill@nationaltrust.org.uk

Bembridge Windmill		M	T	W	T	F	S	S
16 Mar–3 Nov	10:30–5	M	T	W	T	F	S	S

Closes dusk if earlier. Conducted school groups and special
visits March to end October by written appointment.

Birling Gap and the Seven Sisters

East Dean, near Eastbourne,
East Sussex BN20 0AB

Map ② H9

Stretching between Birling Gap and Cuckmere Haven are the gleaming white cliffs of the Seven Sisters, eroded continuously by the sea. They are an impressive sight, and there are some lovely walks across the 242 hectares (600 acres) of Trust open-access downland with spectacular views out to sea.

Eating and shopping: café serving breakfast, lunch, teas and snacks. Small shop. Picnics welcome.

Making the most of your day: events and activities for all ages. Chyngton Farm, Frog Firle Farm, Alfriston Clergy House and Monk's House nearby. **Dogs**: welcome (on leads on beach from June to September).

Looking along the coast at Birling Gap, part of the Seven Sisters cliffs range, East Sussex

Getting here: 189:TV554961. 5 miles west of Eastbourne and 6 miles east of Seaford. **Foot**: on the South Downs Way. **Bus**: times vary throughout year. **Train**: Eastbourne ▣ 6 miles, Seaford ▣ 7 miles. **Road**: between Eastbourne and Seaford, south of A259 and East Dean village. **Parking**: at Birling Gap (pay and display), £2 for half day, £4 for whole day.

Finding out more: 01323 423197 or birlinggap@nationaltrust.org.uk

Birling Gap and the Seven Sisters		M	T	W	T	F	S	S
Countryside								
Open all year		M	T	W	T	F	S	S
Café								
1 Jan–28 Feb	10–4	M	T	W	T	F	S	S
1 Mar–30 Jun	10–5	M	T	W	T	F	S	S
1 Jul–1 Sep	10–6	M	T	W	T	F	S	S
2 Sep–3 Nov	10–5	M	T	W	T	F	S	S
4 Nov–31 Dec	10–4	M	T	W	T	F	S	S

Café closed 24 and 25 December.

Boarstall Duck Decoy

Boarstall, near Bicester,
Buckinghamshire HP18 9UX

Map ② D3

Set in an unspoilt natural environment, this is one of only three duck decoys left in the country.

Finding out more: 01280 817156 or www.nationaltrust.org.uk

Boarstall Tower

Boarstall, near Bicester,
Buckinghamshire HP18 9UX

Map ② D3 🏠🗼❁

Charming 14th-century moated gatehouse set in beautiful gardens.

Finding out more: 01280 817156 or www.nationaltrust.org.uk

The moated Bodiam Castle in East Sussex

Bodiam Castle

Bodiam, near Robertsbridge,
East Sussex TN32 5UA

Map ② I7

One of the most famous and evocative castles in Britain, Bodiam was built in 1385 as both a defence and a comfortable home. The exterior is virtually complete and the walls rise dramatically above the moat. Enough of the ruined interior survives to give an impression of castle life. There are spiral staircases and battlements to explore, and wonderful views across the High Weald, an area of outstanding beauty, from the top of the towers. In the impressive gatehouse is the castle's original wooden portcullis, an extremely rare example of its kind. **Note**: toilets in car park only. Property often used by educational groups during term time.

Eating and shopping: shop selling gifts and local produce. Wharf tea-room. Ice-creams, snacks and drinks available from castle kiosk (seasonal).

Making the most of your day: events, including mid-February challenge, medieval-themed weekend and Santa's Christmas Grotto. Evening events. Family activities throughout school holidays. Film and exhibition. **Dogs**: welcome on leads in grounds only.

Access for all: � of icons   Castle ⬚⬚⬚⬚ Grounds ➡⬚

Getting here: 199:TQ785256. 3 miles south of Hawkhurst. **Foot**: on Sussex Border path. **Ferry**: Bodiam Ferry (seasonal) from Newenden Bridge (A28). **Bus**: 349 from Hastings ➽ to Hawkhurst. **Train**: steam railway (seasonal) from Tenterden ¼ mile; Robertsbridge 5 miles; Battle 10 miles. **Road**: 3 miles east of A21 Hurst Green, between Tunbridge Wells and Hastings. **Parking**: 400 yards, £2.

Finding out more: 01580 830196 or bodiamcastle@nationaltrust.org.uk

Bodiam Castle		M	T	W	T	F	S	S
5 Jan–17 Feb	11–4	·	·	·	·	·	S	S
18 Feb–3 Nov	10:30–5	M	T	W	T	F	S	S
6 Nov–22 Dec	11–4	·	·	W	T	F	S	S
28 Dec–29 Dec	11–4	·	·	·	·	·	S	S

18 February to 3 November, gift shop and tea-room close at 5 most days but at 5:30 during school summer holidays.

The panoramic view from Box Hill in Surrey, above, and a snowy scene, below

Box Hill

Tadworth, Surrey KT20 7LB

Map ② F6

Beautiful countryside and views, woodland with natural play trail; a perfect base to start a leisurely walk with friends, family and dogs or to go cycling. Free walks guides available from our visitor centre.

Eating and shopping: brand-new indoor deli café. Servery for take-away teas and cakes. Small shop selling locally made gifts and souvenirs.

Making the most of your day: cross-country walk to Polesden Lacey. Guided walks and children's events (telephone in advance). School groups welcome. **Dogs**: under close control where sheep grazing.

Access for all: ⊞♿⚒♿♿♿♿
Building ♿♿ Grounds ➡

Getting here: 187:TQ171519. North of Dorking. **Bus**: services to top and foot of hill. **Train**: Box Hill & Westhumble 1½ miles. **Road**: off A24. **Parking**: £3 non-members. Coaches must only approach from east side B2032/B2033; parking at summit.

Finding out more: 01306 885502 or boxhill@nationaltrust.org.uk

Box Hill		M	T	W	T	F	S	S
Countryside								
Open all year		M	T	W	T	F	S	S
Box Tree shop, café, discovery zone and servery								
1 Jan–22 Mar	10–4	M	T	W	T	F	S	S
23 Mar–27 Oct	9–5	M	T	W	T	F	S	S
28 Oct–31 Dec	10–4	M	T	W	T	F	S	S

Shop, café, discovery zone and servery closed 25 December.

Buckingham Chantry Chapel

Market Hill, Buckingham, Buckinghamshire MK18 1JX

Map ② D2

Atmospheric 15th-century chapel, restored by Sir George Gilbert Scott in 1875.

Finding out more: 01280 817156 or www.nationaltrust.org.uk

The Buscot and Coleshill Estates

Coleshill, near Swindon, Wiltshire

Map (2) C4　🖼️🍴✿♿🛏️

These countryside estates on the western borders of Oxfordshire include the attractive, unspoilt villages of Buscot and Coleshill, each with a thriving shop and tea-room. There are circular walks of differing lengths and a series of footpaths criss-crossing the estates. **Note**: toilets in Coleshill estate office yard and next to village shop and tea-room in Buscot.

Eating and shopping: Buscot tea-room offering lunches and afternoon tea. Locally sourced produce served at Coleshill shop and tea-room and The Radnor Arms (award-winning ales and microbrewery).

Making the most of your day: guided walks throughout year. **Dogs**: on leads only.

Getting here: SU239973. Coleshill Village between Faringdon and Highworth. Buscot Village between Faringdon and Lechlade. **Cycle**: NCN45, 10 miles. Regional Route 40: Oxfordshire Cycleway. **Bus**: Swindon to Carterton (passing close Swindon ➡), alight Highworth, 2 miles. **Road**: Coleshill village on B4019. Buscot village on A417. **Parking**: at Buscot village; Coleshill estate office.

Finding out more: 01793 762209 or buscotandcoleshill@nationaltrust.org.uk. Coleshill Estate Office, Coleshill, Swindon, Wiltshire SN6 7PT

The Buscot and Coleshill Estates	Open every day all year
Coleshill Mill open second Sunday of the month: April to October, 2 to 5.	

Buscot Old Parsonage

Buscot, Faringdon, Oxfordshire SN7 8DQ

Map (2) C4　🏚️✿

Beautiful early 18th-century house with small walled garden, on the banks of the Thames. **Note**: administered by a tenant (booking essential). No toilets.

Finding out more: 01793 762209 or www.nationaltrust.org.uk

Schoolchildren on a voyage of discovery at a farm on the Coleshill Estate in Wiltshire

Buscot Park

Faringdon, Oxfordshire SN7 8BU

Map ② C4   🏠 ❖ ⛲

Family home of Lord Faringdon, who continues to care for the property as well as the Faringdon Collection, the family art collection displayed in the house. Consequently, despite the grandeur of their scale, both the house and grounds remain intimate and idiosyncratic and very much a family home. They also continue to change and develop – nothing is preserved in aspic here! Outside, there is a water feature, 'Faux Fall', by David Harber, and 17 life-size terracotta warriors from China. Inside, you can view contemporary paintings by Eileen Hogan and Amelia Roberts, and glassware by Colin Reid and Sally Fawkes. **Note**: administered on behalf of the National Trust by Lord Faringdon.

Eating and shopping: tea-room (not National Trust). Local honey, peppermints, cider, plants and kitchen garden produce (when available). Ice-cream available.

Making the most of your day: occasional events in grounds and theatre (available for hire). Picnics. **Dogs**: in Paddock (overflow car park) only.

Access for all: 🅿 ⓓ ♿ 🚻 ♿ 🎧 ⓙ ⠿ Ⓐ
House 🚶 🍴
Grounds 🚶 ♿ ♿ ➡ ♿ ♿

Getting here: 163:SU239973. Between Faringdon and Lechlade. **Foot**: 4 miles by footpath from Faringdon, 3½ miles from Lechlade. **Bus**: services from Oxford and Swindon to Faringdon and Swindon to Lechlade (passing close Swindon ⇌). **Train**: Oxford 18 miles, Swindon 12 miles. **Road**: on south side of A417. **Parking**: free.

Finding out more: 01367 240932 (Infoline). 01367 240786 or buscotpark@nationaltrust.org.uk. www.buscotpark.com

The Peto Water Garden at Buscot Park in Oxfordshire

Buscot Park	M	T	W	T	F	S	S
House, grounds and tea-room							
3 Apr–27 Sep 2–6	·	·	**W**	**T**	**F**	·	·
Grounds only							
1 Apr–24 Sep 2–6	**M**	**T**	·	·	·	·	·

*House, grounds and tea-room weekend opening: 30 and 31 March, 6 and 7, 20 and 21 April, 4 and 5, 11 and 12, 25 and 26 May, 8 and 9, 22 and 23 June, 13 and 14, 27 and 28 July, 10 and 11, 24 and 25 August, 14 and 15, 28 and 29 September 2 to 6 (tea-room 2:30 to 5:30). Last admission to house one hour before closing. Open Bank Holidays and Good Friday.

Parking charges for non-members may apply

Chartwell

Mapleton Road, Westerham, Kent TN16 1PS

Map ② G6 🏠🌸♿🔔🍴

Chartwell was the much-loved Churchill family home and the place from which Sir Winston drew inspiration from 1924 until the end of his life. The rooms remain much as they were when he lived here, with pictures, books and personal mementoes evoking the career and wide-ranging interests of this great statesman, writer, painter and family man. The hillside gardens reflect Churchill's love of the landscape and nature. They include the lakes he created, Lady Churchill's Rose Garden, the kitchen garden and the Marycot, a playhouse built especially for the youngest Churchill daughter. **Note**: house entrance by timed ticket only (no booking available).

Eating and shopping: large self-service restaurant. Kitchen garden produce available. Kiosk serving light bites, drinks and snacks (busy days only). Shop stocking Churchill memorabilia and local products. Lakeside picnics.

Chartwell, Kent: the light-filled dining room, below, south front, above, and a unique bench, overleaf

Making the most of your day: events, including themed weekends, drop-in family food plot, themed garden days (apples/honey), craft activities. Free talks and tours (selected days). Daily studio talks. Children's trails and activities, and woodland trails (walk sheets available). Regular special restaurant events. Knowledgeable room stewards introduce Sir Winston's family home. Sir Winston's paintings in his fascinating studio. Family trails and playing in the Marycot. Working kitchen garden – with bees and chickens. **Dogs**: on short leads in gardens only.

Access for all:  icons

Building icons Grounds icons

Getting here: 188:TQ455515. 2 miles south of Westerham. **Foot**: Greensand Way. **Bus**: services from Bromley North and Sevenoaks (Sundays and Bank Holidays only). **Train**: Edenbridge 4½ miles. **Road**: left off B2026 after 1½ miles. **Parking**: pay and display (non-members). Gates locked 5, March to October; 4:30 November to 31 December.

Finding out more: 01732 868381 or chartwell@nationaltrust.org.uk

Chartwell		M	T	W	T	F	S	S
House								
2 Mar–3 Nov	11–5	M	T	W	T	F	S	S
Studio								
1 Jan–1 Mar	12–3:30	M	T	W	T	F	S	S
2 Mar–3 Nov	12:30–4:30	M	T	W	T	F	S	S
4 Nov–31 Dec	12–3:30	M	T	W	T	F	S	S
Garden, exhibition, shop and restaurant								
1 Jan–1 Mar	11–4	M	T	W	T	F	S	S
2 Mar–3 Nov	10–5	M	T	W	T	F	S	S
4 Nov–31 Dec	11–4	M	T	W	T	F	S	S
Car park*								
Open all year	9–5	M	T	W	T	F	S	S

*Car park closes at 4 from January to March, November and December, dusk if earlier. Admission to house by timed ticket (places limited), obtain on arrival. Last admission 45 minutes before closing. All winter opening weather permitting. Closed 24 and 25 December. Studio closed 9 January to 29 January. Exhibition closed 23 February to 1 March and 4 November to 16 November.

Chastleton House and Garden

Chastleton, near Moreton-in-Marsh, Oxfordshire GL56 0SU

Map ② C3 icons

A rare gem of a Jacobean country house and garden, Chastleton was created between 1607 and 1612 by a prosperous wool merchant as an impressive statement of wealth and power. Owned by the same increasingly impoverished family until 1991, it remained essentially unchanged for nearly 400 years as the interiors and contents gradually succumbed to the ravages of time. With virtually no intrusion from the 21st century, this fascinating place exudes an informal and timeless atmosphere in a gloriously unspoilt setting. **Note**: timed ticket system for house (limited availability).

Eating and shopping: picnics welcome (in car park only). Plants and garden produce available (subject to availability). Second-hand bookshop. Local publications and souvenirs. No tea-room, but refreshments available from local church (not National Trust) most days.

Clandon Park

West Clandon, Guildford, Surrey GU4 7RQ

Map ② F6

Built *circa* 1730 for the 2nd Lord Onslow by Venetian architect Giacomo Leoni, Clandon Park is one of England's most complete examples of a Palladian mansion. It contains a superb collection of 18th-century furniture, porcelain and textiles, mostly acquired in the 1920s by connoisseur Mrs Gubbay. The wider parkland – still owned by the Onslow family – surrounds the mansion set in intimate gardens, home to a Maori meeting house brought back from New Zealand in 1892. The Onslow family is unique in that they provided three Speakers of the House of Commons.

Chastleton House and Garden in Oxfordshire, above, and Clandon Park in Surrey, below

Making the most of your day: free family explorer packs, croquet on the lawn, garden tours and conservation in action. Themed events. Out-of-hours and Taster Tours on request. **Dogs**: welcome on leads in car park and field opposite house only.

Access for all: ♿️🅿️🚾📷🏛️🎫👓📱
Building 🔥🔥 Garden 🔥

Getting here: 163:SP248291. 4 miles from Moreton-in-Marsh. **Train**: Moreton-in-Marsh 4 miles. **Road**: approach only from A436 between A44 and Stow-on-the-Wold. Follow brown signs, not directions to Chastleton village. **Sat Nav**: follow brown signs. **Parking**: free, 270 yards (short steep hill).

Finding out more: 01494 755560 (Infoline). 01608 674981 or chastleton@nationaltrust.org.uk

Eating and shopping: shop in 19th-century kitchen. Undercroft restaurant (National Trust-approved concession). Picnic area.

Chastleton House and Garden		M	T	W	T	F	S	S
6 Mar–31 Mar	1–4	·	·	**W**	**T**	**F**	**S**	**S**
3 Apr–29 Sep	1–5	·	·	**W**	**T**	**F**	**S**	**S**
2 Oct–3 Nov	1–4	·	·	**W**	**T**	**F**	**S**	**S**
30 Nov–15 Dec	1–4	·	·	·	·	·	**S**	**S**

Entry to the house is by timed ticket (not bookable, places limited). Ticket office open from 12:30. Last entry one hour before closing.

Making the most of your day: events, including conservation demonstrations, behind-the-scenes tours, children's activities, re-enactors and art exhibitions. Surrey Infantry Museum is based here. **Dogs**: assistance dogs only.

Access for all: ⌷⌷⌷⌷⌷⌷⌷⌷⌷⌷
Building ⌷⌷⌷ Grounds ⌷⌷

Getting here: 186:TQ042512. 3 miles east of Guildford. **Foot**: follow drive to reception. **Bus**: from Guildford to Epsom (passing Leatherhead ≋, close Guildford ≋) and Woking ≋. **Train**: Clandon 1 mile. **Road**: West Clandon on A247; from A3 follow signposts to Ripley, join A247 via B2215. **Sat Nav**: may be incorrect – ensure you enter from A247. **Parking**: free, 300 yards.

Finding out more: 01483 222482.
01483 222502 (restaurant) or clandonpark@nationaltrust.org.uk

Clandon Park		M	T	W	T	F	S	S
House, garden, museum, shop and restaurant								
3 Mar–30 Jun	11–5	·	T	W	T	·	·	S
1 Jul–29 Aug	11–5	M	T	W	T	·	·	S
1 Sep–3 Nov	11–5	·	T	W	T	·	·	S
Shop and restaurant*								
5 Nov–28 Nov	12–4	·	T	W	T	·	·	S
1 Dec–23 Dec	12–4	M	T	W	T	·	·	S
Surrey Infantry Museum								
5 Nov–19 Dec	12–4	·	T	W	T	·	·	

Family-friendly offer February half-term. Special opening 24 February. House may be closed 17 March. Open Bank Holiday Mondays, Good Friday and Easter Saturday. Garden may close if waterlogged. *Restaurant booking essential in December, including evening opening 7 to 11.

The Palladio Room at Clandon Park, Surrey

Claremont Landscape Garden, Surrey: a green oasis

Claremont Landscape Garden

Portsmouth Road, Esher, Surrey KT10 9JG

Map ② F6 ▦

Claremont is not a typical garden of herbaceous borders, but a green oasis of trees and shrubs that offers a place where the views always change, the water sparkles and secret glades await. Once the playground of princesses, it's now yours to explore. Garden enthusiasts may recognise some of the famous names from garden history involved in Claremont's creation: Sir John Vanbrugh, Charles Bridgeman, William Kent and 'Capability' Brown. Unexpected things to see are a serpentine lake overlooked by an impressive grass amphitheatre and grotto, as well the camellia terrace, skittle alley and children's play area.

Eating and shopping: licensed tea-room serving light lunches, cakes and cream teas.

Making the most of your day: events, including open-air theatre (July), children's craft workshops and storytelling. Activities, including walks (guided April to October), talks and children's trails (school holidays). **Dogs**: allowed (on short leads) between 1 November and 31 March only.

Access for all:
Grounds

Getting here: 187:TQ128631. 1 mile south of Esher. **Bus**: Kingston to Guildford (passing close Esher). **Train**: Esher 2 miles. **Road**: on east side of A307. **Parking**: free, at entrance.

Finding out more: 01372 467806 or claremont@nationaltrust.org.uk

Claremont Landscape Garden		M	T	W	T	F	S	S
Garden								
1 Jan-31 Jan	10-4	M	T	W	T	F	S	S
1 Feb-24 Mar	10-5	M	T	W	T	F	S	S
25 Mar-31 Oct	10-6	M	T	W	T	F	S	S
1 Nov-24 Dec	10-4	M	T	W	T	F	S	S
26 Dec-31 Dec	10-4	M	T	·	T	F	S	S
Tea-room and shop								
1 Jan-31 Jan	10-3:30	M	T	W	T	F	S	S
1 Feb-24 Mar	10-4:30	M	T	W	T	F	S	S
25 Mar-31 Oct	10-5:30	M	T	W	T	F	S	S
1 Nov-24 Dec	10-3:30	M	T	W	T	F	S	S
26 Dec-31 Dec	10-3:30	M	T	·	T	F	S	S

Closed 25 December. Belvedere Tower open 1 January, 12 to 2, and first weekend each month April to October, 2 to 5. Late night opening 22 June until 9.

Claydon

Middle Claydon, near Buckingham, Buckinghamshire MK18 2EY

Map (2) D3

State rooms within a grand country house that never quite was. Claydon's dazzling 18th-century interiors are among the finest to be found anywhere in England. Chinoiserie, Rococo, Palladian and Neo-classical styles all jostle for position in a house designed to impress. More than 500 years of Verney family history has been played out within these walls. Heroes of the English Civil War, Barbary Coast buccaneers, eccentric 19th-century collectors and Florence Nightingale have all called Claydon home. Set amid 21 hectares (52 acres) of peaceful parkland, with tranquil lake walks and views, Claydon is an inspirational place for all the family. **Note**: gardens (not National Trust) opened by permission of the Verney family. Garden entry charges (including members).

Eating and shopping: second-hand bookshop and Courtyard craft shops and galleries (not National Trust). Carriage House restaurant and Courtyard tea-room (not National Trust). Kitchen garden produce for sale (when in season). Picnics welcome.

There is more than enough space for a game of frisbee at Claydon in Buckinghamshire

Making the most of your day: guided 'taster tours' (except Bank Holidays). Family activity worksheets. All-year exhibitions, 'Claydon – a place in history' and 'Women in history'. **Dogs**: welcome on leads in the park.

Access for all:
House **Grounds**

Getting here: 165:SP720253. In Middle Claydon 13 miles north-west of Aylesbury, 4 miles south-west of Winslow. **Foot**: Bernwood Jubilee Way. **Cycle**: NCN51. **Train**: Aylesbury Parkway 13 miles, Bicester North 13½ miles, Milton Keynes Central, 17 miles. **Road**: signposted A413 (Buckingham), A41 (Waddesdon crossroads). M40 junction 9 (Bicester) follow A41, turn off to Grendon Underwood and Calvert, signposted from Calvert Crossroads. **Parking**: free.

Finding out more: 01296 730349 (Infoline). 01296 730252 (Claydon Estate) or claydon@nationaltrust.org.uk

Claydon		M	T	W	T	F	S	S
House, tea-room, church and bookshop*								
16 Mar–30 Oct	11–5	M	T	W	·	·	S	S
Restaurant								
16 Feb–9 Mar	12–3	·	·	·	·	·	S	·
16 Mar–30 Oct	12–3	M	T	W	·	·	S	S

*House entry by 'taster tours' between 11 and 1 daily every 30 minutes. Visitors are taken through a selection of rooms by an experienced guide. Open Good Friday. The Carriage House Restaurant is open Saturday evenings between 16 February and 26 October.

A 'talking' picture at Claydon, Buckinghamshire

Cliveden

Cliveden Road, Taplow, Maidenhead, Buckinghamshire SL6 0JA

Map (2) E5

Set high above the River Thames with far-reaching views, these beautiful gardens capture the grandeur of a bygone age. Cliveden was a glittering hub of society for centuries, especially when home to Nancy and Waldorf Astor during the early 20th century. 50 years ago Cliveden was engulfed in the 'Profumo Affair' scandal, when it emerged that John Profumo met Christine Keeler here. With spectacular flower displays, miles of walks and a famous maze, it's a perfect place for the whole family to relax and unwind. A short guided tour of the house (now a hotel) is available on certain days. **Note**: mooring charge on Cliveden Reach, £8 per 24 hours (including members), does not include entry.

Eating and shopping: Dovecote coffee house serving morning coffee and afternoon tea. Lunches and snacks available at the Orangery. Doll's House café and toy shop especially for families. Picnic areas. Shop, including plant sales.

Making the most of your day: family and children's activities, including storybook-themed play area and yew-tree maze, play trail in the woods and free seasonal trails around the garden. The introductory film *Cliveden: Camelot on Thames* sets the scene. Events and guided walks. Seasonal floral displays. Boat trips on the Thames show Cliveden from a different view (additional charge). **Dogs**: welcome under close control in woodlands only.

Access for all:
House
Garden

Getting here: 175:SU915851. 2 miles north of Taplow. **Train**: Taplow (not Sunday) 2½ miles; Burnham 3 miles. £1 shop or café voucher for 'green transport' use. **Road**: from M4, exit 7 onto A4 to Maidenhead, from M40, exit 4 onto

A404 to Marlow, follow brown signs. Entrance opposite Feathers Inn. Oversize vehicles, call for details. **Sat Nav**: enter Cliveden Road and SL1 8NS. **Parking**: free.

Finding out more: 01628 605069 (Estate office) or cliveden@nationaltrust.org.uk

Cliveden in Buckinghamshire: the summer parterre, above, Fountain of Love, below, and Long Garden, bottom

Cliveden		M	T	W	T	F	S	S
Woodland								
1 Jan–15 Feb	10–4	M	T	W	T	F	S	S
Garden, woodland and shop								
16 Feb–27 Oct	10–5:30	M	T	W	T	F	S	S
28 Oct–31 Dec	10–4	M	T	W	T	F	S	S
Coffee shop								
16 Feb–27 Oct	10–5	M	T	W	T	F	S	S
28 Oct–31 Dec	10–3:30	M	T	W	T	F	S	S
The Orangery (café)*								
16 Feb–1 Nov	10–5	M	T	W	T	F	S	S
2 Nov–22 Dec	10–3:30	·	·	·	·	·	S	S
Doll's House (café and shop)*								
16 Feb–1 Nov	10–5	M	T	W	T	F	S	S
2 Nov–22 Dec	10–3:30	·	·	·	·	·	S	S
House (part), chapel								
4 Apr–27 Oct	3–5:30	·	·	·	T	·	·	S

Property closed 25 December. Shop closed 25 to 31 December. *Orangery and Doll's House close 3:30, 28 October to 1 November. Admission to house by timed ticket only. Some areas of formal garden may close when ground conditions are poor.

Restored Darnley Mausoleum, Cobham Wood, Kent

Cobham Wood and Mausoleum

near Cobham, Kent

Map ② H5

The atmospheric and wonderfully restored Darnley Mausoleum, designed by James Wyatt, memorably featured in the BBC's *Restoration* programme. The peaceful woodland was once part of the Darnley family's extensive estate and was acquired by the National Trust only recently. **Note**: no vehicle access or parking. No toilets.

Eating and shopping: refreshments and toilets available at Shorne Wood Country Park.

Making the most of your day: guided walks. **Dogs**: under control in wood (stock grazing).

Access for all: Mausoleum

Getting here: 178:TQ694683. At east end of Cobham village. **Foot**: waymarked footpath to mausoleum from Shorne Wood Country Park,

2 miles. **Road**: ½ mile from M2 and A2. Exit A2 at Shorne/Cobham, follow signs to Shorne Wood Country Park. **Sat Nav**: enter DA12 3HX (Shorne Wood Country Park). **Parking**: at Shorne Wood Country Park, pay and display (not National Trust); follow waymarked footpath.

Finding out more: 01474 816764 or cobham@nationaltrust.org.uk. South Lodge Barn, Lodge Lane, Cobham, Kent DA12 3BS

Cobham Wood and Mausoleum
Visit website for opening information.

Dorneywood Garden

Dorneywood, Dorney Wood Road, Burnham, Buckinghamshire SL1 8PY

Map ② E5

House with Rex Whistler decorations and 1930s-style garden. Afternoon tea available. Open on selected afternoons (dates may change at short notice). **Note**: no photography. Booking not required. Ministerial residence, so visitor names are taken for security reasons. Charge including members.

Finding out more: www.nationaltrust.org.uk

Lily pond at Dorneywood Garden in Buckinghamshire

Emmetts Garden

Ide Hill, Sevenoaks, Kent TN14 6BA

Map ② H6

Charming Emmetts – an Edwardian estate owned by Frederic Lubbock – was a plantsman's passion and a much-loved family home. Influenced by William Robinson, the delightful garden was laid out in the late 19th century and contains many exotic and rare trees and shrubs from across the world. After exploring the rose and rock gardens, you can take in the spectacular views and enjoy the glorious shows of spring flowers and shrubs, followed by vibrant autumn colours.

Eating and shopping: Stable tea-room serving sandwiches and cakes. Shop selling variety of plants.

Swathes of bluebells at Emmetts Garden in Kent

Making the most of your day: year-round events. Guided tours (selected days). Children's activities. Walks sheets for surrounding countryside. **Dogs**: on short leads only.

Access for all: ☒☒☒☒☒ ☒☒
Grounds ☒➡☒

Getting here: 188:TQ477524. 4½ miles from Sevenoaks. **Foot**: from Ide Hill (½ mile). Weardale walk from Chartwell (3 miles) – leaflet available. **Bus**: from Sevenoaks (Monday to Friday only), alight Ide Hill, 1½ miles. **Train**: Sevenoaks 4½ miles; Penshurst 5½ miles. **Road**: 1½ miles south of A25 on Sundridge to Ide Hill road, 1½ miles north of Ide Hill off B2042, leave M25 exit 5, then 4 miles. **Parking**: free, 100 yards.

Finding out more: 01732 750367 or emmetts@nationaltrust.org.uk

Emmetts Garden		M	T	W	T	F	S	S
2 Mar–3 Nov	10–5	M	T	W	T	F	S	S
4 Nov–31 Dec	11–4	M	T	W	T	F	S	S

Open Bank Holiday Mondays and Good Friday.
Last admission 45 minutes before closing. Closed 24 and 25 December.

Great Coxwell Barn

Great Coxwell, Faringdon, Oxfordshire SN7 7LZ

Map ② C4

Former monastic barn, a favourite of William Morris, who would regularly bring his guests to wonder at its structure. **Note:** no toilet, narrow access lanes leading to property.

Finding out more: 01793 762209 or www.nationaltrust.org.uk

Greys Court

Rotherfield Greys, Henley-on-Thames, Oxfordshire RG9 4PG

Map ② D5 🏠 ❄ 🍴

An intimate family home and peaceful estate set in the rolling hills of the Chilterns. This picturesque 16th-century mansion and tranquil gardens were home to the Brunner family until recent years. The house exudes a welcoming atmosphere, with a well-stocked kitchen and homely living rooms. The series of walled gardens is a colourful patchwork of interest set amidst medieval ruins. Other buildings from earlier eras include the 12th-century Great Tower and a rare Tudor donkey wheel, in use until the early 20th century.

Eating and shopping: tea-room serving light lunch or tea and cake. Family-inspired shop. Seasonal organic produce from gardens (when available).

Making the most of your day: open-air events and children's workshops. Wider estate walk. Family activities, including explorer packs and garden and house trails. **Dogs:** on estate walk only.

Access for all: 🅿 ♿ 👓 🔊 ✍ 🏠 ♿
House 🏠 Tea-room 🍴 Grounds 🏠

Getting here: 175:SU725834. 2½ miles west of Henley-on-Thames. **Cycle:** on Oxfordshire cycleway. **Train:** Henley-on-Thames 3 miles. **Road:** from Nettlebed mini-roundabout on A4130 take B481. Property signed to the left after about 3 miles. From Henley-on-Thames town centre, follow signs to Badgemore Golf Club towards Peppard (approximately 3 miles from Henley). **Parking:** free, 220 yards.

Finding out more: 01494 755564 (Infoline). 01491 628529 or greyscourt@nationaltrust.org.uk

Greys Court		M	T	W	T	F	S	S
House								
1 Mar–31 Oct*	1–5	M	T	W	T	F	S	S
1 Dec–23 Dec	12–3	M	T	W	T	F	S	S
Garden, tea-room and shop								
1 Mar–31 Oct	11–5	M	T	W	T	F	S	S
Garden and shop								
1 Dec–23 Dec	12–3	M	T	W	T	F	S	S

*Entry to the house by timed ticket only, including members (places limited), only available from ticket office on day. No facility to book. Closed Good Friday. Village fête day (1 September): special opening arrangements apply (charge including members).

Breathtaking planting and mellow stone path in the Peony Walk at Greys Court, Oxfordshire

Grade I-listed Hartwell House Hotel, Buckinghamshire

Hatchlands Park

East Clandon, Guildford, Surrey GU4 7RT

Map ② F6

Hatchlands Park was built in the 1750s for Admiral Boscawen, hero of the Battle of Louisburg. Robert Adam ceilings, with nautical motifs, decorate the house. Today the mansion is a family home, containing tenant Alec Cobbe's superb collection of paintings. Our six rooms also display the Cobbe Collection, Europe's largest collection of keyboard instruments, associated with famous composers such as J. C. Bach, Chopin and Elgar. The mansion is set in informal grounds, with one parterre garden designed by Gertrude Jekyll. The surrounding parkland of more than 160 hectares (400 acres) provides waymarked walks in a tranquil and beautiful setting.

Hartwell House Hotel, Restaurant and Spa

Oxford Road, near Aylesbury, Buckinghamshire HP17 8NR

Map ② E3

The most famous resident of this elegant Grade I-listed stately home (held on long lease from The Ernest Cook Trust) was Louis XVIII, the exiled King of France, who lived here with his Queen and members of his court for five years from 1809. Only one hour from central London, the magnificent grounds include a romantic ruined church, lake, bridge and 36 hectares (90 acres) of parkland.

The house and gardens are already accessible to the public as a hotel, and welcome guests to stay, to dine in the restaurants and to have afternoon tea (booking strongly advised). Please contact hotel directly for best available offer. **Note**: all paying guests to the hotel are welcome to walk in the garden and park.

Finding out more: 01296 747444. 01296 747450 (fax) or info@hartwell-house.com. www.hartwell-house.com

Hatchlands Park, Surrey, is still a family home

Glorious bluebells at Hatchlands Park, Surrey

Eating and shopping: tea-room (National Trust-approved concession) in the original kitchen. Gift shop.

Making the most of your day: children's trails and activities. Stable exhibition. Cobbe Collection Trust concerts. Guided mansion tours most Thursdays. **Dogs**: welcome under close control in designated parkland areas only.

Access for all: 🅿️🚼♿🚻👣🔗🎨🎫📷📱🎧

Building 🔆♿👇 Grounds ♿➡️🚶

Getting here: 187:TQ063516. 2 miles from Clandon. **Bus**: Guildford to Leatherhead (passing Leatherhead ⭑ and close Guildford ⭑). **Train**: Clandon 2 miles, Horsley 2½ miles. **Road**: entry off A246 between Guildford and Leatherhead. **Sat Nav**: recommend following brown signs to main entrance on A246. **Parking**: free, 300 yards.

Finding out more: 01483 222482 or hatchlands@nationaltrust.org.uk

Hindhead Commons and the Devil's Punch Bowl

London Road, Hindhead, Surrey GU26 6AB

Map ② E7

Since the opening of the A3 tunnel, paths, cycle routes and bridleways have been reconnected and natural contours restored. Peace and calm now reign and the glorious landscape, with its carpets of purple heather in the summer and grazing Highland cattle, is there for all to enjoy.

Eating and shopping: café serving hot lunches, sandwiches and cakes.

Making the most of your day: guided walks and talks throughout year. Walks leaflets (available from café). **Dogs**: under very close control during bird-nesting season (March to October).

Access for all: 🅿️♿🚻👣

Café ♿ Grounds ➡️

Getting here: 186:SU890357. At the end of the A333. **Bus**: from Farnham and Haslemere, alight Hindhead crossroads. **Train**: Haslemere 3 miles. **Road**: access via A333 from Hazel Grove roundabout, just south of tunnel. **Parking**: £3 (pay and display or RinGo pay by mobile).

Finding out more: 01428 681050 (rangers). 01428 608771 (café) or hindhead@nationaltrust.org.uk

Hatchlands Park		M	T	W	T	F	S	S
House and garden								
31 Mar–1 Aug	2–5:30	·	T	W	T	·	·	S
2 Aug–30 Aug	2–5:30	·	T	W	T	F	·	S
1 Sep–31 Oct	2–5:30	·	T	W	T	·	·	S
Park walks								
31 Mar–31 Oct	10:30–6	M	T	W	T	F	S	S
Shop and tea-room								
31 Mar–1 Aug	11–5:30	·	T	W	T	·	S	S
2 Aug–30 Aug	11–5:30	·	T	W	T	F	S	S
31 Aug–31 Oct	11–5:30	·	T	W	T	·	S	S

Garden open 11 to 6 on house open days. Timed tickets may be used on Bank Holidays/busy periods. Open Bank Holiday Mondays.

Hindhead Commons		M	T	W	T	F	S	S
Countryside								
Open all year		M	T	W	T	F	S	S
Café								
1 Jan–22 Mar	9–4	M	T	W	T	F	S	S
23 Mar–27 Oct	9–6	·	·	·	·	·	S	S
25 Mar–25 Oct	9–5	M	T	W	T	F	·	·
28 Oct–31 Dec	9–4	M	T	W	T	F	S	S

Café closed 25 December.

Hinton Ampner

Petersfield Road, Hinton Ampner, Alresford,
Hampshire SO24 0NH

Map ② D7

Best known for its magnificent garden and
stunning views to the south, Hinton Ampner
is an elegant country house remodelled in
1960 by Ralph Dutton, the 8th and last
Lord Sherborne, after a devastating fire. It
contains his fascinating collection of Georgian
and Regency furniture, Italian pictures and
objets d'art. The gardens were also laid out by
Ralph Dutton and are widely acknowledged as
a masterpiece of 20th-century design, mixing
formal and informal planting and providing
year-round interest.

Eating and shopping: tea-room serving cakes
and light lunches, made using walled garden
produce. Shop selling gifts, books and garden
products. Plants and produce for sale
(when available).

The Sunken Garden at Hinton Ampner, Hampshire

Making the most of your day: free garden walk
(Tuesdays and Thursdays). House conservation
demonstrations (Tuesdays). Children's quiz
sheet. **Dogs**: assistance dogs only.

Access for all: 🅿️♿🚻♿♿♿✦♿
Building 🏠♿ Grounds 🏠➡♿

Getting here: 185:SU597275. Midway between
Winchester and Petersfield. **Bus**: Winchester
to Petersfield (passing close Winchester ≋)
and passing Petersfield ≋). **Train**: Winchester
9 miles; Alresford (Mid-Hants Railway) 4 miles.
Road: on A272, 1 mile west of Bramdean village,
8 miles east of Winchester. Leave M3 at exit 9
and follow signs to Petersfield. **Parking**: free.

Finding out more: 01962 771305 or
hintonampner@nationaltrust.org.uk.
Hinton Ampner, Alresford,
Hampshire SO24 0LA

Hinton Ampner		M	T	W	T	F	S	S
House								
16 Feb–31 Oct	11–5	M	T	W	T	F	S	S
2 Nov–27 Nov	11–4:30	M	T	W	·	·	S	S
30 Nov–8 Dec	10:30–4	M	T	W	T	F	S	S
Garden, shop and tea-room								
16 Feb–31 Mar	10–5	M	T	W	T	F	S	S
1 Apr–31 Oct*	10–5:30	M	T	W	T	F	S	S
2 Nov–27 Nov	11–5	M	T	W	·	·	S	S
30 Nov–8 Dec	10–4:30	M	T	W	T	F	S	S

*Garden open until 6 from 1 April to 30 October.
Last entry to house and tea-room 20 minutes before closing.

The Homewood

Portsmouth Road, Esher, Surrey KT10 9JL

Map ② F6

Extraordinary Modernist house and landscape
garden, designed in 1938 by the architect
Patrick Gwynne. **Note**: administered on behalf
of the National Trust by a tenant. No toilet.
Additional charge for minibus and guided tour
(including members).

Finding out more: 01372 476424
or www.nationaltrust.org.uk.
c/o Claremont Landscape Garden, Portsmouth
Road, Esher, Surrey KT10 9JG

Hughenden

High Wycombe, Buckinghamshire HP14 4LA

Map ② E4 　🏠🎯🎣🍴

It's hardly surprising that the colourful Victorian Prime Minister, Benjamin Disraeli, fell in love with Hughenden. This handsome home with fine views and woodland walks is still the perfect place to relax and unwind today. His hillside hideaway was HQ for a top-secret operation during the Second World War that put Hughenden high on Hitler's hit list. A replica air-raid shelter, 1940s living room and ice house bring wartime Britain to life. With red kites soaring over ancient woods and views over rolling parkland set in a timeless Chiltern valley, Hughenden is a truly magical place.

Eating and shopping: Stable yard café. Gift shop. Second-hand bookshop. Plant sales.

Making the most of your day: events. Woodland trails. Walled garden. Morning manor guided tour. Free introductory talks. Children's I-Spy sheets. West Wycombe Park nearby. **Dogs**: welcome under close control in park and woodland.

Access for all: 🅿♿🏢🔉🔊🔆📷🖥♿❗🚻🏠 　 Building 🏠🏠♿ 　 Grounds 🏠🏠

Getting here: 165:SU866955. 1½ miles north of High Wycombe. **Foot**: 1½ miles from High Wycombe. **Bus**: from High Wycombe bus station (steep walk to house). **Train**: High Wycombe 2 miles. **Road**: on A4128. Exit 4 M40, take A404 towards High Wycombe, then A4128 towards Great Missenden. **Parking**: free, 200 to 400 yards (waiting possible).

Finding out more: 01494 755565 (Infoline). 01494 755573 or hughenden@nationaltrust.org.uk

Hughenden, Buckinghamshire: the drawing room, above, and Second World War bunker, top

Hughenden		M	T	W	T	F	S	S
Garden, shop and restaurant								
16 Feb–8 Mar	11–4	M	T	W	T	F	S	S
9 Mar–26 Oct	11–5:30	M	T	W	T	F	S	S
27 Oct–31 Dec	11–4	M	T	W	T	F	S	S
House								
16 Feb–8 Mar	11–3	M	T	W	T	F	S	S
9 Mar–26 Oct	12–5	M	T	W	T	F	S	S
27 Oct–31 Dec	11–3	M	T	W	T	F	S	S
Park								
Open all year		M	T	W	T	F	S	S

Occasional early closing for special events and weddings. Closed 25 December.

Ightham Mote

Mote Road, Ivy Hatch, Sevenoaks,
Kent TN15 0NT

Map ② H6 🏠🌸🐕🛏️🍽️

Nearly 700 years of history are encapsulated in this beautiful moated manor house. Every room tells a different story about its owners – from the medieval crypt, to the rare surviving Tudor painted ceiling and Victorian billiard room. The private apartments of Charles Henry Robinson, who gave Ightham Mote to the National Trust in 1985, give a real feel for 1960s American interior design, while interior design of the canine variety can be seen in the extraordinary Victorian dog kennel. The tranquil garden features lakes, an orchard and flower borders. The ancient estate offers breathtaking views of the Kentish countryside. **Note**: very steep slope from reception (lower drop-off point available).

Eating and shopping: Mote Restaurant serving hot lunches, sandwiches, cream teas, cakes and hot, cold, alcoholic and non-alcoholic beverages. Shop selling gifts, local produce and plants.

Making the most of your day: events throughout year including theatre productions, themed restaurant evenings, behind-the-scenes events, arts and crafts courses, countryside walks, outdoor activities and family fun days. **Dogs**: welcome on estate and restaurant patio area.

Access for all: 🅿️♿🚻♿🔊📷📹ℹ️
👓🖼️ Building 🏠🏠🏠🚻♿ Grounds 🏠➡️

Getting here: 188:TQ584535. Between Sevenoaks and Borough Green 1¾ miles south of A25. **Bus**: from Sevenoaks Thursdays and Fridays, other days alight Ivy Hatch, ¾ mile. Sevenoaks to Gravesend, alight Ightham Common, 1½ miles. **Train**: Borough Green and Wrotham 3½ miles; Hildenborough 4 miles; Sevenoaks 6 miles. **Road**: 6 miles north of Tonbridge on A227; 6 miles south of Sevenoaks on A25; 16 miles west of Maidstone on A20/A25. **Parking**: 200 yards. £2 charge for non-members.

Ightham Mote, Kent: 14th-century moated manor house

Finding out more: 01732 810378 (extension 100) or ighthammote@nationaltrust.org.uk

Ightham Mote		M	T	W	T	F	S	S
House								
1 Mar–31 Oct*	11–5	M	T	W	T	F	S	S
1 Dec–23 Dec**	11–3	M	T	W	T	F	S	S
Shop, restaurant and garden								
1 Mar–31 Oct*	11–5	M	T	W	T	F	S	S
1 Dec–31 Dec***	11–3	M	T	W	T	F	S	S
Estate								
Open all year	Dawn–dusk	M	T	W	T	F	S	S

*Tuesdays: booked groups only. **December: partial gardens, courtyard, library, ground-floor access, visitor reception and conservation exhibition, dressed for Christmas. Restaurant may not fully open during private functions. ***Closed 24 and 25 December.

Atmospheric Knole, Kent: during 600 years it has been a palace, royal possession and aristocratic treasure house

King's Head

King's Head Passage, Market Square, Aylesbury, Buckinghamshire HP20 2RW

Map ② E3

Historic public house with a pleasant family atmosphere. The King's Head is one of England's best-preserved coaching inns. Dating back to 1455, the building has many fascinating architectural features, including rare stained-glass windows, exposed wattle and daub and the original stabling for the inn. **Note**: Farmers' Bar leased by Chiltern Brewery.

Eating and shopping: award-winning Farmers' Bar serving local food and ales.

Access for all: 🚻♿️🅿️
Building 🏠

Getting here: 165:SP818137. At top of Market Square in the centre of Aylesbury. **Foot**: access through cobbled lane near the war memorial. **Train**: Aylesbury 400 yards. **Parking**: no onsite parking. Car parks in town centre (not National Trust).

Finding out more: 01296 718812 (Farmers' Bar). 01280 817156 (National Trust) or kingshead@nationaltrust.org.uk

King's Head		
Normal pub opening hours apply. Closed 25 December. For Great Hall tea-room opening times telephone 01296 718812.		

Knole

Sevenoaks, Kent TN15 0RP

Map ② H6

This year Knole will share secrets uncovered during our latest repairs to this extraordinary and atmospheric building, which has evolved over 600 years as an archbishops' palace, royal residence and aristocratic treasure house. We'd like to show you our conservation research and share our passion for our collections of 17th-century royal furniture, paintings, tapestries, silver and ceramics – inspiring objects among the most important in the world. We will be revealing plans to open attics and tower rooms and transform Knole, the beloved home of author Vita Sackville-West and the inspiration for Virginia Woolf's novel *Orlando*. **Note**: building works may affect certain rooms and objects on display.

Eating and shopping: shop selling local produce and books, gifts and children's pocket-money toys. Brewhouse tea-room in Knole's original brewery.

Making the most of your day: conservation talks, tours and handling sessions. Guided walks in our parkland, a Site of Special Scientific Interest. Park Experience Room. Changing art exhibitions. Family holiday activities, including Tudor dressing-up days, historic crafts, games and trails. Ightham Mote and Chartwell nearby. **Dogs**: welcome in park on leads.

Access for all: 📶📶📶📶📶📶📶📶📶
📶📶 House 📶📶📶 Grounds 📶➡️📶

Getting here: 188:TQ532543. 1½ miles from Sevenoaks. **Foot:** entrance by Sevenoaks Library, or as road details. **Bus:** from surrounding area to Sevenoaks, ¾-mile walk. **Train:** Sevenoaks 1½ miles. **Road:** leave M25 at exit 5 (A21). Park entrance south of Sevenoaks town centre off A225 Tonbridge Road (opposite St Nicholas church). **Sat Nav:** use TN13 1HU and carry on to park entrance. **Parking:** 60 yards, available when house, visitor centre or tea-room open, otherwise parking in nearby town centre.

Finding out more: 01732 462100 or knole@nationaltrust.org.uk

Knole		M	T	W	T	F	S	S
House								
9 Mar–3 Nov	12–4	·	**T**	**W**	**T**	**F**	**S**	**S**
Tea-room								
5 Jan–3 Mar	11–4	·	·	·	·	·	**S**	**S**
Visitor centre, Orangery, tea-room, shop								
9 Mar–3 Nov	10:30–5	·	**T**	**W**	**T**	**F**	**S**	**S**
6 Nov–22 Dec	11–4	·	·	**W**	**T**	**F**	**S**	**S**
Garden								
2 Apr–24 Sep	11–4	·	**T**	·	·	·	·	·

Open Bank Holiday Mondays. Timed tickets may be in operation on certain days. Car park: gates open 10:15, close 6. Vehicles not admitted when whole of property is closed. Park open daily for pedestrians. Tea-room open 1 January.

The graceful inner courtyard at Knole, below, and Anthony van Dyke portrait, above

Lamb House

West Street, Rye, East Sussex TN31 7ES

Map ② J8　🏠❄️

Fine brick-fronted house with literary associations – Henry James and E. F. Benson lived here – and large beautiful garden. **Note:** administered and largely maintained on the National Trust's behalf by a tenant. No toilets.

Finding out more: 01580 762334 or www.nationaltrust.org.uk

Leith Hill

Leith Hill, near Coldharbour village, Dorking, Surrey

Map ② F7

There's probably the best view in the South East from the top of the tower; at 1,000 feet high, you can see all the way from London to the seaside. On the ground there are some wonderful walks through woodland and rare rhododendron plantations. **Note**: no toilet.

Eating and shopping: teas, coffees and cakes available (not National Trust). Picnics welcome.

Making the most of your day: free walks leaflets (available from Tower, Landslip and Rhododendron Wood car parks). **Dogs**: under close control in Rhododendron Wood, heathland and farmland during March to July.

Access for all: Tower 🔲

Getting here: 187:TQ139432. 1 mile south-west of Coldharbour. **Bus**: Holmbury St Mary 2½ miles. **Train**: Holmwood 2½ miles, Dorking 5½ miles. **Road**: off A29/B2126. **Parking**: designated areas along road at foot of hill (no vehicle access to summit). Rhododendron Wood £3 a car for non-members.

Finding out more: 01306 712711 or leithhill@nationaltrust.org.uk

Leith Hill	M	T	W	T	F	S	S
Countryside							
Open all year	M	T	W	T	F	S	S
Tower and tea kiosk							
4 Jan–31 Mar	10–4	M	·	·	·	F	S	S
1 Apr–30 Sep	10–5	M	·	·	·	F	S	S
4 Oct–30 Dec	10–4	M	·	·	·	F	S	S

Tower and tea kiosk open daily during school holidays and all Bank Holidays, except 25 December.

Long Crendon Courthouse

Long Crendon, Aylesbury, Buckinghamshire HP18 9AN

Map ② D4

14th-century Court House with a wealth of local history – the second building acquired by the National Trust. **Note**: village exhibition on display. Extremely steep stairs. No toilet.

Finding out more: 01280 817156 or www.nationaltrust.org.uk

Monk's House

Rodmell, Lewes, East Sussex BN7 3HF

Map ② G8

Novelist Virginia Woolf's country home and retreat, a charming weatherboarded cottage – featuring the room where she created her best-known works.

Finding out more: 01273 474760 or www.nationaltrust.org.uk

You can see all the way to London in one direction and the sea in another from the top of the tower at Leith Hill, Surrey

Mottisfont

near Romsey, Hampshire SO51 0LP

Map ② C7 🏠❄️🍴🍵

Once across the crystal clear river, visitors enter a piece of paradise. Ancient trees, bubbling brooks and rolling lawns frame this lovely old house. An 18th-century home with a medieval priory at its heart, Mottisfont inspired a 1930s dream of creativity. Artists came here to relax and create works, some of which are still visible in our historic rooms. This tradition continues today, along with major exhibitions in our top-floor gallery. Outside, carpets of spring bulbs, a walled rose garden, rich autumn leaves and a colourful winter garden make Mottisfont a feast for the senses all year round. **Note**: national collection of old-fashioned roses (usually flowering June).

Eating and shopping: Kitchen Café serving meals and cakes. Ice-cream parlour. Spacious shop. Second-hand books. Plant sales.

Mottisfont, Hampshire: the south front, below, and magnificent rose garden in June, above

Making the most of your day: open-air theatre and events throughout the year. Free daily guided walk and talks. Family fun activities, including building dens, 'make and take' in the creative play space and summer quest trail. Changing exhibitions in the art gallery. Seasonal variety in the Winter Garden, with 60,000 spring bulbs and late summer borders. Wider estate to explore on foot or by bike. **Dogs**: welcome on short leads in most of grounds and garden.

Access for all: 🅿️🏠♿🚻🏛️🔄📷🖼️💺📷
Building 🏠🏠♿ Grounds 🏠➡️

Getting here: 185:SU327270. 4½ miles north of Romsey. **Foot**: on Testway long-distance path. Clarendon Way 2 miles north. **Cycle**: on Testway. **Train**: Dunbridge 1½ miles. **Road**: signposted off A3057 Romsey to Stockbridge. Also signposted off B3087 Romsey to Broughton and B3084. **Parking**: free.

Finding out more: 01794 340757 or mottisfont@nationaltrust.org.uk

Mottisfont		M	T	W	T	F	S	S
Garden, shop, café and art gallery								
Open all year	10–5*	M	T	W	T	F	S	S
House								
1 Mar–3 Nov	11–5	M	T	W	T	F	S	S

*Art gallery opens at 11. Gallery closes for short periods to change exhibitions. Closed 24 and 25 December. Closes dusk if earlier.

Mottistone Manor Garden

Mottistone, near Brighstone,
Isle of Wight PO30 4EA

Map (2) C9

Set in a sheltered valley, this magical garden is full of surprises, with shrub-filled banks, hidden pathways and colourful herbaceous borders. Surrounding an attractive Elizabethan manor house (tenanted so not open), this 20th-century garden is experimenting with a Mediterranean-style planting scheme to take advantage of its southerly location. Other surprises include a young olive grove, a small organic kitchen garden and a traditional tea garden set alongside The Shack, a unique cabin retreat designed as their summer drawing office by architects John Seely (2nd Lord Mottistone) and Paul Paget. There are also delightful walks across the adjoining Mottistone Estate. **Note**: manor house open two days a year.

Eating and shopping: shop selling gifts, books, cards and postcards. Plant stall. Second-hand books. Tea garden serving ice-cream, hot and cold drinks, soup, sandwiches, cake and light refreshments (not National Trust). Picnic table.

Making the most of your day: family events and garden tours. Flowerpot trail and estate walks. Newtown Old Town Hall and The Needles Old Battery and New Battery nearby. **Dogs**: welcome on leads.

Access for all:
The Shack **Garden**

Getting here: 196:SZ406838. At Mottistone. **Foot**: 1 mile north of coastal path; 1 mile south of Tennyson Trail. **Cycle**: NCN67. On the 'Round the Island' cycle route. **Ferry**: Yarmouth (Wightlink) 5 miles (0871 376 1000); East Cowes (Red Funnel) 16 miles (0844 844 9988). **Bus**: Newport to Totland. **Road**: between Brighstone and Brook on B3399. **Parking**: free, 50 yards.

Finding out more: 01983 741302 or mottistonemanor@nationaltrust.org.uk

Mottistone Manor Garden		M	T	W	T	F	S	S
17 Mar–31 Oct	11–5	M	T	W	T	·	·	S

Closes dusk if earlier. Manor House open two days only: Sunday 26 May (members only). Guided tours 9:30 to 12 by timed ticket (available on day), free-flow 1 to 5. Monday 27 May open 11 to 5 (additional charges apply).

A fabulous border at Mottistone Manor Garden on the Isle of Wight

The Needles Old Battery and New Battery

West High Down, Alum Bay,
Isle of Wight PO39 0JH

Map ② C9

Looking out over the Needles on the Isle of Wight

Perched high above the Needles, amid acres of unspoilt countryside, is the Needles Old Battery, a Victorian fort built in 1862 and used throughout both World Wars. The Parade Ground has two original guns, and the fort's fascinating military history is brought to life with displays and models plus a series of vivid cartoons by acclaimed comic book artist Geoff Campion. An underground tunnel leads to a searchlight emplacement with dramatic views over the Needles rocks. The New Battery, further up the headland, has an exhibition on the secret British rocket tests carried out there during the Cold War. **Note**: steep paths and uneven surfaces. Spiral staircase to tunnel. Toilet at Old Battery only.

Eating and shopping: clifftop tea-room serving soup, sandwiches, cakes and light refreshments. Picnic tables (Parade Ground). Guardroom shop selling postcards, gifts and souvenirs. Refreshments, snacks and ice-creams available at New Battery kiosk.

Making the most of your day: family events. Family activity packs, inspector trail and soldier trail. Clifftop walks to Tennyson Monument and beyond. **Dogs**: welcome on leads although assistance dogs only in tea-room.

Access for all: ⬛⬛⬛⬛⬛⬛⬛
Old Battery ⬛⬛⬛⬛ New Battery ⬛

Getting here: 196:SZ300848. Alum Bay.
Foot: Alum Bay ¾ mile, well-surfaced path.
Cycle: NCN67, ½ mile. 'Round the Island' route. **Ferry**: Yarmouth 5 miles (0871 376 1000); East Cowes 16 miles (0844 844 9988).
Bus: Newport to Alum Bay, then ¾ mile. Needles Breezer from Yarmouth and Alum Bay (March to October), member discount

available. **Road**: no vehicular access. West of Freshwater Bay (B3322). **Parking**: no onsite parking. Limited disabled parking by arrangement. Alum Bay ¾ mile (not National Trust, minimum £4). Freshwater Bay 3½ miles (not National Trust), or Highdown (SZ325856) 2 miles, both across Downs.

Finding out more: 01983 754772 or needlesoldbattery@nationaltrust.org.uk

The Needles Batteries		M	T	W	T	F	S	S
Tea-room								
5 Jan–3 Mar	11–3	·	·	·	·	·	S	S
18 Feb–24 Feb	11–3	M	T	W	T	F	S	S
9 Nov–15 Dec	11–3	·	·	·	·	·	S	S
Old Battery and tea-room								
16 Mar–3 Nov	10:30–5	M	T	W	T	F	S	S
New Battery*								
16 Mar–3 Nov	11–4	·	T	·	T	·	S	S

Old Battery closes dusk if earlier. Property closes in high winds, telephone on day of visit to check. *Open other days where possible. 12 May: no disabled vehicular access due to Walk the Wight. 1 June: Old Battery early opening (6:30) for Round the Island Yacht Race.

Newtown Old Town Hall

Newtown, near Shalfleet,
Isle of Wight PO30 4PA

Map (2) C9

Tucked away in a tiny hamlet adjoining the National Nature Reserve, this small and quirky 17th-century building is the only remaining evidence of Newtown's former importance. It's hard to believe that this tranquil corner of the island once held what were often turbulent elections before sending two Members to Parliament. **Note**: nearest toilet in car park.

Eating and shopping: postcards and souvenirs available.

Making the most of your day: children's quiz sheet. Exhibitions by local artists. Walks around adjoining National Nature Reserve. Outdoor family activities (bookable) run by Newtown Warden from nearby Visitor Point (01983 531622).

Access for all: ⬚⬚⬚⬚⬚⬚
Building ⬚

Getting here: 196:SZ424905. Between Newport and Yarmouth. **Cycle**: NCN67, ½ mile. **Ferry**: Yarmouth (Wightlink) 5 miles (0871 376 1000); East Cowes (Red Funnel) 11 miles (0844 844 9998). **Bus**: Newport to Yarmouth, alight Barton's Corner, Shalfleet 1 mile. **Road**: 1 mile north of A3054. **Parking**: free 15 yards.

Finding out more: 01983 531785 or oldtownhall@nationaltrust.org.uk

Newtown Old Town Hall		M	T	W	T	F	S	S
17 Mar–30 Jun	2–5	·	T	W	T	·	·	S
1 Jul–29 Aug	2–5	M	T	W	T	·	·	S
1 Sep–24 Oct	2–5	·	T	W	T	·	·	S

Last admission 15 minutes before closing. Closes dusk if earlier than 5. Open Bank Holiday Mondays.

A crisp winter's day at Nuffield Place, Oxfordshire

Nuffield Place

Huntercombe, near Henley-on-Thames,
Oxfordshire RG9 5RY

Map (2) D5

Home of Britain's greatest philanthropist, William Morris, Lord Nuffield, the founder of Morris Motor Cars and one of the richest men in the world. The house and collection provide a glimpse into the lifestyle of this modest millionaire. Comprising everyday objects, it reflects the tastes of the 1930s.

Eating and shopping: Coronation Café serving light lunches and afternoon tea. Shop selling unique Nuffield Place products and 1930s collection.

Making the most of your day: woodland trails and gardens. **Dogs**: on leads in woodland.

Access for all: ⬚

Getting here: 175:SU679878. At Huntercombe, between Wallingford and Henley-on-Thames. **Foot**: Ridgeway National Trail adjacent to property. **Bus**: Wallingford to Henley-on-Thames. **Train**: Henley-on-Thames, 7 miles and Reading, 12 miles. **Road**: on A4130 between Wallingford and Henley-on-Thames. **Parking**: free.

Finding out more: 01491 641224 or nuffieldplace@nationaltrust.org.uk

Nuffield Place		M	T	W	T	F	S	S
House, garden and tea-room*								
27 Mar–3 Nov	11–5	·	·	W	T	F	S	S
Shop								
27 Mar–3 Nov	11:30–4	·	·	W	T	F	S	S

*House closes at 4, tea-room closes at 4:30. Closed 28 April and 30 June. Tea-room serves light lunches only.

Nymans

Handcross, near Haywards Heath,
West Sussex RH17 6EB

Map ② G7

In the late 19th century, the unusually creative
Messel family bought the Nymans Estate in
the beautiful High Weald landscape of Sussex
with the intention of making a dream country
home. Inspired by the setting and the soil, they
created one of the country's great gardens,
with experimental designs and new plants from
around the world. Nymans became a garden
lovers' house, and the Messels entertained
family and friends, enjoyed relaxing and
playing in the garden, and picnicking and
walking in the woods. Partially destroyed by
fire in 1947, the house and ruins sit within a
romantic and picturesque setting.

Eating and shopping: large shop selling local
products. Plant and Garden Centre, including
Nymans Collection of plants propagated by the
nursery. Café and tea garden. Refreshments
kiosk. Second-hand bookshop.

Nymans, West Sussex: the Forecourt Garden, above,
and the glorious Walled Garden, below

Playing cricket at Nymans, West Sussex

Making the most of your day: events all year for adults and families, including art exhibitions, garden and creative hands-on workshops in our rustic potting shed. There are also theatre and evening events, guided walks, school holiday trails and free activities every day. Family activities include a bamboo jungle, weekend workshops, trails and geocaching. **Dogs**: welcome in the woodland only.

Access for all: ⏸🅿️🆔🚻♿🅰️🎧💻🔊🅰️
House 🚶♿🚼🅰️
Garden ♿➡️🅰️🅰️

Getting here: 187:TQ265294. Handcross, 5 miles south of Crawley. **Foot**: Balcombe 5 miles. **Cycle**: NCN20. **Bus**: Brighton to Crawley and Haywards Heath to Crawley, stop outside Nymans. **Train**: Haywards Heath 9 miles, Three Bridges 5 miles, Crawley 5 miles. **Road**: off London to Brighton M23/A23. **Parking**: free.

Finding out more: 01444 405250 or nymans@nationaltrust.org.uk

Nymans		M	T	W	T	F	S	S
Garden, woods, restaurant, shop and plant centre								
1 Jan–28 Feb	10–4	M	T	W	T	F	S	S
1 Mar–31 Oct	10–5	M	T	W	T	F	S	S
1 Nov–31 Dec	10–4	M	T	W	T	F	S	S
House								
1 Mar–31 Oct	11–3	M	T	W	T	F	S	S
Gallery in house and second-hand bookshop								
Open all year	11–3	M	T	W	T	F	S	S

Gallery closes for short periods to change exhibitions.
Restaurant last orders 15 minutes before closing.
Property closed 25 and 26 December.

Oakhurst Cottage

Hambledon, near Godalming, Surrey GU8 4HF

Map ② E7 🏠❄️

Timber-framed 16th-century cottage, containing objects spanning 400 years, with a delightful cottage garden.
Note: no toilet. Nearest visitor facilities at Winkworth Arboretum (5 miles approximately). Access by booked guided tour only and limited to a maximum of six visitors in the cottage at any one time.

Finding out more: 01483 208936 or www.nationaltrust.org.uk

Old Soar Manor

Plaxtol, Borough Green, Kent TN15 0QX

Map ② H6 🏠

Rare remaining structure of a late 13th-century knight's dwelling, with part of a solar chamber, barrel-vaulted undercroft and garderobe.
Note: no toilet or restaurant. Narrow lanes, limited off-road parking.

Finding out more: 01732 810378 or www.nationaltrust.org.uk

Owletts

The Street, Cobham, Gravesend, Kent DA12 3AP

Map ② H5 🏠❄️🍽️

The family home of Sir Herbert Baker, the architect who redesigned the Bank of England.

Finding out more: 01732 810378 or www.nationaltrust.org.uk

Petworth House and Park

Petworth, West Sussex GU28 0AE

Map ② E7 🏚♿▼

Nestling in the South Downs National Park is one of Britain's finest stately homes, set within a beautiful deer-park landscaped by 'Capability' Brown. The magnificent country house is home to world-famous paintings, many by J. M. W. Turner, Van Dyck, Reynolds and Blake, together with ancient and Neo-classical sculpture and intricate woodcarvings by Grinling Gibbons. In contrast to the opulence of the house are the servants' quarters where life 'below stairs' was very different. Additional private rooms open on weekdays by kind permission of Lord and Lady Egremont. **Note**: additional charge for Christmas fair (including members).

Eating and shopping: Servants' Hall coffee shop and Audit Room restaurant. Gift shop selling presents, and children's books and toys.

Making the most of your day: events and activities, including talks, guided walks and behind-the-scenes tours. Family multimedia guide and trails, plus children's activity baskets in house. Family multimedia guide. Multimedia tours and downloadable app. **Dogs**: under close control in Petworth Park. Assistance dogs only in Pleasure Ground.

Access for all: 🅿♿🚻ᵂᶜ🔔🎧📷🏠 Ⅵ 🚹 👓🅰 **Building** ♿🏠🔽

Getting here: 197:SU976218. In centre of Petworth. **Foot**: access from Petworth and A272. **Bus**: services from Worthing to Midhurst and Horsham to Petworth. **Train**: Pulborough 5¼ miles. **Road**: on A272/A283. **Sat Nav**: use GU28 9LR. **Parking**: on A283, 700 yards. Charge for non-members.

Finding out more: 01798 343929 (Infoline). 01798 342207 or petworth@nationaltrust.org.uk

Petworth House and Park		M	T	W	T	F	S	S
House*								
16 Mar–6 Nov	11–5	M	T	W		·	S	S
Pleasure Ground, shop and restaurant								
12 Jan–13 Mar	10:30–3:30	M	T	W		·	S	S
16 Mar–6 Nov	10:30–5**	M	T	W	T	F	S	S
9 Nov–18 Dec	10:30–3:30	M	T	W		·	S	S
21 Dec–22 Dec	10:30–3:30	·	·	·	·	·	S	S

*On Thursdays and Fridays the house is closed, but Snapshot Tours are available on first-come first-served basis. Open Good Friday. Extra rooms shown weekdays from 1: Monday (not Bank Holiday Mondays), White and Gold Room and White Library; Tuesday and Wednesday, three bedrooms on first floor. **Pleasure Ground closes at 6.

The west front of Petworth House and Park in West Sussex, one of Britain's finest stately homes

Pitstone Windmill

Ivinghoe, Buckinghamshire

Map ② E3　☒☎

One of the oldest windmills in the UK, with stunning views. **Note**: no toilet. At the end of a rough track.

Finding out more: 01442 851227 or www.nationaltrust.org.uk

Polesden Lacey

Great Bookham, near Dorking, Surrey RH5 6BD

Map ② F6　🏛❋☎🛏🍽

This country retreat, with glorious views across the rolling Surrey Hills and acres of countryside waiting to be explored, was home to famous Edwardian hostess Mrs Greville, who entertained royalty and the celebrities of her time. The house has stunning interiors and contains Mrs Greville's fabulous collection of art and ceramics. The beautiful gardens have something for every season, including climbing roses, herbaceous borders and a winter garden. Our free interactive garden guide will help you make the most of your visit and there are waymarked walks, including across Ranmore Common – a designated Site of Special Scientific Interest. **Note**: 'Mrs Greville's House at Christmas', December weekends, additional charge (including members).

Eating and shopping: Courtyard restaurant. Coffee shop and deli. Shops selling souvenirs, gifts and new outdoors range. Plant sales. Shops and restaurant are outside pay perimeter.

Making the most of your day: new for 2013, the house is open every day from March to October, with small group tours weekday mornings. Free daily garden tours, live jazz every Sunday (June to August) and weekend sneak peek house tours (January, February

An Edwardian country estate, Polesden Lacey in Surrey is surrounded by beautiful gardens and extensive parkland

and November). Special activities, including dressing-up in the house, geocaching, croquet and clock golf. Special family activities in school holidays. Waymarked walks. Holiday cottage. **Dogs**: on leads in designated areas, under close control on landscape walks, estate and farmland.

Access for all: 🅿🅓♿♿♿♿♿♿◻♿
👁📷 House 🔥🏠♿　Grounds 🏠➡🚃♿

Getting here: 187:TQ136522. 5 miles north-west of Dorking. **Foot**: North Downs Way within ¾ mile. **Bus**: Guildford ⇄ to Epsom, alight Great Bookham, 1½ miles. **Train**: Boxhill & Westhumble 2 miles; Dorking 4 miles. **Road**: 2 miles south of Great Bookham, off A246 Leatherhead to Guildford road. **Parking**: 200 yards (pay and display).

Finding out more: 01372 458203 (Infoline). 01372 452048 or polesdenlacey@nationaltrust.org.uk

The elegant library at Polesden Lacey, above, and a portrait of the hostess, Mrs Greville, right

Polesden Lacey		M	T	W	T	F	S	S
House tours (spaces limited)								
5 Jan–24 Feb	11–3:30	·	·	·	·	·	S	S
4 Mar–1 Nov*	11–12:30	M	T	W	T	F	·	·
9 Nov–24 Nov	11–3:30	·	·	·	·	·	S	S
28 Dec–29 Dec	11–3:30	·	·	·	·	·	S	S
House								
4 Mar–1 Nov*	12:30–5	M	T	W	T	F	·	·
2 Mar–3 Nov	11–5	·	·	·	·	·	S	S
30 Nov–22 Dec**	11–4	·	·	·	·	·	S	S
Gardens, restaurant, shop and coffee shop								
1 Jan–15 Feb	10–4	M	T	W	T	F	S	S
16 Feb–3 Nov*	10–5	M	T	W	T	F	S	S
4 Nov–31 Dec*	10–4	M	T	W	T	F	S	S
Car park								
Open all year	7:30–6:30	M	T	W	T	F	S	S

*Closed 19 March, 24 and 25 December. **Over the four weekends running up to Christmas the house is open for a special Christmas event: additional charge for all visitors, including members.

Priory Cottages

1 Mill Street, Steventon, Abingdon,
Oxfordshire OX13 6SP

Map ② C5

Now converted into two houses, these former monastic buildings were gifted to the National Trust by the famous Ferguson's Gang. **Note**: Priory Cottage South only open. Administered by a tenant (booking essential). No toilet.

Finding out more: 01793 762209 or www.nationaltrust.org.uk

Quebec House

Quebec Square, Westerham, Kent TN16 1TD

Map ② G6

This intimate 18th-century family home, with its pretty garden, was the boyhood home of James Wolfe. Visitors can uncover the glory of General Wolfe's great victory at Quebec, explore both sides of the conquest of Canada and reflect on the tragedy of Wolfe's death and the art it inspired.

Eating and shopping: tea-room. Coach House shop selling local food, Quebec House-themed products and gifts. Ice-cream available.

Making the most of your day: events, including special talks, children's activities, living history and family trails. Exhibition.

Access for all: 🚻 🧑‍🦽 🔊 🖥 🎧 ⠿ 📷
Building 🏛️ 🚪
Grounds 🏛️ ➡️ 🚪

Getting here: 187:TQ449541. At east end of Westerham. **Bus**: services from Bromley North 🚌 (passing Bromley South 🚌) and Sevenoaks 🚌; also from Tunbridge Wells 🚌 (Sundays only). **Train**: Sevenoaks 4 miles; Oxted 4 miles. **Road**: on north side of A25, facing junction with B2026 Edenbridge road. M25 exit 5 or 6. **Parking**: on A25, 80 yards (not National Trust) – footpath to house.

Finding out more: 01732 868381 or quebechouse@nationaltrust.org.uk

Quebec House		M	T	W	T	F	S	S
House								
2 Mar–3 Nov	1–5	·	·	W	T	F	S	S
9 Nov–22 Dec	1–4	·	·	·	·	·	S	S
Garden and exhibition								
2 Mar–3 Nov	12–5	·	·	W	T	F	S	S
9 Nov–22 Dec	1–4	·	·	·	·	·	S	S

Open Bank Holiday Mondays.

Quebec House, Kent: pretty garden and church beyond

The mirror-like water of the River Wey in Surrey, on a frosty winter's day

River Wey and Godalming Navigations and Dapdune Wharf

Navigations Office and Dapdune Wharf, Wharf Road, Guildford, Surrey GU1 4RR

Map ② F6 🏠🛏️👕🍴

A surprising haven in the heart of Surrey where you can relax on a boat trip, climb aboard a restored barge, tie a sailor's knot or enjoy scenic walks. Our visitor centre at Dapdune Wharf in Guildford brings to life the stories of this historical waterway. You and your family can have fun at one of our many events, let the children explore, build dens on the island, or raid our dressing-up box. The Navigations meander through 20 miles of Surrey countryside with towpath all the way; you can walk it in chunks, looking out for resident wildlife. **Note**: mooring and fishing fees (including members).

Eating and shopping: small tea-room serves sandwiches, cakes, ice-cream and drinks. Small shop with plant sales. Picnic areas at Dapdune Wharf.

Making the most of your day: year-round events, including events for children at Dapdune and guided walks along towpath and beyond. Guildford Festival Boat Gathering in July. Overnight moorings available. **Dogs**: on leads at Dapdune Wharf and lock areas; elsewhere under control.

Access for all: 🅿️🚾♿🚻💺🅿️•••📷🏛️
Grounds 🏛️

Getting here: 186:SU993502. In Wharf Road, ½ mile from Guildford town centre. **River**: visiting craft can enter from the Thames at Shepperton. Slipways at Guildford/Pyrford. **Foot**: towpath from town centre to Dapdune Wharf. **Bus**: frequent services, alight at Cricket Ground on Woodbridge Road. **Train**: Addlestone ➤, Byfleet & New Haw, Guildford, Farncombe and Godalming, all close to the Navigations. **Road**: Dapdune Wharf on Wharf Road to rear of Surrey Cricket Ground, off Woodbridge Road, A322 Guildford. **Parking**: at Dapdune Wharf.

Finding out more: 01483 561389 or riverwey@nationaltrust.org.uk

River Wey and Dapdune Wharf		M	T	W	T	F	S	S
Dapdune Wharf								
16 Mar–26 May	11–5	M	·	·	T	F	S	S
27 May–2 Jun	11–5	M	T	W	T	F	S	S
3 Jun–4 Aug	11–5	M	·	·	T	F	S	S
5 Aug–31 Aug	11–5	M	T	W	T	F	S	S
1 Sep–27 Oct	11–5	M	·	·	T	F	S	S
28 Oct–3 Nov	11–5	M	T	W	T	F	S	S

River trips 11 to 4 (conditions permitting). Access to towpath during daylight hours all year.

Runnymede

Egham, near Old Windsor, Surrey

Map ② F5

In 1215 Runnymede was witness to King John's sealing of the Magna Carta, on the banks of the River Thames. Set within the beautiful natural landscape are various memorials by Maufe, Jellicoe and Lutyens, commemorating moments in world history. **Note**: toilets available during tea-room opening hours. Mooring and fishing fees apply (including members).

Eating and shopping: tea-room (not National Trust).

Making the most of your day: guided walks and events, including Easter Egg trails. River boat trips available with French Brothers Boat Hire (01784 439626). **Dogs**: under close control or on leads near livestock.

Access for all: 🅿️♿🚻🔊🚶 Estate office 🏢 Grounds 🚶♿♿

Getting here: SU996731. A308 between Egham and Old Windsor. **Foot**: 1¼ miles of Thames Path, National Trail. **Cycle**: 1¼ miles of Thames Path. **Bus**: services from Heathrow to Slough. Alight Old Windsor, Bells of Ouzeley, walk back along A308 towards Egham for ¼ mile. **Train**: Egham ⇌, 1½ miles. **Road**: M25 junction 13, 2 miles along A308 towards Old Windsor. **Parking**: either side of A308, pay and display. Riverside car park open seasonally.

Finding out more: 01784 432891 or runnymede@nationaltrust.org.uk. Runnymede Estate Office, North Lodge, Windsor Road, Egham, Old Windsor, Berkshire SL4 2JL

Runnymede		M	T	W	T	F	S	S
Memorials car park (hard-standing)								
2 Jan–3 Mar	8:30–5	M	T	W	T	F	S	S
4 Mar–29 Sep	8:30–7	M	T	W	T	F	S	S
30 Sep–31 Dec	8:30–5	M	T	W	T	F	S	S
Riverside car park (grass/seasonal)*								
4 Mar–29 Sep	10–7	M	T	W	T	F	S	S

*Open when conditions permit. Both car parks may close dusk if earlier. Closed 1 January, 25 and 26 December.

St John's Jerusalem

Sutton-at-Hone, Dartford, Kent DA4 9HQ

Map ② H5

13th-century chapel surrounded by a tranquil moated garden, once part of the former Commandery of the Knights Hospitallers. **Note**: occupied as a private residence, maintained and managed by a tenant on behalf of the National Trust.

Finding out more: 01732 810378 (c/o Ightham Mote) or www.nationaltrust.org.uk

Sandham Memorial Chapel

Harts Lane, Burghclere, near Newbury, Hampshire RG20 9JT

Map ② C6 ⊞❋

An outstanding series of large-scale paintings by acclaimed artist Stanley Spencer is to be found in this modest red-brick building. Inspired by his experiences as a First World War medical orderly and soldier, and peppered with personal and unexpected details, these extraordinarily detailed paintings are considered among his finest achievements. **Note**: no toilet or card payment facility. No artificial lighting, so bright days best for viewing.

Eating and shopping: books, postcards, locally made gifts and home-grown plants for sale. Picnics welcome in garden.

Making the most of your day: reference folders, children's quiz and handling kit available. **Dogs**: in grounds on leads only.

Access for all: ♿🔊📷⋯📷 Building 🚶♿ Grounds 🚶♿

Modest Sandham Memorial Chapel, Hampshire

Getting here: 174:SU463608. 4 miles south of Newbury. **Bus**: 'demand-responsive' from Newbury (0845 6024135). **Train**: Newbury 4 miles. **Road**: ½ mile east of A34. Exit A34 at Tothill services. **Parking**: in lay-by opposite, on road between church and village hall or village car park (¼ mile).

Finding out more: 01635 278394 or sandham@nationaltrust.org.uk

Sandham Memorial Chapel		M	T	W	T	F	S	S
2 Mar–24 Mar	11–3						S	S
27 Mar–29 Sep	11–4:30			W		F	S	S
5 Oct–3 Nov	11–3						S	S
10 Nov	10–3							S

Open Bank Holiday Mondays, 11 to 4:30. Major restoration work may affect opening times from mid-September (contact property before travelling).

The ruins of the romantic 14th-century moated Scotney Castle in Kent, are set in wonderful gardens

Scotney Castle

Lamberhurst, Tunbridge Wells, Kent TN3 8JN

Map ② I7

Scotney Castle has one of the most picturesque gardens in England, with two celebrated former homes on one site. There are newly opened rooms in the Victorian mansion and ruins of the 14th-century moated castle, which is the focal point of this truly romantic garden. Beautiful displays of rhododendrons, azaleas and kalmia can be seen in May and June with trees and shrubs providing brilliant autumnal colour. The 310-hectare (770-acre) estate, which along with the garden is a Site of Special Scientific Interest, is open all year and offers a variety of walks through parkland, woodland and farmland.

Eating and shopping: tea-room serving lunch, sandwiches and cream teas. Picnic area kiosk serving light refreshments. Scotney Ale and honey available. Plant sales.

Making the most of your day: a wide range of activities and events throughout the year – including open-air theatre, music, lecture lunches and family activities. Estate and wildlife walks – a full events programme is available. **Dogs**: welcome on leads around estate, assistance dogs only in the garden.

Access for all: ☐☐☐☐☐☐☐☐
House ☐☐☐ **Grounds** ☐➡☐

Getting here: 188:TQ688353. Outskirts of Lamberhurst village. **Foot**: links to local footpath network. **Cycle**: NCN18, 3 miles. **Bus**: service from Tunbridge Wells to Lamberhurst. **Train**: Wadhurst 5½ miles. **Road**: signposted from A21 at Lamberhurst. **Parking**: main car park 130 yards (limited parking), overflow 440 yards.

Finding out more: 01892 893820 (Infoline). 01892 893868 or scotneycastle@nationaltrust.org.uk

Scotney Castle		M	T	W	T	F	S	S
Garden, Old Castle, shop and tea-room*								
16 Feb–3 Nov	11–5:30	M	T	W	T	F	S	S
4 Nov–23 Dec	11–3	M	T	W	T	F	S	S
26 Dec–31 Dec	11–3	M	T		T	F	S	S
House								
16 Feb–3 Nov	11–5	M	T	W	T	F	S	S
Estate walks								
Open all year		M	T	W	T	F	S	S

*Shop and tea-room closes at 5, 16 February to 3 November. House and garden last admission one hour before closing. All visitors require timed ticket to visit house (places limited, early sell-outs possible). Property may close during adverse weather.

Scotney Castle, Kent: a picture-book castle

Shalford Mill

Shalford, near Guildford, Surrey GU4 8BS

Map ②E6

Shalford Mill is a lucky survivor, telling the story of the decline of traditional village work and life. **Note**: no toilet. No parking. Regular tours.

Finding out more: 01483 561389 or www.nationaltrust.org.uk

Sheffield Park and Garden

Sheffield Park, East Sussex TN22 3QX

Map ②G7

This informal landscape garden was laid out in the 18th century by 'Capability' Brown and further enhanced early in the 20th century by its owner, Arthur G. Soames. The four larger lakes form the centrepiece. In spring, there are colourful shows of daffodils and bluebells. Rhododendrons and azaleas are beautiful in early summer. Autumn brings lovely foliage colours from the many trees and shrubs, some quite rare. Winter walks can also be enjoyed in this garden for all seasons. Visitors can now also explore South Park and East Park, areas of historic parkland with countryside views.

Eating and shopping: Coach House restaurant serving lunch and tea. Catering buggy in garden. Shop selling local products. Plant sales.

Making the most of your day: family fun activities all year, with extra activities every day of school holidays. Twice-weekly garden tours on Tuesdays and Thursdays. Woodland play trail on South Park for families. Cricket matches most weekends May to September. Make a day of it with the Bluebell Railway, connecting service through East Grinstead Station – new from April. **Dogs**: welcome in South or East Park. Assistance dogs only in garden.

Sheffield Park and Garden in East Sussex: one of the four larger lakes, above, and Top Bridge, below

Access for all: ♿🚻♿🅿️🔄🎧🔆👓 🔆

Reception ♿🔄

Garden ♿➡️♿🔄

Getting here: 198:TQ415240. Midway between East Grinstead and Lewes. **Bus**: service from close Lewes ➡ (Saturday only) and Uckfield (Monday, Wednesday, Friday only). **Train**: Bluebell Railway link from East Grinstead ➡ to Sheffield Park ➡ ½ mile; Uckfield 6 miles; Haywards Heath 7 miles. **Road**: 5 miles north-west of Uckfield, on east side of A275 (between A272 and A22). **Parking**: free.

Finding out more: 01825 790231 or sheffieldpark@nationaltrust.org.uk

Sheffield Park and Garden in spring

Sheffield Park and Garden		M	T	W	T	F	S	S
Garden, restaurant and shop								
1 Jan–3 Mar	10:30–4	M	T	W	T	F	S	S
4 Mar–3 Nov	10:30–5:30	M	T	W	T	F	S	S
4 Nov–31 Dec	10:30–4	M	T	W	T	F	S	S
Parkland								
Open all year	Dawn–dusk	M	T	W	T	F	S	S

Garden, shop and restaurant closed 25 December.
Last admission into the garden is one hour before closing or dusk if earlier.

Sissinghurst Castle

Biddenden Road, near Cranbrook,
Kent TN17 2AB

Map (2) I7

Sissinghurst Castle is a ruin of an Elizabethan manor house gently seated in the beautiful Weald of Kent. Once a prison to captured French seamen during the Seven Years War, a poor house and latterly a working farm, it gained international fame in the 1930s when Vita Sackville-West and Harold Nicolson created a garden here. The estate, perfect for wildlife spotting and walking, also comprises our organic vegetable garden.

Eating and shopping: Granary restaurant and coffee shop, both serving home-grown fruit and vegetables. Shop selling local products, crafts and gifts, including the White Garden range. Plants propagated and grown on site available from our garden shop.

Making the most of your day: events all year, including open-air theatre, annual Smallholders' Fair, garden suppers and late-night summer garden opening. Prisoners of war exhibition. Activities, including dawn chorus walks and Ranger-led nature trails. 182-hectares (450 acres) of ancient woodland. Panoramic views across the Wealden countryside from tower. Library containing the Trust's most significant collection of 20th-century literature. Smallhythe Place, Lamb House and Stoneacre nearby.

Dogs: welcome on estate. Assistance dogs only in garden and vegetable garden.

Access for all: 🅿️🐕♿🚾🔞🔞📷📖♿ 👁️🅰️ Building 🔞♿♿ Grounds 🔞♿➡️

Getting here: 188:TQ810380. 1 mile east of Sissinghurst village. **Foot**: from Sissinghurst village past church to footpath on left signposted Sissinghurst Castle (uneven terrain). **Cycle**: NCN18. **Bus**: from Maidstone to Hawkhurst (passing Staplehurst ➡), alight Sissinghurst. **Train**: Staplehurst 5 miles. **Road**: on Biddenden Road, off A262. **Parking**: 315 yards, £2 (non-members).

Sissinghurst Castle, Kent: statue of Dionysus, above, and stunning summer blooms, below

The Elizabethan Tower at
Sissinghurst Castle

Finding out more: 01580 710700 or
sissinghurst@nationaltrust.org.uk

Sissinghurst Castle		M	T	W	T	F	S	S
Garden								
1 Mar–3 Nov	11–5:30	M	T	W	T	F	S	S
1 Dec–31 Dec	11–3:30	M	T	W	T	F	S	S
Shop and restaurant								
1 Mar–3 Nov	10:30–5:30	M	T	W	T	F	S	S
4 Nov–31 Dec	11–4	M	T	W	T	F	S	S
Vegetable garden								
Open all year	10:30–5:30	M	T	W	T	F	S	S
Estate								
Open all year	Dawn–dusk	M	T	W	T	F	S	S

Shop, restaurant and garden closed 24 and 25 December.

Smallhythe Place

Smallhythe, Tenterden, Kent TN30 7NG

Map ② I7   🏠 ❄ 🔔 🍷

Home of Victorian actress Ellen Terry from
1899 to 1928 and containing her fascinating
theatre collection, this half-timbered house
(below) was built in the early 16th century
when Smallhythe was a thriving shipbuilding
yard. Ellen Terry's rose garden, the orchard,
nuttery and working Barn Theatre are in
the grounds.

Eating and shopping: vintage-style tea-room
(licensed) attached to Barn Theatre selling
sandwiches, cakes and drinks.

Making the most of your day: open-air
theatre, indoor plays and music in Barn
Theatre. Smallhythe Music and Beer Festival
(September). Exhibition. Sissinghurst
Castle, Lamb House and Stoneacre nearby.
Dogs: allowed on leads in grounds.

Access for all: 🚽 🖥 ♿ ⠿ 🔎
Building 🔲🔲 Grounds 🔲➡️

Getting here: 189:TQ893300. 2 miles south
of Tenterden. **Bus**: from Rye to Tenterden.
Train: Rye 8 miles; Appledore 8 miles; Headcorn
10 miles. **Road**: on east side of Rye road (B2082).
Parking: free (not National Trust), 50 yards.

Finding out more: 01580 762334 or
smallhytheplace@nationaltrust.org.uk

Smallhythe Place		M	T	W	T	F	S	S
2 Mar–30 Oct	11–5*	M	T	W	·	·	S	S

*Tea-room opens 11:30 to 4:30. Open Good Friday.
Last admission 4:30 or dusk if earlier.

South Foreland Lighthouse in Kent is dramatically situated on the White Cliffs and is a historic landmark

South Foreland Lighthouse

The Front, St Margaret's Bay, Dover, Kent CT15 6HP

Map ② K6

This distinctive, historic landmark, dramatically situated on the White Cliffs, offers unrivalled views and has a fascinating tale to tell. A beacon of safety, guiding ships past the infamous Goodwin Sands, it was the first lighthouse powered by electricity and is the site of the first international radio transmission. **Note**: no access for cars.

Eating and shopping: Mrs Knott's tea-room in former lighthouse keeper's cottage. Shop selling ice-creams and gifts.

Making the most of your day: guided tours and hands-on displays. **Dogs**: in grounds only.

Access for all: 🔊🗣️📷📺♿.:🅿

Building 🏠 Grounds 🏔

Getting here: 179:TR359433. On coast, 1 mile from St Margaret's. **Foot**: from Dover White Cliffs Visitor Centre 2½ miles, or St Margaret's 1 mile. **Cycle**: NCN1, ½ mile. **Bus**: to St Margaret's, alight Bay Hill 1 mile via Lighthouse Road. **Train**: Dover 3 miles. **Road: no vehicular access**. **Parking**: no onsite parking. Nearest at White Cliffs, 2-mile clifftop walk, or St Margaret's 1 mile.

Finding out more: 01304 852463 or southforeland@nationaltrust.org.uk

South Foreland Lighthouse		M	T	W	T	F	S	S
10 Mar–31 Mar	11–5:30	M	·	·	·	F	S	S
1 Apr–14 Apr	11–5:30	M	T	W	T	F	S	S
15 Apr–26 May	11–5:30	M	·	·	·	F	S	S
27 May–2 Jun	11–5:30	M	T	W	T	F	S	S
3 Jun–21 Jul	11–5:30	M	·	·	T	F	S	S
22 Jul–8 Sep	11–5:30	M	T	W	T	F	S	S
9 Sep–27 Oct	11–5:30	M	·	·	·	F	S	S
28 Oct–3 Nov	11–4	M	T	W	T	F	S	S

Admission by guided tour, last tour at 5.

Sprivers Garden

Horsmonden, Kent TN12 8DR

Telephone 01892 893820 (Scotney Castle) for information.

Standen

West Hoathly Road, East Grinstead,
West Sussex RH19 4NE

Map ② G7   🏠✳️🛏️🍴

Standen is the story of family life set against a backdrop of the Arts and Crafts Movement. The design of the house is a monument to the combined genius of architect Philip Webb and his friend William Morris, and is filled with art, ceramics and textiles from the period. You can follow the story of the Beale family in 1925 throughout the house. Standen's garden restoration project will continue in 2013 with lots of work to see and get involved with. The top of the gardens offers wonderful views, and footpaths lead you into acres of woodland and countryside. **Note**: tours to top of water tower, charge (including members).

Eating and shopping: shop selling gifts inspired by William Morris. Barn Restaurant. Fresh kitchen garden produce available. Plant sales.

Pretty corner of a bedroom at Standen, West Sussex

Making the most of your day: guided 'restoration tours' of garden. Woodland family play area. Nearby Bluebell Railway has services to Sheffield Park and Garden. **Dogs**: welcome in woodland areas and outside restaurant.

Access for all: 🅿️🚻♿🔶♿📷📽️📶📷
House 🔶♿♿
Gardens 🔶➡️♿

Getting here: 187:TQ389356. 2 miles south of East Grinstead. **Foot**: Sussex Border Path. **Cycle**: NCN21, 1¼ miles. **Bus**: from East Grinstead to Crawley (passing Three Bridges). **Train**: East Grinstead 2 miles; Kingscote (Bluebell Railway) 2 miles. **Road**: just south of East Grinstead – brown signs from town centre and B2110 (Turners Hill Road). **Parking**: free, 200 yards.

Finding out more: 01342 323029 or standen@nationaltrust.org.uk

Standen		M	T	W	T	F	S	S
Garden, Barn Restaurant and shop*								
16 Feb–3 Nov	10:30–5:30	M	T	W	T	F	S	S
9 Nov–24 Nov	10:30–4	·	·	·	·	·	S	S
30 Nov–24 Dec	10:30–4	M	T	W	T	F	S	S
House								
16 Feb–3 Nov	11–4:30	M	T	W	T	F	S	S
9 Nov–24 Nov	11–3	·	·	·	·	·	S	S
30 Nov–24 Dec	11–3	M	T	W	T	F	S	S

*Shop opens at 11, Barn Restaurant and shop close 30 minutes earlier. Admission to house by timed guided tour only at 11 to 1:30 on Monday to Friday, 16 February to 28 March, and Mondays and Tuesdays throughout the year (excluding Bank Holidays).

Stoneacre

Otham, Maidstone, Kent ME15 8RS

Map ② I6   🏠✳️

Captivating 15th-century timber-framed house restored by the Arts and Crafts designer Aymer Vallance, surrounded by a beautiful garden. **Note**: administered by tenants on behalf of the National Trust. No toilets.

Finding out more: 01622 863247 or www.nationaltrust.org.uk

Stowe

Buckingham,
Buckinghamshire MK18 5EQ

Map ② D2 🏠❄♨🔔🍴

At Stowe visitors can step back in time. When you visit New Inn, our recently restored coaching inn, you will be following in the footsteps of 18th-century tourists. While in the gardens, new trail maps will help you explore and we have plenty of space for youngsters to run and play. With more than 40 temples and monuments, the gardens have beautiful lakes and vistas with ever-changing scenes throughout the seasons. There is also an endless variety of walks to enjoy.

Eating and shopping: café serving cakes, soups and scones. New shop selling gifts, jewellery, plants and local products, including Stowe Ale. Picnics welcome in wildflower paddock outside New Inn.

Making the most of your day: events, walks, family activities and talks throughout the year. Wide range of trails, including new gardens trail. Scenic walk with glimpses of the parkland and Stowe House. Farmhouse kitchen garden to explore. Newly restored 18th-century parlour rooms in New Inn. Stowe House's state rooms (not National Trust) also open. Family cycle trail. **Dogs**: welcome on leads.

Access for all: 🅿🧸♿🚾♿📷📷
Visitor centre 🏠🔺♿ Grounds 🏠➡♿

One of the many temples at Stowe, Buckinghamshire, above, and relaxing beside a lake, below

Getting here: 152:SP681364. 1½ miles north-west of Buckingham. **Foot**: footpath up Stowe Avenue from Buckingham. **Bus**: Cambridge to Oxford, stops Buckingham, 1½ miles. **Train**: Bicester North 9 miles; Milton Keynes Central 14 miles. **Road**: off A422 Buckingham to Banbury road. From M40 take exits 9 to 11, from M1 exits 13 or 15a. **Parking**: free (£2 non-members).

Finding out more: 01280 817156 or stowe@nationaltrust.org.uk

Stowe		M	T	W	T	F	S	S
Gardens, shop, café and parlour rooms								
1 Jan–31 Mar	10–4	M	T	W	T	F	S	S
1 Apr–20 Oct	10–6	M	T	W	T	F	S	S
21 Oct–31 Dec	10–4	M	T	W	T	F	S	S
Parkland								
Open all year	Dawn–dusk	M	T	W	T	F	S	S

Last entry to the gardens is recommended 90 minutes before closing or dusk if earlier. 25 May: landscape gardens closed; visitor centre, parkland, café and shop open. Closed 25 December. May close in severe weather conditions.

Uppark House and Garden

South Harting, Petersfield,
West Sussex GU31 5QR

Map ② E8

Uppark is a place of faded Georgian grandeur, with beautiful interiors and Grand Tour collection all surrounded by a charming garden with amazing views. Over time it has been home to scandal and fame involving the Prince Regent, a young H. G. Wells, Emma Hamilton and her first and last love, and lots of parties.

Eating and shopping: shop selling local food products. Restaurant.

Making the most of your day: house introductory talks. House and garden trails. Free garden history tours (Thursday). Lecture lunch programme (March and November). Petworth House and Hinton Ampner nearby. **Dogs**: on leads on woodland walk only. Please note: no shaded parking.

Access for all: ⓟₐ Ⓓₐ 🚾 ♿ ⅱ 🅿 🅅ₜ ♿ ·· Ⓐ
House 👨‍🦽 ⅱ 👪 ⬇
Gardens 👨‍🦽 🏛 ➡ ⬇

Getting here: 197:SU775177. 5 miles south-east of Petersfield. **Foot**: South Downs Way within ¾ mile. **Bus**: Petersfield ⊛ to Chichester ⊛. **Train**: Petersfield 5½ miles. **Road**: on B2146, 1½ miles south of South Harting. **Parking**: free, 300 yards.

Finding out more: 01730 825857 (Infoline). 01730 825415 or uppark@nationaltrust.org.uk

Uppark House and Garden		M	T	W	T	F	S	S
House								
17 Mar–3 Nov	12:30–4:30	M	T	W	T	.	.	S
House taster tours*								
17 Mar–3 Nov	11–12:30	M	T	W	T	.	.	S
Garden, shop and restaurant								
17 Mar–3 Nov	11–5	M	T	W	T	.	.	S
House, garden, shop and restaurant								
17 Nov–22 Dec	11–3	.	.	.	.	.	.	S

*Numbers limited (Bank Holiday Sundays, Mondays and Good Friday house free-flow from 11). Open Good Friday. Also open Saturday 7 December. Garden tours every Thursday from April to October. Print Room open first Wednesday of each month (times as house).

The charming kitchen at Uppark House and Garden, West Sussex: a place of faded Georgian elegance

The Vyne in Hampshire has royal connections dating back to Henry VIII and has inspired numerous writers and artists

The Vyne

Vyne Road, Sherborne St John,
Basingstoke, Hampshire RG24 9HL

Map ② D6 🏯➕❄🏃🍴☂

An intimate family home steeped in history, The Vyne has royal connections dating back to Henry VIII. It contains, and has inspired, art, architecture and writers, including Jane Austen and J. R. R. Tolkien. The peaceful gardens are perfect for lakeside strolls or picnics on the sweeping lawn, and there is also a walled garden to explore. The ancient woodlands are abundant in wildlife and glorious in every season, from spring, when there are carpets of bluebells, to autumn, with its colourful leaves. **Note**: occasional room closures for essential conservation work and filming.

Eating and shopping: well-stocked shop selling local produce and peat-free plants. Second-hand bookshop. Tudor Brewhouse tea-room.

Making the most of your day: events and free garden tours and children's trails. Waymarked woodland walks and permanent orienteering course. **Dogs**: welcome on short leads in woodlands and most of gardens. Assistance dogs only in house and walled garden.

Access for all:
Building 🧑‍🦽♿ Grounds 🧑‍🦽♿

Getting here: 175/186:SU639576. 4 miles north of Basingstoke, between Bramley and Sherborne St John. **Cycle**: NCN23, 1 mile. **Train**: Basingstoke 4 miles. **Parking**: free, ⅓-mile walk through gardens from visitor reception to house.

Finding out more: 01256 883858 or thevyne@nationaltrust.org.uk

The Vyne		M	T	W	T	F	S	S
Gardens								
2 Jan–15 Feb	11–3	M	T	W	T	F	S	S
16 Feb–24 May	11–5	M	T	W	T	F	S	S
25 May–1 Sep	11–6	M	T	W	T	F	S	S
2 Sep–3 Nov	11–5	M	T	W	T	F	S	S
4 Nov–22 Dec	11–3	M	T	W	T	F	S	S
House and second-hand bookshop*								
16 Feb–3 Nov	12–4	M	T	W	T	F	S	S
Tea-room and shop								
16 Feb–3 Nov	11–5	M	T	W	T	F	S	S
House, tea-room and shop								
7 Nov–22 Dec	11–3	·	·	·	T	F	S	S
Woods								
Open all year	Dawn–dusk	M	T	W	T	F	S	S

*House and second-hand bookshop open 11 to 4:30 at weekends. Admission to house by timed ticket, available on arrival. House opens weekend hours on Bank Holiday Mondays and Good Friday. Property may close during adverse weather conditions. Car park closes at 6 or dusk if earlier and closed on 25 December.

Waddesdon Manor

Waddesdon, near Aylesbury,
Buckinghamshire HP18 0JH

Map ② D3   🏛️ 🍴 ✦ 🔔 📷 ☂️

This Renaissance-style château was built by
Baron Ferdinand de Rothschild to display his
outstanding collection of art treasures and to
entertain the fashionable world. The 45 rooms
on view combine the highest quality French
furniture and decorative arts from the
18th century, with superb English portraits
and Dutch Old Masters. The Victorian garden
is considered one of the finest in Britain, with
its parterre, seasonal displays, fountains and
statuary. At its heart lies the aviary, stocked
with species once part of Baron Ferdinand's
collection. There is a contemporary art
gallery in the Coach House at the Stables.

Note: managed by a Rothschild family
charitable trust. House entrance by
timed tickets only.

Eating and shopping: three licensed
restaurants (not National Trust). Snacks and
drinks available at the Summerhouse or Coffee
Bar. Shops, plant centre and old-fashioned
sweet shop at the Stables.

Making the most of your day: wide range
of free activities on aspects of the house,
collection and special exhibitions with experts.
Guided walks in the gardens, Wildlife Explorer
Trails and talks about the work of the aviary.
Rolling presentations on the Rothschilds and
Waddesdon. Special interest days, wine tastings,
family events, jazz evenings, car days and food
markets and fairs. **Dogs**: assistance dogs only.

Access for all: 🅿️♿ 🚻 ♿ ♿ ♿ ♿ 📷 🖼️ 🅰️
Building 🏛️ ⬆️ ♿
Grounds 🏛️ ➡️ ♿

When seen from the air, the full magnificence of Waddesdon Manor in Buckinghamshire becomes apparent

The Pink Parterre at Waddesdon Manor, Buckinghamshire

Getting here: 165:SP740169. 6 miles north-west Aylesbury. **Bus**: from Aylesbury. **Train**: Aylesbury Vale Parkway 4 miles; Aylesbury 6 miles. **Road**: access via Waddesdon village, on A41; M40 (westbound) exit 6 or 7 via Thame and Long Crendon or M40 (eastbound) exit 9 via Bicester. **Parking**: free.

Finding out more: 01296 653226 or waddesdonmanor@nationaltrust.org.uk

Waddesdon Manor		M	T	W	T	F	S	S
Gardens, aviary, woodland playground, shops, restaurants								
5 Jan–24 Mar	10–5						S	S
16 Feb–24 Feb	10–5	M	T	W	T	F	S	S
27 Mar–22 Dec	10–5			W	T	F	S	S
27 Dec–31 Dec	10–5	M	T			F	S	S
House and wine cellars								
27 Mar–25 Oct	12–4			W	T	F		
30 Mar–27 Oct	11–4						S	S
13 Nov–20 Dec	12–4			W	T	F		
16 Nov–22 Dec	11–4						S	S
27 Dec–31 Dec	12–4	M	T			F	S	S
Bachelors' Wing								
27 Mar–25 Oct	12–4			W	T	F		

Recommended last admission to house one hour before closing. Open Bank Holiday Mondays. Open 2 April, 16, 17 and 23 December. Closed 23 to 26 December. House operates by timed-ticket system (including members), available from ticket office or online at www.waddesdon.org.uk (tickets limited). To guarantee entry during busy periods, especially over Christmas and Bank Holidays, please book house entry tickets. Admission to house must include a garden ticket.

Wakehurst Place

Ardingly, Haywards Heath, West Sussex RH17 6TN

Map ② G7

Open throughout the year, Wakehurst is the country estate of the Royal Botanic Gardens, Kew, and the National Trust's most-visited property. This beautiful botanic garden is internationally significant for its collections and also its vital scientific research and plant conservation. Enjoy visiting woodland and lakes, formal gardens, the Elizabethan mansion and Kew's Millennium Seed Bank. In 2010, Wakehurst marked an international conservation milestone, conserving the seeds of 10 per cent of the world's plant species. The new target is 25 per cent by 2020. **Note**: funded and managed by the Royal Botanic Gardens, Kew. National Trust UK members free.

Eating and shopping: Stables Restaurant. Seed Café serving sandwiches and cakes. Gift shop (not National Trust). Plant centre.

Making the most of your day: free guided tour and informative walk around the botanical gardens. Events and activities, including courses and talks – bat evenings, seasonal

soup and stroll, photography workshops, plus kingfisher and badger watching (charge applies). Loder Valley Nature Reserve with wetland and meadowland (admission limited). Natural play areas and Adventurous Journeys trail for children and families. Winter festival events, with the country's tallest Christmas tree, carols evening and Santa's Winter Wonderland. **Dogs**: assistance dogs only.

Access for all: 🅿️♿🚻♿♿ Building ♿♿
Grounds ♿➡️♿♿

Getting here: 187:TQ339314. 3 miles south of Turners Hill. **Foot**: footpath from Balcombe (4 miles). **Bus**: from Haywards Heath to Crawley, passing Haywards Heath ➕ and Three Bridges ➕. **Train**: Haywards Heath 6 miles; East Grinstead 6 miles. **Road**: M23 junction 10, on B2028 near Ardingly. **Parking**: 50 yards.

Finding out more: 01444 894066 or wakehurst@kew.org. www.kew.org

Wakehurst Place		M	T	W	T	F	S	S
1 Jan–28 Feb	10–4:30*	M	T	W	T	F	S	S
1 Mar–31 Oct	10–6*	M	T	W	T	F	S	S
1 Nov–31 Dec	10–4:30*	M	T	W	T	F	S	S

*Mansion and Millennium Seed Bank closes one hour earlier. Seed Café closes 5:30 March to October, 4:15 November to 1 January, 4 from 2 January to February. Stables Restaurant closes 5 from March to October, 3:45 November to February. Property closed 24 and 25 December. Shop closed Easter Sunday. UK National Trust members free (reciprocal agreements made between the Trust and other parties do not apply).

Millennium Seed Bank at Wakehurst Place, West Sussex

The mansion at Wakehurst Place, above, and flame-like autumn hues, below

West Green House Garden

West Green, Hartley Wintney, Hampshire RG27 8JB

Map ② D6

A critically acclaimed series of elegant gardens containing a major collection of follies, a famous potager and subtly coloured borders. **Note**: maintained on behalf of the National Trust by Marylyn Abbott. Facilities not National Trust.

Finding out more: 01252 845582 or www.nationaltrust.org.uk

The exquisite mansion at West Wycombe Park, Buckinghamshire, is surrounded by a serene landscape garden

West Wycombe Park and Village

West Wycombe, Buckinghamshire HP14 3AJ

Map ② E4

Alongside this historic village lies an exquisite country mansion. This lavish home and serene landscape garden reflect the wealth and personality of its creator, the infamous Sir Francis Dashwood, founder of the Hellfire Club. Still home to the Dashwood family and their fine collection, it remains a busy, private estate. **Note**: opened in partnership with the National Trust.

Eating and shopping: refreshments available at George and Dragon public house, Village Community Library, West Wycombe Garden Centre and Hellfire Caves (not National Trust). Variety of shops in National Trust village. Picnics welcome on West Wycombe Hill.

Making the most of your day: centuries-old village high street with intriguing cottages, coaching inns and courtyards. **Dogs**: welcome on West Wycombe Hill. Assistance dogs only in park.

Access for all: 🅿♿🏬🆔🚾🎨🚶👀
Building ♿🔼

Getting here: 175:SU828947. 2 miles west of High Wycombe. **Foot**: circular walk links West Wycombe, Bradenham, Hughenden Manor. **Bus**: from High Wycombe. **Train**: High Wycombe 2½ miles. **Road**: south of Oxford road (A40). **Parking**: 250 yards.

Finding out more: 01494 755571 (Infoline). 01494 513569 or westwycombe@nationaltrust.org.uk

West Wycombe Park and Village	M	T	W	T	F	S	S
House and grounds							
2 Jun–29 Aug 2–6	M	T	W	T	.	.	S
Grounds only							
1 Apr–29 Aug 2–6	M	T	W	T	.	.	S

Last admission 45 minutes before closing. Entry to the house on weekdays is by guided tour/timed ticket in June, July and August. A free-flow system operates on Sundays and Bank Holidays.

The White Cliffs of Dover

Langdon Cliffs, Upper Road, Dover, Kent CT16 1HJ

Map ② K7 🏠🍴🛍️🐾☕

There can be no doubt that The White Cliffs of Dover are one of this country's most spectacular natural features. They are an official icon of Britain and have been a symbol of hope and freedom for centuries. You can appreciate their beauty and enjoy their special appeal through the seasons by taking one of the dramatic clifftop walks, which offer unrivalled views of the busy English Channel and the French coast. While here, learn more about the fascinating military and penal history of The White Cliffs and savour the rare flora and fauna only found on this chalk grassland. **Note**: toilets only available when Visitor Centre is open.

Eating and shopping: shop selling souvenirs, gifts and outdoor goods. Coffee shop serving light lunches and afternoon tea.

The White Cliffs of Dover, Kent, have been a symbol of hope and freedom for centuries

Making the most of your day: self-guided walks for adults and activity sheets for children. Events and guided walks throughout year. **Dogs**: under close control at all times (stock grazing).

Access for all: 🅿️ ♿ 🚾 🔦 ♿ 🚶 ⁝• 🅰️
Visitor centre ♿♿ Grounds ♿

Getting here: 138:TR336422. **Foot**: signed pathways from port, station and town centre. On the Saxon Shore Way path. **Cycle**: NCN1. **Bus**: alight Castle Hill. 1 mile along Upper Road (no footpath). **Train**: Dover Priory 2½ miles. **Road**: A2, take A258 towards Dover town. After 1 mile turn left into Upper Road. A20, follow signs for castle and turn right into Upper Road past castle entrance. **Sat Nav**: use CT15 5NA.

Finding out more: 01304 202756 or whitecliffs@nationaltrust.org.uk

The White Cliffs of Dover		M	T	W	T	F	S	S
Visitor Centre								
1 Jan–3 Mar	11–4	M	T	W	T	F	S	S
4 Mar–21 Jul	10–5	M	T	W	T	F	S	S
22 Jul–1 Sep	10–5:30	M	T	W	T	F	S	S
2 Sep–3 Nov	10–5	M	T	W	T	F	S	S
4 Nov–31 Dec	11–4	M	T	W	T	F	S	S
Car park								
1 Jan–3 Mar	8–6	M	T	W	T	F	S	S
4 Mar–3 Nov	8–7	M	T	W	T	F	S	S
4 Nov–31 Dec	8–6	M	T	W	T	F	S	S

Visitor Centre closed 24, 25 and 26 December.
Car park closed 24 and 25 December.

White Horse Hill

Uffington, Oxfordshire

Map ② C4 🏛🖼🖐

The oldest dated chalk figure in the country and an Iron Age hill fort. **Note**: archaeological monuments under English Heritage guardianship. No toilet.

Finding out more: 01793 762209 or www.nationaltrust.org.uk

Winchester City Mill

Bridge Street, Winchester, Hampshire SO23 0EJ

Map ② D7 🏛🍴♿🍵

A rare surviving example of an urban working corn mill, Winchester City Mill is powered by the fast-flowing River Itchen, which can be seen passing underneath, thrilling our visitors. Rebuilt in 1743 on a medieval mill site, it remained in use until the early 20th century. The National Trust undertook an ambitious restoration project and the mill resumed grinding flour in March 2004. With hands-on activities for families and audio-visual displays about milling and the rich wildlife in the area, the City Mill is a lively and informative place for all ages to enjoy. **Note**: nearest toilet 220 yards (not National Trust).

Eating and shopping: shop selling local produce, gifts and books and our freshly milled wholemeal flour.

Making the most of your day: events. Activities for families and children (school holidays). Milling and baking demonstrations and workshops. **Dogs**: assistance dogs only.

Access for all: 🐕♿📷🖼🧏‍♂️👁🅰
Building ♿

Getting hands-on at Winchester City Mill in Hampshire

Getting here: 185:SU487294. At foot of High Street, beside City Bridge. **Foot**: South Downs Way, King's Way, Itchen Way. **Bus**: from surrounding areas. **Train**: Winchester 🚆 1 mile. **Road**: junction 9 north M3, junction 10 south M3. **Sat Nav**: do not use. **Parking**: Chesil car park or park and ride, St Catherine's to Winchester.

Finding out more: 01962 870057 or winchestercitymill@nationaltrust.org.uk

Winchester City Mill		M	T	W	T	F	S	S
4 Jan–17 Feb	11–4	M	·	·	·	F	S	S
18 Feb–1 Dec	10–5	M	T	W	T	F	S	S
2 Dec–23 Dec	10:30–4	M	T	W	T	F	S	S
Open 1 January 11 to 4.								

Winkworth Arboretum

Hascombe Road, Godalming, Surrey GU8 4AD

Map ② F7 ❂🔼

Bursts of colour excite the senses at every turn in this natural landscape. There are more than 1,000 different shrubs and trees, many of them rare, and every day brings something new. Spring has the most impressive displays, with the magnolias, bluebells and azaleas flowering, while in autumn the colour of the foliage is stunning. In summer this tranquil place is ideal for the family to explore and picnic. **Note**: steep slopes; banks of lake and wetlands only partially fenced.

Eating and shopping: small, friendly tea-room serving light lunches and afternoon tea.

Making the most of your day: events, including walks and talks throughout year (send stamped addressed envelope for details). **Dogs**: welcome on leads.

Access for all: P🅿️♿🚻♿ Grounds ♿➡️

Getting here: 169/170/186:SU990412. 2 miles south-east of Godalming. **Bus**: Guildford to Cranleigh (passing close Godalming ➤). **Train**: Godalming 2 miles. **Road**: near Hascombe, on east side of B2130. **Parking**: free, 100 yards.

Finding out more: 01483 208477 or winkwortharboretum@nationaltrust.org.uk

Winkworth Arboretum		M	T	W	T	F	S	S
Arboretum								
1 Jan–31 Jan	10–4	M	T	W	T	F	S	S
1 Feb–24 Mar	10–5	M	T	W	T	F	S	S
25 Mar–31 Oct	10–6	M	T	W	T	F	S	S
1 Nov–24 Dec	10–4	M	T	W	T	F	S	S
26 Dec–31 Dec	10–4	M	T	.	T	F	S	S
Tea-room								
1 Jan–31 Jan	10–3:30	M	T	W	T	F	S	S
1 Feb–24 Mar	10–4:30	M	T	W	T	F	S	S
25 Mar–31 Oct	10–5:30	M	T	W	T	F	S	S
1 Nov–24 Dec	10–3:30	M	T	W	T	F	S	S
26 Dec–31 Dec	10–3:30	M	T	.	T	F	S	S

Arboretum may be closed in bad weather.
Closed 25 December. Car park gates locked at 6.

Autumn at Winkworth Arboretum in Surrey

Woolbeding Gardens

Midhurst, West Sussex GU29 9RR

Map ② E7/8 ❖

Woolbeding is a modern garden masterpiece, with constantly evolving colour-themed garden rooms surrounding the house, plus a woodland garden. A gentle walk over open pastureland provides views of the River Rother and leads to the landscape garden, which includes a Chinese-style bridge, waterfall and stumpery. **Note: booking essential**. Access by minibus only (booking also essential).

Making the most of your day: nearby properties include Petworth House and Park, Uppark House and Hinton Ampner. **Dogs**: assistance dogs only.

Access for all: P♿ 🚻♿ ♿ Reception ♿♿
Garden 🚶 ➡ ♿

Getting here: SU872227. 8¾ miles from Petersfield and Haslemere. **Foot**: various footpaths to gardens. **Bus**: services from Petersfield 🚂 to Midhurst. **Train**: Petersfield 🚂 8¾ miles. **Parking**: no onsite or local parking. Access by minibus only (booking essential).

Finding out more: 01730 811960 (April to September). 01798 342207 (October to March) or woolbedinggardens@nationaltrust.org.uk

Woolbeding Gardens		M	T	W	T	F	S	S
4 Apr–27 Sep	10:30–4:30	·	·	·	**T**	**F**	·	·

Admission by appointment, booking essential on 01730 811960. Access by park and ride only.

Woolbeding Gardens in West Sussex is a modern masterpiece, with colour-themed garden rooms

London

Butterfly spotting in the Great Meadow at Osterley Park and House, Middlesex – the 'palace of palaces'

'A Chelsea Interior' by Robert Tait, 1857, shows the parlour at Carlyle's House, Chelsea, frozen in time

Carlyle's House

24 Cheyne Row, Chelsea, London SW3 5HL

Map ② F5

Charles Dickens said: 'I would go further to see Carlyle than any man alive!' Carlyle's House tells the intriguing story of the mysterious 'Sage of Chelsea' and his extraordinary influence on the Victorian era. Authentic and evocative, this unusual property is amazing and inspiring.

Access for all: 🦽📷👓 **Building** 🚶🧍
Grounds 🦽

Getting here: 176:TQ272777. Cheyne Row off Cheyne Walk, behind Carlyle's statue between Albert Bridge and Battersea Bridge. **Bus**: frequent services along King's Road to Carlyle Square, walk down Bramerton Street or Glebe Place to Cheyne Row. **Underground**: Sloane Square or South Kensington, 1 mile. **Parking**: limited metered street parking.

Finding out more: 020 7352 7087 or carlyleshouse@nationaltrust.org.uk

Carlyle's House		M	T	W	T	F	S	S
9 Mar–3 Nov	11–5	·	·	**W**	**T**	**F**	**S**	**S**

Open Bank Holiday Mondays.

Eastbury Manor House

Eastbury Square, Barking, London IG11 9SN

Map ② G5

Brick-built Tudor house, completed about 1573 and little altered since. Early 17th-century wall-paintings showing fishing scenes and a cityscape grace the former Great Chamber. Exposed timbers in the attic, fine original spiral oak staircase in the turret, soaring chimneys, cobbled courtyard and peaceful walled garden with bee-boles. **Note**: managed by the London Borough of Barking and Dagenham.

Eastbury Manor House, Barking: little altered since 1573

Fenton House and Garden in Hampstead: a cabinet of curiosities waiting to be discovered

Eating and shopping: garden tea-room serving drinks, sandwiches and snacks.

Making the most of your day: guided tours. Themed family days first Saturday of month – homemade cakes and costumed guides. School holiday activities. Children's Saturday workshops. Candlelit tours (last Tuesday of month, October to March). **Dogs**: in grounds only on leads.

Access for all: 🅿️ 🚻 ♿ 🍴 🎫 🎨 VT 📷 •• 🖼️
Building 🏠 ♿ Courtyard 🏠 ♿ Grounds 🏠

Getting here: 177:TQ457838. In Eastbury Square. **Cycle**: LCN15, ¾ mile, local link. **Bus**: frequent services. **Train**: Barking, 1½ miles. **Underground**: Upney, 750 yards. **Road**: A13, then signposted from A123 Ripple Road. **Parking**: free, in adjacent street.

Finding out more: 020 8227 5216 or eastburymanor@nationaltrust.org.uk

Eastbury Manor House		M	T	W	T	F	S	S
House								
4 Feb–26 Feb	10–4	M	T	·	·	·	·	·
4 Mar–31 Oct	10–4	M	T	W	T	·	·	·
4 Nov–17 Dec	10–4	M	T	·	·	·	·	·
Café and garden								
4 Feb–19 Dec	10–3:30	M	T	W	T	·	·	·

Also open every first and second Saturday of the month from 2 February. Closed Bank Holiday Mondays.

Fenton House and Garden

Hampstead Grove, Hampstead, London NW3 6SP

Map ② G4 🏠 ❄️ 🍴

A cabinet of curiosities, this 1686 town house is brimming with world-class decorative and fine art collections ranging from the 16th to the 20th centuries. Housed within elegant interiors are musical instruments, ceramics, paintings, textiles and furniture, gathered by eccentric collectors whose passions drove them to amass these objects from across the globe. There are panoramic views across London from the top-floor balcony, while outside it is delightful to stroll around our intimate 0.8-hectare (two-acre) grounds, which include a 300-year-old orchard and kitchen garden, a rose garden and formal terraces and lawns. Further afield lie historic Hampstead and the Heath.

Eating and shopping: small shop area selling local and National Trust items, garden plants and produce.

Making the most of your day: free introductory talks. Garden events, including annual Apple Weekend. Joint tickets with 2 Willow Road available. **Dogs**: assistance dogs only.

Access for all:
Building Grounds

Getting here: 176:TQ262860. In Hampstead village, near Whitestone Pond. **Bus**: frequent services pass nearby. **Train**: Hampstead Heath (Overground) 1 mile. **Underground**: Hampstead (Northern Line) 300 yards. **Parking**: very limited parking, pay and display (including members).

Finding out more: 020 7435 3471 or fentonhouse@nationaltrust.org.uk. Fenton House, Windmill Hill, London NW3 6RT

Fenton House and Garden		M	T	W	T	F	S	S
2 Mar–3 Nov	11–5			W	T	F	S	S
30 Nov–22 Dec	11–4						S	S

Open Bank Holiday Mondays.

George Inn

The George Inn Yard, 77 Borough High Street, Southwark, London SE1 1NH

Map (2) G5

Copper pots hanging in the George Inn, Southwark

This public house, dating from the 17th century, is London's last remaining galleried inn. **Note**: leased to a private company (please telephone to book a table).

Finding out more: 020 7407 2056 or www.nationaltrust.org.uk

Ham House and Garden

Ham Street, Ham, Richmond-upon-Thames, Surrey TW10 7RS

Map (2) F5

One of London's best-kept secrets, this atmospheric Stuart mansion nestles on the banks of the river in leafy Richmond-upon-Thames. Virtually unchanged for 400 years, it is internationally recognised for its superb collection of textiles, furniture and art which have remained in the house for centuries. Largely the vision of Elizabeth Murray, Countess of Dysart, who was deeply embroiled in the politics of the English Civil War and subsequent restoration of the monarchy, Ham House and Garden is an unusually complete survival of the 17th century. It is reputed to be one of the most haunted houses in Britain. **Note**: for conservation reasons, some rooms have low light levels.

Discovering Ham House and Garden in Surrey

Eating and shopping: Orangery Café serving dishes made using kitchen garden produce and homemade cakes. Shop selling local crafts, gifts, books, toys, plants and gardening accessories.

Making the most of your day: events and activities, including regular ghost tours and free garden tours. Hands-on basement area and interactive discovery room. Family house and garden trails. **Dogs**: assistance dogs only.

Access for all: 🅿️ 💺 ♿ 🚻 📷 💻 ♿ ∷
🅰️ Building ♿ Café ♿
Grounds ♿ ➡️ ♿

Getting here: 176:TQ172732. On south bank of Thames, between Richmond, 1½ miles, and Kingston, 3 miles. **Foot**: Thames Path passes entrance. **Cycle**: NCN4. **Ferry**: seasonal foot/bike ferry from Twickenham towpath (by Marble Hill House). **Bus**: services from Richmond ≥ and Kingston ≥. **Train**: Richmond, 1½ miles. **Underground**: Richmond, 1½ miles. **Road**: west of A307. From Richmond Park take Ham Gate exit. Accessible from M3, M4 and M25. **Sat Nav**: takes you to stables on Ham Street nearby.

Ham House and Garden, Surrey: the Cherry Garden

Parking: free, 400 yards (not National Trust).

Finding out more: 020 8940 1950 or hamhouse@nationaltrust.org.uk

Ham House and Garden		M	T	W	T	F	S	S
House tours*								
16 Feb–7 Mar	12–3:30	M	T	W	T	.	S	S
House								
9 Mar–14 Jul	12–4	M	T	W	T	.	S	S
15 Jul–8 Sep	12–5	M	T	W	T	F	S	S
9 Sep–3 Nov	12–4	M	T	W	T	.	S	S
Below stairs only								
1 Dec–31 Dec**	12–3	M	T	W	T	.	S	S
Garden, shop and café								
5 Jan–10 Feb	11–4	.	.	.	.	.	S	S
16 Feb–7 Mar	11–4	M	T	W	T	.	S	S
9 Mar–14 Jul	11–5	M	T	W	T	.	S	S
15 Jul–8 Sep	11–6	M	T	W	T	F	S	S
9 Sep–3 Nov	11–5	M	T	W	T	.	S	S
9 Nov–30 Nov	11–4	.	.	.	.	.	S	S
1 Dec–31 Dec**	11–4	M	T	W	T	.	S	S

House, garden, shop and café open Good Friday.
*30-minute guided tours of selected rooms only, no free-flow. Entry by timed ticket available on the day. Last tour at 3. **Closed 24 and 25 December.

Morden Hall Park

Morden Hall Road, Morden, London SM4 5JD

Map ② G5　🏠🚻🚲🔄🎫🚶

With diverse landscapes and hidden histories, Morden Hall Park is a green oasis in suburbia, giving visitors a glimpse back to a country estate with an industrial heart. This tranquil former deer-park is one of the few remaining estates that lined the River Wandle during its industrial heyday. The river meanders through the park, creating a haven for wildlife, and snuff mills still survive – one is now a Learning Centre. The Victorian Stableyard has been restored and is now open to visitors. It is powered using renewable energy and has interactive and changing exhibitions. **Note**: May Fair and other special events, admission charges apply (including members).

Eating and shopping: Riverside café and ice-cream parlour in stables. Gift shop. Second-hand bookshop. Craft sales in stableyard and old garden stores. Garden centre (not National Trust).

Making the most of your day: events, including walks, talks and open-air theatre. Exhibitions. Trails. Family activities (Thursdays, school holidays). New natural play area.
Dogs: welcome on leads around buildings and mown grass, under close control elsewhere.

Access for all: 🅿🎧♿🔈📷🚗♿✦🅰
Building 🔄♿♿　Grounds ♿➡

Getting here: 176:TQ261684. Near Morden town centre. **Foot**: Wandle Trail from Croydon or Carshalton to Wandsworth. **Cycle**: NCN20 passes through. **Bus**: frequent services from surrounding areas. **Train**: Tramlink to Phipps Bridge, on park boundary ½ mile. **Underground**: Morden, 500 yards. **Road**: off A24, and A297 south of Wimbledon, north of Sutton. **Parking**: free, 25 yards (not National Trust), next to garden centre.

Finding out more: 020 8545 6850 or mordenhallpark@nationaltrust.org.uk

Morden Hall Park		M	T	W	T	F	S	S
Park, estate, car park, shop and café*								
Open all year		M	T	W	T	F	S	S
Second-hand bookshop								
2 Jan–24 Dec	11–3	M	T	W	T	F		
5 Jan–22 Dec	12–4						S	S
Stableyard café								
5 Jan–22 Dec	10–4						S	S
27 Mar–1 Nov	11–4			W	T	F		
Stables craft stalls								
2 Feb–22 Dec	11–4						S	S
3 Apr–20 Dec	11–4			W	T	F		
Stables exhibition								
2 Jan–22 Dec	11–3	M	T	W	T	F	S	S

*Car park and rose garden open 8 to 6, shop and café open 10 to 5. Car park, shop and café closed 25 and 26 December. Stableyard café opening dependent on weather.

Morden Hall Park, with its pretty bridge over the River Wandle, provides welcome green space in South London

Osterley Park and House, Middlesex: 'palace of palaces'

Osterley Park and House

Jersey Road, Isleworth, Middlesex TW7 4RB

Map ② F5

Once described as 'the palace of palaces' and surrounded by gardens, park and farmland, Osterley is one of the last surviving country estates in London. Created in the late 18th century by architect and designer Robert Adam for the wealthy Child family to entertain and impress their friends and clients, it continues to impress today. Explore the dazzling interior with handheld audio-visual guides or downloadable iPhone app, which bring the house to life in a completely new way. Retreat from urban life in the delightful gardens, now restored to their 18th-century glory, and park – perfect for picnics and leisurely strolls.

Eating and shopping: Stables tea-room and tea terrace. Gift shop. Plant sales. Second-hand bookshop. Farm shop (not National Trust). Lakeside ice-cream and snack kiosk (National Trust-approved concession). Picnics welcome in park.

Making the most of your day: family activities, including dressing-up and tours. Family trails. Park and lake walks (free leaflet). Cycling in park (shared paths). Closer-to-nature wildlife walks. **Dogs**: allowed on leads in park only.

Access for all: House ⬛ Garden ⬛

Getting here: 176:TQ146780. Between Hammersmith and Hounslow. **Cycle**: links to London Cycle Network. **Bus**: services to within 1 mile. **Train**: Isleworth 1½ miles. **Underground**: Osterley (Piccadilly Line) 1 mile. **Road**: A4 between Hammersmith and Hounslow. Brown signs between Gillette Corner and Osterley Underground; from west M4, exit 3 then A312/A4 towards London. Main gates on Jersey Road. **Sat Nav**: use TW7 4RD. **Parking**: 400 yards.

Finding out more: 020 8232 5050 or osterley@nationaltrust.org.uk

Osterley Park and House		M	T	W	T	F	S	S
House and garden*								
16 Feb–28 Mar	12–4	M	T	W	T	F	S	S
29 Mar–30 Sep	11–5	M	T	W	T	F	S	S
1 Oct–1 Nov	12–4	M	T	W	T	F	S	S
2 Nov–15 Dec	12–4						S	S
Tea-room, shop and second-hand bookshop								
16 Feb–28 Mar	12–4:30	M	T	W	T	F	S	S
29 Mar–30 Sep	11–5:30	M	T	W	T	F	S	S
1 Oct–31 Oct	12–4:30	M	T	W	T	F	S	S
1 Nov–15 Dec	12–4:30			W	T	F	S	S
Park and car park**								
2 Jan–28 Mar	8–6	M	T	W	T	F	S	S
29 Mar–30 Sep	8–7:30	M	T	W	T	F	S	S
1 Oct–31 Dec	8–6	M	T	W	T	F	S	S

*House: only basement floor open every Monday and Tuesday, 16 February to 1 November. Last entry one hour before stated closing time. **Park and car park open Christmas Day, Boxing Day and New Year's Day 11 to 4.

Rainham Hall

The Broadway, Rainham, Havering,
London RM13 9YN

Map ② H5

Charming Georgian house with some surprising features and newly restored garden and orchard. **Note**: owing to planned restoration work, property may be closed from June. Please check website before travelling. No toilet.

Finding out more: 020 8303 6359
or www.nationaltrust.org.uk

The east front of the Red House, Kent,
which was commissioned, created
and lived in by William Morris

Red House

Red House Lane, Bexleyheath, Kent DA6 8JF

Map ② H5 🏛🌼

The only house commissioned, created and lived in by William Morris, founder of the Arts and Crafts Movement, Red House is a building of extraordinary architectural and social significance. When it was completed in 1860, it was described by Edward Burne-Jones as 'the beautifullest place on earth'. Only recently acquired by the Trust, the house is not fully furnished, but the original features and furniture by Morris and Philip Webb, stained glass and paintings by Burne-Jones, the bold architecture and a simple garden add up to a fascinating and rewarding place to visit.

Eating and shopping: shop selling Morris-related gifts and souvenirs. Second-hand bookshop. Coach House tea-room serving light refreshments. Picnics welcome in orchard.

Making the most of your day: events, including Easter Fun, summer arts and crafts fair, autumn Apple Day and carols at Christmas. Family fun (school holidays). Games in garden. Exhibition. **Dogs**: assistance dogs only.

Access for all: 🅿️🚻📷📖📷📷
Building 📷 Grounds 📷➡️

Getting here: 177:TQ481750. In Bexleyheath.
Bus: services from central London. All stop at Upton Road. **Train**: Bexleyheath ≋, ¾ mile.
Road: M25 junction 2 to A2 for Bexleyheath. Exit Danson interchange and follow A221 Bexleyheath.
Sat Nav: DA6 8HL – Danson Park car park.
Parking: nearest parking at Danson Park 1 mile. Charge at weekends and Bank Holidays.

Finding out more: 020 8304 9878 or redhouse@nationaltrust.org.uk

Red House		M	T	W	T	F	S	S
20 Feb–3 Nov	11–5		·	·	**W**	**T**	**F**	**S**	**S**
8 Nov–22 Dec	11–5		·	·	·	·	**F**	**S**	**S**

Guided tours at 11, 11:30, 12, 12:30 and 1 (booking essential). Free-flow 1:30 until 5 (booking not required). Last admission 45 minutes before closing. Last serving in tea-room 4:30. Open Bank Holiday Mondays.

Sutton House and Breakers Yard

2 and 4 Homerton High Street, Hackney, London E9 6JQ

Map ② G4 🏛️🔺⛩️

Built in 1535 by Sir Ralph Sadleir, prominent courtier of Henry VIII, Sutton House retains much of the atmosphere of a Tudor home despite some alterations by later occupants, including Huguenot silkweavers and squatters. An outdoor space revealing the recent car breakers yard history opens later this year.

The Little Chamber at Sutton House, Hackney

Eating and shopping: tea-room serving cream teas. Second-hand bookshop. Gift shop. Static ice-cream van (Breakers Yard).

Making the most of your day: events for all ages, including themed family days. Craft fairs. Monthly Sunday guided tours (February to November). **Dogs**: assistance dogs only.

Access for all: 🅿️🚻🚻📷📷📷📖📷📷📷
Building 📷📷📷📷

Getting here: 176:TQ352851. At the corner of Isabella Road and Homerton High Street. **Cycle**: NCN1, 1¼ miles.
Bus: frequent local services. **Train**: Hackney Central ¼ mile; Hackney Downs ½ mile.
Underground: Bethnal Green.
Parking: no onsite parking. Limited metered parking on adjacent streets.

Finding out more: 020 8986 2264 or suttonhouse@nationaltrust.org.uk

Sutton House		M	T	W	T	F	S	S
7 Feb–20 Dec	10:30–5	·	·	·	**T**	**F**	·	·
9 Feb–22 Dec	12–5	·	·	·	·	·	**S**	**S**
1 Apr–10 Apr	10:30–5	**M**	**T**	**W**	·	·	·	·
22 Jul–4 Sep	10:30–5	**M**	**T**	**W**	·	·	·	·

Open Bank Holiday Mondays and Good Friday. Open seven days a week during summer holidays and Easter break. Property is regularly used by local community groups – the rooms will always be open as advertised, but call if you would like to visit during a quiet time. Occasional 'Museum Lates' opening.

575 Wandsworth Road

575 Wandsworth Road, Lambeth,
London SW8 3JD

Map ② G5 🏠

Modest terraced house, transformed into a work of art, with a breathtaking hand-carved fretwork interior. **Note**: no toilet. Access by guided tour only (booking fee for non-members).

Access for all: House 👨‍🦽🚻

Getting here: 176:TQ292761. Between Clapham and Vauxhall. **Bus**: frequent local services stop outside. **Train**: Wandsworth Road 🚆 220 yards or Clapham Junction 🚆 1¼ miles. **Underground**: Clapham Common ½ mile. **Parking**: no onsite parking.

Finding out more: 0844 249 1895 (bookings). 020 7720 9459 or 575wandsworthroad@nationaltrust.org.uk

575 Wandsworth Road		M	T	W	T	F	S	S
2 Mar–3 Nov	Times vary		·	**W**	·	**F**	**S**	**S**

Admission by guided tour only, booking essential (places limited). Evening tours only on Wednesdays. House will be closed the last Sunday of every month.

575 Wandsworth Road, Lambeth

2 Willow Road

Hampstead, London NW3 1TH

Map (2) G5

This late 1930s house, an architect's vision of the future, paints a vivid picture of the creative and social circles in which Ernö Goldfinger and his artist wife moved. You can explore the intimate and evocative interiors, with its innovative designs, intriguing personal possessions and impressive 20th-century art collection. **Note**: nearest toilet at local pub.

Eating and shopping: property-related items available.

Making the most of your day: events, including late openings, walks and tours. Fenton House nearby (joint tickets available). **Dogs**: assistance dogs only.

Access for all: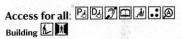
Building

Getting here: 176:TQ270858. **Foot**: signposted from Hampstead Heath Overground ¼ mile or from Hampstead Underground ½ mile. **Bus**: frequent services pass nearby. **Train**: Hampstead Heath ¼ mile. **Underground**: Hampstead (Northern Line) ½ mile. **Parking**: very limited parking, pay and display (charge including members).

Finding out more: 020 7435 6166 or 2willowroad@nationaltrust.org.uk

2 Willow Road		M	T	W	T	F	S	S
2 Mar–3 Nov	11–5			**W**	**T**	**F**	**S**	**S**

Open Bank Holiday Mondays. Entry by guided tour only at 11, 12, 1 and 2 (places limited with tickets available on the day). Morning tours: Wednesday to Friday are occasionally booked by groups, so please call before visit. 3 to 5, self-guided viewing (timed entry when busy).

National Trust
Partner

London partners

'National Trust Partner' is an exciting new venture between the National Trust and a selection of small, independent heritage attractions and museums within London. The Partnership aims to bring enhanced benefits to National Trust members living in London or for those visiting the capital for a day out, helping to provide increased opportunities to explore our rich and diverse heritage

Entry charges: 50 per cent discount for members on presentation of a valid membership card. For full visiting information (and access), please see individual National Trust Partner websites.

Benjamin Franklin House

The world's only remaining home of Benjamin Franklin, featuring a unique 'Historical Experience'.

Underground: Charing Cross or Embankment.

Finding out more: 020 7925 1405 or www.benjaminfranklinhouse.org

Danson House

Beautiful Georgian villa with sumptuous interiors built for pleasure and entertaining.

Overground: Bexleyheath.

Finding out more: 020 8303 6699 or www.bexleyheritagetrust.org.uk/dansonhouse

Dr Johnson's House

Late 17th-century townhouse, once home to lexicographer and wit, Samuel Johnson.

Underground: Chancery Lane or Blackfriars.

Finding out more: 020 7353 3745 or www.drjohnsonshouse.org

Foundling Museum

Nationally important collection of 18th-century art, interiors, social history and music.

Underground: Russell Square, King's Cross St Pancras or Euston.

Finding out more: 020 7841 3600 or www.foundlingmuseum.org.uk

The Fan Museum

Unique collection of more than 4,000 fans, housed in elegant Georgian buildings.

Overground: Cutty Sark (DLR) or Greenwich.

Finding out more: 020 8305 1441 or www.thefanmuseum.org.uk

Hall Place and Gardens

Stunning Tudor house with magnificent gardens.

Overground: Bexley.

Finding out more: 01322 526 574 or www.bexleyheritagetrust.org.uk/hallplace

Keats House

House where Romantic poet John Keats lived from 1818 to 1820.

Underground: Hampstead or Belsize Park.
Overground: Hampstead Heath.

Finding out more: 020 7332 3868 or www.keatshouse.cityoflondon.gov.uk

Leighton House Museum

Restored home of Victorian painter Lord Leighton, with priceless Islamic tile collection.

Underground: High Street Kensington or Holland Park.

Finding out more: 020 7602 3316 or www.leightonhouse.co.uk

Museum of Brands

Journey through consumer culture, from Victorian times to the present day.

Underground: Notting Hill Gate.

Finding out more: 020 7908 0880 or www.museumofbrands.com

The Old Operating Theatre Museum

Atmospheric medical survival, hidden in the timber-framed Herb Garret of St Thomas's Church.

Underground: London Bridge.
Overground: London Bridge.

Finding out more: 020 7188 2679 or www.thegarret.org.uk

East of England

A moment to savour: peaceful
Danbury Common, Essex

Outdoors in the East of England

The East of England is a region of contrasts and character. It is made up of some very individual and distinct counties, each with their own feel, landscape and qualities. From wide open beaches and rolling heathland to mysterious inlets and estuaries, this is a region you can explore on foot, by bike or boat at your own pace. Our people are welcoming, our nature is abundant and the fresh air makes this area a little slice of heaven.

Right: **enjoying a gentle cycle ride at Blickling Estate, Norfolk**

Open all year
The vast choice of landscapes, gardens, coast and countryside in the East of England offers you the opportunity to get outdoors and closer to nature all year round. Whether you are a fair-weather walker or a seriously hardy enthusiast, every month brings its own pleasures and surprises – be it puddles to jump in, nature to watch, or views to be inspired by. Depending on your mood, you can do as much or as little as takes your fancy – it's your choice.

Every compass point has its gems. From Dunstable Downs in the west, with its magnificent views, Orford Ness and its secret military past in the east, Blakeney Point and its iconic wildlife in the north, to Rayleigh Mount and its importance to the local community in the south, the variety of places means that the only difficulty you'll have is in deciding where to start.

The adventure starts here

You don't have to be a nature lover to appreciate the vast stretches of coastline and wide open spaces of countryside in our region. We have more than 100 years of experience in maintaining the fragile balance between offering access to our special places and conserving their uniqueness for future generations to enjoy.

We understand that people want to enjoy the outdoors for many different reasons: for play, for beauty, for nature or for spiritual refreshment. That's why at places such as Wicken Fen, in Cambridgeshire, there are numerous quiet spots where some of the incredible 8,000 or so varieties of wildlife and plant life can be spotted. Booming bitterns, emperor dragonflies, yellow brimstone butterflies and cranes can all be seen if you stop for a moment and look around you.

Meanwhile the more adventurous can take a boat trip along the ancient lode waterways with one of our friendly staff to see the Fen from a duck's point of view!

Above: horse riding on Danbury Common, Essex
Below buttercups at Takeley Hill, Hatfield Forest in Essex

No need to break the bank

Having a good time doesn't need to cost the Earth. From getting on your bike to chasing through the leaves, we've come up with some great ways to enjoy the wonderful landscape without breaking the bank. Down the road from Wicken you'll find Hatfield Forest, which was one of England's great royal hunting forests during the Middle Ages. The magnificent ancient trees bear witness to the many people who have enjoyed themselves in their shade over the centuries. You can follow in their footsteps as you explore the peace and tranquillity of this special place, while in spring you can also enjoy the breathtaking spectacle of about half a billion buttercups!

Bikes, beaches and beasties
Brancaster Millennium Activity Centre on the North Norfolk coast is an ideal base from which to discover this popular part of our coastline. If you join one of the one-day courses during the school holidays, you can explore the beach, dunes and creeks with our experienced team. Have a go at kayaking, go on a coastal safari or take to two wheels to head further afield and get some exercise at the same time!

Dunstable Downs in Bedfordshire boasts awe-inspiring views across the beautiful countryside and was once the venue for the Whipsnade Games. In 1929 you could have taken part in aeroplane balloon bursting, horse jumping in pairs or a six-a-side motorbike football match! These days visitors tend to enjoy themselves in slightly less whacky ways. Kite flying is a popular pastime here, as the wind coming up the hill nearly always ensures some lift for your kite – whether you're a first-timer or an expert in aerobatics.

Right: the Lifeboat House at Blakeney Point, Norfolk
Opposite top: Danbury Common, Essex

Right: **Blake's Wood, Essex,** in spring
Below: **fishing fun at Hatfield Forest, Essex**

Just over 200 years ago, the famous landscape designer Humphry Repton put the finishing touches to his favourite work, Sheringham Park in Norfolk. This is acclaimed as one of his masterpieces and today it retains its splendour. If you wander through the parkland you can enjoy stunning views down to the sea – you may even see a steam train running along the coast in the distance. If you look closer you'll also see that the park is home to a multitude of wildlife during the day and the night. Special events allow you to get your torch out and wander through the famous rhododendrons to spot some of the more elusive night-time creatures.

People power

The beauty of our coast, countryside, parkland and gardens is that sometimes it feels like you have them to yourselves – as there isn't another soul in sight. But if you are lucky enough to bump into one of our Rangers, they will be more than happy to share their passion for the places they look after. Our volunteers are all keen to help too – especially if you find them hard at work in one of our many gardens.

If you take a stroll at Ickworth in Suffolk down to the picturesque walled garden, it is easy to imagine what a bustling place it once was. You can hear from our Rangers about work in the parklands or wander through the basement and learn how the engine-room of the great house relied on the produce coming from the gardens and park.

Wimpole's parkland and farm is a real case in point – you can explore the acres of rolling parkland on your own, admiring the views while following one of the many paths, or you can visit the farm where our team will inspire you to find out more about where your food comes from and how it has shaped the development of one of Cambridgeshire's most important estates. However you feel like exploring, we know that we can help you do it in your own way – and in the best way!

Why not try…?

A stay at one of our unique holiday cottages
Our holiday cottages are set in some of the most stunning locations. You can stay in the grounds of a grand country estate or the centre of a picturesque village. Once our gates close at the end of the day, you have exclusive behind-the-scenes access, as well as a fantastic base for a peaceful, restful retreat.

An adventure on two wheels
Many of our places are opening new routes for exploring on two wheels. Cycling gives a different perspective on our countryside, whether you want to raise your heart rate as you race along, or take a more gentle pace. Don't worry if you've arrived without bikes, you can now hire them at Blickling Hall and Wicken Fen.

Digging out those walking boots
In autumn this year we will be celebrating our second walking festival, so this is the perfect time to explore the outdoors. There will be a number of different walks available across the region which will take you through some of our fascinating countryside. You can join one of our Rangers on a guided walk, or download a walk from our website and take off on your own. Whatever your preference, join us on foot this autumn.

Anglesey Abbey, Gardens and Lode Mill

Quy Road, Lode, Cambridge,
Cambridgeshire CB25 9EJ

Map ③ G7 🏠🖼️✳️🔔🍴

A passion for tradition and style inspired Lord Fairhaven to transform a run-down country house and desolate landscape. Visitors stepping into his elegant home will journey back to the golden age of country-house living. A generous host, Lord Fairhaven loved to entertain, and enjoyed a life of horse-racing and shooting. His guests were treated to a luxurious stay, surrounded by rare and fabulous objects. The celebrated garden, with its working watermill and wildlife discovery area, offers captivating views, vibrant colour and delicious scents in every season. There are also sweeping avenues, classical statuary and beautiful flower borders to enjoy.

Eating and shopping: Redwoods Restaurant. Shop selling local products and Lode Mill flour. Plant centre.

Making the most of your day: exhibitions, activities and events all year. Family trails and adventure packs. Room cards and volunteer room guides. **Dogs**: assistance dogs only.

Access for all: 🅿️♿🚻🔛👜📷📺♿:·🔵
Abbey and mill 🔧♿
Grounds ♿▶️👓♿

Getting here: 154:TL533622. 6 miles north-east of Cambridge. **Foot**: Harcamlow Way from Cambridge. **Cycle**: NCN51, 1¼ miles. **Bus**: from Cambridge (frequent services link Cambridge 🚉 and bus station). Alight at Lode Crossroads. **Train**: Cambridge 6 miles. **Road**: on B1102. Signposted from A14, junction 35. **Parking**: free, 50 yards.

Finding out more: 01223 810080 or angleseyabbey@nationaltrust.org.uk

Anglesey Abbey		M	T	W	T	F	S	S
House								
13 Mar–3 Nov	11–5			W	T	F	S	S
23 Jul–1 Sep	11–5		T	W	T	F	S	S
House (guided tours, spaces limited)								
12 Mar–16 Jul	11–3		T					
3 Sep–29 Oct	11–3		T					
5 Nov–31 Dec	12–3		T					
Lode Mill								
2 Jan–22 Dec	11–4			W	T	F	S	S
Garden, restaurant, shop and plant centre								
1 Jan–28 Mar	10:30–4:30	M	T	W	T	F	S	S
29 Mar–3 Nov	10:30–5:30	M	T	W	T	F	S	S
4 Nov–31 Dec	10:30–4:30	M	T	W	T	F	S	S

Mill and house open on Bank Holiday Mondays. Timed tickets on busy days. Last entry to house/bookshop 4. Summer tours every 30 minutes 11 to 2:30; winter: 12 and 1:30. Property closed 24 to 26 December. Snowdrop season: 21 January to 24 February.

Snowdrops at Anglesey Abbey, Cambridgeshire

Blakeney National Nature Reserve, Norfolk, where the sky goes on forever and the coastline is pure and unspoilt

Blakeney National Nature Reserve

Morston Quay, Quay Road, Morston, Norfolk NR25 7BH

Map (3) I3

Wide open spaces and uninterrupted views of this unspoilt coastline make for an inspiring visit, at any time of the year. The ebb and flow of the tide, covering pristine saltmarsh or exposing the harbour, combined with the constantly changing light of Norfolk's big skies, create beautiful and memorable scenery. **Note**: nearest toilet at Morston Quay and Blakeney Quay (not National Trust).

Eating and shopping: refreshments and seafood stall (not National Trust) at Morston Quay. Seafood, including Morston mussels from local suppliers (not National Trust). Nearby pubs and hotels (not National Trust) offering locally themed menus.

Making the most of your day: activities, including guided walks. Interpretation panels about this coastal environment – Information Centres (Morston Quay and Lifeboat House on Blakeney Point). Seabirds/seals at Blakeney Point. Coastal path and downloadable walks. **Dogs**: some restrictions (particularly Blakeney Point), 1 April to mid-August.

Access for all: 🚾 🆅🆃
Information centre 🏢   Lifeboat House ♿

Getting here: 133:TG000460. **Foot**: Norfolk Coast Path passes. **Cycle**: Norfolk Coast Cycleway Regional Route 30 runs along minor road above coast. **Ferry**: to Blakeney Point. **Bus**: Cromer ≋ to Hunstanton. **Train**: Sheringham 8 miles. **Road**: Morston Quay, Blakeney and Cley all off A149 Cromer to Hunstanton road. **Parking**: pay and display (members free) at the Green Way Stiffkey Saltmarshes, Morston Quay and Blakeney Quay (administered by Blakeney Parish Council). Quayside car parks liable to flooding.

Finding out more: 01263 740241 or blakeneypoint@nationaltrust.org.uk. Norfolk Coast Office, Friary Farm, Cley Road, Blakeney, Norfolk NR25 7NW

Blakeney	M	T	W	T	F	S	S
Nature Reserve							
Open all year	M	T	W	T	F	S	S
Lifeboat House (Blakeney Point)							
25 Mar–29 Sep	Dawn–dusk	M	T	W	T	F	S	S

*Lifeboat House and toilets (Blakeney Point) open dawn to dusk. Refreshment kiosk (not National Trust) and Information Centre at Morston Quay open according to tides and weather.

Blickling Estate

Blickling, Norwich, Norfolk NR11 6NF

Map ③ J4 [icons]

Setting off on a cycle ride at Blickling

Nobody ever forgets their first sight of Blickling. For four centuries, the 1,902-hectare (4,700-acre) estate has been at the heart of this north Norfolk community, offering a home to many – from the Boleyn family to the RAF. Come and walk in the footsteps of lords and ladies, cooks, butlers, gardeners and scullery maids – all of whom have left their mark. After exploring the atmospheric Long Gallery, with its nationally important book collection, you can relax in the stunning 22-hectare (55-acre) garden; then ramble or cycle through the parkland to find the hidden pyramid. One day is never enough.

Eating and shopping: two cafés and restaurant. Large second-hand bookshop. Stamp shop, gift shop, plant centre and pub (not National Trust).

Making the most of your day: events and activities for all ages, including local art, craft and photography exhibitions, quizzes and trails, living history performances, open-air theatre and music concerts. Free house and garden tours. Fishing, guided and waymarked parkland walks (walk guides available from visitor reception), cycle maps and cycle hire. RAF Museum. Felbrigg Hall nearby.
Dogs: welcome on leads in park and woods. Assistance dogs only in formal gardens.

One day is never enough to explore the huge Blickling Estate in Norfolk

The atmospheric Long Gallery at Blickling

Access for all: 🅿️ 🏠 🚻 ♿ 🎫 🔌 🎧 📷 •• 🅾️
House 🔥 🏠 ♿
Gardens 🏛️ ➡️ 🎨 ♿

Getting here: 1½ miles north-west of Aylsham. **Foot**: Weavers' Way (Aylsham, 1½ miles), Queen Anne's Walk from Market Place. **Cycle**: Regional Route 33. **Train**: North Walsham (9 miles), Wroxham (13 miles). Bure Valley Railway (seasonal). **Road**: on B1354, signposted off A140 Norwich/Cromer. **Parking**: 400 yards.

Finding out more: 01263 738030 or blickling@nationaltrust.org.uk

Blickling Estate		M	T	W	T	F	S	S
Historic park and woodland								
Open all year	Dawn–dusk	M	T	W	T	F	S	S
Gardens, shop and cafés								
2 Jan–7 Jan	10:15–4	M		W	T	F	S	S
10 Jan–15 Feb	10:15–3				T	F	S	S
16 Feb–3 Nov	10:15–5:30	M	T	W	T	F	S	S
7 Nov–22 Dec	10:15–4				T	F	S	S
House								
16 Feb–24 Feb	11–3:30	M	T	W	T	F	S	S
2 Mar–10 Mar	11–3						S	S
16 Mar–3 Nov	12–5	M		W	T	F	S	S
9 Nov–15 Dec	11–3						S	S

Last entry to house one hour before closing. House also open on the following Tuesdays during school holidays: 2 and 9 April, 28 May, 30 July, 6, 13, 20 and 27 August, 3 September, 29 October. Cycle hire available at weekends and daily during school holidays. Muddy Boots café open until 3 on 24, 26 and 31 December, and 1 January 2014. During weekends in November, the house opens for bookable 'behind-the-scenes' tours only.

Bourne Mill

Bourne Road, Colchester, Essex CO2 8RT

Map ③ I8   🏛️

Delightful piece of late Elizabethan playfulness built for banquets and converted into a mill, still with working waterwheel. **Note**: no toilet. Limited parking in mill grounds.

Finding out more: 01206 572422 or www.nationaltrust.org.uk

Brancaster Estate

Beach Road, Brancaster, Norfolk

Map ③ H3   🏛️ 🍴 🚗 🐾 🛏️

Famous for its mussels, the fishing village of Brancaster Staithe lies on the shores of the beautiful north Norfolk coast. Visitors can find out about the history of the fishing industry at Brancaster Quay, visit Branodunum Scheduled Ancient Monument or stroll along Brancaster beach. **Note**: nearest toilet Brancaster beach. Scolt Head Island National Nature Reserve managed by Natural England.

Eating and shopping: Brancaster mussels and fresh fish available. Pubs at Brancaster Staithe (not National Trust).

Making the most of your day: downloadable walks. Family adventure day or week at Brancaster Millennium Activity Centre (holiday periods). **Dogs**: welcome, but some restrictions apply at Brancaster beach from May to mid-August.

Access for all: Grounds 🏛️

Getting here: 132:TF800450. Halfway between Wells and Hunstanton. **Foot**: Norfolk Coast Path passes property. **Cycle**: Regional Route 30 runs along ridge above coast. **Bus**: from Sheringham 🚆 to Hunstanton. **Road**: on A149.

Sat Nav: use PE31 8AX (Beach Road), P31 8BW (Brancaster Staithe). **Parking**: Beach Road, Brancaster (not National Trust), charge including members. Limited parking at Brancaster Staithe, subject to tidal flooding.

Finding out more: 01263 740241 or brancaster@nationaltrust.org.uk. Norfolk Coast Office, Friary Farm, Cley Road, Blakeney, Norfolk NR25 7NW

Brancaster Estate	Open every day all year

Brancaster Millennium Activity Centre

Dial House, Harbour Way, Brancaster Staithe, Norfolk PE31 8BW

Map ③ H3

The 400-year-old Dial House is a residential activity centre for school and family groups; however, our adventurous activities and field studies can also be enjoyed by day visitors.

A great venue for meetings and training sessions, as well as an ideal base for exploring the north Norfolk coast and countryside.

Eating and shopping: meals prepared using locally sourced produce whenever possible (some grown in our garden). Small ethical gift shop.

Making the most of your day: coastal activities, including taster sessions in kayaking, sailing and raft building. Workshops. Guided tours.

Access for all: 🚻 Centre 🦽🏞️

Getting here: 132:TF792444. Halfway between Wells and Hunstanton. **Foot**: Norfolk Coast Path passes. **Cycle**: Regional Route 30 runs along ridge above coast. **Bus**: service from Sheringham ⬜ to King's Lynn ⬜. **Road**: on A149 coast road. **Parking**: limited parking within Harbour Way, Brancaster Staithe.

Finding out more: 01485 210719 or brancaster@nationaltrust.org.uk

Brancaster

Please contact the centre for more information on residential group bookings, courses and activities.

Children prepare for an adventure at Brancaster Millennium Activity Centre in Norfolk

Coggeshall Grange Barn

Grange Hill, Coggeshall, Colchester,
Essex CO6 1RE

Map ③ I8

One of the largest medieval timber-framed
buildings in Europe, with oak timbers soaring
into a cathedral-like roof spanning 800 years.

Finding out more: 01376 562226
or www.nationaltrust.org.uk

Dunstable Downs, Chilterns Gateway Centre and Whipsnade Estate

Whipsnade Road, Dunstable,
Bedfordshire LU6 2GY

Map ③ E8

Acres of space to enjoy with fabulous views
over the Vale of Aylesbury and along the
Chiltern Ridge. Dunstable Downs is in an Area
of Outstanding Natural Beauty because of
its chalk grassland, rich in wildlife. There are
many ideas for walks and family days out at
the Gateway Centre. **Note**: Chilterns Gateway
Centre owned by Central Bedfordshire Council
and managed by the National Trust.

Eating and shopping: shop selling mementoes,
maps and guidebooks. Café serving
Bedfordshire Clanger and other dishes.

Making the most of your day: new natural
play area (Chute Wood). Waymarked routes,
multi-user trail to Five Knolls and regular
guided walks. Kite-flying. Events throughout
year, including annual kite festival. **Dogs**: under
close control, on leads near livestock.

Dunstable Downs, Bedfordshire: breathtaking views

Access for all: [icons]
Chilterns Gateway Centre [icons] Dunstable Downs ➡

Getting here: 165/166:TL002189. 7 miles from
Luton. **Cycle**: bridleway from West Street,
Dunstable, and Whipsnade. **Bus**: services
from surrounding towns. **Train**: Luton
7 miles. **Road**: on B4541 west of Dunstable.
Sat Nav: for older equipment use LU6 2TA.
Parking: Dunstable Downs, off B4541 (pay and
display); Whipsnade crossroads (Whipsnade
Heath), junction of B4541 and B4540.

Finding out more: 01582 500920 or
dunstabledowns@nationaltrust.org.uk

Dunstable Downs		M	T	W	T	F	S	S
Chilterns Gateway Centre								
1 Jan–3 Mar	10–4	M	T	W	T	F	S	S
4 Mar–3 Nov	10–5	M	T	W	T	F	S	S
4 Nov–31 Dec	10–4	M	T	W	T	F	S	S
Downs								
Open all year		M	T	W	T	F	S	S

Chilterns Gateway Centre closes dusk if earlier and closed
24 and 25 December. Car park adjacent to Centre locked
dusk in winter and 6 in summer. Opening times extended
in summer.

Examining bugs and beasties at Dunwich Heath and Beach in Suffolk: a rare and precious habitat

Dunwich Heath and Beach

Dunwich, Saxmundham, Suffolk IP17 3DJ

Map ③ K6 🔦♨️🏛️🐕‍🦺🍴🍽️🍵

Tucked away on the Suffolk coast, Dunwich Heath offers peace and quiet and a true sense of being at one with nature. A rare and precious habitat, the heath is in an Area of Outstanding Natural Beauty and home to species such as the Dartford warbler and nightjar. Quiet and serene, wild and dramatic, this is an inspiring visit whatever the time of year. From July to September, the heath is alive with colour – its patchwork of pink and purple heather and coconut-scented gorse is an unmissable experience. **Note**: parking restrictions may operate at times of extreme fire risk.

Eating and shopping: clifftop tea-room serving lunch and cakes (gluten-free choices and children's menu). Coastal-themed shop.

Making the most of your day: self-guided trails and guided walks. Family activities, including geocaching, nature and smugglers' trails. Family Tracker Packs. SeaWatch buildings with telescopes and wildlife identification

charts. Children's play area. **Dogs**: allowed under close control, restrictions apply.

Access for all: 🅿️ 🅳 ♿ 🚻 ⛽ 🅿️ 🎵
Buildings 🏛️♿ Grounds ➡️🐕

Getting here: 156:TM476685. 1 mile south of Dunwich. **Foot**: Suffolk Coast and Heaths Path and Sandlings Walk. **Cycle**: on Suffolk coastal cycle route. **Bus**: demand-responsive bus from Darsham 🚆 and Saxmundham (booking essential, 01728 833526). **Train**: Darsham 6 miles. **Road**: signposted from A12. From Westleton/Dunwich road, turn right 1 mile before Dunwich village into Minsmere road, then 1 mile to Dunwich Heath. **Parking**: 150 yards (pay and display).

Finding out more: 01728 648501 or dunwichheath@nationaltrust.org.uk

Dunwich Heath and Beach		M	T	W	T	F	S	S
Heath								
Open all year	Dawn–dusk	M	T	W	T	F	S	S
Tea-room and shop								
5 Jan–17 Feb	10:30–4						S	S
18 Feb–24 Feb	10:30–4	M	T	W	T	F	S	S
2 Mar–31 Mar	10:30–4			W	T	F	S	S
1 Apr–29 Sep	10:30–5	M	T	W	T	F	S	S
2 Oct–27 Oct	10:30–5			W	T	F	S	S
28 Oct–3 Nov	10:30–4	M	T	W	T	F	S	S
9 Nov–22 Dec	10:30–4						S	S

Open Bank Holiday Mondays. Tea-room and shop closing times vary and limited service in early and late season.

Carpet of heather at Dunwich Heath and Beach

Elizabethan House Museum

4 South Quay, Great Yarmouth,
Norfolk NR30 2QH

Map ③ K5

An amazing hands-on museum that will enthrall and fascinate all ages. The museum reflects the life and times of the families who lived in this 16th-century quayside building, from Tudor right through to Victorian times. **Note**: house managed by Norfolk Museums and Archaeology Service.

Eating and shopping: small shop.

Making the most of your day: activity-packed toy room for children and hands-on activities, including Tudor dressing-up costumes.

Access for all:
Building 🚹♿

Getting here: 134:TG523073. On Great Yarmouth's South Quay. **Train**: Great Yarmouth ½ mile. **Road**: from A47 follow town centre signs, then brown South Quay signs. From A12 follow brown signs. **Parking**: free at South Quay or town centre (pay and display), not National Trust.

Finding out more: 01493 855746 or elizabethanhouse@nationaltrust.org.uk

Elizabethan House Museum		M	T	W	T	F	S	S
1 Apr–31 Oct	10–4	M	T	W	T	F		
6 Apr–27 Oct	12–4						S	S

Felbrigg Hall, Gardens and Estate

Felbrigg, Norwich, Norfolk NR11 8PR

Map ③ J4

This 'bountiful estate' really lives up to its name. Felbrigg Hall is full of delights, a surprising mixture of opulence and homeliness where every room has something to feed the imagination. The decorative and productive walled garden, traditionally providing fruit and vegetables for the kitchens of the Hall, now supplies produce to the brasserie, flowers for the Hall and inspiration to visitors. The rolling landscape park with a lake, 211 hectares (520 acres) of woods and miles of waymarked trails, is a great place to explore nature, spot wildlife or just to get away from it all.

Eating and shopping: Carriages Brasserie using walled garden produce. Tea-room serving cakes and snacks. Gift shop. Plant sales. Second-hand bookshop.

Making the most of your day: children's trails. Events, including Chilli Fiesta, the Hall at Harvest and Hall at Christmas. **Dogs**: on leads in parkland when stock grazing, under close control in woodland.

Access for all: 🅿♿♿🚻♿♿👁️🅰️
Hall ♿🅱️ Grounds ♿♿➡️🚜

Cascades of wisteria at Felbrigg Hall, Norfolk

Getting here: 133:TG193394. Felbrigg, 2 miles from Cromer. **Foot**: Weavers' Way runs through property. **Cycle**: Regional Route 30. **Train**: Cromer or Roughton Road, both 2½ miles. **Road**: 2 miles from Cromer; off B1436, signposted from A148 and A140. **Sat Nav**: gives poor directions, follow brown signs. **Parking**: £2.50 non-members.

Finding out more: 01263 837444 or felbrigg@nationaltrust.org.uk

Felbrigg Hall		M	T	W	T	F	S	S
House and bookshop								
2 Mar–3 Nov	11–5	M	T	W	·	·	S	S
22 Jul–30 Aug	11–5	M	T	W	T	F	S	S
Gardens								
2 Mar–3 Nov	11–5:30	M	T	W	T	F	S	S
Refreshments and shop								
2 Mar–3 Nov	10:30–5:30	M	T	W	T	F	S	S
Gardens, refreshments, shop and bookshop								
7 Nov–15 Dec	11–3	·	·	·	T	F	S	S
Refreshments, shop and bookshop								
5 Jan–24 Feb	11–3	·	·	·	·	·	S	S
Parkland								
Open all year	Dawn–dusk	M	T	W	T	F	S	S

House open Good Friday, times as above. 25 July to 30 August: access to some areas of house may be limited on Thursdays and Fridays.

Tucking into a tasty treat at Felbrigg Hall, Gardens and Estate in Norfolk

Flatford: Bridge Cottage

Flatford, East Bergholt, Suffolk CO7 6UL

Map ③ I8

The hamlet of Flatford nestles by the River Stour, surrounded by the countryside of Dedham Vale, the inspiration for Constable's iconic paintings. Our exhibition will tell you more about Constable's paintings, then you can explore the countryside or row along the river. **Note**: no public access to Field Studies Council – Flatford Mill, Valley Farm and Willy Lott's house.

Eating and shopping: riverside tea-room serving light lunches and cakes. Shop selling gifts and Constable souvenirs.

Making the most of your day: guided tours of Constable's painting locations. Waymarked walks. Family activity trail. Exhibition.

Access for all: 🅿️ 🅱️ 🚻 🏠 🔍 📷 📋 ⦂ 🅰️
Building 🏠 ♿
Grounds 🏠 🛤️ ♿

Getting here: 168:TM075333. ½-mile south of East Bergholt. **Foot**: accessible from East Bergholt, Dedham and Manningtree. **Bus**: frequent services from Colchester. **Train**: Manningtree 1¾ miles by footpath, 3½ miles by road. **Road**: south of East Bergholt off B1070. **Parking**: 200 yards.

Finding out more: 01206 298260 or flatfordbridgecottage@nationaltrust.org.uk

Flatford: Bridge Cottage		M	T	W	T	F	S	S
5 Jan–3 Mar	10:30–3:30	·	·	·	·	·	S	S
6 Mar–31 Mar	10:30–5	·	·	W	T	F	S	S
1 Apr–28 Apr	10:30–5	M	T	W	T	F	S	S
29 Apr–29 Sep	10:30–5:30	M	T	W	T	F	S	S
30 Sep–3 Nov	10:30–5	M	T	W	T	F	S	S
6 Nov–22 Dec	10:30–3:30	·	·	W	T	F	S	S

Property may close early from October to March in bad weather. The visitor information centre is closed weekdays in March, November and December.

Why not visit us on foot or by public transport? See pages 6 and 374

Hatfield Forest, Essex, has survived better than any other medieval hunting forest in existence

Hatfield Forest

near Bishop's Stortford, Essex

Map ③ G8

Hatfield Forest has survived better than any other medieval hunting forest on Earth. The ancient trees, some of which are over 1,000 years old, are magnificent living sculptures under which descendants of the herd of fallow deer introduced in the 12th century still roam. Whether you are looking for somewhere for the children to let off steam, a place to exercise, or somewhere tranquil to walk where you can reflect and learn about this intriguing setting, you are sure to find what you are looking for in this special place.

Eating and shopping: shop selling local gifts and Hatfield Forest venison and rabbit. Café. Sustainable woodland products available.

Making the most of your day: events. Tracker Packs and trail guide. Bike hire. Rowing boat hire. Powered mobility vehicle and all-terrain pushchair available. New guidebook and mobile app with handsets free to hire. **Dogs**: welcome. On leads near livestock and in lake area.

Access for all: ⓟ ♿ ⌨ 🅿 ⓐ
Grounds ♿ ➡ ♿ ⌨

Getting here: 167:TL547203. 4 miles east of Bishop's Stortford. **Foot**: Flitch Way from Braintree. Three Forests Way and Forest Way pass through. **Cycle**: Flitch Way. **Bus**: Saffron Walden to Stansted Airport, alight Takeley Street, 1 mile. **Train**: Stansted Airport 3 miles. **Road**: from M11 exit 8, take B1256 towards Takeley and follow signs. **Parking**: charge (non-members).

Finding out more: 01279 874040 (Infoline). 01279 870678 or hatfieldforest@nationaltrust.org.uk. Hatfield Forest Estate Office, Takeley, Bishop's Stortford, Hertfordshire CM22 6NE

Hatfield Forest		M	T	W	T	F	S	S
Countryside and kiosk car park								
Open all year	Dawn–dusk	M	T	W	T	F	S	S
Car parks								
5 Jan–24 Feb	10–3:30						S	S
2 Mar–3 Nov	9–5						S	S
4 Mar–1 Nov	10–5	M	T	W	T	F		
2 Nov–29 Dec	10–3:30						S	S
Café								
2 Jan–28 Feb	10–3:30			W	T	F	S	S
1 Mar–3 Nov	9–5	M	T	W	T	F	S	S
6 Nov–29 Dec	10–3:30			W	T	F	S	S
Shop								
5 Jan–24 Feb	10–3:30						S	S
1 Mar–3 Nov	10–5	M	T	W	T	F	S	S
9 Nov–29 Dec	10–3:30						S	S

Car parks, café and shop open daily during February and December school holidays, 10 to 3:30. Car parks open from 9 daily during summer school holidays and Bank Holidays. Café closed 25 December. Shop closed 25 and 26 December.

Heigham Holmes

Martham Staithe, Ferrygate Lane,
Martham, Norfolk

Map ③ K5

Remote island nature reserve, with grazing
marshes and ditches, supporting wildlife
typical of this important and vast broadland
landscape. **Note**: admission limited to guided
group visits (charge applicable including
members) due to restricted access via floating
river crossing. Booking essential (visit website).

Finding out more: 01263 740241
or www.nationaltrust.org.uk.
Norfolk Coast Office, Friary Farm, Cley Road,
Blakeney, Norfolk NR23 7NW

Horsey Windpump

Horsey, Great Yarmouth, Norfolk NR29 4EF

Map ③ K4

This striking windpump offers stunning
views over Horsey Mere and this mysterious
broadland landscape, full of exceptional
wildlife. Here you'll find a great introduction
to the Broads – whether you want to go for a
walk, visit the beach or just enjoy a cup of tea.
Note: surrounded by Horsey Estate –
managed by the Buxton family. Building
work to replace stock/sails.

Eating and shopping: Horsey Staithe Stores
(next to Horsey Windpump) serving light
refreshments and selling local gifts,
souvenirs and books.

There are wonderful views over Horsey Mere and the Broads from Horsey Windpump in Norfolk

Making the most of your day: staff at Horsey Staithe Stores will provide visit ideas. Boat trips (not National Trust) across Horsey Mere (holiday periods). **Dogs**: welcome on leads (wildlife and livestock).

Access for all: 🅿♿🚻♿♿🔲♫@
Windpump ♿♿♿ Grounds ♿➡

Getting here: 134:TG457223. 15 miles north of Great Yarmouth; 4 miles north-east of Martham. **Road**: off B1159 south of Horsey village. **Parking**: 50 yards, pay and display.

Finding out more: 01263 740241 or horseywindpump@nationaltrust.org.uk. Norfolk Coast Office, Friary Farm, Cley Road, Blakeney, Norfolk NR25 7NW

Horsey Windpump		M	T	W	T	F	S	S
Horsey Windpump								
2 Mar–24 Mar	10–4:30	·	·	·	·	·	S	S
25 Mar–3 Nov	10–4:30	M	T	W	T	F	S	S
Horsey Staithe Stores								
2 Mar–24 Mar	10–4:30	·	·	·	·	·	S	S
25 Mar–3 Nov	10–4:30	M	T	W	T	F	S	S

Open all Bank Holidays between 2 March and 3 November. Car park open all year, dawn to dusk.

Houghton Mill

Houghton, near Huntingdon, Cambridgeshire PE28 2AZ

Map ③ F6 🖼🚻♿🅰

Situated in a stunning riverside setting and full of excellent hands-on activities for all the family, this five-storey historic building is the last working watermill on the Great Ouse. You can watch a milling demonstration and buy some of our flour, ground in the traditional way by water-powered millstones. **Note**: milling demonstrations (Sundays and Bank Holidays, 1 to 5) subject to river levels.

Eating and shopping: riverside tea-room serving snacks and scones. Second-hand bookshop. Freshly ground Houghton Mill wholemeal flour available.

Houghton Mill, Cambridgeshire: discovering grinding

Making the most of your day: family events, including open-air theatre and hands-on baking days. Children's trails and activities and summer holiday events. **Dogs**: welcome in the grounds, please keep them on a lead. Access to countryside via public footpaths.

Access for all: 🅿♿🚻♿🔲🔲♫:
Building ♿♿ Grounds ➡

Getting here: 153:TL282720. 3½ miles from Huntingdon. **Foot**: on the Ouse Valley Way. **Cycle**: NCN51. **Bus**: services Cambridge to Huntingdon (passing close Huntingdon ≷). **Train**: Huntingdon 3½ miles. **Road**: signposted off A1123. **Parking**: 20 yards, pay and display.

Finding out more: 01480 301494 or houghtonmill@nationaltrust.org.uk

Houghton Mill		M	T	W	T	F	S	S
Mill								
23 Mar–27 Oct	11–5	·	·	·	·	·	S	S
25 Mar–25 Sep	1–5	M	T	W	·	·	·	·
Tea-room								
23 Mar–25 Sep	11–5	M	T	W	·	·	S	S
28 Sep–27 Oct	11–5	·	·	·	·	·	S	S

Open Bank Holiday Mondays, plus Good Friday 11 to 5. Caravan and campsite: open March to October; managed by the Caravan Club (01480 466716). Car park closes 8 or dusk if earlier. Toilets: as tea-room but closed Thursday and Friday.

Ickworth

The Rotunda, Horringer, Bury St Edmunds,
Suffolk IP29 5QE

Map ③ H7

A grand place for a truly entertaining day
out. The impressive central Rotunda – a
magnificent showcase commissioned by
the 4th Earl of Bristol to house his priceless
treasures, collected on tours around Europe in
the 18th century – is a marvel. For 200 years,
the eccentric and sometimes infamous Hervey
family added to the treasures inside and out,
creating the first and finest Italianate garden in
England. After walking in the tranquil parkland,
you can experience 1930s domestic service in
the newly restored servants' basement, and
share the real stories and memories of former
staff who kept this country estate running.
Note: for wedding, conference and banqueting
facilities telephone 01284 735957;
Ickworth Hotel 01284 735350.

The exterior of Ickworth, Suffolk, showing the Rotunda,
above and below. Bottom, tea in the housekeeper's room

Eating and shopping: West Wing
restaurant. Porter's Lodge serving snacks
and refreshments. Gift shop. Second-hand
bookshop. Plant and garden centre.

Making the most of your day: events and
activities all year, including 'Ickworth Lives'
exhibition and Living History days, open-air
theatre and wood fair. Paintings by Titian,
Velázquez, Reynolds and Gainsborough, as
well as Georgian silver collection. Guided and
waymarked walks – walk guides (available
from visitor reception). Cycle routes.
Play areas. **Dogs**: welcome on leads near
livestock and close to house. Assistance dogs
only in Italianate gardens.

Access for all: ♿ symbols
House ♿ symbols West Wing ♿ symbols
Grounds ♿ symbols

Getting here: 155:TL810610. 3 miles south-
west of Bury St Edmunds. **Foot**: 4½ miles via
footpaths from Bury St Edmunds. **Bus**: from
Bury St Edmunds to Haverhill. **Train**: Bury St
Edmunds 3 miles. **Road**: from A14 take junction
42 towards Westley; on west side of A143.

Lavenham Guildhall

Market Place, Lavenham, Sudbury,
Suffolk CO10 9QZ

Map ③ I7 ⬚⬚

Located at the heart of Lavenham, the Guildhall of Corpus Christi tells the story of one of the best-preserved and wealthiest towns in Tudor England. When you step inside this fine timber-framed building, you will learn about the importance of the Guild and Lavenham's famous blue cloth, as well as the people who have used the Guildhall through history. Be sure to treat yourself to one of the delicious homemade cakes before exploring the picturesque streets of Lavenham, lined with more than 320 houses of historic interest, quaint shops, quirky tea-rooms and award-winning restaurants.

Parking: 200 yards.

Finding out more: 01284 735270 or ickworth@nationaltrust.org.uk

Eating and shopping: tea-room serving ploughman's lunches and cream teas. Shop selling local gifts, souvenirs, books and plants.

Making the most of your day: children's activities, including house trails and Tudor dressing-up costumes. Guided walks and talks (summer). Events. Local history exhibition.

Access for all: 🅿️🚻🅿️📖🎨📷🅰️
Guildhall 🚶♿   Garden 🚶♿

Ickworth		M	T	W	T	F	S	S
Parkland, woods and children's playground								
Open all year	8–8	M	T	W	T	F	S	S
Italianate Gardens								
1 Jan–14 Mar	10–4	M	T	W	T	F	S	S
15 Mar–1 Nov	10–5:30	M	T	W	T	F	S	S
2 Nov–31 Dec	10–4	M	T	W	T	F	S	S
Rotunda								
15 Mar–1 Nov*	11–5	M	T	·	·	F	S	S
21 Mar–31 Oct	12–3	·	·	·	T	·	·	·
2 Nov–15 Dec**	11–4	·	·	·	·	·	S	S
Plant and garden shop								
15 Mar–1 Nov	11:30–5:30	M	T	W	T	F	S	S
West Wing, shop, restaurant and second-hand bookshop								
1 Jan–14 Mar	10:30–4	M	T	W	T	F	S	S
15 Mar–1 Nov	10:30–5	M	T	W	T	F	S	S
2 Nov–31 Dec	10:30–4	M	T	W	T	F	S	S
Porter's Lodge Outdoor Café								
5 Jan–10 Mar	10–4	·	·	·	·	·	S	S
15 Mar–1 Nov	10–5	M	T	·	T	F	S	S
2 Nov–29 Dec	10–4	·	·	·	·	·	S	S

*Tours only until lunchtime, free-flow only on busy days.
**Limited opening in November, only basement weekends in December. Last entry to Rotunda 60 minutes before closing. Property closed 25 December. Limited catering available 24 and 26 December. Parkland closes 8 or dusk if earlier.

Tudor Guildhall of Corpus Christi at Lavenham, Suffolk

Getting here: 155:TL916493. In Market Place, off the main High Street. **Foot**: 4-mile 'Railway Walk' links Lavenham with Long Melford. **Cycle**: South Suffolk Cycle Route A1. **Train**: Sudbury 7 miles. **Road**: A1141 and B1071. **Parking**: free in village.

Finding out more: 01787 247646 or lavenhamguildhall@nationaltrust.org.uk

Lavenham Guildhall		M	T	W	T	F	S	S
Guildhall, tea-room and shop								
2 Mar–24 Mar	11–4	·	·	W	T	F	S	S
25 Mar–3 Nov	11–5	M	T	W	T	F	S	S
9 Nov–1 Dec	11–4	·	·	·	·	·	S	S
Shop								
5 Jan–24 Feb	11–4	·	·	·	·	·	S	S
5 Dec–22 Dec	11–4	·	·	·	T	F	S	S
Tea-room								
5 Dec–22 Dec	11–4	·	·	·	T	F	S	S

Parts of Guildhall may close occasionally for community use.

Melford Hall

Long Melford, Sudbury, Suffolk CO10 9AA

Map (3) I7

For almost five centuries the picturesque turrets of Melford Hall have dominated Long Melford's village green. Devastated by fire in 1942, the house was brought back to life by the Hyde Parker family and it remains their much-loved family home to this day. Their interior decoration and furnishings chart the changing tastes and fashions of two centuries, but it is the stories of family life at Melford – from visits by their relation Beatrix Potter with her menagerie of animals, to children sliding down the grand staircase on trays – that make this house more than just bricks and mortar.

Eating and shopping: small tea-room or Park Room serving sandwiches and cream teas. Gatehouse shop selling souvenirs, gifts, second-hand books, souvenir story book and plants.

Making the most of your day: walks, talks and family events (April to October). Children's spot-it quiz and park trail. Some annual events in park are not National Trust. **Dogs**: on leads in car park and park walk only.

Family fun on the lawn at Melford Hall, Suffolk

Access for all: 🅿️ 🚻 ♿ 🔌 🎧 📷 🏠 ♿ 🔸 🅰️
Building ♿ ♿ ♿ ♿ Grounds ♿ ♿

Getting here: 155:TL867462. 14 miles from Bury St Edmunds, 4 miles from Sudbury. **Bus**: from Sudbury and Bury St Edmunds (Mondays to Saturdays). Nearest stop The Bull Hotel. **Train**: Sudbury 4 miles. **Road**: entrance to car park and grounds opposite village green. **Parking**: free.

Finding out more: 01787 376395 (Infoline). 01787 379228 or melford@nationaltrust.org.uk

Melford Hall		M	T	W	T	F	S	S
30 Mar–31 Oct	1–5	·	·	W	T	F	S	S

Also open on Bank Holiday Mondays. Closed Good Friday.

Orford Ness National Nature Reserve

Orford, Woodbridge, Suffolk

Map ③ K7 ⬛⬛⬛⬛⬛

This wild remote shingle spit, the largest in Europe, can only be reached by ferry. The stunning landscape has a history that will both delight and intrigue. Although an internationally important nature reserve, the site is littered with unusual, often forbidding, buildings from a sometimes disturbing past. **Note**: steep, slippery steps. 'Pagodas' accessible on guided events only. Ferry charge (including members).

Eating and shopping: freshly caught fish available at quay. Local smokehouses (not National Trust). Bring own food and drink to reserve.

Making the most of your day: guided tours and events (booked only). Crossings limited (arrive early to avoid disappointment). **Dogs**: assistance dogs only.

Access for all:
Buildings 🔲 Grounds 🔲➡

Getting here: 169:TM425495. Orford on Suffolk coast, east of Ipswich. **Foot**: Suffolk Coast Path and Sandlings Walk nearby on mainland. **Cycle**: Regional Route 41, 1 mile. **No cycling onsite**. **Ferry**: only access to Ness via National Trust ferry *Octavia*. **Bus**: local service from Woodbridge (passing Melton ➡). Bookable demand-responsive service (0845 604 1802). **Train**: Wickham Market 8 miles. **Road**: 10 miles east of A12 (B1094/1095), 12 miles north-east of Woodbridge (B1152/1084). **Parking**: Quay Street, 150 yards, pay and display (not National Trust).

Finding out more: 01728 648024 (Infoline). 01394 450900 or orfordness@nationaltrust.org.uk. Quay Office, Orford Quay, Orford, Woodbridge, Suffolk IP12 2NU

Orford Ness		M	T	W	T	F	S	S
30 Mar–29 Jun	10–2						S	
2 Jul–28 Sep	10–2		T	W	T	F	S	
5 Oct–26 Oct	10–2						S	

The only access is by National Trust ferry from Orford Quay, with boats crossing regularly to the Ness between 10 and 2 only, the last ferry leaving the Ness at 5. Some routes only open seasonally.

Orford Ness National Nature Reserve, Suffolk: remote and wild, with an intriguing, sometimes disturbing, history

The impossibly romantic 15th-century Oxburgh Hall, Norfolk, contains treasures and secrets

Oxburgh Hall

Oxborough, near Swaffham, Norfolk PE33 9PS

Map ③ H5 🏠 ✚ ✿ 🍴

No one ever forgets their first sight of Oxburgh. This romantic, moated manor house was built by the Bedingfeld family in the 15th century and they have lived here ever since. Inside, visitors can learn about the family's Catholic history, and see the secret priest's hole. There is also astonishing needlework by Mary, Queen of Scots, and a private chapel, built with reclaimed materials. Outside, you can climb up the original spiral stairs to the Tudor gatehouse roof and enjoy panoramic views, then follow the woodcarving trails in the gardens and woodlands. **Note**: major electrical rewiring February/March, so access to parts of the house may be restricted.

Eating and shopping: Old Kitchen tea-room. Picnic area. Kiosk (seasonal) serving light refreshments. Gift shop selling local Norfolk products. Plant sales. Second-hand bookshop.

Making the most of your day: free garden tours (open days). Free children's trails in house and garden. Year-round events. Woodland walks and nature trails. **Dogs**: assistance dogs only.

Access for all: 🅿️ 🛗 🚻 👨‍🦽 🎨 💻 📹 🚶
Hall 🔽 👨‍🦽 🚪 ♿ Chapel 👨‍🦽 Garden 👨‍🦽➡️♿

Getting here: 143:TF742012. In Oxborough village. **Train**: Downham Market, 10 miles, then taxi; no public transport. **Road**: 7 miles south-west of Swaffham and 3 miles from A134 at Stoke Ferry; 17 miles south of King's Lynn. **Parking**: free.

Finding out more: 01366 328258 or oxburghhall@nationaltrust.org.uk.
Oxborough, King's Lynn, Norfolk PE33 9PS

Oxburgh Hall		M	T	W	T	F	S	S
House, garden, shop and tea-room								
9 Mar–20 Mar	11–5	M	T	W	·	·	S	S
23 Mar–14 Apr	11–5	M	T	W	T	F	S	S
15 Apr–22 May	11–5	M	T	W	·	·	S	S
25 May–2 Jun	11–5	M	T	W	T	F	S	S
3 Jun–24 Jul	11–5	M	T	W	·	·	S	S
27 Jul–1 Sep	11–5	M	T	W	T	F	S	S
2 Sep–2 Oct	11–5	M	T	W	T	·	S	S
5 Oct–27 Oct	11–4	M	T	W	T	·	S	S
28 Oct–3 Nov	11–4	M	T	W	T	F	S	S
Garden, shop and tea-room								
5 Jan–10 Feb	11–4	·	·	·	·	·	S	S
16 Feb–6 Mar	11–4	M	T	W	·	·	S	S
9 Nov–22 Dec	11–4	·	·	·	·	·	S	S

February and March: due to essential electrical rewiring works, access to parts of the house may be restricted.

Paycocke's House and Garden

25 West Street, Coggeshall,
Colchester, Essex CO6 1NS

Map (3) I8

Fine half-timbered Tudor merchant's house, with a beautiful and tranquil cottage garden. Visitors can follow the changing fortunes of the house over its 500 years of history, as it went from riches to rags, and see how it was saved from demolition and restored to its former glory.

Eating and shopping: gift shop and plant sales. Courtyard café serving cream teas, drinks and ice-creams. Picnics welcome.

Making the most of your day: children's trail. Children's activities during events. Guided tours (on request). **Dogs**: in garden only.

Access for all: 🅳🦻📖�🅐
Building 🔼 Grounds 🦽

Getting here: 168:TL848225. 400 yards from Coggeshall centre. **Bus**: from Colchester to Braintree (passing Marks Tey ≋). **Train**: Kelvedon 2½ miles. **Road**: 5½ miles east of Braintree. On south side of West Street. **Parking**: Grange Barn (½ mile) until 4:30. Limited roadside parking.

Finding out more: 01376 561305 or paycockes@nationaltrust.org.uk

Paycocke's		M	T	W	T	F	S	S
3 Apr–3 Nov	11–5		·	W	T	F	S	S
Open Bank Holiday Mondays.								

Paycocke's House and Garden, Essex, was built by a wealthy Tudor merchant and has seen its fortunes rise and fall

Peckover House and Garden

North Brink, Wisbech, Cambridgeshire PE13 1JR

Map ③ G5 🏛️✂️🛏️♿☂️

Peckover House is a secret gem, an oasis hidden away in an urban environment. A classic Georgian merchant's town house, it was lived in by the Peckover family for 150 years. The Peckovers were staunch Quakers, which meant they had a very simple lifestyle, yet at the same time they ran a successful private bank. Both facets of their life can be seen as you wander through the house and gardens. The gardens themselves are outstanding – a huge area of sensory delight, complete with orangery, summerhouses, croquet lawn and rose garden with more than 60 varieties of roses.

Eating and shopping: tea-room in the barn. Gift shop in old banking wing. Second-hand bookshop. Plant sales.

Making the most of your day: Bechstein piano to play. Free garden tours. Croquet (summer). Children's handling collection and trails. Behind-the-scenes tours (selected days). Octavia Hill's birthplace nearby. **Dogs**: assistance dogs only.

Access for all: 🅿️♿WC🚻🎭☐VT♿
House ♿🚻   Garden ♿➡️🔎

Getting here: 143:TF458097. West of Wisbech town centre on north bank of River Nene. **Foot**: from Chapel Road car park walk up passageway to left of W-Four restaurant, turn right by river. Peckover House is 160 yards on right. **Cycle**: NCN1, ¼ mile. **Bus**: from Peterborough ➡ to Lowestoft; and King's Lynn (passing close King's Lynn ➡). **Train**: March 9½ miles. **Road**: B1441. **Sat Nav**: enter PE13 1RG for nearest car park. **Parking**: free in town, nearest is Chapel Road (not National Trust), 270 yards.

Finding out more: 01945 583463 or peckover@nationaltrust.org.uk

Peckover House and Garden		M	T	W	T	F	S	S
Garden, shop and tea-room								
16 Feb–24 Feb	12–4	.	.	.	.	.	S	S
2 Mar–3 Nov	12–5	M	T	W	.	.	S	S
House								
2 Mar–3 Nov	1–5	.	M	T	W	.	S	S
House, garden, shop and tea-room								
14 Dec–18 Dec	12–6	M	T	W	.	.	S	S

Shop open as garden, but closes at 4:30, 2 March to 3 November. Garden and tea-room open at 11 during Wisbech Rose Fair 3 to 6 July. Property also open on the following Thursdays and Fridays during school holidays: 28, 29 March, 4, 5, 11 and 12 April, 30, 31 May, 31 October and 1 November and during Wisbech Rose Fair 4 and 5 July.

Peckover House and Garden, Cambridgeshire, is an oasis hidden away in an urban environment

Ramsey Abbey Gatehouse

Abbey School, Ramsey, Huntingdon, Cambridgeshire PE26 1DH

Map ③ F6

This former gatehouse is all that remains of the once-great Benedictine abbey at Ramsey. **Note**: on school grounds, please respect school security. Exterior can be seen all year. No toilets.

Finding out more: 01480 301494 or www.nationaltrust.org.uk

Rayleigh Mount

Rayleigh, Essex

Map ③ I10

Medieval motte and bailey castle site, with adjacent windmill housing historical exhibition. **Note**: exhibition in windmill operated by Rochford District Council.

Finding out more: 01284 747500 or www.nationaltrust.org.uk

St George's Guildhall

29 King Street, King's Lynn, Norfolk PE30 1HA

Map ③ H5

The largest surviving medieval guildhall in England, with many original features – now a theatre. **Note**: managed by King's Lynn and West Norfolk Borough Council and King's Lynn Arts Centre Trust.

Finding out more: 01553 779095. 01553 764864 (box office) or www.nationaltrust.org.uk

Shaw's Corner

Ayot St Lawrence, near Welwyn, Hertfordshire AL6 9BX

Map ③ F9

Playwright, politician, philosopher and wit George Bernard Shaw lived in this Edwardian villa for over 40 years from 1906. Today, his home remains much as he left it. As you explore, enjoying the beautiful early 20th-century interiors, you will find fascinating links with the literary and theatrical past. **Note**: access roads very narrow.

Eating and shopping: souvenir shop. Second-hand bookshop. Ice-cream and soft drinks available in garden. Pre-1950s varieties of plants for sale.

Making the most of your day: events, including open-air performances of George Bernard Shaw's plays (summer). **Dogs**: assistance dogs only.

Access for all: ⬚⬚⬚⬚⬚ House ⬚⬚⬚
Grounds ⬚⬚⬚

Getting here: 166:TL194167. 5 miles from Harpenden. **Cycle**: NCN12, 1 mile. **Bus**: nearest bus stops Blackmore End (infrequent) and Wheathampstead, both a 2-mile walk down narrow country lanes without pavements. **Train**: Welwyn North 4½ miles; Welwyn Garden City 6 miles; Harpenden 5 miles. **Road**: A1(M) exit 4 or M1 exit 10. Signposted from B653 Welwyn Garden City to Luton road near Wheathampstead, and from B656 at Codicote. **Parking**: free small car park, 30 yards (unsuitable for large vehicles).

Finding out more: 01438 829221 (Infoline). 01438 820307 or shawscorner@nationaltrust.org.uk

Shaw's Corner		M	T	W	T	F	S	S
9 Mar–3 Nov	12–5:30*	·	·	**W**	**T**	**F**	**S**	**S**

*House open 1 to 5. Open Bank Holiday Mondays.
Closes earlier for open-air theatre events in June and July.

Walking past one of the 80 species of rhododendron at Sheringham Park in Norfolk

Sheringham Park

Upper Sheringham, Norfolk NR26 8TL

Map ③ J4 ✳️🍴🏛️🏠

Walking through this 405-hectare (1,000-acre) estate visitors are met by breathtaking views of the north Norfolk coast created by landscape gardener Humphry Repton 200 years ago. The garden has 80 species of rhododendron and azalea, which provide colour for most of the year, peaking in May to early June. An extensive network of paths allows you to explore a variety of habitats and spot wildlife, including birds, reptiles, butterflies and three species of deer. The peace and quiet of the park is interrupted only by birdsong, and provides a superb antidote to the outside world. **Note**: Sheringham Hall is privately occupied. April to September: limited access by written appointment with leaseholder.

Eating and shopping: souvenir shop. Plant sales. Courtyard Café serving cream teas, sandwiches and ice-cream. Picnics welcome.

Making the most of your day: events, including open-air theatre and various guided walks. Family events during school holidays. Children's activities, including Tracker Packs, mini-beast hunting and environmental art. Gazebo tower offers unrivalled views. **Dogs**: on leads near livestock and visitor facilities.

Access for all: ♿🏢🚻🍴🔲🚶⬚⬛🅿️ Building 🚶♿ Grounds 🚶➡️📷♿

Getting here: 133:TG135420. 2 miles south-west of Sheringham. **Foot**: Norfolk Coastal Path. **Cycle**: Regional Route 30, 1½ miles south. **Bus**: request stop at main entrance. **Train**: Sheringham 2 miles. **Road**: Cromer 5 miles, Holt 6 miles. Main entrance at junction A148/B1157. **Parking**: 60 yards, £4.80 (pay and display).

Finding out more: 01263 820550 or sheringhampark@nationaltrust.org.uk. Visitor Centre, Wood Farm, Upper Sheringham, Norfolk NR26 8TL

Sheringham Park		M	T	W	T	F	S	S
Park								
Open all year	Dawn–dusk	M	T	W	T	F	S	S
Visitor centre								
5 Jan–10 Mar	11–4						S	S
16 Mar–29 Sep	10–5	M	T	W	T	F	S	S
30 Sep–3 Nov	10–5	M			T	F	S	S
9 Nov–29 Dec	11–4						S	S
Courtyard Café								
16 Mar–29 Sep	10–5	M	T	W	T	F	S	S
30 Sep–3 Nov	10–5	M			T	F	S	S

Visitor centre and Courtyard Café: open daily 16 to 24 February and 26 October to 3 November, 10 to 5; 27 to 31 December, 11 to 4.

Sutton Hoo

Tranmer House, Sutton Hoo,
Woodbridge, Suffolk IP12 3DJ

Map ③ J7

Undisturbed for 1,300 years, an Anglo-Saxon King and his treasured possessions were unearthed days before the outbreak of the Second World War, changing perceptions of the past. You can discover more of the fascinating story by exploring the ancient burial mounds. We also have stunning replica as well as original finds from the mounds and a reconstruction of the king's burial chamber. Visitors can sit, touch and relax inside Edith Pretty's country house and enjoy the beautiful seasonal colours of this atmospheric landscape.

Eating and shopping: licensed café. Gift shop selling exclusive ceramics and jewellery. Second-hand bookshop.

Making the most of your day: activities, including living history, behind-the-scenes tours and wildlife/nature walks. Family events and children's play area. 'Let's Dig It'

archaeology trench, quiz/trails and dressing-up box. Exhibitions. **Dogs**: welcome on leads in park and café terrace area only.

Access for all: 🅿️ 🄳 🚾 📶 🅱️ 🖼️ 🔖 ∷
Buildings 🦽🦵 **Grounds** 🦽➡️🗺️🦵

Getting here: 169:TM288487. 1¼ miles from Melton. **Bus**: from Ipswich to Framlingham (passing Melton ☒). **Train**: Melton 1¼ miles, Woodbridge 3 miles. **Road**: on B1083 Melton to Bawdsey, follow signs from A12. **Parking**: 30 yards (pay and display when exhibition closed).

Finding out more: 01394 389700 or suttonhoo@nationaltrust.org.uk

Sutton Hoo		M	T	W	T	F	S	S
1 Jan–4 Jan	11–4	·	T	W	T	F	·	·
5 Jan–10 Feb	11–4	·	·	·	·	·	S	S
16 Feb–24 Feb	11–4	M	T	W	T	F	S	S
2 Mar–17 Mar	11–4	·	·	·	·	·	S	S
20 Mar–31 Mar	10:30–5	·	·	W	T	F	S	S
1 Apr–3 Nov	10:30–5	M	T	W	T	F	S	S
9 Nov–22 Dec	11–4	·	·	·	·	·	S	S
27 Dec–29 Dec	11–4	·	·	·	·	F	S	S
30 Dec–31 Dec	11–4	M	T	·	·	·	·	·

Open Bank Holiday Mondays. Estate walks open daily all year, 9 to 6 (except for some Thursdays, November to end December).

Sutton Hoo, Suffolk: reconstructed warrior's helmet

Theatre Royal Bury St Edmunds

Westgate Street, Bury St Edmunds,
Suffolk IP33 1QR

Map ③ I7 🏠🔔⊤

This Grade I-listed theatre, one of the country's
most significant theatre buildings and the only
surviving Regency playhouse in Britain, will
give you an intimate and unique theatrical
experience. We offer year-round tours and
open door sessions. **Note**: managed by
Bury St Edmunds Theatre Management
Ltd. Admission charges apply to live shows
(including members).

Eating and shopping: gifts and souvenirs on
sale. Light snacks available in Greene Room.

Making the most of your day: tours and
self-guided visits.

Access for all: 📠 📶 Building 🚶🦽

Getting here: 155:TL856637. In Bury St
Edmunds. **Foot**: easily accessible from
town centre. **Train**: Bury St Edmunds
¾ mile. **Road**: Bury St Edmunds is located
just off the A14 east of Cambridge, west of
Ipswich and north of the A134 from Sudbury.
Parking: limited free parking on Westgate
Street, or at Swan Lane car park, 546 yards
(free after 6).

Finding out more: 01284 769505 or
theatreroyal@nationaltrust.org.uk

Theatre Royal Bury St Edmunds		M	T	W	T	F	S	S
15 Jan–30 May	2–4		T		T			
16 Jan–1 Jun	10:30–1			W			S	
5 Jun–27 Jul	10–4			W	T	F	S	S
30 Jul–14 Nov	2–4		T		T			
31 Jul–16 Nov	10:30–1			W			S	

Guided tours: January to May, August to November:
Tuesdays and Thursdays at 2, Wednesdays and Saturdays
at 11, June to July. 'Backstage Past – Access all Eras':
Wednesday to Sunday at 11 and 2. Tours bookable in
advance. Closed 22 June, 13 and 20 July. Call for alterations
in the schedule before visiting. See www.theatreroyal.org
for performance information and booking.

Regency Theatre Royal Bury St Edmunds, Suffolk

Whipsnade Tree Cathedral

Whipsnade, Dunstable, Bedfordshire LU6 2LL

Map ③ E8

Incredible tree cathedral created after the
First World War in a spirit of 'faith, hope and
reconciliation'. **Note**: owned by the National
Trust and administered by the Trustees of
Whipsnade Tree Cathedral. An annual service is
held on the second Sunday in June.

Finding out more: 01582 872406
or www.nationaltrust.org.uk.
Trustees c/o Chapel Farm, Whipsnade,
Dunstable, Bedfordshire LU6 2LL

Wicken Fen National Nature Reserve

Lode Lane, Wicken, Ely,
Cambridgeshire CB7 5XP

Map ③ G6 ⊠⛫⛹

Wicken Fen is Britain's oldest nature reserve and one of Europe's most important wetlands. It supports some amazing wildlife, including more than 8,500 species of plants, birds and dragonflies. The raised boardwalk and lush grass droves allow easy access to a lost landscape of flowering meadows, sedge and reedbeds, where you may see rarities such as hen harriers, water voles and bitterns. The Wicken Fen Vision, an ambitious landscape-scale conservation project, is opening up new areas of land to explore. Our grazing herds of Highland cattle and Konik ponies are helping to create a diverse range of new habitats.

The windpump at Wicken Fen National Nature Reserve, Cambridgeshire, above, and Konik pony, top

Eating and shopping: shop selling local crafts and wildlife books. Café serving soup, 'Fen Docky' and cake. Picnics welcome.

Making the most of your day: trails, including all-weather boardwalk, butterfly walk and longer walking routes which take you deep into the fen. Observation hides allow you to discover seasonal wildlife highlights. Fenman's yard, workshop and cottage bring the history of the fens to life. Dragonfly Centre (summer weekends). Family events all year. Guided boat trips. Cycle hire available – you can cycle to Anglesey Abbey, explore the wider reserve or follow the Lodes Way. Dogs: welcome on leads on reserve and in visitor centre.

Access for all: 🅿️♿🅳♿👜♿📷📹😊🅰️
Building ♿🚹🚻 Grounds ♿🚻

Getting here: 154:TL563705. 3 miles west of Soham. Cycle: NCN11 from Ely; Lodes Way from Anglesey Abbey and local villages. Train: Ely 9 miles. Road: south of Wicken (A1123), 3 miles west of Soham (A142), 9 miles south of Ely, 17 miles north-east of Cambridge via A10. Parking: 120 yards (£2.50 non-members).

Finding out more: 01353 720274 or wickenfen@nationaltrust.org.uk

Wicken Fen		M	T	W	T	F	S	S
Reserve, visitor centre and shop								
Open all year	10–5	M	T	W	T	F	S	S
Café								
2 Jan–10 Feb	10:30–4:30			W	T	F	S	S
11 Feb–3 Nov	10–5	M	T	W	T	F	S	S
6 Nov–29 Dec	10:30–4:30			W	T	F	S	S
30 Dec–31 Dec	10:30–4:30	M	T					
Fen Cottage								
23 Mar–21 Jul	2–5						S	S
27 Mar–17 Jul	11–3			W				
24 Jul–1 Sep	11–5			W	T	F	S	S
4 Sep–30 Oct	11–3			W				
7 Sep–3 Nov	2–5						S	S
Cycle hire								
30 Mar–14 Apr	10–5	M	T	W	T	F	S	S
20 Apr–21 Jul	10–5						S	S
24 Jul–3 Sep	10–5	M	T	W	T	F	S	S
7 Sep–3 Nov	10–5						S	S

Closed 25 December. Access to reserve dawn to dusk. Visitor centre closes dusk in winter. Some paths may close in very wet conditions. Fen Cottage and cycle hire also open Bank Holiday Mondays. Café open 1 January. Last cycle hire 3:30.

Catching tiddlers at Wicken Fen National Nature Reserve in Cambridgeshire

The impressive Wimpole Hall lies at the very heart of the Wimpole Estate in Cambridgeshire

Willington Dovecote and Stables

Willington, Church End, near Bedford,
Bedfordshire MK44 3PX

Map ③ F7

Enjoying a tranquil setting, these outstanding Tudor stone stable buildings and dovecote, were built for Henry VIII's 1541 visit.
Note: no toilet.

Finding out more: 01480 301494
or www.nationaltrust.org.uk

Wimpole Estate

Arrington, Royston, Cambridgeshire SG8 0BW

Map ③ G7

A unique working estate, still guided by the seasons, with an impressive mansion at its heart. We tell the stories of the people who shaped Wimpole, while visitors soak up the atmosphere and take in the spectacular views. Inside the hall, intimate rooms meet with beautiful Georgian interiors. While outside, there are pleasure grounds and a walled garden, bursting with seasonal produce and glorious herbaceous borders. At Home Farm, you can contrast the traditional farmyard with the noisy modern piggery and cattle sheds, while our stockman explains about our rare breeds, your food and our farming.
Note: half-price entry to Home Farm for members (under-fives free).

Eating and shopping: Old Rectory Restaurant and Farm Café serving dishes made with walled garden and Home Farm produce. Shop selling local pottery, gifts, Wimpole rare-breed meat and eggs. Plant sales. Second-hand bookshop.

Making the most of your day: activities, including bat and wildlife walks, free family trails and Tracker Packs. Daily farm activities. Events, including open-air theatre, monthly seasonal market, craft fair and Christmas events. **Dogs**: welcome on leads in park.

Access for all: ♿ 🅿 ♿ ♿ ♿ ♿ ♿ ♿ 🅅🆃 ♿ ♿
Hall ♿ ♿ Farm ♿ ♿
Gardens ♿ ➡ ♿ ♿

Getting here: 154:TL336510. 6 miles north of Royston. **Foot**: Wimpole Way from Cambridge. **Bus**: Arrington 1 mile, Orwell 2 miles. **Train**: Shepreth 5 miles. Taxis from Royston 8 miles. **Road**: 8 miles south-west of Cambridge (A603), 6 miles north of Royston (A1198). Entrance via A603. **Parking**: 275 yards, £2 (non-members).

Finding out more: 01223 206000 or wimpolehall@nationaltrust.org.uk

Wimpole Estate		M	T	W	T	F	S	S
Stable Block (servery, shops and ticket office)								
1 Jan–8 Feb	11–4	M	T	W	T	F	S	S
9 Feb–3 Nov	10–6	M	T	W	T	F	S	S
4 Nov–31 Dec	11–4	M	T	W	T	F	S	S
Home Farm and Farm Café								
5 Jan–3 Feb	11–4	·	·	·	·	·	S	S
9 Feb–3 Nov	10:30–5	M	T	W	T	F	S	S
9 Nov–29 Dec	11–4	·	·	·	·	·	S	S
Garden and Old Rectory Restaurant								
1 Jan–8 Feb	11–4	M	T	W	T	F	S	S
9 Feb–3 Nov	10:30–5	M	T	W	T	F	S	S
4 Nov–31 Dec	11–4	M	T	W	T	F	S	S
Hall								
9 Feb–3 Nov	11–5	M	T	W	T	·	S	S
Hall (guided basement tour)								
9 Nov–29 Dec	11–3	·	·	·	·	·	S	S
Park								
Open all year	Dawn–dusk	M	T	W	T	F	S	S

Home Farm open 1 to 7 January and 27 to 31 December, daily, 11 to 4. Estate closed 25, 26 December except park and stable block (servery and gift shops) open 26 December 11 to 4. Bookshop as shop, but closed Monday mornings.

Visitors get to know one of the residents of Home Farm on the Wimpole Estate in Cambridgeshire

We welcome dogs assisting visitors with disabilities

Midlands

An exuberant swing after a fun family
adventure at Croome, Worcestershire

Outdoors in the Midlands

Above: **Carding Mill Valley, Shropshire**

Set in the very heart of England, the Midlands offers a stunning variety of countryside to explore. From the sweeping hills of Shropshire and open parkland of Clumber Park in Nottinghamshire, to the dramatic landscape of the Peak District and the panoramic views from the Clent Hills – a green haven for Birmingham – there is so much to enjoy.

Beautiful landscapes on your doorstep
We care for some of the Midlands' most iconic and wildlife-rich landscapes, including parts of the Peak District and the Shropshire Hills.

Carding Mill Valley and the Shropshire Hills is an important place for wildlife, geology, landscape and archaeology. If you head to the top of the hills on a clear day, you can see more than 50 miles in every direction. This is the perfect spot to find your own special place, away from the crowds, and take in the beautiful scenery.

Get walking!

Across the Midlands we have a variety of outdoor places where you can enjoy stretching your legs, whether it be on a gentle amble to a long ramble. Take a look at our website and download a walk or pick up a walks leaflet when you visit one of our places.

At the 'Long Mynd' (Long Mountain) in Shropshire, an ancient track, the Portway, extends for ten miles and is home to a wide variety of flora and fauna, including an increasing number of ground-nesting birds – snipe, skylark, curlew and red grouse.

When it comes to ancient trees, Calke Abbey in Derbyshire is one of the Trust's best places to visit. Take a walk around the park and see two oak trees which are more than 1,000 years old!

The Peak District is the second most visited national park in the world and the National Trust cares for about 14,970 hectares (37,000 acres) of iconic land within the National Park area. You can challenge yourself with a brisk walk to the top of Mam Tor and take in the amazing views, or enjoy a leisurely stroll around the picturesque White Peak Estate.

Above:
organic shapes at Mam Tor in the Peak District

We've also got walks you can enjoy as a family. Brockhampton in Herefordshire is a special place to visit throughout the year and there's a 1½-mile route which is partially suitable for pushchairs.

If you love walking and want to reduce your impact on the environment, why not enjoy one of our car-free suggestions? Our website shows many walks in the Peak District that can be reached by train.

You can also take the dog for a stroll at a number of our places, including Clumber Park in Nottinghamshire.

Kinver Edge, in Staffordshire, has a fascinating history, and its woodland sandstone ridge offers dramatic views towards Worcestershire and the Malvern Hills. There's also miles of heathland walking country to explore and the nearby Rock Houses tea-room provides well-earned refreshments after a relaxing walk.

Right:
pond dipping at Clumber Park, Nottinghamshire

Enjoy landscaped woodlands at the Dudmaston Estate in Shropshire, with its many miles of paths, and discover the south Shropshire countryside. Alternatively, a little further north near Shrewsbury, enjoy a walk through the dappled woodland at Attingham Park.

Outdoor play

This is play at its best! Den building, bug hunting, jumping, digging, discovering – our places throughout the Midlands offer plenty of space to let your imagination run wild!

Belton House in Lincolnshire is home to the largest adventure playground in the county, attracting visitors from far and wide to whiz along the zip wire or enjoy the miniature train.

In the Clent Hills in Worcestershire, you'll find a natural play trail nestled into the woodland, or if you venture over to Packwood you can don your favourite boots for our Welly Walk, while elsewhere in the county at Hanbury Hall there's a fun children's play area.

At Sudbury Hall and the Museum of Childhood in Derbyshire you can have an outside adventure in the woodland play area.

Berrington Hall in Herefordshire is home to a dedicated den-building area, where you can get creative and build your own natural roof over your head!

You can also take part in natural play events, from bat and bug hunting to pond dipping and family trails. Or you could bring along a picnic and make up your own games in the fabulous great outdoors?

Relax and enjoy

There are many ways to experience the outdoors in this lovely area – some more active than others. From walking, cycling, camping and picnicking, to the more energetic pursuits of wild swimming, geocaching and den building, there are so many ways you can get out into the fresh air. Why not simply admire the breathtaking views in the Clent Hills or the Peak District – the perfect escape from the hustle and bustle of life.

Find out more

This is just a flavour of the great outdoors in the Midlands, so how can you find out more about our places and the many things you can do when you get there? Some of the best-known places have entries in this *Handbook*, but there are many more.

For information about these, visit **www.nationaltrust.org. uk/midlands**

Above:
the rugged
Longshaw Estate,
Derbyshire
Right: **cycling at Clumber Park, Nottinghamshire**

Why not try…?

Pedal power
Whether you've got a mountain bike, a road bike or no bike at all and you want to hire one, we've got something for you. Explore the mountain bike trails at Carding Mill Valley in Shropshire or hire bikes for the family at Clumber Park in Nottinghamshire and take your pick from more than 20 miles of cycle routes.

Fishing at the Hardwick Estate, Derbyshire
Did you know you can cast a line and enjoy a spot of fishing at many of our places, including the Hardwick Estate?

Wild swimming in Shropshire
You really can take a dip with the National Trust at Carding Mill Valley. Keep an eye out for our wild swimming events throughout the year.

High-tech treasure hunting
Geocaches (or treasure boxes) are hidden in numerous Trust places in the Midlands, including the Clent Hills, Calke Park and the Brockhampton Estate. Why not have a go?

Camping in the Peak District, Derbyshire
Pitch a tent and have a family camping holiday in the Peak District this year. The Trust owns a campsite at Upper Booth Farm in Edale – perfect for enjoying the Peak District's spectacular scenery and getting away from it all.

Stretching your legs
If running is your thing, there are miles of paths to explore across the Midlands – both road routes and cross country. For the competitive runner there are also events throughout the year to put you through your paces.

Attingham Park

Atcham, Shrewsbury, Shropshire SY4 4TP

Map ④ H4 🏠 ✿ 🐾 🚂 ☂

Attingham, Shropshire's leading year-round place to visit, has something to inspire, intrigue and delight everyone, whatever the weather. With acres of parkland and miles of walks, walled kitchen garden and welcoming mansion, Attingham is the perfect all-day trip. Whether you are a family looking for activities both inside and out or someone in search of a traditional, inspirational visit to a historic house plus parkland stroll you'll find it here. Attingham, built for 1st Lord Berwick in 1785, brings the family's stories to life and you can discover how their fortunes rose and fell and how their legacy lives on. **Note**: 'Attingham Re-discovered Goes Through the Roof': project work in Picture Gallery and Nash Staircase.

Eating and shopping: Lady Berwick's waitress-service luncheon and afternoon tea. Mansion tea-room. Carriage House Café. Greedy Pig kiosk. Shops include Butler's Pantry, Stables' shop and bookshop. Picnics welcome.

Making the most of your day: 'Mansion Regency Wednesdays', with costumed room guides. Late summer park opening and open-air theatre. Seasonal events, including Easter, Hallowe'en and Christmas, as well as themed walks and food, craft, garden and harvest fairs. Daily family trails and activities during all school holidays. **Dogs**: welcome on leads in grounds (identified off-lead areas).

Access for all: 🅿 🏛 ♿ 🚻 🔦 🏠 📷 ♿ 🧷
Mansion 🏠🏠 ⬆ 👐   Grounds 🏠 ➡ 🦽 👐

Getting here: 126:SJ550099. In Atcham village. **Foot**: ½ mile along park road from main drive. **Bus**: Shrewsbury to Telford. **Train**: Shrewsbury 5 miles. **Road**: on B4380, 4 miles south-east of Shrewsbury. **Parking**: free, 25 yards approximately from visitor reception.

A costumed interpreter helps some little bakers in the kitchen at Attingham Park in Shropshire

Finding out more: 01743 708123
(Infoline). 01743 708162 or
attingham@nationaltrust.org.uk

Attingham Park		M	T	W	T	F	S	S
Park and reception*								
Open all year	8–7	M	T	W	T	F	S	S
Walled garden, playfield and Carriage House Café **								
Open all year	9–7	M	T	W	T	F	S	S
Mansion								
2 Mar–3 Nov***	10:30–5:30	M	T	W	T	F	S	S
7 Dec–8 Dec	10:30–4	·	·	·	·	·	S	S
14 Dec–23 Dec	10:30–4	M	T	W	T	F	S	S
Mansion winter tours** **								
5 Jan–1 Mar	11–2	·	·	·	·	F	S	S
9 Nov–24 Nov	11–2	·	·	·	·	F	S	S
Lady Berwick's tea-room								
2 Mar–3 Nov	12–5	M	T	W	T	F	S	S
7 Dec–8 Dec	12–4	·	·	·	·	·	S	S
14 Dec–23 Dec	12–4	M	T	W	T	F	S	S

*Park and reception: January to April and October to
December open 9 to 6 or dusk if earlier. **Garden, playfield,
café: January to April and October to December close 6 or
dusk if earlier. ***Mansion: tours only 10:30 to 12:30,
free-flow from 12:30. Last admission one hour before
closing. Bank Holiday weekends: free-flow from 10:30.
****Winter tours: 12, bookable. Mansion tea-room: open
from 11, 16 February to 3 November, 14 to 31 December
and all other weekends. Greedy pig catering kiosk: open
weekends and daily during school holidays (weather
permitting). Mansion Butler's Pantry shop: open when
mansion free-flow. Frost Fair: 29 November to 1 December.
Snowdrop evenings: 22 to 24 February; park walk, garden,
shop, and Greedy Pig open until 8. Property closed
25 December.

The Picture Gallery at Attingham Park

Attingham Park Estate: Cronkhill

near Atcham, Shrewsbury, Shropshire SY5 6JP

Map ④ H5

Delightful Italianate hillside villa designed by
Regency architect John Nash, with views across
the estate. **Note**: property contents belong to
tenants. House, garden and stables open as
part of visit. Open six days a year.

Finding out more: 01743 708162
or www.nationaltrust.org.uk

Attingham Park Estate: Town Walls Tower

Shrewsbury, Shropshire SY1 1TN

Map ④ H4

This last remaining 14th-century watchtower
sits on what were once the medieval fortified,
defensive walls of Shrewsbury. **Note**: no toilet
or car parking and 40 extremely steep steps to
top floor. Open six days a year.

Finding out more: 01743 708162
or www.nationaltrust.org.uk

Looking at pigs in the Walled Garden at Attingham Park

Baddesley Clinton

Rising Lane, Baddesley Clinton,
Warwickshire B93 0DQ

Map ④ K6   🏠✝️♣️🎣🍴

The magic of Baddesley Clinton comes from its secluded, timeless setting deep in its own parkland. Yet its modest scale and homely feel can be deceptive – for a small manor house a surprising amount is known about its inhabitants and their often unexpected lives. This year you can discover the story of the Victorian Quartet: four writers and artists who restored the house they used as a retreat from the modern world. The gardens include medieval fish pools, lakeside walk and walled garden filled with colour whatever the season.

Eating and shopping: Barn Restaurant, newly refurbished. Shop selling seasonal gifts, local foods and plants. Second-hand bookshop.

Making the most of your day: events, including brunch lectures and a Murder Mystery evening. Family Fun every holiday, as well as new playful journeys around the estate and our summer family hub – with games and activities. Activities, including welcome talks and garden tours, plus walking trails around the estate and surrounding countryside. Packwood House and Coughton Court are nearby. **Dogs**: welcome on leads in car park and on public footpaths.

Baddesley Clinton, Warwickshire, above and below, exudes a timeless quality

Access for all: ♿🚻♿🔄📷📷♿ .:
Building 🔆♿♿   Grounds ♿➡️♿

Getting here: 139:SP199723. 7½ miles north-west of Warwick. **Foot**: Heart of England Way crosses property. **Train**: Lapworth, 1½ miles; Birmingham International 9 miles. **Road**: 6 miles south of M42 exit 5; 15 miles south-east of central Birmingham. **Parking**: free, 100 yards.

Finding out more: 01564 783294 or baddesleyclinton@nationaltrust.org.uk

Baddesley Clinton		M	T	W	T	F	S	S
House, grounds, shop and restaurant								
1 Jan–15 Feb	11–4	M	T	W	T	F	S	S
16 Feb–3 Nov	11–5	M	T	W	T	F	S	S
4 Nov–31 Dec	11–4	M	T	W	T	F	S	S

Admission to house by timed ticket on Bank Holidays and busy days, tickets available from reception (not bookable). Closed 25 December.

Belton House

Grantham, Lincolnshire NG32 2LS

Map ③ E4

This classic 17th-century English country house is set in delightful gardens with a magnificent deer-park. The perfect symmetry, opulent decor, fine furnishings and Brownlow family portraits give Belton both grandeur and a more intimate feel. This year we are putting the spotlight on collections and collecting – from the fascinating books in the house, to the stunning specimen trees in the park and specialist planting in the Orangery. There will be special events, with walks, talks and opportunities to take a closer look at many of our treasures and discover more about the people who collected them.

The north front of the perfectly symmetrical Belton House in Lincolnshire

Eating and shopping: Stables Restaurant and Ride Café. Garden and outdoor shop. Gift shop. Second-hand bookshop.

Making the most of your day: events and activities all year, including Paint the Garden, open-air theatre, Food Fayre, Christmas craft market, lantern procession and carols. Daily below-stairs guided tours. Collections-themed events and seasonal talks. Family trails, indoors and out, plus the Trust's largest outdoor adventure playground, with miniature railway rides. Indoor adventure play area. Woolsthorpe Manor, home of Sir Isaac Newton, nearby. **Dogs**: welcome on leads in parkland and stableyard only. Assistance dogs only in garden.

Access for all:
House Grounds

Getting here: 130:SK930395. 3 miles north-east of Grantham. **Bus**: Grantham to Lincoln (passing close to Grantham ≅). **Train**: Grantham 3 miles. **Road**: on A607 Grantham to Lincoln road, signposted from A1. **Parking**: free, 250 yards. Please note: all visitors (including members) must obtain a ticket from visitor reception.

Belton House		M	T	W	T	F	S	S
House								
2 Mar–10 Mar	12:30–5						S	S
13 Mar–3 Nov	12:30–5			W	T	F	S	S
Basement								
1 Jan–1 Mar	11–2	M	T	W	T	F	S	S
2 Mar–3 Nov	11–3	M	T	W	T	F	S	S
4 Nov–31 Dec	11–2	M	T	W	T	F	S	S
Garden, park, restaurant and shop								
1 Jan–1 Mar	10:30–4	M	T	W	T	F	S	S
2 Mar–3 Nov	10:30–5:30	M	T	W	T	F	S	S
4 Nov–31 Dec	10:30–4	M	T	W	T	F	S	S
Adventure playground								
2 Mar–3 Nov	10:30–5:30	M	T	W	T	F	S	S

House open Bank Holiday Mondays (March to October).
House conservation talks 11:30 selected days (March to
October). House: guided tours replace free-flow on selected
days. Timed tickets likely at busy times. Basement entrance
by guided tour only (every 15 minutes). Bellmount Woods:
open daily, access from separate car park. Bellmount Tower
and Boathouse open occasionally. House closes in poor
light. Property closed 25 December.

Enjoying Belton House, Lincolnshire

Benthall Hall

Broseley, Shropshire TF12 5RX

Map (4) I5

Within this fine stone house, you can discover
the history of the Benthall family from the
Saxon period to the present day. Outside, the
garden boasts a beautiful Restoration church,
a restored plantsman's garden, with fabulous
crocus displays in spring and autumn, and an
old kitchen garden. **Note**: Benthall Hall is the
home of Edward and Sally Benthall.

The fine stone Benthall Hall in Shropshire

Eating and shopping: tea-room serving hot
drinks and cakes only.

Making the most of your day: guided walks
and tours of Hall (by arrangement).
Dogs: in park and woodland only.

Access for all: ⬚⬚ ⬚⬚ ⬚⬚ ⬚ Building ⬚

Getting here: 127:SJ658025. 1 mile south-west
of Ironbridge. **Bus**: services from Telford and
Wellington to Much Wenlock. **Train**: Telford
Central 7½ miles. **Road**: 1 mile north-west of
Broseley (B4375), 4 miles north-east of Much
Wenlock, 1 mile south-west of Ironbridge.
Parking: free, 100 yards. Space for one coach.

Finding out more: 01952 882159 or
benthall@nationaltrust.org.uk

Benthall Hall		M	T	W	T	F	S	S
House and tea-room								
2 Feb–24 Feb*	1–4	·	·	·	·	·	S	S
2 Mar–30 Oct	1–5	·	T	W	·	·	S	S
Garden								
2 Feb–24 Feb	1–4:30	·	·	·	·	·	S	S
2 Mar–30 Oct	12:30–5:30	·	T	W	·	·	S	S

*Only the ground floor is open in February. Open Good Friday and Bank Holiday Mondays. Closes dusk if earlier.

Berrington Hall

near Leominster, Herefordshire HR6 0DW

Map ④ H6   🏠✿⚓🛏🍽

Created as the perfect house in the perfect setting, Berrington has many secrets to uncover. Here in one of Henry Holland's first houses, you can explore the family rooms and walk in the servants' footsteps down the back stairs, moving around the house unseen by the family and guests. You will find out what happened to William Kemp, Lord Cawley's butler, and discover the anguish of a grieving mother during the First World War. Alternatively why not join a below-stairs tour to see if you would have liked being a servant at Berrington?

Eating and shopping: shop selling gifts, local products and preserves made from our fruit. Tea-room serving light lunches, afternoon tea and cakes.

Making the most of your day: family events all year. Children's natural play and den-building area. Garden, parkland and architecture tours. House quizzes. Costume collection on view (by appointment). Waymarked estate walks.
Dogs: on leads on estate and in parts of garden.

Access for all: 🅿♿🅿♿🚻♿🏳♿📖🎦♿😊
Building 📷♿   Grounds ♿➡♿

Getting here: 137:SO510637. 3 miles north of Leominster. **Bus**: Ludlow to Hereford (passing close Ludlow ≋ and Leominster), alight Luston, 2 miles. **Train**: Leominster 4 miles. **Road**: 7 miles south of Ludlow, west side of A49.

Parking: free, 30 yards to visitor reception.

Finding out more: 01568 615721 or
berrington@nationaltrust.org.uk

Berrington Hall		M	T	W	T	F	S	S
Below stairs, gardens, park, tea-room and shop								
26 Jan–10 Feb	10–4	·	·	·	·	·	S	S
16 Feb–3 Nov	10–5	M	T	W	T	F	S	S
9 Nov–15 Dec	10–4	·	·	·	·	·	S	S
16 Dec–23 Dec	10–4	M	T	W	T	F	S	S
Mansion tours								
16 Feb–3 Nov	11–1	M	T	W	T	F	S	S
9 Nov–15 Dec	11–1	·	·	·	·	·	S	S
16 Dec–23 Dec	11–1	M	T	W	T	F	S	S
Mansion								
16 Feb–3 Nov	1–5	M	T	W	T	F	S	S
9 Nov–15 Dec	1–4	·	·	·	·	·	S	S
16 Dec–23 Dec	1–4	M	T	W	T	F	S	S

Below stairs, gardens, park, tea-room and shop open 1 January, 10 to 4. Shop: opens at 11 each day. House: ground floor only 9 November to 23 December. Below stairs, gardens, parkland, tea-room and shop: 27 December to 31 December, open 10 to 4.

Berrington Hall, Herefordshire: perfect house and setting

Biddulph Grange Garden

Grange Road, Biddulph, Staffordshire ST8 7SD

Map ④ J2 ❖

This amazing Victorian garden was created by Darwin contemporary, James Bateman, as an extension of his beliefs and scientific interests. His plant collection comes from all over the world – a visit takes you on a journey from an Italian terrace to an Egyptian pyramid, via a Himalayan glen and Chinese-inspired garden. We have a fabulous collection of rhododendrons, as well as a dahlia walk and the oldest surviving golden larch in Britain, brought from China by the great plant hunter Robert Fortune. There is also a woodland nature path and tours of the unrestored Geological Gallery. A garden for all seasons. **Note**: many steps throughout the garden and from the car park.

The Chinese footbridge at Biddulph Grange Garden

Eating and shopping: self-service tea-room. Gift shop. Expanded plant centre.

Making the most of your day: talks, guided tours, events and children's trails throughout year. Summer activities programme.

Access for all: 🅿🖼🖥👓 Building 🏢 Grounds 🏢

Getting here: 118:SJ895591. 1 mile north of Biddulph. **Bus**: from Congleton (passing Congleton ⬛). **Train**: Congleton 2½ miles. **Road**: 3½ miles south-east of Congleton, 7 miles north of Stoke-on-Trent. Access from A527 (Tunstall to Congleton road). Entrance on Grange Road. **Parking**: free, 50 yards.

Finding out more: 01782 517999 or biddulphgrange@nationaltrust.org.uk

Biddulph Grange Garden		M	T	W	T	F	S	S
1 Jan–15 Mar	11–3:30	M	T	W	T	F	S	S
16 Mar–3 Nov	11–5:30	M	T	W	T	F	S	S
4 Nov–24 Dec	11–3:30	M	T	W	T	F	S	S
26 Dec–31 Dec	11–3:30	M	T	·	T	F	S	S

Open Bank Holiday Mondays. Closes dusk if earlier. Closed 25 December.

Chinese temple at Biddulph Grange Garden, Staffordshire

Birmingham Back to Backs

55-63 Hurst Street/50-54 Inge Street, Birmingham, West Midlands B5 4TE

Map ④ J5

An atmospheric glimpse into the lives of the ordinary people who crammed into Birmingham's last surviving court of back to backs: houses built, literally, back to back around a communal courtyard. Our guided tour will take you on a journey in time, from the 1840s through to the 1970s. With fires alight in the grates, and sounds and smells from the past, you will experience an evocative and intimate insight into life and work at the Back to Backs. **Note**: visits by guided tour only (advance booking essential).

Eating and shopping: variety of mementoes available. Traditional 1930s sweetshop (not National Trust).

Making the most of your day: exciting year-round events. Ground-floor tour also available.

Access for all: 🏢🚻🏠🅿️🏛️📖🏪♿📷🅰️
Building 🏠🏠

Getting here: 139:SP071861. In the centre of Birmingham next to the Hippodrome Theatre. **Foot**: easy walking distance of bus and railway stations (follow signs for Hippodrome Theatre). **Cycle**: NCN5. **Bus**: services from Birmingham city centre. **Train**: Birmingham New Street ¼ mile. **Parking**: Arcadian Centre, Bromsgrove Street (not National Trust).

Finding out more: 0121 666 7671 (booking line). 0121 622 2442 or backtobacks@nationaltrust.org.uk

Birmingham Back to Backs		M	T	W	T	F	S	S
5 Feb–22 Dec	10–5		T	W	T	F	S	S

Admission by timed ticket and guided tour only, booking essential. Open Bank Holiday Mondays (but closed next day). During term time property closed 10 to 1 on Tuesdays, Wednesdays and Thursdays for schools. Last tour times vary in winter. Closed 31 August to 6 September.

Discovering the past at Birmingham Back to Backs

Brockhampton Estate

Greenfields, Bringsty, near Bromyard,
Herefordshire WR6 5TB

Map ④ I7

**Two views, above and top, of the timeless
Brockhampton Estate in Herefordshire**

This timeless estate captures the spirit of rural
Herefordshire in 687 hectares (1,700 acres) of
open parkland, traditional orchards, working
farmland and ancient woodland. There
are miles of walks with breathtaking views
across the surrounding countryside to the
Malvern and Clee Hills. Nestled at the heart of
the estate is the picturesque medieval manor
house at Lower Brockhampton. Surrounded
by a moat and borders of seasonal flowers,
the house is entered via a timber-framed
gatehouse. Enjoy the tranquillity as you sit in
the damson orchard or stroll along the nature
trail to discover a rich variety of wildlife.

Eating and shopping: refurbished Old
Apple Store tea-room. Granary shop selling
Herefordshire gifts and award-winning estate
jams, honey and beer. Second-hand bookshop.
Picnics welcome.

Making the most of your day: year-round
events, including ranger-led wildlife walks,
historical re-enactments and medieval
Christmas. Family trails and activities
(school holidays). Natural play trail.
Waymarked walks and orienteering routes.
Guided tours most weekends. **Dogs**: welcome
on leads in grounds, woods and parkland.

Access for all: 🅿️🅳♿🦽🧎🖐️🎒📷♿
Building 🔆♿🔆 Grounds ♿➡️🔆

Getting here: 149:SO682546. 2 miles east of
Bromyard. **Bus**: Worcester to Hereford (passing
Worcester Foregate Street ≋ and close Hereford
≋). **Road**: on Worcester road (A44); house
reached by a narrow road through 1 mile of
woods and park. **Parking**: 50 yards and 1 mile.

Finding out more: 01885 482077 (estate office).
01885 488099 (manor house) or
brockhampton@nationaltrust.org.uk

Brockhampton Estate		M	T	W	T	F	S	S
Estate								
Open all year	10–5	M	T	W	T	F	S	S
Tea-room								
1 Jan–6 Jan	10–4		T	W	T	F	S	S
12 Jan–10 Feb	10–4						S	S
16 Feb–3 Nov	10–5	M	T	W	T	F	S	S
9 Nov–15 Dec	10–4						S	S
16 Dec–22 Dec	10–4	M	T	W	T	F	S	S
27 Dec–31 Dec	10–4	M	T			F	S	S
House, grounds and shop								
16 Feb–3 Nov	11–5	M	T	W	T	F	S	S
9 Nov–22 Dec	11–4						S	S

Calke Abbey, Derbyshire, tells the story of the dramatic decline of a grand country house

Calke Abbey

Ticknall, Derby, Derbyshire DE73 7LE

Map ③ C4

With peeling paintwork and overgrown courtyards Calke Abbey tells the story of the dramatic decline of a grand country-house estate. The house and stables are little restored, with many abandoned areas vividly portraying a period in the 20th century when numerous country estates did not survive to tell their story. Outdoors there are beautiful, yet faded, walled gardens and the orangery, auricula theatre and kitchen gardens to explore. The more adventurous can discover the ancient and fragile habitats of Calke Park and its National Nature Reserve, an excellent area for walking and wildlife. **Note**: everyone requires admission tickets for house and garden, including members (membership cards essential).

Eating and shopping: restaurant serving local produce, including estate-reared meat. Gift shop. Pantry selling local food. Refreshments available from coffee shop kiosk (peak times).

Making the most of your day: events all year, whatever the weather, as well as activities such as guided park or garden walks. Family activities in Squirt's Stable at weekends and during school holidays, from March to October. We also offer Tracker Packs, discovery trails and geocaching. **Dogs**: welcome on leads in park and stables.

Access for all: 🅿🦽♿🚻🔦🔍🎧💻📺👁
Building 🏛♿🔽 Grounds 🏛♿🔽➡

Getting here: 128:SK367226. 10 miles south of Derby. **Bus**: Swadlincote, alight Ticknall, 1½ mile walk through park. **Train**: Derby 9½ miles; Burton-on-Trent 10 miles. **Road**: A514 Ticknall between Swadlincote and Melbourne. M42/A42 junction 13, A50 Derby South. **Parking**: per person park admission for all. 3.6-metre height restriction on archway.

Finding out more: 01332 863822 or
calkeabbey@nationaltrust.org.uk

Calke Abbey		M	T	W	T	F	S	S
Calke Park National Nature Reserve								
Open all year	7:30–7:30	M	T	W	T	F	S	S
House								
23 Feb–3 Nov	11–5	M	T	W	·	·	S	S
Garden and stables								
23 Feb–3 Nov	10–5	M	T	W	T	F	S	S
Restaurant and shop								
Open all year	10–5	M	T	W	T	F	S	S
Themed house tours								
28 Feb–1 Nov	11–4	·	·	·	·	T	F	·

House: Saturday to Wednesday, 11 to 12, entry by guided
conservation tour (places limited); house opens fully at
12:30. House admission by timed ticket for all visitors
(including members), delays occur at peak times. Open for
themed tours Thursday and Friday. Restaurant and shop:
close at 4 January, February, November and closed
25 December. Calke Park closes 7:30 or dusk if earlier.

Calke Abbey, Derbyshire: the Auricula Theatre, above, and fascinated young visitors in the Bird Lobby, below

Members may have to pay on special events days

Canons Ashby

near Daventry, Northamptonshire NN11 3SD

Map ③ D7 🏠➕🏛️✿🏊

Tranquil Elizabethan manor house set in beautiful early 18th-century gardens. Built by the Drydens using remains of a medieval priory, the house and gardens have survived largely unaltered since 1710 and are presented as they were during the time of Sir Henry Dryden, a Victorian antiquary, passionate about the past. The warm welcoming house features grand rooms, stunning tapestries and Jacobean plasterwork, contrasting with the domestic detail of the servants' quarters. Strolling in the historic parkland, visitors will catch glimpses of early medieval landscapes, while a wander through the priory church reveals the story of the canons of Canons Ashby.

Eating and shopping: Stables tea-room and tea-gardens. Coach House shop selling home and garden gifts. Second-hand bookshop (donations welcome).

The Elizabethan manor house of Canons Ashby in Northamptonshire, above, is set in 18th-century gardens, below

Making the most of your day: events all year, including costumed weekends, live music in gardens and priory church, guided walks, Hallowe'en and Christmas. Family fun activities and trails. **Dogs**: on leads in car park, paddock, tea-garden and parkland only.

Access for all: 🅿️♿👓🦽🦼🐕‍🦺💻📹🚶😊
🅰️ Building 🦽🚶🚻♿ Grounds 🦽🚶➡️♿

Getting here: 152:SP577506. In Canons Ashby village, 11 miles south of Daventry. **Foot**: Macmillan long-distance footpath. **Cycle**: NCN70. **Train**: Banbury 10 miles. **Road**: M40 exit 11, then A422 Brackley, M1 junction 16, then A45 towards Daventry, at Weedon turn left onto A5, then follow brown signs. **Parking**: 218 yards.

Finding out more: 01327 861900 or canonsashby@nationaltrust.org.uk

Canons Ashby		M	T	W	T	F	S	S
9 Feb–17 Feb*	11–3	M	T	W	T	F	S	S
23 Feb–10 Mar*	11–3	.	.	.	.	.	S	S
16 Mar–27 Oct**	11–5	M	T	W	.	F	S	S
27 May–2 Jun**	11–5	M	T	W	T	F	S	S
28 Oct–3 Nov**	11–5	M	T	W	T	F	S	S
9 Nov–24 Nov	12–4	.	.	.	.	.	S	S
30 Nov–8 Dec	12–4	M	T	W	T	F	S	S

*Entry to house by tour only. **Taster tours between 11 and 1 (30-minute tours covering three rooms). Free-flow entry to house for all visitors from 1. Tea-room and shop open 30 minutes before whole property.

Carding Mill Valley and the Shropshire Hills

Church Stretton, Shropshire

Map ④ H5

Covering as much as 2,000 hectares (4,942 acres) of heather-covered hills with iconic views of the Shropshire Hills Area of Outstanding Natural Beauty. An important place for wildlife, geology, landscape and archaeology, with excellent visitor facilities and information in Carding Mill Valley.

Eating and shopping: Chalet Pavilion tea-room serving local food, including hot lunches, drinks and ice-cream. Gift shop, maps, guides and pond nets available.

Making the most of your day: events all year. Walks card and walks leaflets available at Information Hut. **Dogs**: under close control (grazing livestock).

Access for all: 🅿️🅳♿🚻🅼🔶

Building ♿ Grounds ♿

Getting here: 137:SO443945. 15 miles south of Shrewsbury. **Bus**: Shrewsbury to Ludlow, alight Church Stretton, 1½ miles. Shuttle bus weekends/Bank Holidays (Easter to October). **Train**: Church Stretton 1 mile. **Road**: west of Church Stretton Valley and A49. **Sat Nav**: use SY6 6JG. **Parking**: 50 yards (pay and display).

Finding out more: 01694 725000 or cardingmill@nationaltrust.org.uk

Carding Mill Valley		M	T	W	T	F	S	S
Countryside								
Open all year		M	T	W	T	F	S	S
Tea-room and shop*								
1 Jan–2 Jan	11–4		T	W				
5 Jan–17 Feb	11–4						S	S
18 Feb–3 Nov	10–5	M	T	W	T	F	S	S
4 Nov–23 Dec	11–4	M				F	S	S
26 Dec–31 Dec	11–4	M	T		T	F	S	S

*Shop opens at 11 on weekdays. Tea-room and shop close at dusk if earlier. Toilets and information hut open 9 to 7 March to October; 9 to 4:15 November to February.

Charlecote Park

Wellesbourne, Warwick,
Warwickshire CV35 9ER

Map ④ K7

Charlecote has been home to the Lucy family since the 12th century. Their stories are told throughout the house by their portraits and the objects they collected from around the world. Today you will see how Mary Elizabeth and her husband George Hammond Lucy spared no expense extending their home and furnishing it in Victorian times. The gardens include a formal parterre, colourful herbaceous planting and shady woodland garden. The wider 'Capability' Brown parkland offers level walks with picturesque views across the River Avon. A herd of fallow deer has been in the park since Tudor times. **Note**: major rewiring project may reduce number of open showrooms until spring.

Eating and shopping: Orangery restaurant serving hot meals and light snacks. Two retail outlets, main shop and gatehouse shop, selling locally sourced produce. Picnics welcome.

By the river at Charlecote Park, Warwickshire

Making the most of your day: events all year. Wide range of guided walks and talks. Children's activities, including Easter Egg and treasure hunts (during the school holidays) and there is a Victorian kitchen, laundry, brew-house and tack room below stairs to explore. The house is festively decorated during weekends in December. **Dogs**: assistance dogs only.

Access for all: Building Grounds

Getting here: 151:SP263564. 1 mile west of Wellesbourne, 5 miles east of Stratford-upon-Avon. **Bus**: Leamington Spa to Stratford-upon-Avon. **Train**: Stratford-upon-Avon, 5 miles; Warwick 6 miles; Leamington Spa 8 miles. **Road**: 6 miles south of Warwick on north side of B4086. **Parking**: free, 300 yards.

Finding out more: 01789 470277 or charlecotepark@nationaltrust.org.uk

Charlecote Park		M	T	W	T	F	S	S
Park, gardens and outbuildings								
Open all year	10:30-5:30	**M**	**T**	**W**	**T**	**F**	**S**	**S**
House								
9 Feb-22 Mar	12-3:30	**M**	**T**	·	**T**	**F**	**S**	**S**
23 Mar-3 Nov	11-4:30	**M**	**T**	·	**T**	**F**	**S**	**S**
9 Nov-22 Dec	12-3:30	·	·	·	·	·	**S**	**S**
Restaurant								
Open all year	10:30-5	**M**	**T**	**W**	**T**	**F**	**S**	**S**
Shop								
Open all year	10:30-5	**M**	**T**	**W**	**T**	**F**	**S**	**S**

Closed 23 to 25 December. House: parts of ground floor only in November and December. Some showrooms closed in February. Park, garden, outbuildings: close at 4 in January, February, November and December. May close at dusk if earlier. Restaurant, shop and Victorian kitchen: close at 3:30 in January, February, November and December.

The drive leading to the turreted Charlecote Park, top, and exploring the extensive gardens, above

Clent Hills

Romsley, Worcestershire

Map ④ J6

Set on the edge of Birmingham and the Black Country, the hills offer a green oasis with panoramic views. **Note**: for play area, toilets and café (not National Trust), park at Nimmings Wood (B62 0NL). Café open Tuesday to Sunday.

Finding out more: 01562 712822 or www.nationaltrust.org.uk

The magnificent lake at Clumber Park, Nottinghamshire, provides excellent fishing opportunities

Clumber Park

Worksop, Nottinghamshire S80 3AZ

Map ③ D2

With 1,537 hectares (3,800 acres) of picturesque parkland and gardens, peaceful woodlands and a magnificent lake, there is plenty of space to explore and relax in at Clumber Park. Although the house was demolished, there are glimpses of its grand past to enjoy. From the 'cathedral in miniature', you can follow in the footsteps of dukes through the pleasure ground to the Walled Kitchen Garden, a beautiful 1.6-hectare (4-acre) garden, which includes a long herbaceous border. There's so much to discover, and you can have a perfect day out with family and friends among Clumber Park's spectacular scenery.

Places may occasionally close for conservation, safety or events

Eating and shopping: café serving snacks, lunch and hot drinks. Gift shop, plus outdoors shop. Plant sales.

Making the most of your day: family events and activities all year, including hands-on wildlife exhibitions in the Discovery Centre. There are also family Tracker Packs and a climbing forest in the play park. You can hire a bike (we have 20 miles of cycle routes). Barkers restaurant offers special gourmet evenings. The Workhouse and Mr Straw's House are nearby. Stay longer at our campsite. **Dogs**: on leads in walled garden, pleasure grounds and grazed areas. Under close control elsewhere.

Access for all: ⬚⬚⬚⬚⬚⬚⬚⬚⬚
Buildings ⬚⬚   Grounds ⬚⬚⬚⬚

Getting here: 120:SK629752. 4½ miles south-east of Worksop. **Cycle**: NCN6. **Bus**: Worksop to Ollerton, alight Carburton, ¾ mile. **Train**: Worksop 4½ miles; Retford 6½ miles.

Road: 1 mile A1/A57, 11 miles M1 junction 30. **Parking**: 200 yards from facilities. 250 yards from Walled Kitchen Garden.

Finding out more: 01909 476592 or clumberpark@nationaltrust.org.uk

Clumber Park		M	T	W	T	F	S	S
Visitor facilities								
1 Jan–22 Mar	10–4	M	T	W	T	F	.	.
5 Jan–24 Mar	9–4	.	.	.	.	.	S	S
25 Mar–1 Nov	10–5	M	T	W	T	F	.	.
23 Mar–3 Nov	9–6	.	.	.	.	.	S	S
4 Nov–31 Dec	10–4	M	T	W	T	F	.	.
2 Nov–29 Dec	9–4	.	.	.	.	.	S	S
Walled Kitchen Garden								
25 Mar–3 Nov	10–5	M	T	W	T	F	S	S
Campsite								
1 Mar–31 Oct		M	T	W	T	F	S	S

Visitor facilities include: café, tea-room, shop, plant sales, cycle hire, chapel, Discovery Centre and children's play areas. Chapel open as visitor facilities except 12 January to 28 March, when closed for conservation cleaning. Open daily except Christmas Day.

Clumber Park boasts fabulous parkland and peaceful woodlands, so there is plenty of space to let off steam

Coughton Court

Alcester, Warwickshire B49 5JA

Map ④ K6 🏛️✝️♣️🔔⊤

Coughton has been home to the Throckmorton family for 600 years. Facing persecution for their Catholic faith, they were willing to risk everything. Their fascinating story is told through 'Cabinets of Curiosities: 600 years of Catholic Treasures' – artefacts and curios that were hidden away, then proudly displayed as the family gained freedom to practise their faith. Coughton is still very much a family home with an intimate feel; in fact the Throckmorton family still live here and they created and manage the stunning gardens, which include a riverside walk, bog garden and beautiful display of roses in the walled garden.

Eating and shopping: restaurant serving lunch and teas. Drinks and ice-cream available from Stables Coffee Bar. Coach House shop selling local food and seasonal gifts. Throckmorton family plant centre.

Historic display in the Tribune at Coughton Court

Making the most of your day: events, including Family Fun every holiday, open-air theatre, exhibitions, Cheese and Pickle and Winter Festivals. Welcome talks. Children's playground and outdoor games. Walking trails. Baddesley Clinton and Packwood House nearby. **Dogs**: welcome on leads in car park only.

Access for all: 📶🅿️♿🚾♿♿🦽🔘📷🖼️📹••
House 🔛🔛♿ **Grounds** 🔛➡️♿

Getting here: 150:SP080604. 2 miles north of Alcester. **Foot**: Arden Way passes close by. **Cycle**: NCN5, ½ mile. **Bus**: services from Redditch, Evesham and Stratford-upon-Avon. **Train**: Redditch 6 miles. **Road**: on A435. **Parking**: free, 150 yards.

Finding out more: 01789 400777 or coughtoncourt@nationaltrust.org.uk

Coughton Court		M	T	W	T	F	S	S
House, shop and restaurant								
9 Mar–24 Mar	11–5						S	S
23 Nov–1 Dec*	11–5	M	T	W	T	F	S	S
House, shop, restaurant and garden								
30 Mar–30 Jun	11–5			W	T	F	S	S
2 Jul–1 Sep	11–5		T	W	T	F	S	S
4 Sep–29 Sep	11–5			W	T	F	S	S
3 Oct–3 Nov	11–5				T	F	S	S
'Cabinets of Curiosity' tours**								
3 Apr–27 Sep	11–11:30			W	T	F		

Open Bank Holidays. Closed Good Friday and 6 July and 21 September. Admission by timed ticket on weekends and busy days. *Coughton Winter Festival, see website for details. **Tours last 35 minutes and focus on parts of the collection, tickets available on arrival.

The opulent Saloon at Coughton Court, Warwickshire

Croft Castle and Parkland

Yarpole, near Leominster,
Herefordshire HR6 9PW

Map ④ H6 🏰🏯✝🏛❄♟♿🚻

Croft Castle is informal, relaxed and family-friendly. Home of the Croft family for nearly 1,000 years, Croft is the place to stroll through miles of woodland trails, picnic on the lawns, enjoy the beautiful scenery of the 607-hectare (1,500-acre) estate and be delighted by the Georgian interiors. You can learn about the family who have made Croft so special, then relax in the walled garden and walk to the Iron Age hill fort at Croft Ambrey, past some of our 300 veteran trees.
Note: parts of property may close in high winds.

Eating and shopping: tea-room serving local beers, fruit juices, ciders, cakes, scones and Sunday roasts. Shop selling local gifts. Plant sales. Second-hand bookshop. Wildlife and gardening gifts available.

Making the most of your day: events, including open-air theatre and historical re-enactments. Family activities, including Easter, Hallowe'en, bird-box making and bug hunting. Castle-inspired play area and family room. Children's trails. Waymarked walks across estate. **Dogs**: on leads in parkland only.

Access for all: 🅿♿🚽🚾♿🔔📷♿
Castle 🅿♿🚶 Grounds 🚶➡♿

Two views of the wonderfully informal Croft Castle and Parkland, Herefordshire, above and below

Getting here: 137:SO455655. 5 miles north-west of Leominster, 9 miles south-west of Ludlow. **Bus**: Ludlow to Hereford, alight Gorbett Bank, 2¼ miles. **Train**: Leominster 7 miles. **Road**: B4362, signposted from Ludlow to Leominster road (A49) and from A4110. **Sat Nav**: use HR6 0BL. **Parking**: 100 yards.

Finding out more: 01568 782120 or croftcastle@nationaltrust.org.uk

Croft Castle and Parkland		M	T	W	T	F	S	S
Tea-room and play area								
5 Jan–24 Feb	10–4	·	·	·	·	·	S	S
Tea-room, shop, garden and play area								
16 Feb–24 Feb	10–4:30	M	T	W	T	F	S	S
2 Mar–3 Nov	10–5	M	T	W	T	F	S	S
9 Nov–22 Dec	10–4:30	·	·	·	·	·	S	S
Castle tours								
16 Feb–24 Feb	10:30–1	M	T	W	T	F	S	S
2 Mar–3 Nov	10:30–1	M	T	W	T	F	S	S
9 Nov–22 Dec	10:30–1	·	·	·	·	·	S	S
Castle								
16 Feb–24 Feb	1–4:30	M	T	W	T	F	S	S
2 Mar–3 Nov	1–5	M	T	W	T	F	S	S
9 Nov–22 Dec	1–4:30	·	·	·	·	·	S	S

*Castle admission between 10:30 and 1 is by tour only (approx 10:30, 11:15, 12 free with entry, book on arrival). Shop: opens 11. Countryside: open daily dawn to dusk. Parkland and woods may close in high winds. Property may be closed in snow. Tea-room open winter weekends 10 to 4.

The ha-ha, with meadow and church beyond at Croome, Worcestershire: now restored to its 18th-century heyday

Always remember your current membership card

Croome

near High Green, Worcester,
Worcestershire WR8 9DW

Map (4) J7

Croome is now a place that is both familiar and unexpected. The parkland has been transformed. Once a garden hidden in the undergrowth, we have restored it to its 18th-century heyday. As you walk through the enchanting shrubberies, you will find dramatic views with temples, bridges, follies and statues waiting around every corner. To get a taste of something different, step into our mansion house, Croome Court. Once close to destruction and then home to an eclectic mix of communities in the 20th century, it is now embarking on an entirely new journey in the 21st century. **Note**: major repair project starting end of year.

Eating and shopping: 1940s-style restaurant and Tapestry Room tea-room. Shop selling gifts, local products, plants and garden ornaments.

Keystone of the Dry Arch Bridge, Croome

Making the most of your day: events and activities all year, including new guided tours of the gardens and house. Family events, such as our themed activity days and event weekends (teddy bear zip wire being just one) in July and August. Trails and children's natural play area. In Croome Court there is the grand ground floor and vaulted basement to explore, as well as the restored wartime buildings. **Dogs**: welcome on leads. Assistance dogs only in house, restaurant and shop (waiting areas provided).

Access for all: [icons]
House [icons] Garden [icons]

Getting here: 150:SO887452. 9 miles south of Worcester. **Bus**: from Worcester to Pershore, alight Ladywood Road/Rebecca Road crossroads, 2 miles. From Worcester to Malvern, alight Kinnersley, 2 miles. **Train**: Worcester/Pershore. **Road**: M5 junction 7. Follow brown signs off B4084 from Pershore or off A38 from Worcester/Upton. **Parking**: free.

Finding out more: 01905 371006 or croomepark@nationaltrust.org.uk. Estate Office, The Builders' Yard, High Green, Severn Stoke, Worcestershire WR8 9JS

The dining room at Croome

Croome		M	T	W	T	F	S	S
Park, restaurant and shop								
1 Jan–15 Feb	10–4	M	T	W	T	F	S	S
16 Feb–3 Nov	10–5:30	M	T	W	T	F	S	S
4 Nov–23 Dec	10–4	M	T	W	T	F	S	S
House								
2 Jan–15 Feb	12–3	M	·	W	T	F	S	S
16 Feb–3 Nov	11–4:30	M	·	W	T	F	S	S
4 Nov–23 Dec	12–3	M	·	W	T	F	S	S
House, park, restaurant and shop								
26 Dec–31 Dec	11–4	M	T	·	T	F	S	S

Access to some areas of park and house may be limited due to winter maintenance.

Cwmmau Farmhouse

Brilley, Whitney-on-Wye,
Herefordshire HR3 6JP

Map (4) G7

Unique early 17th-century black-and-white timbered farmhouse with many original features, including stone-tiled roofs and vernacular barns. **Note**: open eight days a year. Available at other times as holiday cottage (0844 800 2070). Tea, coffee and cake available on open days.

Finding out more: 01568 782120 or www.nationaltrust.org.uk

Dudmaston Estate

Quatt, near Bridgnorth, Shropshire WV15 6QN

Map (4) I5

Enchanting wooded parkland, sweeping gardens and a house with a surprise, Dudmaston is something unexpected in the Shropshire countryside. In the Hall, still a family home by inheritance for over 850 years, you'll find atmospheric family rooms and unexpected art galleries created by the last owners, Sir George and Rachel Labouchere, displaying their differing contemporary and traditional collections. The gardens provide amazing vistas while the orchard is the perfect place to relax. For tranquillity and stunning views of the house, head to the Big Pool and Dingle, while the wider estate provides extensive walking and cycling routes for year-round enjoyment. **Note**: the family home of Mr and Mrs Mark Hamilton-Russell.

Eating and shopping: shop selling everything from gifts to estate charcoal and woodland craft products. Tea-room and Stable Snacks offering lunch and afternoon tea. Ice-cream parlour. Second-hand bookshop.

Making the most of your day: traditional outdoor games and children's woodland playground. Introductory talks and garden tours. Varied events throughout the open season. **Dogs**: welcome on leads in parkland and orchard only.

Access for all:
Building **Grounds**

The Hall on the Dudmaston Estate, Shropshire, is bathed in a magical golden light as the sun sets

The graceful Staircase Hall at Dudmaston

Getting here: 138:SO746887. 4 miles south-east of Bridgnorth. **Foot**: Hampton Loade car park to property. **Ferry**: Severn Valley Railway, via river ferry (occasional service). **Bus**: Bridgnorth to Kidderminster. **Train**: Hampton Loade (Severn Valley Railway) 1½ miles; Kidderminster 10 miles. **Road**: A442. **Parking**: House, Hampton Loade and The Holt (both pay and display).

Finding out more: 01746 780866 or dudmaston@nationaltrust.org.uk

Dudmaston Estate		M	T	W	T	F	S	S
Park, tea-room and shop								
17 Mar–28 Mar	11:30–5	M	T	W	T	·	·	S
31 Mar–30 Sep	11–5:30	M	T	W	T	·	·	S
1 Oct–31 Oct	11:30–5	M	T	W	T	·	·	S
2 Nov–15 Dec**	11:30–4	·	·	·	·	·	S	S
Galleries and second-hand bookshop								
17 Mar–28 Mar	1–5	M	T	W	T	·	·	S
1 Oct–31 Oct	1–5	M	T	W	T	·	·	S
House, galleries and second-hand bookshop*								
31 Mar–30 Sep	1–5:30	M	T	W	T	·	·	S
Garden								
17 Mar–28 Mar	12–5	M	T	W	T	·	·	S
31 Mar–30 Sep	12–5:30	M	T	W	T	·	·	S
1 Oct–31 Oct	12–5	M	T	W	T	·	·	S

*House and galleries open at 2 on Sundays. No entry to the car park before 11. **Dingle, tea-room and shop only open.

Duffield Castle

Milford Road, Duffield, Derbyshire DE56 4DW

Map ③ C4

Remains of one of England's largest 13th-century castles. **Note**: no toilets. Steep steps.

Finding out more: 01332 844052 or www.nationaltrust.org.uk. c/o Kedleston Hall, near Quarndon, Derbyshire DE22 5JH

Farnborough Hall

Farnborough, near Banbury, Oxfordshire OX17 1DU

Map ④ L7

Honey-coloured stone house with stunning library and treasures collected during the Grand Tour, surrounded by landscaped garden with country views. **Note**: occupied and administered by the Holbech family.

Finding out more: 01295 690002 or www.nationaltrust.org.uk

Entrance at Farnborough Hall in Oxfordshire

The Fleece Inn

Bretforton, near Evesham,
Worcestershire WR11 7JE

Map ④ K7

A half-timbered medieval farmhouse which originally sheltered a farmer and his stock, the inn was first licensed in 1848. Fully restored to its former glory, with witches' circles and precious pewter collection, it has developed a reputation for traditional folk music, morris dancing and asparagus.

Eating and shopping: finest local produce. Quality cask ales, including landlord's own. Local ciders and wines. Special asparagus menu between 23 April and 21 June.

Making the most of your day: events, including gigs, morris dancing and weekly folk sessions throughout year. Vintage and classic car events (May to September). Annual Asparagus Auction and festival day, plus annual Apple and Ale Festival (October).

Access for all: **Building**

The medieval Fleece Inn in Worcestershire

Getting here: 150:SP093437. In the village square in the centre of Bretforton. **Bus**: from Evesham to Chipping Campden. **Train**: Evesham 2½ miles. **Road**: 4 miles east of Evesham, on B4035. **Parking**: in village square only (not National Trust).

Finding out more: 01386 831173 or fleeceinn@nationaltrust.org.uk

The Fleece Inn
September: may close Monday and Tuesday, 3 to 6. June, July, August and Bank Holidays: open all day.

Grantham House

Castlegate, Grantham, Lincolnshire NG31 6SS

Map ③ E4

Handsome town house, one of the oldest buildings in Grantham, with riverside walled garden. **Note**: leased by the National Trust and the lessee is responsible for arrangements and facilities. Appointments may be needed.

Finding out more: 01476 564705 or www.nationaltrust.org.uk

Greyfriars' House and Garden

Friar Street, Worcester, Worcestershire WR1 2LZ

Map ④ J7

Set in the heart of historic Worcester, Greyfriars is a stunning timber-framed merchant's house – perfect for getting away from the hustle and bustle. This unique house and garden were rescued by two extraordinary people with a vision to revive this medieval gem and create a peaceful oasis.

Eating and shopping: refreshments served in the tranquil setting of the walled garden. Buy plants grown at nearby Hanbury Hall or pick up a second-hand book.

The Entrance Hall at Gunby Hall, Lincolnshire

Making the most of your day: activities, including garden games for all ages and conservation tours (Friday mornings). Children's activity room. Family events throughout year. **Dogs**: welcome in garden.

Access for all: 🈳️🖼️⚫️ Building 🏛️🖼️👤

Getting here: 150:SO852546. In centre of Worcester on Friar Street. **Bus**: from surrounding areas. **Train**: Worcester Foregate Street ½ mile. **Parking**: at Corn Market, Kings Street and Cathedral Plaza (pay and display). No onsite parking, park and ride service from city outskirts.

Finding out more: 01905 23571 or greyfriars@nationaltrust.org.uk

Greyfriars		M	T	W	T	F	S	S
House and garden								
19 Feb–21 Dec	1–5	·	T	W	T	F	S	·
Conservation tours								
22 Feb–20 Dec	11:30–12:30	·	·	·	·	F	·	·

Admission by timed ticket on busy days.
Open Bank Holiday Mondays.

Gunby Hall and Gardens

Gunby, Spilsby, Lincolnshire PE23 5SS

Map ③ G3

With links to Kipling and Darwin, and regarded by Tennyson as a Haunt of Ancient Peace, this splendid 18th-century house is a hidden gem. There is a magnificent music room, dining room and 3 hectares (8 acres) of grounds, including a wonderful rose garden, immaculate lawns and extensive vegetable gardens. **Note**: fully open for the first time as a National Trust property.

Eating and shopping: Courtyard tea-room offering homemade food, cake, as well as hot and cold drinks.

Making the most of your day: events throughout the year, from Rose Garden Days to Apple Days. Public footpaths run across the wider historic park and estate. **Dogs**: welcome on lead in the gardens and grounds.

Access for all: 📷📶⚫️ Building 🏛️ Grounds 🖼️

Getting here: 274:TF466673. 13 miles east of Horncastle. **Bus**: from Lincoln to Skegness via Horncastle. **Train**: Skegness 7 miles. **Parking**: free, 530 yards from entrance.

Finding out more: 01754 890102 or gunbyhall@nationaltrust.org.uk

Gunby Hall and Gardens		M	T	W	T	F	S	S
Gardens and tea-room								
2 Mar–30 Oct	11–5	M	T	W	·	·	S	S
Hall								
3 Mar–1 May	11–5	·	·	W	·	·	·	S
5 May–28 Aug	11–5	M	T	W	·	·	·	S
1 Sep–30 Oct	11–5	·	·	W	·	·	·	S
Gardens and tea-room								
2 Nov–15 Dec	11–4	·	·	·	·	·	S	S

Property may close at dusk if earlier than times stated due to safety considerations.

Gunby Hall Estate: Monksthorpe Chapel

Monksthorpe, near Spilsby,
Lincolnshire PE23 5PP

Map ③ G3   ⊞

Remote late 17th-century Baptist chapel.

Finding out more: 01754 890102
or www.nationaltrust.org.uk

Hanbury Hall and Gardens

School Road, Hanbury, Droitwich Spa,
Worcestershire WR9 7EA

Map ④ J6   🏠🌸🏊🛏🔔🍴

William and Mary-style house – built in 1701
by Thomas Vernon, lawyer and Whig MP for
Worcester – containing a fascinating mix of
interiors, including the restored Hercules rooms
and re-created Gothic corridor, smoking room
and magnificent staircase wall-paintings by Sir
James Thornhill. Surrounding the house are
eight hectares (20 acres) of re-created early
18th-century gardens and 162 hectares
(400 acres) of park. Features include the
intricately laid out parterre, fruit garden, grove,
orangery, orchard and bowling green. Park walks
lead out into the surrounding countryside.

Eating and shopping: extended gardening
range and plants grown in walled garden
for sale. Tea-room serving meals using local
produce. Outdoor stables café.

Making the most of your day: regular garden
tours and introductory talks. Varied events,
including family activity days, concerts,
open-air theatre, art exhibitions and
themed weekends. Park walks leaflet.
Dogs: in car park and park only.

Hanbury Hall, Worcestershire: magnificent wall-paintings

Access for all: 🅿️♿🚻📖🚻♿🅰️
Building ♿♿♿ Grounds ♿♿➡️

Getting here: 150:SO943637. 4 miles east of Droitwich Spa. **Foot**: public footpaths cross the park. **Bus**: Worcester to Birmingham (passing close Droitwich Spa ▤), alight Wychbold (2 miles via footpaths, 4 miles via lanes). **Train**: Droitwich Spa 4 miles. **Road**: From M5 junction 5 follow A38 to Droitwich; from Droitwich 4 miles along B4090. **Parking**: free, 150 yards.

Finding out more: 01527 821214 or hanburyhall@nationaltrust.org.uk

Hanbury Hall and Gardens		M	T	W	T	F	S	S
House*, gardens, park, shop and tea-room								
5 Jan–11 Feb	11–4	M	·	·	·	·	S	S
House*, gardens, park, shop, tea-room and play area								
16 Feb–30 May	11–5	M	T	W	T	·	S	S
1 Jun–5 Sep	10:30–5	M	T	W	T	F	S	S
7 Sep–4 Nov	11–5	M	T	W	T	·	S	S
9 Nov–22 Dec	11–4	M	·	·	·	·	S	S
Gardens, park, shop and tea-room								
1 Jan	11–4	·	T	·	·	·	·	·
26 Dec–31 Dec	11–4	M	T	·	T	F	S	S

*16 February to 4 November: house admission by guided tour until 1 (last tour leaves at 12:15), 1 to 5 free-flow. Property closed 26 July. 5 January to 11 February, 9 November to 1 December: house admission by tour 11:30 to 3:30 (limited access and tickets). All tour tickets allocated on arrival (non-bookable). 7 to 22 December: limited free-flow access. Admission by timed ticket on busy days. Bank Holiday Mondays: free-flow access, 11 to 5. Property open Good Friday. Property closes dusk if earlier.

Checking the flour at Stainsby Mill in Derbyshire

Making the most of your day: National Mills weekend (May). **Dogs**: on leads in Hardwick Park only.

Hardwick Estate: Stainsby Mill

Doe Lea, Chesterfield, Derbyshire S44 5RW

Map ③ D3 🏠

Fully operational watermill, giving a vivid evocation of the workplace of a 19th-century miller. Flour is ground regularly and is for sale throughout the season. **Note**: nearest toilet at Hardwick Hall.

Eating and shopping: Stainsby freshly milled flour for sale. Restaurant and shop at nearby Hardwick Hall.

Access for all: 📷📖🚻♿🅰️
Building ♿ Grounds ♿♿

Getting here: 120:SK455653. 6½ miles west of Mansfield. **Foot**: Rowthorne Trail and Teversal Trail nearby. **Bus**: from Chesterfield, alight Glapwell 'Young Vanish', 1½ miles. **Train**: Chesterfield 7 miles. **Road**: M1 exit 29, A6175 signposted Clay Cross, first left, left again to Stainsby Mill. **Sat Nav**: do not use. **Parking**: free, limited (not National Trust).

Finding out more: 01246 850430 or stainsbymill@nationaltrust.org.uk

Hardwick Estate: Stainsby Mill		M	T	W	T	F	S	S
16 Feb–3 Nov	10–4	·	·	W	T	F	S	S

Open Bank Holiday Mondays.

The Herb Garden, with the late 16th-century Hardwick Hall beyond, Derbyshire

Please display current sticker for free parking (and show card when asked)

Hardwick Hall

Doe Lea, Chesterfield, Derbyshire S44 5QJ

Map ③ D3　🏠🍴✳️🎒🚪🔔🔊🍷

The Hardwick Estate is made up of stunning houses and beautiful landscapes that have been created by a cast of thousands. It was the formidable Bess of Hardwick who first built Hardwick Hall in the late 16th century. In the centuries since then gardeners, builders, decorators, embroiderers and craftsmen of all kinds have contributed and made Hardwick their creation. We want you to explore and enjoy Hardwick and in the process discover the lives, loves and adventures of the builders of Hardwick. **Note**: Old Hall is owned by the National Trust and administered by English Heritage (01246 850431).

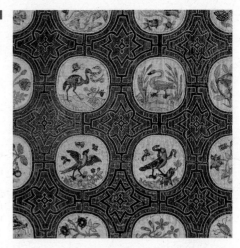

Eating and shopping: Great Barn restaurant. Stable gift shop. Plant sales and outdoor shop.

Making the most of your day: family trails, Tracker Packs and 'Hands-on Hardwick' family activities. Events, including Living History days and Conservation in Action, as well as daily tours and talks (when the house is open), garden tours, fishing and circular walks through the picturesque parkland. **Dogs**: on leads and in park and car park only.

Access for all: 🅿️♿🚻♿♿📷📹♿📷
Hall ♿♿♿　Garden ➡️♿

Getting here: 120:SK463638. 6½ miles west of Mansfield. **Foot**: Rowthorne Trail; Teversal Trail. **Bus**: from Chesterfield, alight Glapwell 'Young Vanish', 1½ miles. **Train**: Chesterfield, 7 miles. **Road**: 8 miles south-east of Chesterfield; via A6175. Leave M1 exit 29, follow brown signs. **Sat Nav**: do not use. **Parking**: 600-space car park.

Finding out more: 01246 850430 or hardwickhall@nationaltrust.org.uk

Hardwick Hall		M	T	W	T	F	S	S
Hall*								
16 Feb–3 Nov	12–4:30	·	·	W	T	F	S	S
Garden, park, shop and restaurant**								
Open all year	9–6	M	T	W	T	F	S	S

*Hall: also open Bank Holiday Mondays (April to August).
**Closed 25 December. Stone Centre opens daily all year round. Christmas opening: 4 to 15 December, Wednesday to Sunday, 11 to 3. Property may close early if weather is bad during winter months.

Hardwick Hall: Blue Bedroom, above, embroidered panel, top

Hawford Dovecote

Hawford, Worcestershire WR3 7SG

Map (4) J6

Picturesque dovecote, which has survived virtually unaltered since the late 16th century, retaining many nesting boxes. **Note**: no toilet or tea-room. Park carefully to one side of lane.

Finding out more: 01527 821214 or www.nationaltrust.org.uk

Kedleston Hall, Derbyshire: the Marble Hall – inspired by Roman architecture – was designed by Robert Adam

Kedleston Hall

near Quarndon, Derby, Derbyshire DE22 5JH

Map (3) C4

Take a trip back in time to the 1760s at this spectacular Neo-classical mansion, framed by historic parkland. Designed for lavish entertaining and displaying an extensive collection of paintings, sculptures and original furnishings, Kedleston is a stunning example of the work of architect Robert Adam. The Curzon family, in residence, have lived at the Hall since the 12th century. Lord Curzon's Eastern Museum is a treasure trove of fascinating objects acquired on his travels in Asia and while Viceroy of India (1899 to 1905). Kedleston was used as a key location for the Hollywood blockbuster *The Duchess*.

Note: medieval All Saints church, containing many family monuments, run by the Churches Conservation Trust.

Eating and shopping: shop selling Kedleston souvenirs and local products. Plant sales. Restaurant serving recipes made using local produce, including Kedleston Park lamb. New garden shop.

Making the most of your day: events, including open-air theatre, antiques and food fairs (not National Trust) and Christmas craft fair. Family activities. Walks, talks and tours, including fishing pavilion, great west stable and pleasure grounds. **Dogs**: on leads in park and pleasure grounds.

Access for all: 🅿️ 🅳 ♿ ⓦⓒ 🔎 🅰️
🔲 📺 🎬 ⏺ 🅰️ Ground floor 🔶 ♿
State floor 🔶 ♿ Grounds ➡️

Getting here: 128:SK312403. 5 miles north-west of Derby, 12 miles south-east of Ashbourne. **Cycle**: parkland roads only. **Bus**: Derby to Ashbourne, summer Saturdays only, otherwise alight the Smithy, 1 mile. **Train**: Duffield 3½ miles; Derby 5½ miles. **Road**: at intersection of A52/ A38, follow A38 (north). Take first exit along Kedleston Road towards Quarndon. **Sat Nav**: may misdirect, follow brown signs instead. **Parking**: 200 yards.

Finding out more: 01332 842191 or kedlestonhall@nationaltrust.org.uk

Kedleston Hall		M	T	W	T	F	S	S
House								
16 Feb–7 Mar*	12–3	M	T	W	T	·	S	S
9 Mar–31 Oct	12–5	M	T	W	T	·	S	S
Park and Pleasure Grounds								
Open all year	10–4	M	T	W	T	F	S	S
9 Mar–31 Oct	10–6	M	T	W	T	F	S	S
Restaurant and shop								
5 Jan–10 Feb	11–3	·	·	·	·	·	S	S
16 Feb–31 Oct	10:30–5	M	T	W	T	·	S	S
22 Jul–1 Sep	10:30–5	M	T	W	T	F	S	S
2 Nov–1 Dec	11–3	·	·	·	·	·	S	S
5 Dec–22 Dec	11–3	·	·	·	T	F	S	S
26 Dec–31 Dec	11–3	M	T	·	T	F	S	S

Last entry to house 45 minutes before closing. *House entry by guided tour only, every 30 minutes from 12 to 3 (spaces limited, booking on day). Open Good Friday. Park closes occasionally November to February. Closed 25 December. 17 to 19 May: large folk festival in parkland.

Kinver Edge and the Rock Houses

Holy Austin Rock Houses, Compton Road, Kinver, near Stourbridge, Staffordshire DY7 6DL

Map ④ I5   🏠 🏛️ 🍴 ♿ 🍽️

The Holy Austin Rock Houses, which were inhabited until the 1950s, are truly unique. Come and find out about the extraordinary people who carved a home for themselves in this famous sandstone ridge. There is an extra treat if you walk onto Kinver Edge – dramatic views stretching across three counties.

The heathland of Kinver Edge, Staffordshire

Eating and shopping: Rock Houses tea-room.

Making the most of your day: Family Explorer Backpacks for hire. Trails and information. Miles of woodland and heathland walks. New events and activities. **Dogs**: on leads within Rock Houses grounds.

Access for all: 🅿️ 🅳 🅰️ 🎬 ⏺ 🅰️
Building 🔶 Grounds 🔶

Getting here: 138:SO836836. Near Kinver village, 4 miles west of Stourbridge. **Bus**: Merry Hill bus station to Kinver. **Train**: Stourbridge town 5 miles. **Road**: Rock Houses signposted from Kinver High Street. **Parking**: by Warden's Lodge, Comber Road for the Edge and Compton Road for the Rock Houses.

Finding out more: 01384 872553 or kinveredge@nationaltrust.org.uk

Kinver Edge and the Rock Houses	M	T	W	T	F	S	S
Rock Houses							
28 Feb–22 Nov	2–4				T	F		
2 Mar–24 Nov	11–4						S	S
Tea-room							
28 Feb–24 Nov	11–4				T	F	S	S
Countryside							
Open all year		M	T	W	T	F	S	S

Open Bank Holiday Mondays. Lower Rock Houses open for guided weekday tours (March to November), by arrangement (groups of ten or over).

The extraordinary Rock Houses, Staffordshire

Kinwarton Dovecote

Kinwarton, near Alcester,
Warwickshire B49 6HB

Map (4) K7

Rare 14th-century circular dovecote with metre-thick walls, hundreds of nesting holes and original rotating ladder. **Note:** stock may be grazing. No toilet.

Finding out more: 01789 400777
or www.nationaltrust.org.uk

Knowles Mill

Dowles Brook, Bewdley,
Worcestershire DY12 2LX

Map (4) I6

Dating from the 18th century, the mill retains much of its machinery, including the frames of an overshot waterwheel. **Note:** mill open daily, but Mill Cottage not open to visitors (please respect the resident's privacy). No toilets or tea-room. No parking at Mill Cottage.

Finding out more: 01527 821214
or www.nationaltrust.org.uk.
Hanbury Hall, School Road, Droitwich Spa,
Worcestershire WR9 7EA

Letocetum Roman Baths and Museum

Watling Street, Wall, near Lichfield,
Staffordshire WS14 0AW

Map (4) K5

Remains of a once-important Roman staging post and settlement, including *mansio* (Roman inn) and bath-house. **Note:** in the guardianship of English Heritage.

Finding out more: 0121 625 6820 (English Heritage) or www.nationaltrust.org.uk

Letocetum Roman Baths in Staffordshire

Lyveden New Bield

near Oundle, Northamptonshire PE8 5AT

Map ③ E6

Set in the heart of rural Northamptonshire, the mysterious Lyveden is a remarkable survival of the Elizabethan age. Visitors can explore Sir Thomas Tresham's garden, which has remained incomplete since work was abandoned in 1605, then learn about the hidden symbols of his Catholic faith and the family's involvement with the infamous Gunpowder Plot. Our audio guide will tell you all about Tresham's dream and the troubled history of one of Northamptonshire's most famous families, then you can stroll through one of the oldest gardens in England and see the atmospheric garden lodge, which was destined never to be finished.

Eating and shopping: ice-cream available. Shop selling drinks and local honey (seasonal). Picnics welcome.

Making the most of your day: garden tours (weekends, May to October). Garden labyrinth and Elizabethan orchard. The Lyveden Way and Rockingham Forest. **Dogs**: welcome on leads only.

Access for all: ♿ 🚻 ♿ ⦿ ⦿
Building ♿ Grounds ♿

Getting here: 141:SP983853. 3 miles east of Brigstock and 4 miles south-west of Oundle.
Foot: Lyveden Way passes though Lyveden and connects with Wadenhoe and Fermyn Woods.
Bus: from Northampton ➤ to Peterborough ➤.
Train: Kettering 10 miles. **Road**: off A6116. From Oundle take A427. **Parking**: free, 100 yards.

Finding out more: 01832 205358 or lyveden@nationaltrust.org.uk

Lyveden New Bield		M	T	W	T	F	S	S
2 Feb–10 Mar	11–4						S	S
13 Mar–27 Oct	10:30–5			W	T	F	S	S
1 May–29 Sep	10:30–5	M	T	W	T	F	S	S
2 Nov–1 Dec	11–4						S	S

Open Bank Holidays. Open Good Friday, 10:30 to 5.

Mysterious Lyveden New Bield, Northamptonshire

Middle Littleton Tithe Barn

Middle Littleton, Evesham,
Worcestershire WR11 8LN

Map (4) K7

The largest and finest restored 13th-century tithe barn in the country. **Note**: no toilet.

Finding out more: 01905 371006
or www.nationaltrust.org.uk

Morville Hall

Morville, near Bridgnorth,
Shropshire WV16 5NB

Map (4) I5

Beautiful stone-built house set in attractive gardens – of Elizabethan origin and enlarged and expanded around 1750. **Note**: admission by written appointment directly to the tenants, Dr and Mrs C. Douglas. Dower House garden also open (not National Trust).

Finding out more: 01746 780838
or www.nationaltrust.org.uk

Children examine a bee-bole in the orchard wall at Moseley Old Hall in Staffordshire

Members may have to pay on special events days

Moseley Old Hall

Moseley Old Hall Lane, Fordhouses,
Wolverhampton, Staffordshire WV10 7HY

Map (4) J5

This atmospheric Elizabethan farmhouse
conceals a priest's hole and hiding places,
where Charles II hid while on the run after
being defeated at the Battle of Worcester in
1651. You can also see the bed on which the
royal fugitive slept and discover how the King
escaped from Cromwell's troops, then find out
about 17th-century domestic life in this friendly
and fascinating historic home. The Hall is an
integral part of the Monarch's Way Trail.

The garden has plant varieties in keeping with
the period and a striking knot garden following
a 17th-century design.

Eating and shopping: tea-room serving light
lunches and cakes. Shop selling gifts and
plants. Second-hand bookshop.

Making the most of your day: events and
activities all year, including tours, family
events, demonstrations and re-creations of
17th-century life. Children's activities on family
event days and Mondays and Tuesdays in
August. Tracker Packs. **Dogs**: welcome on leads
in garden and grounds.

Access for all: ⟦P⟧⟦D⟧⟦WC⟧⟦⟧⟦⟧⟦⟧⟦⟧⟦⟧
House ⟦⟧⟦⟧   **Grounds** ⟦⟧⟦⟧➡⟦⟧

Getting here: 127:SJ932044. 4 miles north
of Wolverhampton. **Bus**: regular service from
Wolverhampton or Cannock; both ½ mile.
Road: south of M54; from north on M6 leave at
exit 11, then A460; from south on M6 and M54
take exit 1. **Parking**: free, no coach parking.

Finding out more: 01902 782808 or
moseleyoldhall@nationaltrust.org.uk

Moseley Old Hall		M	T	W	T	F	S	S
16 Feb–13 Mar	11–3			W			S	S
16 Mar–30 Jun	11–5			W			S	S
1 Jul–8 Sep	11–5	M	T	W			S	S
11 Sep–3 Nov	11–5			W			S	S
6 Nov–22 Dec	11–3			W			S	S

House: opens at 12, with entry by guided tour until 1,
then guided tour or free-flow. No tours on Bank Holiday
Mondays. Open Saturday to Wednesday during all local
half-terms, check dates on website. February, November
and December opening, guided tours.

Moseley Old Hall, Staffordshire, the knot garden

The Old Manor

Norbury, Ashbourne, Derbyshire DE6 2ED

Map (3) B4

Medieval hall featuring a rare king post,
Tudor door and 17th-century Flemish glass.
Note: limited parking (cars only).

Finding out more: 01283 585337
or www.nationaltrust.org.uk

Packwood House

Packwood Lane, Lapworth,
Warwickshire B94 6AT

Map ④ K6 🏠✿🍴☂

Surrounded by beautiful gardens and countryside, Packwood was described by a guest in the 1920s as 'a house to dream of, a garden to dream in'. Lovingly restored at the beginning of the 20th century by Graham Baron Ash, the house contains a wonderful collection of 16th-century furniture and textiles. The newly restored 18th-century gentleman's kitchen garden includes herbs, flowers and vegetables used for dyes, perfumes and medicines as well as food. This year you can explore Packwood's tapestry collection and new artwork in the park. **Note**: closed until late spring, due to building works.

Eating and shopping: gift shop selling seasonal gifts, local foods and plants (many grown here). Light refreshments available from kiosk. New café and visitor centre due to open in the autumn. Picnics welcome.

Making the most of your day: events, including Family Fun every holiday, open-air theatre and evening garden tours. Trails, workshops and talks. Baddesley Clinton and Coughton Court nearby. **Dogs**: welcome on leads in car park and on public footpaths.

Access for all: 🅿️ 🄳 🚾 🏛 ⠿
House 🦽🦼🦽 Grounds 🦽🦼🦽

Getting here: 139:SP174723. 1½ miles from Lapworth. **Foot**: Millennium Way crosses the park. **Bus**: from Birmingham to Stratford-upon-Avon, alight Hockley Heath. **Train**: Lapworth 1½ miles. **Road**: 6 miles south of M42 exit 5, 11 miles south-east of central Birmingham. **Parking**: free, 100 yards.

Finding out more: 01564 782024 or packwood@nationaltrust.org.uk

Packwood House		M	T	W	T	F	S	S
House, shop, garden and park								
1 May–19 Jul	11–5	·	T	W	T	F	S	S
20 Jul–1 Sep	11–5	M	T	W	T	F	S	S
3 Sep–3 Nov	11–5	·	T	W	T	F	S	S
Café, shop and park*								
5 Nov–31 Dec	11–5	·	T	W	T	F	S	S

Open Bank Holiday Mondays with admission to the house by timed ticket (not bookable). *Tours of the house and garden in November and December. Closed 25 December.

Above and top, Packwood House in Warwickshire

Peak District: Dark Peak

near Hope Valley, Derbyshire

Map ③ B2

The estate stretches from the heather-clad moors of Kinder to the gritstone tors of Derwent Edge, from the peat bogs of Bleaklow to the limestone crags of Winnats Pass. The wild Pennine moorlands are of international importance for their populations of breeding birds and mosaic of habitats. Sites of particular interest include Mam Tor, with spectacular views, landslip and prehistoric settlement, and the famous Snake Pass. Kinder Scout, where the Mass Trespass of 1932 took place, is the highest point for 50 miles. The Trust also owns several farms and a café in the beautiful Edale Valley. Note: nearest toilet in adjacent villages and at visitor centres at Ladybower Reservoir, Edale, Castleton.

Eating and shopping: Penny Pot Café in Edale serving breakfast, lunch and tea.

Making the most of your day: events all year. New downloadable walking and audio trails. Geocaching and podcasts available. Waymarked walks. Edale Visitor Centre and information barns. Camp at Upper Booth Farm, Edale. Dogs: on leads at all times from early March to end July.

Access for all: P♿ [WC] [♿] [♿]

Getting here: 110:SK100855. Peak District National Park. Foot: Pennine Way and miles of footpaths. Cycle: Pennine Bridleway and many other routes. Bus: from Sheffield, Bakewell and Manchester to Castleton, Edale and Hope Valley. Train: Edale for Kinder Scout and Mam Tor; Chinley for Kinder Scout west; Hope for Losehill; Bamford for Upper Derwent Valley. Road: A57 Sheffield to Manchester, A625 Hope Valley. Parking: pay and display at Mam Nick (SK123833). Other pay and display at Edale, Castleton, Bowden Bridge, Upper Derwent Valley and Hayfield (not National Trust).

Finding out more: 01433 670368 or peakdistrict@nationaltrust.org.uk. Dark Peak Estate Office, Edale End, Hope Valley, Derbyshire S33 6RF

Above and top, enjoying the Peak District, Derbyshire

Dark Peak		M	T	W	T	F	S	S
Penny Pot Café								
5 Jan–10 Mar	10–4:30						S	S
13 Mar–3 Nov	10–4:30			W	T	F	S	S
1 Jul–1 Sep	10–4:30	M	T	W	T	F	S	S
25 May–15 Sep	8:30–4:30						S	S
9 Nov–22 Dec	10–4						S	S
27 Dec–31 Dec	10–4	M	T			F	S	S
Estate								
Open all year		M	T	W	T	F	S	S

Open all year: Information shelters at Lee Barn (SK096855) and Dalehead (SK101843) in Edale; South Head (SK060854) at Kinder; Edale End (SK161864); Grindle Barns above Ladybower Reservoir (SK189895). Mam Nick car park (SK123832). Dalehead Bunkhouse (01433 670368); camping and bed and breakfast available at some farms.

Peak District: Longshaw and Eastern Moors

Longshaw, near Sheffield, Derbyshire

Map ③ C2

Longshaw offers spectacular views of the Peak District, with ancient woods, meadows, parkland, heather moorland and many unusual sites – from millstone quarries to packhorse routes. The adjacent Eastern Moors, managed in partnership with the RSPB, offers a good network of footpaths and fantastic views.
Note: Moorland Discovery Centre only open to the public for certain events and during school holidays.

Eating and shopping: Longshaw tea-room and shop selling local and wildlife-themed products and dishes made with local and kitchen garden produce.

Making the most of your day: events all year, including seasonal family events and trails. Circular, waymarked walks and woodland and geocaching trail. Wildlife webcams in Visitor Centre. Holiday cottage. **Dogs**: welcome on estate on leads from early March to end of July.

Access for all: ⓟ♿ Ⓓ♿ ☜ ☝ ♿ 🅿 ⓙ
Building 🏢 Grounds ⬇️🏢➡️

Getting here: 110/119:SK266800. 7½ miles from Sheffield. **Foot**: 2 miles Grindleford, 3 miles Hathersage. **Cycle**: from Sheffield via Moss Road and Houndkirk bridleways. **Bus**: services from Sheffield to Castleton ➡️, Matlock and Buxton ➡️. **Train**: Grindleford 2 miles. **Road**: A625 Sheffield to Hathersage road; Woodcroft car park off B6055, near junction with A625. **Parking**: at Haywood (110/119: SK256778), Wooden Pole (110/119: SK267790), Woodcroft (110/119: SK267802). All pay and display.

Finding out more: 01433 637904 (Longshaw). 01433 630316 (Eastern Moors) or peakdistrict@nationaltrust.org.uk. Estate Office, Longshaw Estate, Longshaw, Sheffield, Derbyshire S11 7TZ

Longshaw and Eastern Moors		M	T	W	T	F	S	S
Tea-room and shop								
1 Jan–6 Jan	10:30–4	·	T	W	T	F	S	S
12 Jan–10 Feb	10:30–4	·	·	·	·	·	S	S
11 Feb–3 Nov	10:30–5	·	M	T	W	T	F	S	S
4 Nov–23 Dec	10:30–4	M	T	W	T	F	S	S
27 Dec–31 Dec	10:30–4	M	T	·	·	F	S	S
Estate								
Open all year		M	T	W	T	F	S	S

Last orders in the tea-room 30 minutes before closing.
White Edge Lodge not open to the public (holiday let).
Closed 24 to 26 December.

Peak District, Derbyshire: heather moorland

Peak District: White Peak

Ilam, Ashbourne, Derbyshire and Peak District

Map ③ B3

White Peak Estate is situated in the spectacular setting of the Staffordshire and Derbyshire Peak District. You can explore the rich daleside grasslands and ash woodlands in dramatic Dovedale and enjoy Ilam Park's beautiful location beside the River Manifold. The tea-room has amazing views of Dovedale, and there is a shop and visitor centre with changing exhibitions. We have a caravan site at

Places may occasionally close for conservation, safety or events

Children enjoy the fabulous views while taking a well-earned rest at beautiful Dovedale in Derbyshire

Ilam Park and holiday cottages at Wetton Mill in the magnificent Manifold Valley. This is the perfect base to explore other parts of the White Peak Estate, such as Winster Market House. **Note**: Ilam Hall is let to the Youth Hostel Association.

Eating and shopping: tea-rooms at Manifold, Ilam Park and Wetton Mill (not National Trust). Gift shop at Ilam Park and mobile barn at Dovedale. Peak District farm shop selling award-winning meat.

Making the most of your day: guided walks, talks and exhibitions. New walks postcards (in shop). Downloadable walking trails, geocaches, audio trails and podcasts. **Dogs**: under close control and on leads in areas with livestock.

Access for all: ▣▣▣▣▣▣▣
Ilam Park stableyard ▣▣ Winster Market House ▣
Ilam Park grounds ▣▣▣➡▣

Getting here: 119:SK132507 (Ilam Park), 119:SK152514 (Dovedale), 119:SK241606 (Winster Market House). Ilam Park and Dovedale are 4½ miles north-west of Ashbourne. Winster Market House, Winster village, 4 miles west of Matlock.

Cycle: NCN68, 2 miles. **Bus**: for Ilam and Dovedale: services from Buxton ☰ to Ashbourne, daily, alight Thorpe, 2 miles. For Winster Market House from Bakewell to Matlock ☰, daily. **Parking**: Ilam Park (pay and display).

Finding out more: 01335 350503 or peakdistrict@nationaltrust.org.uk. White Peak Estate Office, Home Farm, Ilam, Ashbourne, Derbyshire DE6 2AZ

White Peak		M	T	W	T	F	S	S
Dovedale mobile barn								
29 Mar–29 Sep	11–5	M	T	W	T	F	S	S
Ilam Park shop								
5 Jan–10 Feb	11–4	·	·	·	·	·	S	S
11 Feb–3 Nov	11–5	M	T	W	T	F	S	S
8 Nov–22 Dec	11–4	·	·	·	·	F	S	S
23 Dec–30 Dec	11–4	M	·	·	T	F	S	S
Ilam Park tea-room								
5 Jan–10 Feb	11–4	·	·	·	·	·	S	S
11 Feb–3 Nov	10:30–5	M	T	W	T	F	S	S
9 Nov–22 Dec	11–4	·	·	·	·	·	S	S
23 Dec–30 Dec	11–4	M	·	·	T	F	S	S
Winster Market House								
30 Mar–3 Nov	11–5	M	T	W	T	F	S	S

Call for shop and tea-room Christmas opening. Closed 24 and 25 December. Ilam Hall: available for overnight accommodation via Youth Hostel Association, 01335 350212. Ilam Bunkhouse open all year.

Priest's House, Easton on the Hill

Easton on the Hill, near Stamford, Northamptonshire PE9 3LS

Map ③ E5　

Small late 15th-century building, with interesting local architecture and museum exploring Easton on the Hill's industrial past.

Finding out more: 01780 762619 or www.nationaltrust.org.uk

Rosedene

Victoria Road, Dodford, near Bromsgrove, Worcestershire B61 9BU

Map ④ J6

Restored 1840s cottage, organic garden and orchard illustrating the mid-19th century Chartist movement. **Note**: available to hire as a 'back to basics' holiday cottage. Visit by booked tours only (first Sunday of March to December).

Finding out more: 01527 821214 or www.nationaltrust.org.uk

Rosedene, Worcestershire: simple Chartist cottage

Shugborough Estate

Milford, near Stafford, Staffordshire ST17 0XB

Map ④ J4

Shugborough is the ancestral home of the Earls of Lichfield. With rumoured connections to the Holy Grail, the 364-hectare (900-acre) classical landscape is peppered with unusual monuments. The fine Georgian mansion house, with magnificent views over riverside garden terraces, features stunning porcelain collections. Costumed characters work in the servants' quarters and farmstead, doing laundry, cheese-making, milling, brewing and baking. It is in these areas that the Staffordshire County Council Museum collections are held, including puppets, reconstructed chemist shop, tailors' shop and Victorian schoolroom. In addition, the newly restored walled garden grows historic varieties of fruit and vegetables. **Note**: run by Staffordshire County Council. Only house and gardens are free to members. Parking pay and display (including members). Refunded on purchase of all-sites ticket.

Eating and shopping: licensed tea-room. Gift shop. Ice-cream parlour. Old-fashioned sweet shop. Craft outlets making and selling handmade goods.

Making the most of your day: events all year, including craft fairs, open-air theatre, themed weekends and family fun. **Dogs**: on leads in parkland and gardens only.

Access for all:
Building　Grounds

Getting here: 127:SJ992225. 6 miles east of Stafford. **Foot**: access from the canal/Great Haywood side of the estate. Estate walks link to towpaths along Trent & Mersey Canal and Staffordshire & Worcestershire Canal and to Cannock Chase trails. On Staffordshire Way. **Bus**: Stafford ☒ to Lichfield ☒. **Train**: Rugeley Trent Valley 3 miles; Stafford 6 miles. **Road**: on A513, entrance at Milford. Signposted from M6 junction 13. **Parking**: £3 (pay and display, including members). Refunded on purchase of an all-sites ticket.

The west front of Shugborough Hall, Staffordshire, seen from across the River Sow at sunset. Samuel Wyatt's extended end pavilions and projecting central bow are all reflected in the water

Finding out more: 0845 459 8900 or shugborough@nationaltrust.org.uk

Shugborough Estate		M	T	W	T	F	S	S
House, servants' quarters, farm, walled garden								
22 Mar–25 Oct	11–5	M	·	W	T	F	S	S
Parkland and gardens								
22 Mar–25 Oct	10–6	M	T	W	T	F	S	S
Tea-room and shop								
22 Mar–25 Oct	11–5	M	T	W	T	F	S	S
Shop								
26 Oct–22 Dec	11–4	M	T	W	T	F	S	S

Access to house by guided tour only 11 to 1.

Staunton Harold Church

Staunton Harold Estate, Ashby-de-la-Zouch, Leicestershire LE65 1RW

Map ③ C4　✠

One of the few churches built between the outbreak of the English Civil War and the Restoration period. **Note**: toilets 500 yards (not National Trust). Parking not National Trust; Staunton Harold Estate, charges apply.

Finding out more: 01332 863822 (Calke Abbey) or www.nationaltrust.org.uk

Mr Straw's House

5-7 Blyth Grove, Worksop,
Nottinghamshire S81 0JG

Map ③ D2

Help us celebrate 90 years since the
Straw family moved into this Edwardian,
semi-detached house, which has remained
virtually unchanged since 1923. The Straws
threw little away and chose to live without
many of the modern comforts we take for
granted. Their eagerness to preserve the house
means that it maintains its original 1920s decor
and everyday objects they cherished. This
life-sized time capsule has delighted guests for
20 years, providing a rare glimpse of treasured
objects from times gone by. As the house is
rather cosy we operate timed tickets and ask
visitors to contact us to avoid disappointment.

Eating and shopping: shop selling jam,
biscuits, plants, souvenirs and gifts. New coffee
area. Picnic benches. Tea and cakes available
in orchard on first Saturday of each month
(provided by Friends of Mr Straw's House).

Making the most of your day: special tours
and events and activity days all year. Exhibition.

Access for all: 👤 ⠿ Ⓐ
Buildings 👤👥 **Garden** 👤

Getting here: 120:SK592802. On private road
in suburbs north of Worksop town centre.
Cycle: NCN6, ¾ mile. **Bus**: from Worksop.
Train: Worksop ⇌. **Road**: follow signs for
Bassetlaw Hospital and Blyth Road (B6045).
Blyth Grove is a small private road off B6045,
just south of Bassetlaw Hospital A and E
entrance. Signposted with black and white sign
at the entrance to Blyth Grove. **Parking**: free.

Finding out more: 01909 482380 or
mrstrawshouse@nationaltrust.org.uk

Mr Straw's House		M	T	W	T	F	S	S
12 Mar–28 Mar	11–5	.	T	W	T	F	S	.
30 Mar–2 Nov	11–5	.	T	W	T	F	S	.

Admission by timed ticket, preferably booked in advance by
telephone or email; on quiet days same-day telephone call
may be sufficient. Last tours start at 4. Closed Good Friday.
November to March: special behind-the-scenes events.

Above and top, Mr Straw's House in Nottinghamshire

Sudbury Hall and the National Trust Museum of Childhood

Sudbury, Ashbourne, Derbyshire DE6 5HT

Map (3) B4

Sudbury, a place to share stories of vision and imagination, where you can enjoy a grand, 17th-century family home and prize-winning museum in one day out. Sudbury Hall is the country home of the Lords Vernon and a stunning example of 17th-century craftsmanship, featuring exquisite plasterwork, wood carvings and classical story-based murals. The Museum of Childhood is a delight for all ages, with something for everyone. You can journey through childhood with our collection, reminisce about the games you used to play, and attend a lesson in the Victorian schoolroom, before having a go at being a chimney sweep.

Eating and shopping: two shops selling toys and gifts. Tea-room serving seasonal menus and latte or cappuccino.

Making the most of your day: for children, there are hands-on toys in the museum, a woodland play area and family activities during the school holidays. We also offer morning tours of the Hall and there are naturalised gardens to enjoy. Kedleston Hall is nearby. **Dogs**: assistance dogs only.

Sudbury Hall, Derbyshire: the magnificent Long Gallery

Having fun at The Museum of Childhood, Derbyshire

Sunnycroft

200 Holyhead Road, Wellington,
Telford, Shropshire TF1 2DR

Map ④ I4   🏠🌼

This rare suburban villa and mini estate, tucked away in Wellington, is an Edwardian time capsule. Its original contents and features will transport you back to the pre-First World War 'country-house' lifestyle. Sunnycroft tells the story of a brewer, a widow and three generations of a local industrialist family. **Note**: no credit or debit card facilities.

Eating and shopping: Smoking Room tea-room serving light lunch and afternoon tea. Second-hand bookshop. Sunnycroft souvenirs available. Picnic on the lawn.

Making the most of your day: events reflecting Sunnycroft's heyday, including traditional Easter Egg hunt, garden fête (July), harvest-themed Michaelmas Fair (September) and Edwardian Christmas. Free guided tours. Children's trails. **Dogs**: welcome on leads in grounds only.

Access for all: 🅿️🅳🅆️🖥️🚷
Building 🔨 Grounds 🦽➡️

Getting here: 127:SJ652109. In Wellington. **Cycle**: NCN81, 1 mile. **Bus**: from Telford (passing Wellington ➤). **Train**: Wellington ½ mile. **Road**: M54 junction 7, follow B5061 towards Wellington. **Sat Nav**: enter address not postcode. **Parking**: free, 150 yards. Additional free parking in Wrekin Road car park (not National Trust).

Finding out more: 01952 242884 or sunnycroft@nationaltrust.org.uk

Sunnycroft		M	T	W	T	F	S	S
5 Jan–24 Feb	10:30–3	·	·	·	·	·	S	S
1 Mar–4 Nov	10:30–5	M	·	·	·	F	S	S
9 Nov–8 Dec	10:30–3	·	·	·	·	·	S	S
14 Dec–22 Dec	10:30–4	M	T	W	T	F	S	S

March to November timed tickets with ten-minute introductory talk, then free-flow. Daily guided tours available (not bookable). Winter entry by guided tour only starting on the hour. Free-flow throughout house for Bank Holiday weekends, Christmas and event days. Last admission to house one hour before closing.

Access for all: 🅿️🅳🖥️♿🔨🦼
🚐🦽🔆🅾️ Hall 🔨♿ Museum 🦽↕️♿
Grounds 🔨🦽

Getting here: 128:SK158322. 6 miles east of Uttoxeter. **Cycle**: NCN54. **Bus**: from Derby or Burton to Uttoxeter. **Train**: Tutbury & Hatton 5 miles. **Road**: 6 miles east of Uttoxeter at junction of A50 Derby to Stoke and A515 Ashbourne. **Parking**: free, 500 yards.

Finding out more: 01283 585305 (Infoline). 01283 585337 or sudburyhall@nationaltrust.org.uk

Sudbury Hall		M	T	W	T	F	S	S
Hall								
16 Feb–3 Nov	1–5	·	·	W	T	F	S	S
Hall tours								
16 Feb–3 Nov	11:30–12	·	·	W	T	F	S	S
2 Apr–29 Oct	11:30–2:30	·	T	·	·	·	·	·
Museum, restaurant and shops								
16 Feb–31 Mar	11–5	·	·	W	T	F	S	S
1 Apr–3 Nov	11–5	M	T	W	T	F	S	S
7 Nov–15 Dec	11–4	·	·	·	T	F	S	S
Christmas event								
7 Dec–15 Dec	11–4	·	·	·	T	F	S	S
Restaurant and shops								
21 Dec–22 Dec	11–4	·	·	·	·	·	S	S
Grounds								
16 Feb–22 Dec	10–5	M	T	W	T	F	S	S

Open Bank Holidays. Last admission 45 minutes before closing (Hall will close early if light level is poor). Hall tours Wednesdays to Sundays between 11:30 and 12 and Tuesdays between 11:30 and 2:30. Not all rooms may be open as part of these tours.

Tattershall Castle

Sleaford Road, Tattershall,
Lincolnshire LN4 4LR

Map ③ F3   🏠🏛️🎣🔔

There are six floors to explore in this stunning red-brick medieval castle built by Ralph Cromwell, Lord Treasurer of England, in 1434. The castle has been a family home, a defensive tower and a cattle shed, before being saved from demolition by Lord Curzon of Kedleston in 1911. This iconic Lincolnshire landmark is a beautiful statement of 15th-century ambition and wealth, architecture and style. It is also a great place for watching the historic planes from the Battle of Britain Memorial Flight, based at nearby RAF Coningsby.

Eating and shopping: Guardhouse shop selling gifts and souvenirs, sandwiches, snacks, drinks and ice-cream. Picnics welcome.

Making the most of your day: events all year, including Hallowe'en walks, Christmas market. Free audio guide. Children's activities. Battle of Britain Memorial Flight Centre tours (weekday) nearby. **Dogs**: assistance dogs only.

Access for all: 🅿️♿️🚻👜📷📷📄
Building 🏠♿️🔓   Grounds 🏠♿️

Getting here: 122:TF211575. 10 miles south-west of Horncastle. **Cycle**: NCN1, 1 mile. **Bus**: from Lincoln to Boston (passing close Lincoln 🚆). **Train**: Ruskington 10 miles. **Road**: on south side of A153. **Parking**: free, 150 yards from entrance.

Finding out more: 01526 342543 or tattershallcastle@nationaltrust.org.uk

Tattershall Castle		M	T	W	T	F	S	S
2 Mar–30 Oct	11–5	M	T	W	·	·	S	S
2 Nov–15 Dec	11–4	·	·	·	·	·	S	S

Opens 1 some Saturdays if hosting a wedding.
Open Good Friday.

The Great Tower at Tattershall Castle, Lincolnshire.
Built in 1434, the castle was narrowly saved from
demolition in 1911 by Lord Curzon of Kedleston

Ulverscroft Nature Reserve

Ulverscroft, Copt Oak,
near Loughborough, Leicestershire

Map ③ D5

Part of the ancient forest of Charnwood, Ulverscroft is especially beautiful during the spring – with heathland and woodland habitats. **Note**: no toilet. Access by permit only from Leicestershire and Rutland Wildlife Trust (0116 272 0444).

Finding out more: 01332 863822
or www.nationaltrust.org.uk

Upton House and Gardens, Warwickshire: a series of full-height windows flood the Long Gallery with light

Upton House and Gardens

near Banbury, Warwickshire OX15 6HT

Map ④ L7

Welcome to Lord and Lady Bearsted's 1930s country residence, set among stunning terraced gardens. The atmosphere of the 1930s lifestyle is evoked by the sparkling art deco interiors, with masterpieces by Bosch, El Greco and Stubbs, iconic Sèvres tableware and 18th-century Chelsea figures – all collected by this millionaire oil magnate. Outside, on the south terrace, you can follow in the footsteps of Lady B's friend and garden designer, Kitty Lloyd Jones, as you stroll across the sweeping lawn, down the terraced Mediterranean banks to the mirror pool, then see what treats there are in the kitchen garden.

The exterior of Upton House and Gardens

Eating and shopping: restaurant serving lunch, morning coffee and afternoon tea. Plant centre. Gift shop selling souvenirs, sweets and books.

Making the most of your day: events, including jazz concerts and art. Garden/house tours. Family activities, including woodland adventures, games, treasure boxes and dressing-up. Displays of tulips (April), National Collection of Asters (September). Holiday cottages.
Dogs: assistance dogs only in grounds.

Access for all: ♿ 🅿️ 🖼️ ♿ 🚻 🔍 📷 💺 📖 ♿
:·: 🅰️ Building 🔁🔁🔁 Grounds 🔁🔁🔁

Getting here: 151:SP371461. On the edge of the Cotswolds, between Banbury and Stratford-upon-Avon. **Foot**: Footpath SM177 runs adjacent to property, Centenary Way ½ mile, Macmillan Way 1 mile. **Cycle**: NCN5, 5 miles. Oxfordshire Cycle Way 1½ miles. **Train**: Banbury 7 miles. **Road**: On A422, 7 miles north of Banbury, 12 miles south-east of Stratford-upon-Avon. Signed from junction 12 M40. **Parking**: 300 yards.

Finding out more: 01295 670266 or uptonhouse@nationaltrust.org.uk

Upton House and Gardens		M	T	W	T	F	S	S
House, gardens, shop and restaurant*								
12 Jan–10 Feb	12–4	·	·	·	·	·	S	S
16 Feb–21 Jul	11–5	M	T	W	·	F	S	S
22 Jul–1 Sep	11–5	M	T	W	T	F	S	S
2 Sep–3 Nov	11–5	M	T	W	·	F	S	S
4 Nov–22 Dec	12–4	M	·	·	·	F	S	S
Exhibition, Winter Walk, shop and restaurant								
1 Jan–6 Jan	12–4	·	T	W	T	F	S	S
26 Dec–31 Dec	12–4	M	T	·	T	F	S	S

*12 January to 10 February: house open with guided tours (limited access and numbers). 16 February to 3 November: house open with taster tours 11 to 1, free-flow 1 to 5. Timed tickets to all house tours available on arrival (non-bookable). Bank Holidays: house open 11 to 5 by timed tickets. 4 November to 10 February: gardens open as Winter Walk. Garden access may be restricted in wet weather.

The Weir

Swainshill, Hereford, Herefordshire HR4 7QF

Map ④ H7   🏛️ 🌸 ♨️

Stunning riverside garden and walled garden with sweeping views along the River Wye. Spectacular all year round, with drifts of spring bulbs which give way to summer wild flowers, followed by autumn colour and a walled garden full of fruit and vegetables. Worth a visit any time of year. **Note**: sturdy footwear recommended.

Eating and shopping: self-service tea and coffee available. Picnics welcome at the riverside picnic sites.

Making the most of your day: children's days (school holidays). Open-air theatre.
Dogs: assistance dogs only in garden (allowed on leads in car park).

Access for all: 🚻 Grounds 🔁🔁

Getting here: 149:SO438418. 5 miles west of Hereford. **Bus**: to Hereford and then taxi. **Train**: Hereford 5 miles. **Road**: on A438. **Parking**: free.

Finding out more: 01981 590509 (Infoline). 01568 782120 (Croft office) or theweir@nationaltrust.org.uk

The Weir		M	T	W	T	F	S	S
9 Feb–17 Feb	11–4	M	T	W	T	F	S	S
18 Feb–3 Nov	11–5	M	T	W	T	F	S	S

Last admission 45 minutes before closing.

Glasshouse at The Weir, Herefordshire

Wichenford Dovecote

Wichenford, Worcestershire WR6 6XY

Map (4) I7

Small but striking 17th-century half-timbered dovecote at Wichenford Court. **Note**: no access to Wichenford Court (privately owned). No toilet or tea-room. Please consider local residents when parking.

Finding out more: 01527 821214 or www.nationaltrust.org.uk

Wightwick Manor and Gardens

Wightwick Bank, Wolverhampton, West Midlands WV6 8EE

Map (4) J5

Wightwick Manor was the haven of a romantic industrialist. With its timber beams and barley-twist chimneys, gardens of wide lawns, yew hedges and roses, rich William Morris furnishings and exquisite Pre-Raphaelite paintings, Wightwick is in every way an idyllic time capsule of Victorian nostalgia for medieval England. If you delve deeper, you will find stories of the remarkable politician who fought social injustice and European Fascism and felt the need to share this unique property with the nation. More than 75 years since that gift, the magic and warmth of the home is as enthralling and enchanting as ever. **Note**: house entry by timed ticket for all (only available from reception in car park).

Eating and shopping: shop with William Morris and Arts and Crafts-inspired ranges and plant centre. New tea-room in stable block serving hot food made with kitchen garden produce.

Making the most of your day: family activities at holidays and weekends. Exhibitions in the Malthouse. Specialist tours and talks during the week and saucy late-night tours for adults only! **Dogs**: welcome on leads in garden.

Access for all: ⬛⬛⬛⬛⬛⬛⬛⬛⬛
Manor ⬛⬛⬛ Gardens ⬛⬛⬛➡

Getting here: 139:SO869985. 3 miles west of Wolverhampton. **Foot**: via Staffordshire & Worcestershire Canal. **Cycle**: as foot. **Bus**: regular services from Wolverhampton and Bridgnorth, alight Wightwick Bank stop on Bridgnorth Road beside Mermaid pub. **Train**: Wolverhampton 3 miles. **Road**: access A454 from junction with A4150 (ring road). From A41 follow brown signs on the B4161. **Sat Nav**: use WV6 8BN. **Parking**: free, entrance off A454.

Wightwick Manor and Gardens, West Midlands: enjoying the gardens, right, and the Great Parlour, above

Finding out more: 01902 761400 or
wightwickmanor@nationaltrust.org.uk

Wightwick Manor and Gardens		M	T	W	T	F	S	S
Garden, tea-room and shop								
1 Jan–15 Feb	11–4	M	T	W	T	F	S	S
16 Feb–3 Nov	11–5	M	T	W	T	F	S	S
4 Nov–31 Dec	11–4	M	T	W	T	F	S	S
House								
2 Jan–15 Feb	12–4	M	·	W	T	F	S	S
16 Feb–30 Jun	12–5	M	·	W	T	F	S	S
1 Jul–1 Sep	12–5	M	T	W	T	F	S	S
2 Sep–3 Nov	12–5	M	·	W	T	F	S	S
4 Nov–30 Dec	12–4	M	·	W	T	F	S	S

This year we will be trialling new combinations of tours and free-flow when visiting the house and we welcome visitors' feedback on these trials. Last entry to house one hour before closing, 30 minutes in July and August. Property closed 25 December. A reduced number of rooms will be visible during January and February.

Wilderhope Manor

Longville, Much Wenlock, Shropshire TF13 6EG

Map (4) H5

Beautiful Elizabethan manor house, restored by John Cadbury in 1936, surrounded by farmland managed for landscape and wildlife. **Note:** popular youth hostel, so access to some rooms may be restricted. Open on Sundays throughout the year and Wednesdays during April to September.

Finding out more: 01694 771363 (Hostel Warden YHA) or www.nationaltrust.org.uk

Woolsthorpe Manor

Water Lane, Woolsthorpe by Colsterworth, near Grantham, Lincolnshire NG33 5PD

Map (3) E4

A small manor house but the birthplace of a great mind – Sir Isaac Newton, world-famous scientist, mathematician, alchemist and Master of the Royal Mint. During the plague years of 1665–7, he returned to the family farm and produced some of his most important work on physics and mathematics here, including his crucial experiment to split white light into a spectrum of colours. Today you can still see the famous apple tree and explore some of Newton's ideas for yourself in the Science Discovery Centre.

Eating and shopping: small coffee shop and shop in ticket office. Second-hand book stall.

Making the most of your day: events, including regular 'Tales from Woolsthorpe' and science talks. Hands-on Science Discovery Centre. National Science Week (March), Apple Day (October). Summer holiday workshops. Belton House only 12 miles. **Dogs:** welcome in car park only.

Woolsthorpe Manor, Lincolnshire: Sir Isaac Newton's great work on mathematics

Access for all: [icons] P D WC [icons] ☐ ☐ ▦ ⓐ

House [icons] 🦽 ▦ 🚹 ♿   Discovery Centre ▦ ♿

Grounds ▦ ➡ ♿

Getting here: 130:SK924244. Close A1, 8 miles south of Grantham. **Foot**: footpath from Colsterworth. **Bus**: Grantham to South Witham. **Train**: Grantham. **Road**: note Woolsthorpe by Colsterworth, not Woolsthorpe near Belvoir. Brown signs from A1. From Melton take B676 towards Colsterworth, follow brown signs. **Parking**: free, 50 yards.

Finding out more: 01476 860338 or woolsthorpemanor@nationaltrust.org.uk. 23 Newton Way, Woolsthorpe by Colsterworth, near Grantham, Lincolnshire NG33 5NR

Woolsthorpe Manor		M	T	W	T	F	S	S
Manor house								
15 Feb–24 Mar	11–3	·	·	W	T	F	S	S
25 Mar–3 Nov	11–5	M	·	W	T	F	S	S
Science Discovery Centre, coffee shop and grounds								
15 Feb–24 Mar	11–3	·	·	W	T	F	S	S
25 Mar–3 Nov	11–5	M	T	W	T	F	S	S

Timed tickets may be in operation at busy times. The manor house has limited lighting and on dark days may close early.

Eating and shopping: shop selling specialist publications and souvenirs. Produce from vegetable garden for sale.

Making the most of your day: family activities. Children's trails and games. Living history days, tours and exhibitions.

The Workhouse, Southwell

Upton Road, Southwell, Nottinghamshire NG25 0PT

Map ③ D3

This is the most complete workhouse in existence. While immersing yourself in the unique atmosphere of the building, you can find out about the Reverend Becher, the founder of The Workhouse, and learn about the true stories of the 19th-century poor. While exploring the segregated work yards, day rooms, dormitories, master's quarters and cellars, you can reflect on how society dealt with poverty through the centuries, right up to the modern day. Outside there is a re-created 19th-century vegetable garden to discover.

The Workhouse, Southwell, Nottinghamshire, above

Access for all: [icons] P D WC [icons] ☐ ▧ ☐ ☐ ▥ ▦ ⠿ ⓐ

Building [icons] 🦽 ▦ 🚹 ♿   Grounds ▦ ➡ ♿

Getting here: 120:SK712543. Nottingham 13 miles. **Foot**: Robin Hood Trail. **Cycle**: National Byway. **Bus**: services from Newark, Nottingham and Mansfield. **Train**: Newark Castle 7 miles; Newark North Gate 7½ miles; Nottingham 13 miles. **Road**: 13 miles from Nottingham on A612 and 8 miles from Newark via A617 and A612. **Parking**: free, 200 yards.

Finding out more: 01636 817260 or theworkhouse@nationaltrust.org.uk

The Workhouse, Southwell		M	T	W	T	F	S	S
27 Feb–27 Oct	12–5	·	·	W	T	F	S	S
30 Oct–3 Nov	12–4	·	·	W	T	F	S	S

Guided tour of the outside and other buildings at 11. No booking is required but numbers are limited. Open Bank Holidays. Last admission one hour before closing.

North West

Off-road adventure and challenging
cycling action at Wasdale, Cumbria

Outdoors in the North West

Here in the North West we are lucky enough to have some of Britain's finest landscapes and wildlife, as well as a fascinating industrial heritage. We also offer amazing hospitality and great food and drink – an irresistible combination.

Above: **the Lake District and Cumbria offer unbeatable biking**
Top right: **Low Wray Campsite, Cumbria, on the shore of Windermere, has stunning views**

The Lake District and Cumbria

For pure drama and internationally renowned beauty, the Lake District is unbeatable. Whether you want a gentle stroll and splash in the prettiest of tarns, a challenging hike to the wildest of mountaintops, or a demanding downhill cycle ride across rugged terrain, we've got the lot. Our Rangers will tell you there's nowhere more inspiring – it's the perfect place to share adventures, capture amazing memories and return home spiritually refreshed.

The Trust looks after one quarter of the Lake District, encouraging access and promoting enjoyment of this magnificent landscape. We care for England's highest mountain, Scafell Pike, and its deepest lake, Wastwater, as well as most of the central fells and major valleys, and more than 20 lakes and tarns. The Lake District Appeal exists to help protect this stunning landscape. For more details visit **www.nationaltrust.org.uk/lakedistrict**

One of our greatest supporters was Beatrix Potter, whose love of the area is legendary. She left us 1,600 hectares (4,000 acres)

and 14 farms when she died in 1943. But we also have links to dozens of inspirational characters, not least the poet William Wordsworth and Canon Hardwicke Rawnsley, one of the founders of the National Trust.

Our flora and fauna is spectacular – some of the rarest species in the UK are thriving in our valleys and woodlands, and on our fell tops and crag sides. So, whether you love wildlife or views with a wow factor, or seek tranquillity or adrenaline-fuelled thrills, you'll find them all in Cumbria.

Camp in the Lake District

Low Wray Campsite
Lying on the quiet western shore of Windermere, you won't find more spectacular lake and fell views. We've got a new reception area and shop, refurbished toilet and shower blocks, a family picnic play area, fun orienteering course, bike hire and guided adventure activities. We're in the heart of Beatrix Potter country, so you can enjoy many beautiful walks from here, visit fascinating Wray Castle or catch the boat to Ambleside.

Great Langdale Campsite
This is the adventure heartland of the Lake District; so there's no better location for fell walkers and thrill seekers alike. We've just bought the neighbouring Sticklebarn pub, so now you can get expert advice on where to go and what to see, alongside a great pint and locally sourced food – all provided by our team behind the bar. Just a few miles from Ambleside and convenient for the other Lakes' attractions, this is a great base in a stunning location.

Wasdale Campsite
Valleys don't get more impressive than this. The campsite is a mere stone's throw from dramatic Wastwater, where the famed pyramidal peak of Great Gable is reflected in its waters. It's perfect for walkers, as Scafell Pike and some of the most exciting of high-fell walking routes are within striking distance. This is a remote place where peace and tranquillity reign – though if you want some extra comfort, you can now book an electric hook-up for your tent. Pitches for all our campsites can be booked online.

Camping pods
For those who prefer something a little bit more luxurious than a tent, we've got pods on Low Wray, Great Langdale and Wasdale Campsites. For details call 015394 63862 or visit **www. ntlakescampsites.org.uk**

Why not try...?

Following our Rangers' top tips
We've got a fantastic new selection of Ranger guides, featuring everything from walks around a secret Lakeland tarn to exhilarating cycle rides in the Yewdale Valley, as well as hikes through giant trees at Aira Force, and climbing in the Langdales. Visit **www.ntlakesoutdoors.org.uk** to see all our Rangers' ideas for things to do in the outdoors and to catch up on the latest news, or buy one of *Our Ranger Guides* – available at our information points.

A day without the car
Enjoy the freedom of leaving the car behind and catching the local bus, train or boat – there's no better way to enjoy the view. Or try a bike trail – there are gentle paths and high-speed downhill tracks galore. For details telephone Traveline (see page 6) or ask our Rangers for the best routes.

Discover Morecambe Bay

There are few things more exhilarating than striding up to the magnificent limestone peak of Arnside Knott on the Cumbrian coast, with its amazing views of Morecambe Bay, or strolling through Jack Scout or Eaves Wood in Silverdale, home to a fantastic variety of wild flowers and butterflies.

Why not check out the limestone pavement of Holme Park Fell, close to junction 36 of the M6, when it is ablaze with gorse, heather and wild flowers in May and June? It's home to numerous birds, bees and insects, all thriving in its craggy and impressive nooks and crannies.

Or you could visit the Heysham Coast, a sandstone headland with ruins of the 8th-century St Patrick's Chapel and unique rock-cut graves, some intriguingly body-shaped.

The high, grass-covered sand dunes of Sandscale Haws, near Barrow, make the perfect backdrop for a day at the beach. One fifth of Britain's natterjack toads, a nationally rare species, live here happily.

Not only that, but Sandscale Haws is also a haven for a rich variety of birds, including shelducks, eider ducks, goldeneyes and plovers – the population swells to more than 20,000 when wintering waterfowl come to visit.

Above: **distinctive red-clad Rangers at Wasdale, Cumbria**
Below left: **mountain biking at Wasdale, Cumbria**

Lake District car parks	
Buttermere	
Lanthwaite Wood	NY 149 215
Buttermere	NY 172 173
Honister Pass	NY 225 135
Borrowdale	
Seatoller	NY 246 137
Rosthwaite	NY 257 148
Bowderstone	NY 254 167
Watendlath	NY 276 164
Kettlewell	NY 269 196
Great Wood	NY 272 213
Ullswater	
Aira Force	NY 401 201
Glencoyne Bay	NY 387 188
Wasdale	
Wasdale Head	NY 182 074
Langdale	
Blea Tarn	NY 295 043
Old Dungeon Ghyll	NY 285 062
Stickle Ghyll	NY 295 064
Elterwater	NY 329 047
Coniston	
Glen Mary	SD 321 998
Tarn Hows	SD 326 995
Windermere	
Red Nab	SD 385 995
Harrowslack	SD 388 960
Ash Landing	SD 388 955
West coast	
Sandscale Haws	SD 199 758

Cheshire, Merseyside and Lancashire

We have many places close to Liverpool and Manchester, so you can combine a visit to the city (or escape it) with one to an array of countryside, parkland and garden destinations – many open all year. The Stubbins Estate and Holcombe Moor are some of our great open spaces north of Bury, with Dunham, Lyme and Quarry Bank Mill offering acres of parkland and walking trails.

To the west, in Cheshire, you can explore Alderley Edge, a very special sandstone ridge. There are endless views of the Cheshire Plain. At Bickerton you'll also see the wild ponies we're using to graze our land. While Helsby Hill has a vista across the Mersey Estuary to Liverpool. For more great scenery, stretching towards the Peak District, head to The Cloud, a great rocky heathland at Timbersbrook, near Congleton.

Right: **Bank House Farm, Silverdale, Lancashire**
Below: **Derwentwater, Cumbria**

History buffs can step back in time at Bickerton Hill and Helsby's Bronze Age forts, while romantics can watch the sun rise over the Peckforton Hills from Bulkeley Hill Wood. Further south lies the folly of Mow Cop. Built in 1754, it is famed as the birthplace of Primitive Methodism and stands in romantic ruin. While at Daresbury, near Warrington, is the site of Lewis Carroll's birthplace, kindly donated to the National Trust by the Lewis Carroll Birthplace Trust. Here you can find the 'footprint' of Daresbury Parsonage, where the author was born in 1832, while nearby Daresbury Church has a stained-glass window featuring Carroll and his Wonderland characters.

Why not try…?

A stay in one of our unique holiday cottages
These range from luxurious large homes to quirky, cosy hideaways – some are right on the lake shore, while others have sweeping views.

A foodie treat
Some of the finest food in the land is grown on Trust farms in this region. Be sure to try local specialities such as damson dishes at Sizergh, venison from the parks at Lyme, Dunham and Tatton, or Herdwick lamb from our farms in Cumbria.

Acorn Bank's lovely garden gives us home-grown herbs and the most amazing apples, and there are also endless cheeses to savour in Cheshire.

Don't forget to look out for our meat in Booths supermarkets – field-to-fork doesn't come much fresher than this.

Acorn Bank

Temple Sowerby, near Penrith,
Cumbria CA10 1SP

Map (6) E7

At the heart of the Eden Valley, with spectacular views across to the Lake District, Acorn Bank is a tranquil haven with an almost forgotten industrial past. There are walled gardens, sheltering a medicinal herb collection, and traditional orchards. A path leads through woodland, along the Crowdundle Beck, to the watermill, now working again after more than 70 years. You can also explore the wider estate with its hidden gypsum-mining remains and abundance of wildlife. The unfurnished 17th-century, sandstone house is partially open to the public for the first time, with the shop and tea-room within it. **Note**: access to fragile grass paths may be restricted after wet weather.

Eating and shopping: tea-room serving local produce, the garden's herbs and fruit, cakes and scones. Plant sales. Shop selling local and national products.

Making the most of your day: Apple Day in October (charge, including members). Woodland trails and new wildlife hide. Watermill machinery operating (most weekend afternoons). **Dogs**: welcome on leads on woodland walks/garden courtyard. Apple Day: assistance dogs only.

Acorn Bank in Cumbria: a tranquil haven

Access for all: ▢▢▢▢▢▢▢▢▢▢
Mill ▢▢ House ▢▢
Grounds ▢▢▢▢▢

Getting here: 91:NY612281. 6 miles east of Penrith. **Foot**: public footpath from Temple Sowerby. **Cycle**: NCN7, 6 miles. **Bus**: Penrith to Kirkby Stephen, to within 1 mile. **Train**: Langwathby 5 miles; Penrith 6 miles. **Road**: 1 mile from A66. **Parking**: free.

Finding out more: 017683 61893 or acornbank@nationaltrust.org.uk

Acorn Bank		M	T	W	T	F	S	S
House, garden, watermill, woodland walks and shop								
9 Feb–10 Mar	10–5	·	·	·	·	·	S	S
16 Mar–3 Nov	10–5	M	·	W	T	F	S	S
Tea-room								
9 Feb–10 Mar	11–4:30	·	·	·	·	·	S	S
16 Mar–3 Nov	11–4:30	M	·	W	T	F	S	S

Aira Force and Ullswater

near Watermillock, Penrith, Cumbria

Map (6) D7

Ullswater is truly breathtaking. With its beautiful lake nestled among towering fells, this valley begs to be explored. The tumbling waterfall of Aira Force drops an impressive 65 feet and can be reached by strolling through ancient woodland and landscaped glades. The perfect place for a family walk and picnic.

Eating and shopping: Aira Force tea-room (not National Trust) by car park. Side Farm tea-room (Trust farm) in Patterdale.

Making the most of your day: numerous walks. Canoe launching at Glencoyne car park. **Dogs**: under close control (stock grazing).

Access for all: ▢▢

Getting here: 90:NY401203. 7 miles south of Penrith. **Cycle**: NCN71, 2 miles. **Bus**: from Penrith ▢ to Patterdale. **Train**: Penrith 10 miles.

Aira Force and Ullswater in Cumbria

Parking: two car parks at Aira Force and Glencoyne Bay (pay and display).

Finding out more: 017684 82067 or ullswater@nationaltrust.org.uk. Tower Buildings, Watermillock, Penrith, Cumbria CA11 0JS

Aira Force and Ullswater	Open every day all year

Alderley Edge

Nether Alderley, Macclesfield, Cheshire

Map (5) D8

The dramatic red sandstone escarpment of Alderley Edge has views over the Cheshire Plain and the Peak District. There are woodland paths and walks to Hare Hill. Alderley Edge is designated an SSSI for its geological interest, and has a history of copper mining dating back to the Bronze Age.

Eating and shopping: Wizard Tea-room (weekends and some Bank Holidays only) and Wizard Inn at Alderley Edge (neither National Trust).

Making the most of your day: guided walks at Alderley Edge throughout summer. **Dogs**: under close control. On leads where livestock present (particularly during bird-nesting season).

Access for all: 🅿️🚻♿🎎 Grounds ♿➡️

Getting here: Alderley Edge 118:SJ860776. The Cloud 118:SJ905637; Mow Cop 118:SJ857573; Bickerton Hill 117:SJ498529; Bulkeley Hill 117:SJ527553; Helsby Hill 117:SJ492754; Lewis Carroll's Birthplace 118:SJ593805; Maggoty's Wood 118:SJ889702; Burton Hill Wood SJ317743; Caldy Hill SJ223855; Heswall Fields SJ245824; Thurstaston Common SJ248845; Mobberley Fields SJ789801. **Parking**: at some properties (roadside elsewhere); pay and display at Alderley Edge.

Finding out more: 01625 584412 or alderleyedge@nationaltrust.org.uk. c/o Cheshire Countryside Office, Nether Alderley, Macclesfield, Cheshire SK10 4UB

Alderley Edge		M	T	W	T	F	S	S
Countryside								
Open all year	Dawn–dusk	M	T	W	T	F	S	S
Car park								
1 Jan–31 Mar	8–5	M	T	W	T	F	S	S
1 Apr–31 May	8–5:30	M	T	W	T	F	S	S
1 Jun–30 Sep	8–6	M	T	W	T	F	S	S
1 Oct–31 Dec	8–5	M	T	W	T	F	S	S

Far-reaching views at Alderley Edge, Cheshire

Allan Bank and Grasmere

Allan Bank, Grasmere, Ambleside,
Cumbria LA22 9QB

Map (6) D8

A National Trust experience like no other,
Allan Bank is a place to relax in front of a
warm fire with a cup of tea while the children
play. Once home to William Wordsworth and
National Trust founder Canon Rawnsley, Allan
Bank was rescued from the ravages of fire in
2011. Now partially restored and undecorated,
the house offers you the opportunity to see and
touch the many layers of this home's fascinating
history. Take the time to explore the intriguing
woodland and soak up the stunning views.

Eating and shopping: Grasmere Shop
and Information Centre selling a range of
local gifts, snacks, books, maps and guides.
Light refreshments available at Allan Bank.
Picnics welcome.

**Allan Bank, Cumbria: touch the many layers of this home's
fascinating history**

Making the most of your day: walks around
Grasmere and Rydal Water, and Easedale Tarn.
Children's indoor activities. **Dogs**: welcome
under control.

Access for all: ⃞⃞⃞⃞⃞
Allan Bank ⃞⃞⃞ Countryside ⃞

Getting here: 90:NY333076. Allan Bank: in
centre Grasmere. Grasmere: 4 miles north of
Ambleside. **Foot**: 437 yards from the Red Lion
Hotel/Miller Howe Café in centre of village
(slight gradient before house). **Bus**: services
from Keswick and Windermere to Bowness.
Road: A591 to Ambleside, continuing to
Grasmere. **Parking**: three pay and display car
parks in Grasmere village (not National Trust).

Finding out more: 015394 35143 or
grasmere@nationaltrust.org.uk

Allan Bank and Grasmere		M	T	W	T	F	S	S
Allan Bank								
18 Mar–3 Nov	10–5	M	T	W	T	F	S	S
4 Nov–23 Dec	10–4	M	T	W	T	F	S	S
Grasmere Shop and Information Centre								
18 Mar–3 Nov	9:30–5	M	T	W	T	F	S	S
4 Nov–31 Dec	10–4	M	T	W	T	F	S	S
Countryside								
Open all year		M	T	W	T	F	S	S

Grasmere Shop and Information Centre: 1 January to
17 March – opening times vary. Closed 25 to 26 December.

Windermere in Cumbria is perfect for outdoor fun

Ambleside and Windermere

near Windermere, Cumbria

Map ⑥ D8

The bustling Lakeland towns of Windermere and Ambleside are situated around England's longest lake. With fells, woodland, lakeshore parks and a Roman fort on offer, this part of the Lake District is a great option for families looking for fun in the great outdoors.

Making the most of your day: Galava Roman fort. Seasonal displays of azaleas, rhododendrons and camellias at Stagshaw Gardens. Bridge House, Ambleside's smallest building. Townend nearby. **Dogs**: welcome under close control (stock grazing).

Access for all: Bridge House

Getting here: 90:NY375046. **Ferry**: from Newby Bridge to Ambleside and Bowness. **Bus**: services from Windermere ☒. During the season open-top buses run regularly from Bowness to Ambleside. **Train**: Windermere, direct trains from/to Manchester Airport and Oxenholme. **Road**: Troutbeck is signposted east of A591 Windermere to Ambleside road. **Parking**: limited, at Stagshaw Gardens.

Finding out more: 015394 63803 or windermere@nationaltrust.org.uk. The Hollens, Grasmere, Ambleside, Cumbria LA22 9QZ

Ambleside and Windermere		M	T	W	T	F	S	S
Countryside								
Open all year		M	T	W	T	F	S	S
Stagshaw Gardens								
16 Mar–31 Jul	Dawn–dusk	M	T	W	T	F	S	S
Bridge House, please call for details.								

Arnside and Silverdale

near Arnside, Cumbria

Map ⑤ C4

Overlooking Morecambe Bay, this is species-rich limestone grassland, woodland, wet meadow, scree and scrub. Arnside Knott and Eaves Wood are renowned for their butterflies. Jack Scout is one of only two cliffs between North Wales and Cumbria. Breeding ground for songbirds and feeding places for weary migrant birds passing through.

Eating and shopping: variety of small cafés in and around Arnside and Silverdale villages (not National Trust).

Making the most of your day: species-rich habitats and haven for butterflies. Easy walking at The Lots in Silverdale. Stunning views and fabulous sunsets over Morecambe Bay. **Dogs**: welcome under control (stock grazing).

Access for all: 🚶♿

Getting here: 97:SD450774 Arnside Knott; 97:SD471759 Eaves Wood. Arnside Knott: 500 yards south-west of Arnside. Eaves Wood: 800 yards east of Silverdale village. **Foot**: Lancashire Coastal Way. **Cycle**: Lancashire Cycleway on Regional Route 90. **Bus**: services from Kendal to Silverdale and Kendal to Arnside. **Train**: Silverdale, 800 yards; Arnside, 1,000 yards. **Road**: Arnside: B5282 from the A6 at Milnthorpe; Silverdale: from A6, between Carnforth and Milnthorpe, follow signs to Silverdale. **Parking**: at Arnside Knott and Eaves Wood.

Finding out more: 01524 702815 or arnsidesilverdale@nationaltrust.org.uk. Morecambe Bay Properties Office, Bank House Farm, Silverdale, Carnforth, Cumbria LA5 0RE

Arnside and Silverdale	Open every day all year

The Beatles' Childhood Homes

Woolton and Allerton, Liverpool

Map ⑤ C8

A combined tour to Mendips and 20 Forthlin Road, the childhood homes of John Lennon and Paul McCartney, is your only opportunity to see inside the houses where the Beatles met, composed and rehearsed many of their earliest songs. You can walk through the back door into the kitchen and imagine John's Aunt Mimi cooking him his tea, or stand in the spot where Lennon and McCartney composed 'I Saw Her Standing There'. Join our custodians on a fascinating trip down memory lane in these two atmospheric period houses, so typical of Liverpool life in the 1950s. **Note**: access to these houses is by National Trust minibus tour only (charge including members).

Inside 20 Forthlin Road, Liverpool

Eating and shopping: guidebooks and postcards available at both houses and Speke Hall shop. Speke Hall's Home Farm restaurant serving local produce.

Making the most of your day: departures from convenient pick-up points (city centre and Speke Hall). Our comfortable minibus and easy online booking service allow you to relax, as we take the strain out of visiting.

Arnside and Silverdale, Cumbria: view of Morecambe Bay

Members may have to pay on special events days

Access for all: Building

Getting here: 108:SJ422855. No direct access by car or on foot to either house. Access is via minibus tour (advance booking essential) from Liverpool city centre or Speke Hall. **Parking**: for morning tours numerous public car parks in city centre (not National Trust). For afternoon tours, parking at Speke Hall.

Finding out more: 0844 800 4791 (Infoline). 0151 427 7231 (booking line) or thebeatleshomes@nationaltrust.org.uk

The Beatles' Childhood Homes	M	T	W	T	F	S	S
23 Feb–24 Nov	·	·	**W**	**T**	**F**	**S**	**S**

*Admission by guided tour only. Times and pick-up locations vary. Please visit website or call for details and to book tickets.

Beatrix Potter Gallery

Main Street, Hawkshead, Cumbria LA22 0NS

Map (6) D8

This unique gallery space occupies the charming 17th-century building which once served as the office of Beatrix Potter's solicitor husband. We display an annually changing exhibition of rarely seen original Potter artwork from the National Trust collection. This year we celebrate the centenary of Potter's wedding to William Heelis and the publication of *The Tale of Pigling Bland*. 1913 was a busy year for Beatrix. You can see her original 'Pigling Bland' artwork and family photographs and discover how she wrote this delightful story while preparing for her wedding. She even included her pet pigs in the tale. **Note**: nearest toilet 300 yards in main village car park (not National Trust).

Eating and shopping: shop in Hawkshead, 50 yards, selling local products (online shop at www.shop.nationaltrust.org.uk/beatrixpotter). Meals and refreshments available in Hawkshead village (not National Trust).

Making the most of your day: children's activities and family story corner. Exhibition. Audio points and touchscreens. Hill Top and Wray Castle nearby. **Dogs**: assistance dogs only.

Access for all: Building

Getting here: 96:SD352982. Main Street, Hawkshead village, by Red Lion pub. **Bus**: Windermere to Coniston. Cross Lakes shuttle Bowness to Hawkshead. **Train**: Windermere 6½ miles. **Road**: B5286 from Ambleside, 4 miles; B5285 from Coniston, 5 miles. **Parking**: 300 yards (pay and display), not National Trust.

Finding out more: 015394 36355 (gallery). 015394 36471 (shop) or beatrixpottergallery@nationaltrust.org.uk

Beatrix Potter Gallery		M	T	W	T	F	S	S
Gallery								
9 Feb–21 Mar	10:30–3:30	**M**	**T**	**W**	**T**	·	**S**	**S**
23 Mar–23 May	10:30–5	**M**	**T**	**W**	**T**	·	**S**	**S**
25 May–30 Aug	10:30–5	**M**	**T**	**W**	**T**	**F**	**S**	**S**
31 Aug–3 Nov	10:30–5	**M**	**T**	**W**	**T**	·	**S**	**S**
Shop								
5 Jan–3 Feb	10–4	·	·	·	·	·	**S**	**S**
9 Feb–24 May	10–5	**M**	**T**	**W**	**T**	**F**	**S**	**S**
25 May–30 Aug	10–5:30	**M**	**T**	**W**	**T**	**F**	**S**	**S**
31 Aug–3 Nov	10–5	**M**	**T**	**W**	**T**	**F**	**S**	**S**
6 Nov–22 Dec	10–4	·	·	**W**	**T**	**F**	**S**	**S**

Open various Fridays throughout the year. At busy periods, timed entry system in operation.

Beatrix Potter Gallery, Cumbria

Borrowdale

near Keswick, Cumbria

Map (6) D7

Spectacular landscape around Derwentwater, where the Trust cares for much of the valley, including Derwentwater, its islands and Georgian manor, Watendlath hamlet, Bowder Stone, Friar's Crag, Ashness Bridge and Castlerigg Stone Circle. Brandelhow Park was the first piece of the Lake District to be safeguarded by the Trust from development.

Eating and shopping: lakeside shop selling local souvenirs. Tenant-run cafés at Rosthwaite, Watendlath and Stonethwaite. Flock Inn, Rosthwaite, serving local Herdwick lamb. Free-range eggs available at Ashness or Stonethwaite farms.

Making the most of your day: events all year. Downloadable trails. Open days at Derwent Island House and Force Crag Mine. **Dogs**: welcome throughout valley under close control (particularly at lambing time).

Access for all: 🅿️🅳♿ **Grounds** ♿

Getting here: 90:NY250160. **Cycle**: NCN71 (C2C). **Ferry**: Keswick Launch around Derwentwater, 017687 72263. **Bus**: Keswick to Seatoller. **Train**: Penrith 18 miles. **Road**: B5289 from Keswick. **Parking**: at Great Wood, Watendlath, Kettlewell, Bowder Stone, Rosthwaite, Seatoller, Honister. Coach parking by prior arrangement at Seatoller only. Limited parking at Catbells.

Borrowdale, Cumbria: Friar's Crag at Derwentwater

Finding out more: 017687 74649 or borrowdale@nationaltrust.org.uk. Bowe Barn, Borrowdale Road, near Keswick, Cumbria CA12 5UP

Borrowdale	M	T	W	T	F	S	S
Countryside							
Open all year	M	T	W	T	F	S	S
Shop and information centre							
9 Feb–26 Oct	10–5	M	T	W	T	F	S	S

Open days for Force Crag Mine and Derwent Island House are available on our website.

Buttermere, Ennerdale and Whitehaven Coast

near Cockermouth and Whitehaven, Cumbria

Map (6) C7

The beautiful lakes of Buttermere, Crummock Water and Loweswater are surrounded by dramatic high fells, in some of the north-west Lake District's most stunning scenery. Over the fells lie 'Wild Ennerdale' and the Whitehaven coast, where we and our partners are working to allow a wilder landscape to evolve.

Eating and shopping: pubs and cafés in Buttermere, Loweswater, Ennerdale villages and Whitehaven town. Picnics welcome.

Making the most of your day: events and activities all year in Buttermere and Ennerdale valleys and on Whitehaven coast. Circular lakeshore ambles, dramatic ridge-line walks and coastal paths. Off-road cycling in Ennerdale and Whitehaven coast. **Dogs**: welcome throughout valleys and coastline under close control (particularly at lambing time).

Access for all: Grounds ♿

Getting here: 89:NY180150. 8 miles south of Cockermouth. **Bus**: from Keswick and Cockermouth to Buttermere; and Whitehaven to Ennerdale. **Train**: Whitehaven. **Road**: off the A595. **Parking**: at Honister Pass, Buttermere village, Lanthwaite Wood near

Crummock Water and by Ennerdale Water (not National Trust) and in Whitehaven.

Finding out more: 017687 74649 or buttermere@nationaltrust.org.uk.
Bowe Barn, Borrowdale, Keswick, Cumbria CA12 5UP

Buttermere and Ennerdale	Open every day all year

Coniston and Little Langdale

near Coniston, Cumbria

Map (6) D8

The area around Coniston and Little Langdale covers a large area of some of the Lake District's most scenic woodland, water and fells. There are lots of routes to and from Coniston village and the accessible Blea Tarn in Little Langdale also has superb views and fine walking.

Eating and shopping: numerous places (not National Trust) to eat in area, particularly in

Stunning scenery on the River Liza, which feeds into Ennerdale Water at Ennerdale, Cumbria

Coniston – some linked with National Trust tenants. Refreshments generally available at Tarn Hows. Trust shop in nearby Hawkshead.

Making the most of your day: paths and bridleways around Coniston. Cruises on Steam Yacht *Gondola*, disembarking at Monk Coniston jetty for a walk through Monk Coniston grounds to Tarn Hows. **Dogs**: on leads (stock grazing).

Access for all: 🅿♿

Getting here: 90:NY295043 for Blea Tarn; Little Langdale, 5 miles north of Coniston. **Bus**: Ambleside to Coniston via Hawkshead. **Road**: A593 from Ambleside to Coniston; B5285 from Hawkshead; minor road to Little Langdale. **Parking**: Glen Mary 90/97:SD320998; Blea Tarn 90:NY295043.

Finding out more: 015394 41456 or coniston@nationaltrust.org.uk.
Boon Crag, Coniston, Cumbria LA21 8AQ

Coniston and Little Langdale	Open every day all year

Dalton Castle

Market Place, Dalton-in-Furness,
Cumbria LA15 8AX

Map (6) D9

Eye-catching 14th-century tower built to assert
the authority of the Abbot of Furness Abbey.
Note: opened on behalf of the National Trust
by the Friends of Dalton Castle.

Finding out more: 015395 60951
or www.nationaltrust.org.uk

Dunham Massey

Altrincham, Cheshire WA14 4SJ

Map (5) D8

Set in a magnificent deer-park, this Georgian
house tells the story of the owners and servants
who lived here. You can discover the salacious
scandals of the 7th Earl of Stamford, who
married Catherine Cocks, a former bare-back
circus rider, and the 2nd Earl of Warrington,
so enamoured with his wife that he wrote
anonymously on the desirability of divorce!
These, and other fascinating stories, are waiting
to be uncovered at this treasure-packed house.
Dunham Massey has one of the North's great
gardens, including Britain's largest winter garden
and a spectacular new rose garden opening in
late spring. **Note**: all visitors require a white entry
ticket (free to members), from visitor reception.

Eating and shopping: Stables Restaurant
serving lunch and cakes. Shop selling gifts
and local products.

Making the most of your day: free guided tours
and walks. Family fun. School holiday activities.
Cycling for under fives. 'Faithful and Obedient?'
exhibition. **Dogs**: welcome on leads in deer-park
and estate walks.

Access for all: [icons] House [icons] Grounds [icons]

Getting here: 109:SJ735874. 3 miles south-
west of Altrincham. **Foot**: Trans-Pennine Trail
and Bridgewater Canal. **Cycle**: NCN62, 1 mile.
Bus: Altrincham and Warrington, stops at main
gates. **Train**: Altrincham 3 miles; Hale 3 miles.
Road: off A56: M6 J19; M56 J7. **Parking**: 200
yards. March to October shuttle buggy service
most days between car park and visitor facilities.

Finding out more: 0161 942 3989 (Infoline).
0161 941 1025 or
dunhammassey@nationaltrust.org.uk

Dunham Massey, Cheshire: the north front, left, and fallow deer resting in sunshine on the lawn, above

Fell Foot Park

Newby Bridge, Windermere,
Cumbria LA12 8NN

Map (6) D9

The views of Lake Windermere are truly breathtaking! This is a magical environment for families and friends to enjoy a relaxed lunch around the boathouses, picnic or barbecue near the lakeshore or take to the water in a rowing boat. A perfect place for children to play safely! **Note**: launch/slipway facilities available for a wide variety of craft (charges apply).

Eating and shopping: Boathouse Café serving drinks and snacks. Retail corner offering a small selection of children's games, gifts and local food. Picnics welcome.

Making the most of your day: rowing boats and kayaks for hire April to October (weather permitting). Events. Adventure playground. **Dogs**: welcome on leads.

Access for all: 🅿♿👶♿🚻♿   Grounds ♿

Getting here: 96/97:SD381869. On southern tip of Lake Windermere. **Ferry**: from Lakeside (seasonal). **Bus**: from Ambleside to Barrow, stops outside park. From Kendal to Barrow, alight Newby Bridge. **Train**: Grange or Windermere. **Road**: 1 mile north of Newby Bridge on A592. **Parking**: charges (non-members). Coach access difficult (booking essential).

Finding out more: 015395 31273 or fellfootpark@nationaltrust.org.uk

Dunham Massey		M	T	W	T	F	S	S
House*								
23 Feb–3 Nov	11–5	M	T	W	·	·	S	S
Garden**								
1 Jan–22 Feb	11–4	M	T	W	T	F	S	S
23 Feb–3 Nov	11–5:30	M	T	W	T	F	S	S
4 Nov–31 Dec	11–4	M	T	W	T	F	S	S
Restaurant and shop								
1 Jan–22 Feb	10:30–4	M	T	W	T	F	S	S
23 Feb–3 Nov	10:30–5	M	T	W	T	F	S	S
4 Nov–31 Dec	10:30–4	M	T	W	T	F	S	S
Park*								
Open all year	9–5	M	T	W	T	F	S	S
Mill								
23 Feb–3 Nov	12–4	M	T	W	·	·	S	S
White Cottage***								
24 Feb–27 Oct	2–5	·	·	·	·	·	·	S

*Last entry at 4. House open Good Friday. **Winter: closes at 4 or dusk if earlier. Contact property for June evening openings of Rose Garden. ***March to October: gates open until 7:30. Property closed 20 November for staff training and 25 December (including park). ****Open last Sunday each month, booking essential (0161 928 0075).

Fell Foot Park		M	T	W	T	F	S	S
Park								
1 Jan–17 Mar	9–5	M	T	W	T	F	S	S
18 Mar–27 Oct	8–8	M	T	W	T	F	S	S
28 Oct–31 Dec	9–5	M	T	W	T	F	S	S
Boathouse Café								
9 Feb–17 Mar	11–3:30	M	T	W	T	F	S	S
18 Mar–3 Nov	10–4:30	M	T	W	T	F	S	S

Boat hire available from 18 March to 3 November, daily, 11 to 4. Weather permitting. Times of opening for catering facilities may vary according to weather conditions.

Formby

near Formby, Liverpool

Map ⑤ B7

This ever-changing sandy coastline set between the sea and Formby town offers miles of walks through the woods and dunes. You may glimpse a rare red squirrel or see a historic landscape levelled for asparagus. Prehistoric animal and human footprints can sometimes be found in silt beds on the shoreline.
Note: toilets close 5:30 in summer, 4 in winter.

Eating and shopping: ice-creams, soft drinks and coffee from mobile van.

Making the most of your day: guided walks and awareness days. Circular and longer walks linked to the Sefton Coastal Path. Formby Point audio guide trail. **Dogs**: under close control (vulnerable wildlife).

Access for all:  Grounds

Getting here: 108:SD275080. 2 miles west of Formby, 6 miles south of Southport. **Foot**: Sefton Coastal Footpath. **Cycle**: NCN62, 3 miles. **Train**: Freshfield 1 mile. **Road**: 2 miles off A565. Follow brown signs from roundabout at north end of Formby bypass. **Sat Nav**: use L37 1LJ. **Parking**: width restriction 3 yards. Minibuses: £10, coaches: £25.

Finding out more: 01704 878591 or formby@nationaltrust.org.uk.
Countryside Office, Blundell Avenue, Formby, Liverpool L37 1PH

Formby		M	T	W	T	F	S	S
Car park								
1 Jan–27 Jan	9–4	M	T	W	T	F	S	S
28 Jan–31 Mar	9–4:30	M	T	W	T	F	S	S
1 Apr–27 Oct	9–5:30	M	T	W	T	F	S	S
28 Oct–31 Dec	9–4	M	T	W	T	F	S	S
Countryside								
Open all year	Dawn–dusk	M	T	W	T	F	S	S

Closed 25 December. Long queues for car parks in peak season.

Gawthorpe Hall

Burnley Road, Padiham, near Burnley, Lancashire BB12 8UA

Map ⑤ D6

This imposing house is set in the heart of urban Lancashire. In the 19th century, Sir Charles Barry created the opulent interiors we see today. The Hall displays more than 500 textiles from the Rachel Kay-Shuttleworth collection, including needlework, lace and embroidery. The grounds are popular with dog walkers. **Note**: financed and run in partnership with Lancashire County Council.

Eating and shopping: tea-room serving light snacks.

Making the most of your day: events all year, including open-air theatre (July) and Victorian Christmas. **Dogs**: under close control in grounds.

Access for all:
Building   Grounds

The beach at Formby, Liverpool

Imposing Gawthorpe Hall, Lancashire

Getting here: 103:SD806340. On outskirts of Padiham. **Foot**: driveway from Burnley Road (no footpath). **Bus**: frequent buses from Burnley bus station. **Train**: Rose Grove, Burnley Barracks and Burnley Manchester Road stations nearby. **Road**: on A671. From M65 exit 8 towards Clitheroe then Padiham. **Parking**: 150 yards, narrow access road (passing places).

Finding out more: 01282 771004 or gawthorpehall@nationaltrust.org.uk

Gawthorpe Hall		M	T	W	T	F	S	S
House								
23 Mar–3 Nov	12–5	·	·	W	T	F	S	S
Tea-room								
23 Mar–3 Nov	11–5	·	·	W	T	F	S	S
Grounds								
Open all year	8–7	M	T	W	T	F	S	S

Hall and tea-room also open Bank Holidays.
Opening times are subject to change.

Eating and shopping: Sticklebarn pub serving food cooked with Lakeland produce and local ales. Shop at campsite.

Making the most of your day: fell walking, mountain biking, ghyll scrambling, rock climbing and bouldering. Campsite. **Dogs**: welcome under control.

Access for all: ♿ 🏠 📶
Sticklebarn pub 🔜 📶 Grounds 📶

Getting here: 89/90:NY294064. Great Langdale valley starts 4 miles west of Ambleside. **Foot**: network of local footpaths and Coast to Coast route. **Cycle**: NCN37, then links from Skelwith Bridge to Elterwater. **Bus**: services from Ambleside to Langdale. **Road**: A591 to Ambleside, A593 to Skelwith Bridge, B5343 to Great Langdale. **Parking**: three car parks.

Finding out more: 015394 63823 (Property Office). 015394 35665 (Grasmere Information Centre). 015394 37356 (Sticklebarn pub) or grasmere@nationaltrust.org.uk. Central and East Lakes Property Office, The Hollens, Grasmere, Cumbria LA22 9QZ

Great Langdale		M	T	W	T	F	S	S
Sticklebarn*								
Open all year	12–11	M	T	W	T	F	S	S
Countryside								
Open all year		M	T	W	T	F	S	S

*Sticklebarn: food served all day until 9. Open from 9 to 11 during school holidays. Closed 23 to 27 December. Closes at 10:30 on Sundays.

Sticklebarn in Great Langdale, Cumbria

Great Langdale

near Ambleside, Cumbria

Map ⑥ D8 ➕ 🍴 🏛 🔊 ♿ 🛏 🏕 🍴

Spectacular mountain scenery in the heart of the Lakes. Traditional Lakeland farms nestle in the valley bottom beneath towering fells. Wonderful walks and adventures for outdoor enthusiasts with walking routes to suit all abilities. So, take a deep breath and prepare to be inspired.

The Hardmans' House

59 Rodney Street, Liverpool, Merseyside L1 9EX

Map (5) B8

Step back in time and experience the 1950s. In this time capsule of post-war years, you will glimpse the life of an extraordinary couple. Renowned photographer E. Chambré Hardman and his talented wife Margaret lived and worked together in this remarkable Georgian house for 40 years, keeping everything, changing nothing. **Note**: admission by guided tour only – booking advised.

The Hardmans' House in Rodney Street, Liverpool

Eating and shopping: shop selling unique photographic prints, postcards and guidebooks.

Making the most of your day: tours (book your place to avoid disappointment). Virtual tour of house. Children's quiz trail.

Access for all: [icons] **Building** [icons]

Getting here: 108:SJ355895. Rodney Street is off Hardman Street and Upper Duke Street, Liverpool. **Foot**: follow fingerposts '59 Rodney Street'. Visitor entrance on Pilgrim Street. **Bus**: frequent services from surrounding area. **Train**: Liverpool Lime Street. **Parking**: no onsite parking. Car parks at Anglican Cathedral and Slater Street NCP.

Finding out more: 0151 709 6261 or thehardmanshouse@nationaltrust.org.uk

The Hardmans' House		M	T	W	T	F	S	S
13 Mar–26 Oct	11–3:30		·	**W**	**T**	**F**	**S**	·

Admission by timed ticket only, including members. Visitors advised to book, as tickets on the day are subject to availability. Open Bank Holiday Mondays.

Hare Hill

Over Alderley, Macclesfield, Cheshire SK10 4PY

Map (5) D8

This woodland garden provides the ideal habitat for a wide variety of native wildlife, while also boasting ornamental ponds, impressive collections of rhododendrons, azaleas and other fine specimen shrubs and waterside plantings. At its heart is the delightful walled garden – a tranquil place to reflect and relax.

Eating and shopping: hot drinks vending machine. Picnics welcome.

Making the most of your day: walks, hare sculpture trail and bird hide. **Dogs**: under close control on estate only.

Access for all: [icons] Grounds [icons]

Enjoying the colour at Hare Hill, Cheshire

Getting here: 118:SJ873763. 2½ miles from Alderley Edge and Prestbury. **Train**: Alderley Edge and Prestbury, both 2½ miles. **Road**: between Alderley Edge and Macclesfield (B5087). **Parking**: not suitable for coaches.

Finding out more: 01625 584412 or harehill@nationaltrust.org.uk

Hare Hill	M	T	W	T	F	S	S
9 Mar–3 Nov	10–5		T	W	T	F	S	S

Open Bank Holiday Mondays. Last admission one hour before closing. Car park closes at 5.

Hawkshead and Claife Viewing Station

near Hawkshead, Cumbria

Map ⑥ D8

Hawkshead village, home to the Beatrix Potter Gallery, is surrounded by beautiful countryside, perfect for walks and exploration. Why not start your adventure at Claife Viewing Station on Windermere lakeshore, then take the lakeshore path to Wray Castle? Have a paddle, soak up the views... enjoy a great day out! **Note**: toilets at Ferry House (near Claife Viewing Station) and in Hawkshead.

Eating and shopping: numerous catering options and shopping opportunities in and around Hawkshead village, including Hawkshead Trust gift shop (internet shop at www.shop.nationaltrust.org.uk/beatrixpotter).

Making the most of your day: Beatrix Potter Gallery in Hawkshead. National Trust campsite on lakeshore at Low Wray (90:NY372012). Walks in the countryside that inspired Beatrix Potter. **Dogs**: allowed in countryside, under close control. Assistance dogs only on guided walks and tours.

Access for all: 🦽

Getting here: 96/97:SD352982. Hawkshead 6 miles south-west of Ambleside. **Foot**: many footpaths. **Ferry**: Windermere car and passenger ferry; Ferry House to Ferry Nab. Cross Lakes Experience (not National Trust) 01539 448600. **Bus**: Windermere ≡ to Coniston. **Parking**: Ash Landing (near ferry) and Harrowslack, near Lake Windermere.

Finding out more: 015394 41456 or hawkshead@nationaltrust.org.uk. Boon Crag, Coniston, Cumbria LA21 8AQ

Hawkshead and Claife	Open every day all year

Hawkshead Courthouse (not staffed): access from 23 March to 3 November by key from the National Trust shop in Hawkshead. Free admission but no parking facilities.
Claife Station and courtyard: free entry, not always staffed.

Hawkshead village in the Lake District, Cumbria: home to the Beatrix Potter Gallery

Hill Top

Near Sawrey, Hawkshead, Ambleside,
Cumbria LA22 0LF

Map ⑥ D8 🎫 🍴 ❖

Hill Top is a time capsule of Beatrix Potter's life. Full of her favourite things, the house appears as if Beatrix had just stepped out for a walk. Every room contains a reference to a picture in a 'tale'. The lovely garden is a haphazard mix of flowers, herbs, fruit and vegetables. Hill Top is a small house and a timed-ticket entry system is in operation to avoid overcrowding and to protect the fragile interior. Hill Top can be very busy and visitors may sometimes have to wait to enter the house. **Note**: tickets cannot be booked and **early sell-outs** are possible, especially during school holidays.

Hill Top is a time capsule of Beatrix Potter's life

Eating and shopping: internet shop www.shop.nationaltrust.org.uk/beatrixpotter or mail-order service (contact hilltop.shop@nationaltrust.org.uk or 01539 436801). Hill Top shop selling Potter books and collectables. Sawrey House Hotel and Tower Bank Arms serving meals and refreshments.

Making the most of your day: why not visit by boat, bus, boot or bike? 'Windermere Cross Lakes Experience' website (not National Trust). Children's free garden trail. Downloadable local walks. Beatrix Potter Gallery nearby. **Dogs**: assistance dogs only.

Access for all: 📷 🏠 🚶 ♿ 📷
House 🏠♿ Shop 🏠 Garden 🏠 ➡

Getting here: 96/97:SD370955. 2 miles south of Hawkshead, in Near Sawrey hamlet; 3 miles from Bowness via ferry. **Foot**: off-road path from ferry (2 miles), marked. **Ferry**: seasonal service from Bowness Pier 3 (01539 448600 for details). **Bus**: regular service, plus seasonal service from Bowness Pier 3. **Train**: Windermere 4½ miles via vehicle ferry. **Road**: B5286 and B5285 from Ambleside (6 miles), B5285 from Coniston (7 miles). **Parking**: limited.

Finding out more: 015394 36269 or hilltop@nationaltrust.org.uk

Hill Top		M	T	W	T	F	S	S
House								
9 Feb–21 Mar	10:30–3:30	M	T	W	T	·	S	S
23 Mar–23 May	10:30–4:30	M	T	W	T	·	S	S
25 May–29 Aug	10–5:30	M	T	W	T	·	S	S
31 Aug–3 Nov	10:30–4:30	M	T	W	T	·	S	S
Shop and garden								
9 Feb–22 Mar	10:15–4	M	T	W	T	F	S	S
23 Mar–24 May	10–5	M	T	W	T	F	S	S
25 May–30 Aug	9:45–5:45	M	T	W	T	F	S	S
31 Aug–3 Nov	10–5	M	T	W	T	F	S	S
4 Nov–24 Dec	10–4	M	T	W	T	F	S	S

House open various Fridays throughout the year. Entry by timed ticket (limited). Small car park. Access to garden and shop free during opening hours. Shop closes at 1 on 24 December.

Beatrix Potter's bedroom at Hill Top, Cumbria

Entry is still possible at most places up to 30 minutes before closing

Keld Chapel

Keld Lane, Shap, Cumbria CA10 3NW

Map ⑥ E7 🏠

16th-century chapel, linked to Shap Abbey.
Note: no facilities. Access daily (for key,
see the notice on chapel door).

Finding out more: 015395 69816
or www.nationaltrust.org.uk

Little Moreton Hall

Congleton, Cheshire CW12 4SD

Map ⑤ D9 🏠✝🏛❖

A Cheshire icon not to be missed! This quirky
black and white Tudor hall, surrounded by a
moat, is brought to life through free guided tours
and Tudor festivals throughout the year. You
can take a peek at Tudor life with our costumed
guides as you explore this charming and quirky
property. Our small orchard, pretty knot garden
and large front lawn provide the perfect setting
for relaxing and enjoying time with friends and
family. Our new visitor facilities include a larger
shop located in the car park and delightful
tea-room and popular restaurant within the Hall.

Eating and shopping: Little Tea Room.
Brewhouse Restaurant. Shop selling local
ice-cream and gifts.

Making the most of your day: free guided
tours and costumed interpreters. Tudor
festivals all year, including Midsummer,
Michaelmas and Yuletide. Open-air theatre.
Children's activities, including Tudor games
and costumes to try on. **Dogs**: on leads in
car park and front lawn only.

Access for all: 🅿️🅳♿🚻♿🅿️📷📷📹♿
👁️📷 Building ♿♿♿♿ Grounds ♿♿➡️

Getting here: 118:SJ832589. 4 miles south-west
of Congleton. **Foot**: leave Macclesfield

Distinctive Little Moreton Hall in Cheshire

Canal at bridge 86. Directions from towpath.
Bus: services Alsager to Congleton (passing
close to Kidsgrove), infrequent (not Sundays).
Train: Kidsgrove 3 miles; Congleton 4 miles.
Road: East side of A34. M6 exit 17 follow
signs for Congleton and join A34 southbound
(signed Newcastle) from Congleton.
Parking: 100 yards.

Finding out more: 01260 272018 or
littlemoretonhall@nationaltrust.org.uk

Little Moreton Hall		M	T	W	T	F	S	S
16 Feb–24 Feb	11–4	·	·	W	T	F	S	S
2 Mar–10 Mar	11–4	·	·	·	·	·	S	S
13 Mar–30 Jun	11–5	·	·	W	T	F	S	S
1 Jul–1 Sep	11–5	M	T	W	T	F	S	S
7 Sep–3 Nov	11–5	·	·	W	T	F	S	S
9 Nov–22 Dec	11–4	·	·	·	·	·	S	S

Open Bank Holiday Mondays.

Lyme Park, House and Garden

Disley, Stockport, Cheshire SK12 2NR

Map (5) E8 🏠✚❀♨🛏

At Lyme there is a picture of a servants' ball, which was painted at the height of the Edwardian age when this great sporting estate was enjoying a golden era. It captures a moment when Lyme was at its best; however, life would never be the same again after the tragedy of the Great War. You can explore lavish interiors and view treasures and beautiful gardens set against sweeping moorland, then dip into experiences of a vanished age. What was life like before the ball had ended? **Note**: owned and managed by the National Trust but partly financed by Stockport Metropolitan Borough Council.

Eating and shopping: restaurant serving lunch. Coffee shop. Refreshments and light meals from Servants' Hall. Gift, plant and bookshop.

Making the most of your day: family activities, including toys to play with, costumes to try on and books to read. Children's playscape, Crow Wood. CD sets the scene as you drive to the house. Newly opened butler's rooms. New walks leaflets. **Dogs**: under close control in park only (on leads in some areas).

Access for all: 🅿♿♿🚻♿♿📷🆚👓♿
House 🚶♿ Grounds 🚶♿♿

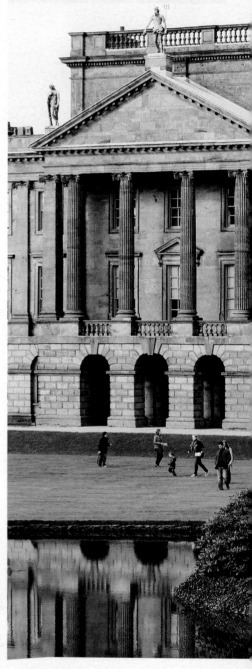

Lyme Park, House and Garden, Cheshire: an Edwardian painting of a servants' ball, above left, and an autumnal view of the imposing façade

We welcome dogs assisting visitors with disabilities

A quiet corner of the garden at Lyme Park

Getting here: 109:SJ965825. 1 mile from Disley. **Foot**: northern end Gritstone Trail. **Bus**: frequent services to entrance from Stockport and Buxton. **Train**: Disley ½ mile. **Road**: off A6 only. **Parking**: 200 yards from house.

Finding out more: 01663 762023 or lymepark@nationaltrust.org.uk

Lyme Park		M	T	W	T	F	S	S
Garden, 'Nuffin like a Puffin' exhibition and shop								
5 Jan–17 Feb	11–3	·	·	·	·	·	S	S
House, restaurant and shop								
25 Feb–27 Oct	11–5	M	T	·	·	F	S	S
Garden								
23 Feb–27 Oct	11–5	M	T	W	T	F	S	S
Park								
Open all year	8–6	M	T	W	T	F	S	S
Coffee shop								
Open all year	11–4	M	T	W	T	F	S	S
Plant sales and Timber Yard shop								
5 Jan–17 Feb	11–4	·	·	·	·	·	S	S
23 Feb–27 Oct	10:30–5	M	T	W	T	F	S	S
2 Nov–29 Dec	11–4	·	·	·	·	·	S	S

Closed 25 December. Last entry to house 4.

Nether Alderley Mill

Congleton Road, Nether Alderley, Macclesfield, Cheshire SK10 4TW

Map (5) D8

This charming rustic mill is one of only four virtually complete corn mills in Cheshire.

Finding out more: 01625 527468 or www.nationaltrust.org.uk

Quarry Bank Mill and Styal Estate

Styal, Wilmslow, Cheshire SK9 4LA

Map ⑤ D8

At Quarry Bank at Styal you can discover the compelling story of mill workers, entrepreneurs and the Industrial Revolution. There are hand-spinners working, the clatter of machinery and the hiss of steam engines – we also have Europe's most powerful working waterwheel. Guided tours take you to the Apprentice House, which housed the pauper children who worked in the mill. In the stunning garden, you can follow our progress with our Upper Garden Project. Nearby Styal village, built by the Gregs to house the mill workers, is still a thriving community. There are also woodland walks along the beautiful River Bollin.

Ironing the old-fashioned way at Quarry Bank Mill

Eating and shopping: shop selling gifts, mementoes and glass cloths produced in the mill. Plant sales. Mill Café serving lunch and afternoon tea. Coffee and ice-cream available from the Pantry. Picnic facilities.

Making the most of your day: events, including guided walks and open-air theatre. School holiday activities and trails for all the family. Family tours of the Apprentice House (summer) and children's play areas. Cycle route. **Dogs**: under close control on estate. On lead only in mill yard.

Access for all: 🅿️ 🚻 🚾 ⛎ 🅿️ 🖼 🎦 ⠿ ♿
Building 🔥 🏛 ♿   Grounds 🏛 ➡️ 🚲

Getting here: 109:SJ835835. 1½ miles north of Wilmslow. **Cycle**: NCN6, 1½ miles. RCR85, ½ mile. **Bus**: service from Manchester Airport station and Wilmslow stations. **Train**: Manchester Airport 2 miles; Wilmslow 2 miles; Styal (limited service) ½ mile. **Road**: off B5166, 2 miles from M56, exit 5. Signs from A34 and M56. **Parking**: 200 yards.

Quarry Bank Mill and Styal Estate, Cheshire: discovering the mill's story, above left, and the striking garden set in a valley

Finding out more: 01625 445896 (Infoline).
01625 527468 or
quarrybankmill@nationaltrust.org.uk

Quarry Bank Mill and Styal Estate		M	T	W	T	F	S	S
Mill and Apprentice House								
1 Jan–6 Jan	11–3:30	·	T	W	T	F	S	S
12 Jan–15 Feb	11–3:30	·	·	W	T	F	S	S
16 Feb–3 Nov	11–5	M	T	W	T	F	S	S
6 Nov–29 Dec	11–3:30	·	·	W	T	F	S	S
Garden								
16 Feb–3 Nov	10:30–5	M	T	W	T	F	S	S
Shop, café and ticket/information office								
1 Jan–6 Jan	10:30–4	·	T	W	T	F	S	S
12 Jan–15 Feb	10:30–4	·	·	W	T	F	S	S
16 Feb–3 Nov	10:30–5	M	T	W	T	F	S	S
6 Nov–29 Dec	10:30–4	·	·	W	T	F	S	S

Property closed 7 to 11 January for essential maintenance.
Closed 25 December, open daily 26 December to 6 January.
Apprentice House guided tours: timed tickets only,
available from ticket office (early arrival advised).

Rufford Old Hall, Lancashire, seen from the garden

Rufford Old Hall

200 Liverpool Road, Rufford, near Ormskirk,
Lancashire L40 1SG

Map ⑤ C6 🏠✴♿⬆🍴

Lancashire's magnificent Tudor Great Hall, with
its later additions, was home to the Hesketh
family until 1936. If you stand in front of the
moveable screen you can imagine a young Will
Shakespeare entertaining Sir Thomas Hesketh
and his guests in 1581. The drawing room,
overlooking the beautiful formal gardens, has
a table set for afternoon tea with Lady Hesketh.
You can find out about the children in the
portrait in the schoolroom, and what life was
like for them in the 1920s, then discover the
Hesketh family's lives, loves and fortunes, both
here and in America. **Note**: additional charges
for some events (including members).

Eating and shopping: tea-room serving local
food. Shop. Plant centre. Picnics welcome.

Making the most of your day: garden tours.
Daily quizzes and trails for children. Giant
chess, jenga, croquet or boules. Family
activities (school holidays). **Dogs**: on leads
in courtyard and woodland only.

Access for all: 🅿♿🚾♿♿📷📷📷♿
Building 🏠♿♿♿ **Grounds** 🏠♿♿➡♿

Getting here: 108:SD462161. ½ mile from
Rufford. **Foot**: on Leeds/Liverpool Canal
towpath. Enter via main drive. **Bus**: services
from Southport to Chorley and Preston to
Ormskirk. **Train**: Rufford ½ mile; Burscough
Bridge 2½ miles. **Road**: on A59. From M6
junction 27, follow signs for Parbold then
Rufford. **Parking**: on site.

Finding out more: 01704 821254 or
ruffordoldhall@nationaltrust.org.uk

Rufford Old Hall		M	T	W	T	F	S	S
House, garden, shop and tea-room								
16 Feb–6 Mar	11–4	M	T	W	·	·	S	S
9 Mar–28 Jul	11–5	M	T	W	·	·	S	S
29 Jul–1 Sep	11–5	M	T	W	T	·	S	S
2 Sep–30 Oct	11–5	M	T	W	·	·	S	S
2 Nov–15 Dec	11–4	·	·	·	·	·	S	S

Tudor Great Hall occasionally closed until 1. Open
Good Friday. Car park closes 30 minutes after times above.

Sandscale Haws National Nature Reserve

near Barrow in Furness, Cumbria

Map ⑥ D9

High, grass-covered sand dunes, home to some of the UK's rarest plants and animals.

Finding out more: 01229 462855 or www.nationaltrust.org.uk. Morecambe Bay Properties, Bank House Farm, Silverdale, Carnforth, Cumbria LA5 0RE

Sizergh in Cumbria, stands proud in its natural setting

Sizergh

Sizergh, near Kendal, Cumbria LA8 8AE

Map ⑥ E8

Sizergh – one family, one estate and more than 700 years of history. This much-loved family home stands proud in its natural setting. Still inhabited by the Strickland family, Sizergh has many tales to tell and certainly feels lived in, with centuries-old portraits sitting alongside modern family photographs. You can explore its gardens or venture into the 647 hectares (1,600 acres) of beautiful estate to spot the rich and diverse wildlife which also makes it their home. The atmosphere here is timeless, and it is an unexpected treasure at the gateway to the Lake District. **Note**: Sizergh is a family home, consequently there are some opening restrictions.

Eating and shopping: licensed café. Shop selling local products and plants. Strickland Arms pub and Low Sizergh tea-room. Picnics available.

Making the most of your day: events all year. Activities, including estate walks, garden trail and house quizzes for children. Elizabethan carvings of international significance. Kitchen garden, with hens and bees. Bird hide and feeding area. National Trust's largest limestone rock garden. Footpaths through estate, guided walks and orienteering.
Dogs: welcome in car park and estate footpaths. Assistance dogs only in house and garden.

Access for all: Building Grounds

Getting here: 97:SD498878. 3½ miles south of Kendal. **Cycle**: NCN6 and RCR20.
Bus: near to stops, Keswick to Lancaster, Kendal to Arnside. **Train**: Oxenholme 3 miles.
Road: M6 junction 36 then A590. From Lake District, take A591 south and then A590.
Sat Nav: use LA8 8DZ. **Parking**: 250 yards.

Finding out more: 015395 60951 or sizergh@nationaltrust.org.uk

Sizergh		M	T	W	T	F	S	S
House								
10 Mar–3 Nov	1–5	M	T	W	T	·	·	S
Garden, café and shop								
5 Jan–10 Feb	11–4	·	·	·	·	·	S	S
11 Feb–17 Feb	11–4	M	T	W	T	F	S	S
23 Feb–9 Mar	11–4	·	·	·	·	·	S	S
10 Mar–3 Nov	11–5	M	T	W	T	F	S	S
4 Nov–31 Dec	11–4	M	T	W	T	F	S	S
Estate								
Open all year	9–5	M	T	W	T	F	S	S

Two guided house tours also available 12 to 1 (places limited, £1 per person – can be booked or taken on the day). A timed-ticket system will be in operation on Sundays, school and Bank Holidays. Some parts of garden are closed Fridays and Saturdays and during January, February, November and December. Closed 25 December.

Inlaid commode and portrait in the Old Dining Room at Sizergh, left, and colourful poppies on the Top Terrace, above

Speke Hall, Garden and Estate, Liverpool: a Tudor manor house with Victorian interiors, set in gardens and woods

For all enquiries telephone 0844 800 1895 (seven days a week)

Speke Hall, Garden and Estate

Speke, Liverpool L24 1XD

Map ⑤ C8 🎟️🔩🔆♨️🔔

A rare example of a Tudor manor house with Victorian interiors and original William Morris wallpaper. In this beautiful building, which has witnessed more than 400 years of turbulent history, you can uncover hidden Tudor secrets, take a guided tour or play billiards. Speke Hall is surrounded by gardens and woodland with seasonal displays of rhododendrons, daffodils and bluebells. There is a maze to explore or you can enjoy a bracing walk with stunning views of the Welsh hills. A perfect oasis from modern life. **Note**: administered and financed by the National Trust, assisted by a grant from National Museums Liverpool.

Eating and shopping: local gifts, products and plants available. Home Farm restaurant serving regional specialities, such as Scouse Pie and Wet Nelly.

Making the most of your day: events all year, including Easter, Hallowe'en, Christmas, open-air theatre and themed Tudor and Victorian events, as well as period-costume guided tours. Gardens and woodland walks. Maze and restored kitchen garden. Children's playground and special activities. **Dogs**: on leads in woodland and on signed estate walks.

Access for all: 🅿️🅳🖼️🆒🔦📷🎁🖥️📱
👓🅰️ Hall 📶♿🔽 Grounds 🏢➡️🚗🔽

Getting here: 108:SJ419825. 8 miles south of city centre. **Cycle**: NCN62. **Bus**: Liverpool Airport bus, within 1 mile of entrance. **Train**: Liverpool South Parkway 2 miles. **Road**: adjacent to Liverpool Airport. 1 mile off A561. From M62 junction 6, A5300; M56 junction 12. Signs from city centre.

Finding out more: 0844 800 4799 (Infoline). 0151 427 7231 or spekehall@nationaltrust.org.uk

Speke Hall, Garden and Estate		M	T	W	T	F	S	S
20 Feb–24 Feb	11–4	·	·	W	T	F	S	S
2 Mar–17 Mar	11–4	·	·	·	·	·	S	S
20 Mar–28 Jul	11–5	·	·	W	T	F	S	S
30 Jul–1 Sep	10:30–5	·	T	W	T	F	S	S
4 Sep–27 Oct	11–5	·	·	W	T	F	S	S
2 Nov–8 Dec	11–4	·	·	·	·	·	S	S

House: entry before 12:30 by guided tour only (places limited); free-flow access from 12:30. Hall open Bank Holiday Mondays. Some rooms under covers 20 February to 17 March for conservation reasons. Car park closes 30 minutes after times stated above.

Bluebells carpet woodland at Speke Hall, above, and a detail of the ornate library fireplace, top

Steam Yacht Gondola

Coniston Pier, Lake Road,
Coniston, Cumbria LA21 8AN

Map (6) D8   🛥🔔🚻

Steam Yacht Gondola, with her sumptuous, upholstered saloons, is the perfect way to view Coniston's spectacular scenery from the lake. You can sail to Monk Coniston jetty at the north of the lake, then walk through the Monk Coniston garden to Tarn Hows. There is a circular walk of four miles or you can disembark at Brantwood to visit Ruskin's home. **Note**: all sailings subject to weather conditions. No toilet on scheduled sailings. Full fare applies to all passengers including members.

Eating and shopping: Bluebird Café, Coniston Pier serving local, freshly prepared food. Disembark at Brantwood jetty for Jumping Jenny's licensed café. Catering provided for private hires. Gondola souvenirs available on board.

Making the most of your day: cruises and guided walks. Events, including evening Campbell and *Bluebird* talks. **Dogs**: in outside areas only.

Access for all: 🅿♿🚾🅱🔊📷   Gangway 🚶♿

Getting here: 96:SD307970. Sails from Coniston Pier (½ mile from Coniston village). **Bus**: from Windermere ≷. **Train**: Foxfield, not Sunday, 10 miles; Windermere 10 miles via vehicle ferry. **Road**: A593 from Ambleside. Pier is at end of Lake Road, turn immediately left after petrol station if travelling south from centre of Coniston village. **Parking**: 50 yards, pay and display, at Coniston Pier (not National Trust).

Finding out more: 01539 432733 or sygondola@nationaltrust.org.uk. Low Wray Campsite, Low Wray, Ambleside, Cumbria LA22 0JA

Steam Yacht Gondola

Daily sailing 27 March to 1 November. Please visit website or call for sailing timetable. Piers at Coniston, Monk Coniston, Parkamoor and Brantwood (not National Trust).

Steam Yacht Gondola on Coniston, Cumbria

Beautiful countryside and majestic mountain views at peaceful Tarn Hows in the Lake District, Cumbria

Tarn Hows

Coniston, Cumbria

Map (6) D8

Stunning Tarn Hows offers an accessible circular (1¾ miles) walk through beautiful countryside with majestic mountain views. A great place to walk and picnic, or to begin your wider Lake District countryside adventure. There are also rare Belted Galloway cattle and sturdy Herdwick sheep grazing by the tarn.

Eating and shopping: local hot food 'Heritage Meats' and ice-cream vans onsite. Numerous catering options, particularly in Coniston and Hawkshead. Trust shop in nearby Hawkshead.

Making the most of your day: Steam Yacht Gondola cruises on Coniston. Accessible circular walk around tarn. Wray Castle nearby. **Dogs**: on leads at Tarn Hows (stock grazing).

Access for all: 🅿️♿🚻♿

Getting here: 90/96:SD326995. 2 miles north-east of Coniston and north-west of Hawkshead. **Foot**: from Coniston and Hawkshead. **Cycle**: on road (please note no cycling around tarns). **Bus**: service from Hawkshead to Coniston drops off a mile away. **Road**: signposted from B5285. **Parking**: free.

Finding out more: 015394 41456 or tarnhows@nationaltrust.org.uk

Tarn Hows	Open every day all year

Tatton Park

Knutsford, Cheshire WA16 6QN

Map (5) D8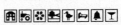

Tatton Park, Cheshire: a complete historic estate

This is one of the most complete historic estates open to visitors. The early 19th-century Wyatt house sits amid a landscaped 400-hectare (1,000-acre) deer-park and is opulently decorated, providing a fine setting for the Egerton family's collections of pictures, books, china, glass, silver and specially commissioned Gillows furniture. The theme of Victorian grandeur extends into the garden, with its Fernery, Orangery, Rose Garden, Tower Garden, Pinetum, Walled Garden with glasshouses, plus Italian and Japanese gardens (viewed from its perimeter). Other features include a 1930s working rare breeds farm, a children's play area, speciality shops, as well as a restaurant and deer-park.

Note: managed and financed by Cheshire East Council. For tours, RHS show, Christmas and other events supplementary charges may apply (including members).

Eating and shopping: shops at Tatton's Stableyard selling local and estate produce and gifts and souvenirs. The Stables Restaurant serving local dishes.

Making the most of your day: www.tattonpark.org.uk for events. Members – free admission to house and gardens only, half-price to farm, car entry charge. Old Hall special openings. 'The Magic of Beatrix Potter at Tatton Park', 23 March to 28 July. Dogs: on leads at farm and under close control in park only.

Access for all: 🅿️ 🚻 ♿ 🔋 📷 🖼️ 🚼 ⠿ 🅐
Building 🦽🧑‍🦽♿👁️ Grounds 🦽🧑‍🦽➡️🚳

Getting here: 109/118:SJ745815. 2 miles north of Knutsford, 4 miles south of Altrincham.
Cycle: Cheshire Cycleway. Bus: buses to Knutsford, then 2 miles. Train: Knutsford 2 miles. Road: 5 miles from M6, junction 19; 3 miles from M56, junction 7, signposted on A556. Sat Nav: use WA16 6SG.
Parking: car entry charge (including members).

Finding out more: 01625 374435 (Infoline). 01625 374400 or tatton@cheshireeast.gov.uk. www.tattonpark.org.uk.

Tatton Park		M	T	W	T	F	S	S
Parkland								
1 Jan–22 Mar	11–5		T	W	T	F	S	S
23 Mar–27 Oct	10–7	M	T	W	T	F	S	S
29 Oct–31 Dec	11–5		T	W	T	F	S	S
Mansion								
23 Mar–29 Sep	1–5		T	W	T	F	S	S
1 Oct–27 Oct	12–4		T	W	T	F	S	S
Gardens and restaurant								
1 Jan–22 Mar	11–4		T	W	T	F	S	S
23 Mar–27 Oct	10–6	M	T	W	T	F	S	S
29 Oct–31 Dec	11–4		T	W	T	F	S	S
Farm								
5 Jan–17 Mar	11–4						S	S
23 Mar–27 Oct	12–5		T	W	T	F	S	S
2 Nov–29 Dec	11–4						S	S
Shops								
1 Jan–22 Mar	12–4		T	W	T	F	S	S
23 Mar–27 Oct	11–5	M	T	W	T	F	S	S
29 Oct–31 Dec	12–4		T	W	T	F	S	S

Open Bank Holiday Mondays. Closed 25 December. Attractions: last admission one hour before closing. Mansion open for Christmas events during December (charge including members). Guided mansion tours Tuesday to Sunday 23 March to 29 September at 12 by timed ticket available from garden entrance after 10:30 (places limited), small charge including members. Old Hall special opening arrangements. Advisable to check opening times before visiting.

A timeless scene in the landscaped deer-park at Tatton Park in Cheshire

Members may have to pay on special events days

The south front of Townend, Cumbria, above, and a young visitor is entranced by a miniature chair, below

Townend

Troutbeck, Windermere, Cumbria LA23 1LB

Map (6) D8

The Brownes of Townend were just an ordinary farming family, but their home and belongings bring to life more than 400 years of extraordinary stories. You will understand why Beatrix Potter described Troutbeck Valley as her favourite as you approach this traditional stone and slate farmhouse. Once inside, you are welcomed into the farmhouse kitchen, which has a real fire burning most days and a quirky collection of domestic tools. Exploring further, you can marvel at the intricately carved furniture and discover why the collection of books belonging to a farming family is of international importance.

Eating and shopping: selection of postcards and souvenirs available. Second-hand books. Plant sales.

Making the most of your day: rag-rug making. Live interpretation. Children's trail. Guided tours. Downloadable circular walks.

Access for all:

Building Grounds

Getting here: 90:NY407023. 3 miles south-east of Ambleside at south end of Troutbeck village. **Bus**: services from Windermere ⊠, alight Troutbeck Bridge, 1½ miles. **Train**: Windermere 2½ miles. **Road**: off A591 or A592. **Parking**: free, 300 yards. Not suitable for coaches or campervans.

Finding out more: 015394-32628 or townend@nationaltrust.org.uk

Townend		M	T	W	T	F	S	S
House tours*								
9 Mar–3 Nov	11–1	·	·	W	T	F	S	S
House								
9 Mar–3 Nov	1–5	·	·	W	T	F	S	S

*11 to 1 entry by guided tour only at 11 and 12 (places limited, first come, first served). Open Bank Holiday Mondays. May close early due to poor light. Property less busy at weekends.

Wasdale, Eskdale and Duddon

near Seascale, Cumbria

Map ⑥ D8

Below Scafell Pike, England's highest mountain, lies Wastwater, England's deepest lake, with its majestic screes. The National Trust owns the valley farms, campsite, lake, surrounding mountains and nearby Nether Wasdale Estate. There are delightful riverside and mountain paths to follow in Upper Eskdale and the ever-changing Duddon Valley to explore.

Eating and shopping: shop at campsite.

Making the most of your day: Hardknott Roman fort. England's highest mountain. Wasdale campsite.

Dogs: under close control (stock grazing).

Access for all: Grounds 🏞

Getting here: NY152055. Wasdale 5 miles east of Seascale; Eskdale 3 miles east of Ravenglass; Duddon 3 miles west of Broughton-in-Furness. **Train**: Ravenglass for Eskdale; Foxfield for Duddon; Seascale for Wasdale. **Road**: Wasdale 5 miles east of A595, turning at Gosforth. Eskdale, 6 miles east of A595, turning at Holmrook. Duddon 3 miles north of A595, turning at Duddon Bridge near Broughton-in-Furness. **Parking**: at Wasdale Head.

Finding out more: 01946 726064 or wasdale@nationaltrust.org.uk.
The Lodge, Wasdale Hall, Wasdale, Cumbria CA20 1ET

Wasdale, Eskdale and Duddon	Open every day all year

Wordsworth House and Garden

Main Street, Cockermouth, Cumbria CA13 9RX

Map ⑥ C7 🏠✦

At this beautiful, homely property you can step back to the 1770s and experience life as William Wordsworth and his sister Dorothy might have. There is a warm welcome from the Wordsworths' servants and you can find out more about the restoration of the house, cellars and garden. William's beloved garden inspired many of his poems and contains 18th-century flowers, fruit and vegetables – all used in the house. We have a beautiful summerhouse on the terrace walk and an audio unit plays poetry and accounts of the great 2009 flood. There are daily talks, recipe tastings and children's holiday activities.

Eating and shopping: shop selling Wordsworth and local souvenirs. Café serving light lunches and cakes.

Making the most of your day: activities, including talks, harpsichord music, garden tours, cooking demonstrations, Georgian tastings, games and crafts. Costumed servants. Family activities (school holidays). Dressing-up and traditional toys.

Access for all: 🚻♿🏷️🖼️🎧📷🅥🔊 :: Ⓐ
Building 👆✦♿ Grounds 👆♿

Getting here: 89:NY118307. In centre of Cockermouth. **Foot**: entrance on Main Street, not side gate on Low Sand Lane. **Cycle**: NCN71 (C2C) and NCN10 (Reivers) pass door. **Bus**: from Penrith ➡ or Keswick to Cockermouth, and Workington to Cockermouth. **Train**: Workington 8 miles; Maryport 6½ miles. **Road**: off A66, on Cockermouth Main Street. **Parking**: town centre car parks. Long-stay car park signposted as coach park (not National Trust), 300 yards, Wakefield Road. Walk back over footbridge to house.

Finding out more: 01900 820884 (Infoline). 01900 824805 or wordsworthhouse@nationaltrust.org.uk

Wordsworth House and Garden		M	T	W	T	F	S	S
House, garden and café*								
9 Mar–3 Nov	11–5		M	T	W	T	.	S	S
Shop								
2 Jan–12 Jan	10:30–4:30	M	T	W	T	F	S	.
9 Mar–3 Nov	10–5	M	T	W	T	F	S	S
4 Nov–23 Dec	10:30–4:30	M	T	W	T	F	S	.

*Café: open 10:30 to 4:30. House: last entry 4.
Timed tickets may operate on busy days.

Wordsworth House and Garden, Cumbria: experience life as it was lived in William Wordsworth's day

Wray Castle

Low Wray, Ambleside, Cumbria LA22 0JA

Map (6) D8 （icons）

Set in beautiful grounds on Lake Windermere's western shore, with its own boathouse and jetty, you can explore this amazing mock-gothic castle inside and outside, whatever the weather. Although empty of original furniture, it has something for all the family – feel free to run around and make noise! Not the usual National Trust visit, so check out our website for more information about the changing activities at this exciting, newly opened National Trust property.

Eating and shopping: café in castle serving locally produced snacks. Small souvenir shop. Picnics welcome on lakeshore.

Wray Castle, Cumbria, on the banks of Lake Windermere

Making the most of your day: children's activities, including dressing-up, trails and cardboard castle building. Exhibition at Beatrix Potter Gallery (Hawkshead) nearby.

Access for all: 〔icons〕 Castle 〔icons〕

Getting here: 96/97:NY375010. 3½ miles south-west of Ambleside. **Foot**: lakeside path and bridleway from car ferry, 4 miles. **Cycle**: as by foot. **Ferry**: from Ambleside or Brockhole (015394 32225 or www.windermere-lakecruises.co.uk). **Train**: Windermere, 8 miles via Ambleside. **Road**: from Ambleside A593 into B5285 and road signposted to Wray. **Parking**: pay and display (non-members).

Finding out more: 015394 33250 or wraycastle@nationaltrust.org.uk

Wray Castle		M	T	W	T	F	S	S
Castle								
23 Mar–3 Nov	10–5	M	T	W	T	F	S	S
8 Nov–22 Dec	10:30–4	·	·	·	·	F	S	S
Grounds								
Open all year	Dawn–dusk	M	T	W	T	F	S	S

Yorkshire and North East

Sinuous curves and rocky crags on the Pennine Way in the Yorkshire Dales, North Yorkshire

Outdoors in Yorkshire and the North East

Yorkshire and the North East are places of dramatic contrasts, each with a character and charm entirely its own.

Yorkshire has more countryside within National Parks than any other region. Walk alongside dry-stone walls through green valleys in the Yorkshire Dales or adventure across wild moorland and rocky crags in the North York Moors.

In the North East you can explore unspoilt coastline and rugged countryside in Northumberland, or discover tranquil woodlands and beautifully restored beaches around Durham.

Add to this a Roman World Heritage Site, the historic Holy Island and one of Europe's most exciting nature reserves, and you get a sense of the great outdoor adventures just waiting to be had.

A pleasure ground for walking
The Yorkshire Dales are a pleasure ground for walkers, with endless routes to explore. The Trust cares for 3,000 hectares (7,500 acres) of the Dales and has waymarked walks for all abilities. From riverside beauty spots and picturesque villages in Upper Wharfedale, to limestone uplands and flower-rich hay meadows around Malham Tarn.

At Hardcastle Crags in West Yorkshire you can enjoy beautiful woodland walks alongside tumbling streams. Follow miles of footpaths through deep ravines, and if you visit in late spring you'll see the woodland carpeted with bluebells.

Over at the edge of the North York Moors, you'll find gentle trails around the iconic Roseberry Topping. If you walk 350 yards to the summit, you will be rewarded with spectacular views across industrial Teesside, the moors and coastline.

Following ancient footsteps

Two thousand years ago a rugged stretch of Northumberland countryside was at the forefront of the Roman Empire. Today, Hadrian's Wall is a World Heritage Site surrounded by fantastic landscapes with breathtaking views, perfect for exploring on foot. We protect six miles of the wall, including Housesteads Fort, one of the best-preserved sections of the ramparts.

For a gentler stroll, the ancient woodland at Allen Banks and Staward Gorge has miles of tranquil footpaths to explore – look out for the remains of a medieval pele-tower on the way.

For downloadable walks in all these places and more, visit **www.nationaltrust.org.uk/walks**

Adventure for all

If you're looking to get active in the outdoors then look no further – we've got it all in Yorkshire and the North East.

The colossal rock formations at Brimham Rocks have more than 470 different climbs for beginners and experts alike – all with views over the Nidderdale Area of Outstanding Natural Beauty. Or feel the freedom of cycling in the fresh air, whether you're a thrill-seeking mountain biker or looking for a gentle pedal.

Follow the northern section of the Pennine Cycleway close to Hadrian's Wall or have an urban adventure on a route around Ormesby Hall near Middlesbrough, with views of the Transporter Bridge and River Tees.

Above:
Hadrian's Wall,
Northumberland,
hugs the
contours of
the landscape
Left:
Brimham Rocks,
North Yorkshire

The endless landscapes of the Yorkshire Dales have uplands that are perfect for off-road mountain biking alongside limestone pavements and fells around Malham Tarn and Upper Wharfedale. Families wanting gentler routes will find the flatter paths around the Tarn are absolutely ideal.

Hard-hat adventure waits in the depths beneath the Dales, where our Rangers will take you to explore caves, ghylls and mine tunnels. And from scrambling below ground to soaring above it, what could be more inspiring than getting a bird's-eye view over Marsden Moor in West Yorkshire? Buckstones is a perfect base for paragliding or hang-gliding – the ultimate dare-devil sports.

Silver sands and Jurassic coast

There's no better natural refreshment than a blast of sea air. And with 33 miles of coastline in our care, you'll find the perfect seaside stroll or coastal adventure in this diverse region.

Why not escape to unspoilt sandy beaches in Northumberland, where an iconic coastal castle is never far away? Or listen to the crashing waves along the shore at Horden Beach in County Durham, which marks the 500th mile acquired through the Trust's Neptune Coastline Campaign.

Or you could explore the Yorkshire coast, with tidal rock pools to investigate and stunning clifftop views to savour. Halfway between Whitby and Scarborough sits the village of Ravenscar, where you can stroll along the cliffs for commanding views of the bay below. Yorkshire's Jurassic coast is the best place in the region to hunt for fossils; dinosaur remains were discovered nearby and ammonites are regularly found on the shoreline.

Above:
looking towards Lindisfarne Castle, Northumberland
Below:
puffins on Staple Island, one of the Farne Islands, Northumberland

Rare and special nature

You'll find one of Europe's finest seabird reserves on the Farne Islands, just off the Northumberland coast. If you visit during the breeding season (May to June), you will encounter more than 100,000 nesting birds, including guillemots, eider ducks and friendly-faced puffins. Or you may enjoy the thrill of meeting some other special inhabitants: England's largest colony of grey seals welcomes more than 1,000 newborn pups here every autumn.

Or you could head inland to Northumberland's vast woodland, one of the few sanctuaries in England for our threatened native red squirrels. If you stay very quiet, you may spot one scurrying through the woods around Allen Banks, Cragside and Wallington.

With so much land in National Parks, it's not surprising that there's an abundance of rare and special nature in Yorkshire. We care for several reserves where you can get close to beautiful and endearing wildlife.

Marsden Moor is an area so rich in birdlife it's been designated as an International Special Protection Area. Why not see if you can spot a golden plover, red grouse, curlew, snipe or twite?

The boardwalk around the National Nature Reserve at Malham Tarn takes you to a unique community of rare plants, birds and insects. There's a bird hide and opportunities for pond dipping, while in late June and July you can join a guided walk and see a glorious display of flowers. Also, as the highest glacial lake in England, the Tarn itself is a natural wonder.

Below:
dawn at Malham, North Yorkshire

Why not try…?

Staying in a characterful cottage
With so much to do, a day is never enough. Rent one of our cottages and you will not want to leave. Stay among the dunes of the Northumberland coast, in a cosy hideaway on the dramatic Cragside Estate or sleep under stylish canvas in a yurt at Gibside. You can even stay in the Old Coastguard Station at Robin Hood's Bay or find the perfect walkers' getaway at a cottage in the Dales. **www. nationaltrustcottages. co.uk**

Exploring Holy Island's castle and crags
Holy Island is a treasure, with the magnificent Lindisfarne Castle as its centrepiece. Once a Tudor fort, the castle sits on a rocky crag that can be seen for miles along the Northumberland coastline. Stroll along the headland and explore the village – just remember to keep an eye on the tides which cover the causeway!

Rock climbing at Brimham Rocks
Get hands-on with the rocks at Brimham. There are tough climbs for the more experienced or taster days for beginners. The rocks are named after their shapes, so you may be taking on the Dancing Bear or negotiating with the Cheese Grater!

Walking along Hadrian's Wall
Lace up your boots and walk in the steps of Roman soldiers. Take in the amazing sights on the way to Milecastle 37 and the infamous Sycamore Gap, and visit Housesteads Fort for an insight into Roman military life.

A winter adventure at Roseberry Topping
When the snow falls, there's a new world of fun waiting outdoors. Wrap up warm and grab a sledge then head for Roseberry Topping on the edge of the North York Moors, where the slopes at the foot of the hill are perfect for sliding and snowball fights.

Something new all year round
Fancy getting active, but would rather join an organised event than go it alone? Our Rangers and volunteers run events all year round designed to make the most of our great landscapes. There is so much to do, from mountain biking and climbing, to family activities such as den building and rock-pooling.

Visit our websites **www.nationaltrust.org.uk/ yorkshire** and **www.nationaltrust.org.uk/ northeast** for the latest events. Alternatively, you can connect with us on Facebook and Twitter – search for NTYorkshire and NorthEastNT.

Allen Banks and Staward Gorge

Bardon Mill, Hexham, Northumberland

Map ⑥ F5

This spectacular gorge and river cuts through the largest area of ancient woodland in the county. There are miles of waymarked walks, the remains of a medieval pele-tower and a reconstructed Victorian summerhouse. Within the North Pennines Area of Outstanding Natural Beauty.

Eating and shopping: numerous picnic spots, either at Allen Banks car park, in the woodland or by the river.

Making the most of your day: guided walks and family activities, including Forest Schools, tree trail and workshops on fungi and woodland birds. **Dogs**: welcome under close control.

Access for all: 🚻 ♿

Grounds 🌳

Getting here: 86:NY799640. 1½ miles from Bardon Mill, 3 miles west of Haydon Bridge, 5½ miles east of Haltwhistle. **Foot**: public and permitted rights of way. **Cycle**: NCN72, 2½ miles. **Bus**: services from Carlisle to Newcastle upon Tyne, alight ½ mile. **Train**: Bardon Mill 1½ miles. **Road**: ½ mile south of A69. **Sat Nav**: avoid using. **Parking**: pay and display at Allen Banks. 3.3-metre height restriction.

Finding out more: 01434 344218 or allenbanks@nationaltrust.org.uk. Housesteads Farm, Haydon Bridge, Hexham, Northumberland NE47 6NN

Allen Banks and Staward Gorge	M	T	W	T	F	S	S
Open every day all year	Dawn–dusk						

Beningbrough Hall and Gardens

Beningbrough, York, North Yorkshire YO30 1DD

Map ⑤ G4

Beautiful gardens, parkland walks and an intriguing house to explore. Beningbrough is a great place to relax and be inspired all year round. Enjoy colourful Edwardian borders, working Victorian walled garden, labyrinth and family trails. Meet the most powerful and influential people of the 18th century in our outstanding portrait collection. In an imaginative partnership with the National Portrait Gallery, paintings and sculptures are brought to life throughout historic rooms and hands-on galleries in the Italian-inspired house. Furniture and ceramics complement a grand interior, where the people in the portraits would feel at home– you may even meet a few!

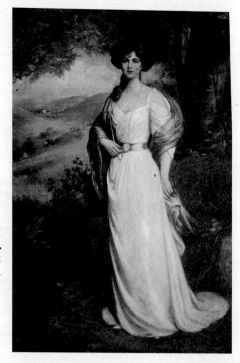

Portrait of the Countess of Chesterfield at Beningbrough Hall, North Yorkshire. The Chesterfields bought the house in 1917 and furnished it lavishly

Members may have to pay on special events days

Enjoying the last rays of sunshine in the garden at Beningbrough Hall, North Yorkshire

Eating and shopping: Walled Garden Restaurant serving hot lunches and snacks. Shop selling souvenirs, gifts, garden and lifestyle products and plants.

Making the most of your day: family-friendly events and Artrageous! workshops. Living history and hidden house tours. Interactive galleries. Guided garden walks, wilderness play area and parkland. Christmas experience. Anniversary display, interpretation and activities on life at Beningbrough during the Second World War. **Dogs**: assistance dogs only in gardens and grounds, dogs on leads welcome in parkland.

Access for all: 🅿️ 🅳 🚾 ♿ 📷 👁️ 🅰️
Mansion 👤 ♿ ⬆️ ♿ Stable block ♿ ♿
Grounds 👤 ♿ ➡️ ♿

Getting here: 105:SE516586. 8 miles north-west of York. **Foot**: beside River Ouse. **Cycle**: NCN65. **Bus**: infrequent service to Newton-on-Ouse, approximately 1 mile. **Train**: York, 8 miles. **Road**: signposted off A59 and A19. **Parking**: free.

Finding out more: 01904 472027 or beningbrough@nationaltrust.org.uk

Beningbrough Hall and Gardens		M	T	W	T	F	S	S
House, galleries, gardens, shop and restaurant*								
1 Mar–30 Jun	11–5:30		T	W	T	F	S	S
1 Jul–1 Sep	11–5:30	M	T	W	T	F	S	S
3 Sep–3 Nov	11–5:30		T	W	T	F	S	S
Galleries, gardens, shop and restaurant**								
5 Jan–17 Feb	11–3:30						S	S
19 Feb–24 Feb	11–3:30		T	W	T	F	S	S
9 Nov–29 Dec	11–3:30						S	S

*House and galleries open 12 to 5. On occasion, house access by guided tour only. **Galleries open 11:30 to 3:30. Open Bank Holiday Mondays, 26 December and 1 January 2014.

The productive garden at Beningbrough Hall

Children explore the fantastically shaped Brimham Rocks in North Yorkshire

Braithwaite Hall

East Witton, Leyburn, North Yorkshire DL8 4SY

Map (5) E3

Beautiful 17th-century tenanted farmhouse in Coverdale. **Note**: no toilet. Open June to September (visits by arrangement in advance with the tenant).

Finding out more: 01969 640287 or www.nationaltrust.org.uk

Bridestones, Crosscliff and Blakey Topping

Staindale, Dalby, Pickering, North Yorkshire YO18 7LR

Map (5) I3

Spectacular all year, the Bridestones are a geological wonder – with moorland vistas, woodland walks and grassy valleys. **Note**: nearest toilets at Staindale Lake car park. Dalby Forest drive starting 2½ miles north of Thornton le Dale – toll charges (including members).

Finding out more: 01723 870423 or www.nationaltrust.org.uk. c/o Peakside, Ravenscar, Scarborough, North Yorkshire YO13 0NE

Brimham Rocks

Summerbridge, Harrogate, North Yorkshire HG3 4DW

Map (5) F4

Fantastically shaped rocks, formed more than 320 million years ago. A great day out for families, climbers or anyone looking to enjoy fresh air, beautiful walks and fantastic views over the Nidderdale Area of Outstanding Natural Beauty. **Note**: beware cliff edges. Nearest toilets 600 yards from car park.

Eating and shopping: shop selling books, gifts and local produce. Refreshments and ice-cream kiosk. Picnic tables.

Making the most of your day: exhibition (in the visitor centre) on the rocks, social history and conservation. Family activities and events. Guided walks. **Dogs**: under control and on leads on moorland April to June (ground-nesting birds).

Access for all: ⬚⬚⬚⬚⬚⬚⬚⬚
Building ⬚⬚ Grounds ➡

Getting here: 99:SE206650. 10 miles south-west of Ripon. **Foot**: Nidderdale Way passes through. **Cycle**: Way of the Roses route passes entrance. **Bus**: from Harrogate: to Brimham Rocks, May to October; to Pateley Bridge, alight Summerbridge, 2 miles. **Road**: 11 miles from Harrogate off B6165, 4 miles from Pateley Bridge off B6265. **Sat Nav**: gives approximate location. **Parking**: free.

Finding out more: 01423 780688 or
brimhamrocks@nationaltrust.org.uk

Brimham Rocks		M	T	W	T	F	S	S
Countryside								
Open all year	8–dusk	M	T	W	T	F	S	S
Visitor centre, shop and kiosk								
16 Feb–24 Feb	11–5	M	T	W	T	F	S	S
2 Mar–24 Mar	11–5	·	·	·	·	·	S	S
30 Mar–14 Apr	11–5	M	T	W	T	F	S	S
4 May–19 May	11–5	·	·	·	·	·	S	S
25 May–29 Sep	11–5	M	T	W	T	F	S	S
5 Oct–20 Oct	11–5	·	·	·	·	·	S	S
26 Oct–3 Nov	11–5	M	T	W	T	F	S	S
9 Nov–29 Dec	11–4	·	·	·	·	·	S	S

Visitor centre, shop and kiosk open Bank Holiday 29 March and 6 May. Also open 26 December and 1 January 2014.

Access for all: ♿ 🅿️ 📶 🚻 👁️ 🔊 ❓ ♿ 👓

Building ♿♿♿   Grounds ♿♿

Getting here: 88:NZ075627. Close to south bank of River Tyne. **Bus**: Newcastle to Hexham (passes Newcastle ≋), alight Mickley Square, ¼ mile. **Train**: Stocksfield 1½ miles; Prudhoe 1½ miles. **Road**: 11 miles west of Newcastle and east of Hexham; follow brown sign off A695 at Mickley Square on to Station Bank. **Parking**: free, 100 yards.

Finding out more: 01661 843276 or cherryburn@nationaltrust.org.uk

Cherryburn		M	T	W	T	F	S	S
16 Feb–30 Jun	11–5	M	T	·	T	F	S	S
1 Jul–1 Sep	10–5	M	T	W	T	F	S	S
2 Sep–3 Nov	11–5	M	T	·	T	F	S	S

Cherryburn

Station Bank, Mickley, Stocksfield,
Northumberland NE43 7DD

Map ⑥ G5   🏠 🔧 📷 ♣ 🐾 🍴

Thomas Bewick, the wood engraver and naturalist who revolutionised print art in Georgian England, was born in this tiny cottage, a farmstead with glorious views over the Tyne Valley. In the traditional 19th-century farmhouse (the later home of the Bewick family), there is an unrivalled collection of Bewick's work and exhibition about his life. He was possibly Northumberland's greatest artist, and you can follow his wood blocks on their journey to the print room, where regular Sunday afternoon demonstrations bring alive this intricate craft. Outside, the delightful cottage gardens and paddock walk are perfect for picnicking or playing.

Eating and shopping: prints from original Bewick engravings, local produce, gifts and books for sale. Farmhouse kitchen serving drinks, snacks and homemade cakes. Farmyard picnic area.

Making the most of your day: regular print demonstrations. Guided walks. Events, including Folk in the Farmyard. Family activities and trails.
Dogs: welcome on short leads in garden and grounds (free-range hens in farmyard).

Thomas Bewick's Cherryburn, Northumberland

Cragside

Rothbury, Morpeth, Northumberland NE65 7PX

Map ⑥ G3 🏠 🛗 ✴ 🍴 🛏 ⌂

Trip the light fantastic to the home where modern living began. Lord and Lady Armstrong used their wealth, art and science in a most ingenious way, and Cragside house was the first in the world to be lit by hydroelectricity – making it a wonder of the Victorian age. Outside, their shared passion for landscaping and gardening was daring and engineered on a spectacular scale. There are towering North American conifers and great drifts of rhododendrons, as well as rocky crags and tumbling water. The house is one of the finest examples of Arts and Crafts workmanship in the country. **Note**: challenging terrain and distances. Stout footwear essential.

Eating and shopping: licensed tea-rooms serving refreshments, hot meals, cream teas and ice-cream. Plant sales.

Making the most of your day: hydroelectric engineering collection and fantasy landscape. Rhododendron labyrinth. Six-mile drive through woodland. Walks for all ages and abilities, from family strolls to strenuous hikes. Family activities and special events throughout the season. Courtesy bus between key features. **Dogs**: welcome on leads on estate only.

Access for all: 🅿️ 🅳 ⛪ 🚹 🔔 🛗 📷 VT ⛰
⛱ 🅰 House ♿ 🔔 Visitor centre ♿ ♿ 🔔
Estate 🔔 ▶

Getting here: 81:NU073022. 13 miles south-west of Alnwick. **Bus**: to nearby Rothbury, with connections from Newcastle, Monday to Saturday. Special summer Sunday service to property. **Road**: on B6341, 15 miles north-west of Morpeth on Coldstream road (A697). Turn left on to B6341 at Moorhouse Crossroads, entrance 3 miles on left.
Parking: free, nine car parks throughout estate.

Finding out more: 01669 620333 or cragside@nationaltrust.org.uk

Cragside, Northumberland, inside and out

Cragside		M	T	W	T	F	S	S
House								
1 Mar–29 Mar	1–5	·	T	W	T	F	·	·
2 Mar–31 Mar	11–5	·	·	·	·	·	S	S
1 Apr–14 Apr	11–5	M	T	W	T	F	S	S
16 Apr–24 May	1–5	·	T	W	T	F	·	·
20 Apr–26 May	11–5	·	·	·	·	·	S	S
27 May–2 Jun	11–5	M	T	W	T	F	S	S
4 Jun–19 Jul	1–5	·	T	W	T	F	·	·
8 Jun–21 Jul	11–5	·	·	·	·	·	S	S
22 Jul–2 Sep	11–5	M	T	W	T	F	S	S
3 Sep–25 Oct	1–5	·	T	W	T	F	·	·
7 Sep–27 Oct	11–5	·	·	·	·	·	S	S
28 Oct–3 Nov	11–5	M	T	W	T	F	S	S
Gardens and woodland*								
1 Mar–3 Nov	10–7	:	T	W	T	F	S	S
8 Nov–22 Dec	11–4	·	·	·	·	F	S	S

House open Bank Holiday Monday 11 to 5. Entry is controlled (queueing at busy times). Last admission one hour before closing. *Gardens and woodland open Mondays when house is open. Last admission 5, close at 7 or sunset if earlier. Open 16 to 24 February: house (ground floor only) 12 to 4, gardens and woodland 11 to 4.

Places may occasionally close for conservation, safety or events

and unwind. Younger visitors can let off steam in the natural play areas, including a mud pie kitchen for budding chefs.

Eating and shopping: tea-room. Plant sales area and shop.

Making the most of your day: family trails. Exhibitions. Open-air theatre. Herb interpretation area. Walking for Health. **Dogs**: assistance dogs only.

Access for all: 🅿🅳♿👷🔧🎧💷🖥📷📱··🅰
Building 🔧♿🔧 **Grounds** 🔧

Getting here: 104:SE079421. 1 mile north-east of Keighley. **Bus**: Bradford Interchange ⬛ to Keighley, alight Granby Lane. **Train**: Keighley 1½ miles. **Road**: on south side of Bradford Road in Riddlesden. A629 relief road from Shipley and Skipton signed for East Riddlesden Hall. **Parking**: free, 100 yards.

Finding out more: 01535 607075 or eastriddlesden@nationaltrust.org.uk

East Riddlesden Hall		M	T	W	T	F	S	S
House, shop and tea-room								
16 Feb–24 Feb	10:30–4:30	M	T	W	·	·	S	S
2 Mar–10 Mar	10:30–4:30	·	·	·	·	·	S	S
16 Mar–3 Nov	10:30–4:30	M	T	W	·	·	S	S
Shop and tea-room								
9 Nov–22 Dec	11–4	·	·	·	·	·	S	S

Open Good Friday. Entry to house may be by guided tour. Last admission to tea-room 15 minutes before closing.

Dunstanburgh Castle

Craster, Alnwick, Northumberland NE66 3TT

Map ⑥ H3 🏯🗺

Iconic castle ruin occupying a commanding position with spectacular views of the Northumberland coastline.
Note: managed by English Heritage.

Finding out more: 01665 576231 or www.nationaltrust.org.uk

East Riddlesden Hall

Bradford Road, Riddlesden, Keighley, West Yorkshire BD20 5EL

Map ⑤ E5 🏛✿🌱♨🎭

East Riddlesden Hall boasts an excellent story of survival. For generations, the estate was a hive of farming activity. Today, visitors can step into the shoes of a 17th-century merchant and wander through the house and gardens. Inside the intimate rooms you'll discover fascinating stories, furniture and textiles, brought to life by our room guides. The romantic award-winning gardens are the perfect place to relax

The 17th-century East Riddlesden Hall, West Yorkshire

Farne Islands

Northumberland

Map (6) H2

Probably the most exciting seabird colony in England. Visitors to the islands have unrivalled views of 23 nesting species, including 37,000 pairs of puffins, Arctic terns and guillemots. There is also a large grey seal colony, with more than 1,000 pups born every autumn. **Note**: basic toilet facilities on Inner Farne only. Access by boat from Seahouses (charge including members).

Eating and shopping: shop in Seahouses.

Making the most of your day: Lindisfarne Castle nearby.

Access for all: ☑️♿️ Grounds 🏞️

Getting here: 75:NU230370. 2 to 5 miles off the Northumberland coast. **Cycle**: NCN1, ¾ mile from Seahouses harbour. **Ferry**: daily from Seahouses harbour, weather permitting. **Bus**: Newcastle ≋ to Alnwick ≋ and to Berwick, alight Seahouses, 1½ miles. **Train**: Chathill, 4 miles (not Sundays). **Parking**: in Seahouses opposite harbour (pay and display), not National Trust.

Puffin on the Farne Islands, Northumberland

Finding out more: 01665 721099 (Infoline). 01289 389244 (Lindisfarne Castle) or farneislands@nationaltrust.org.uk

Farne Islands		M	T	W	T	F	S	S
Both Islands								
29 Mar–30 Apr	10:30–6	M	T	W	T	F	S	S
1 Aug–31 Oct	10:30–6	M	T	W	T	F	S	S
Staple Island								
1 May–31 Jul	10:30–1:30	M	T	W	T	F	S	S
Inner Farne Island								
1 May–31 Jul	1:30–5	M	T	W	T	F	S	S

Landings only on Inner Farne and Staple Islands. Seahouses information centre and shop open all year, 10 to 5.

Fountains Abbey and Studley Royal Water Garden

Fountains, Ripon, North Yorkshire HG4 3DY

Map (5) F4

Monastic ruin or romantic folly? The breathtakingly designed landscape of the Aislabies, now a World Heritage Site with more than 800 years of history, includes the ruins of the once-wealthy and powerful Fountains Abbey. You can step back in time to see how the abbey ruins became a spectacular folly for 18th-century visitors as you journey through these gardens of pleasure. You will need plenty of time to explore the 323 hectares (800 acres) of medieval deer parkland, formal Georgian water gardens, Victorian high Gothic church, Jacobean manor house and monastic grounds, including the only surviving Cistercian corn mill. **Note**: cared for in partnership with English Heritage.

Eating and shopping: restaurant serving estate-reared venison. Lakeside and abbey tea-rooms. Large shop.

Making the most of your day: events all year, including open-air theatre and re-enactment weekends. Abbey's story told at the Porter's Lodge. Family activities and floodlit evenings. Children's play area. Garden with follies, ponds and classical statues. New bird hide.

The romantic ruins of the once-wealthy and powerful Fountains Abbey in North Yorkshire

Guided tours and wildlife walks.
Dogs: welcome on short leads only.

Access for all: 🅿️ 👥 🚾 🍴 🛗 📷 🔊 👓 📱
Building 👥♿ 🔲 **Grounds** ♿➡️ 🚶♿

Getting here: 99:SE271683. 4 miles west of Ripon. **Foot**: public footpaths and bridleways. **Cycle**: signed on-road cycle loop. On Way of the Roses route. **Bus**: from Leeds, York, Yorkshire Dales and Harrogate to Ripon and Fountains Abbey. **Train**: Harrogate, 12 miles. **Road**: off B6265 to Pateley Bridge, signed from A1 (M) junction 48/50, A61 north of Harrogate. **Parking**: free at visitor centre. Pay and display at Studley Royal deer-park.

Finding out more: 01765 608888 or fountainsabbey@nationaltrust.org.uk

Fountains Abbey		M	T	W	T	F	S	S
Abbey and Water Garden								
1 Jan–31 Jan	10–5	M	T	W	T	·	S	S
1 Feb–28 Mar	10–5	M	T	W	T	F	S	S
29 Mar–26 Oct*	10–6	M	T	W	T	F	S	S
27 Oct–31 Dec	10–5	M	T	W	T	·	S	S
Hall, mill, shop and restaurant								
1 Jan–31 Jan	10–4	M	T	W	T	·	S	S
1 Feb–28 Mar	10–4	M	T	W	T	F	S	S
29 Mar–26 Oct	10–5	M	T	W	T	F	S	S
27 Oct–31 Dec	10–4	M	T	W	T	·	S	S
Deer-park								
Open all year	7–9	M	T	W	T	F	S	S
St Mary's Church								
29 Mar–30 Sep	12–4	M	T	W	T	F	S	S

Last admission one hour before closing. Property closed 24 and 25 December. Studley Royal shop and tea-room opening times vary. *25 July to 29 August: abbey and Water Garden open until 9 on Thursdays.

George Stephenson's Birthplace

Wylam, Northumberland NE41 8BP

Map ⑥ G5

The humble birthplace of railway pioneer George Stephenson – whose family lived in just one room. Our costumed guide tells the story of how challenging life was for mining families, such as George's, which once squeezed into this now charming cottage, set in a pretty garden near the River Tyne.

Eating and shopping: Stephenson tea-room and tea garden serving light snacks and cakes. Souvenirs and books for sale.

Making the most of your day: rooms decorated as in 1781, the year of Stephenson's birth. River views and wildlife. Cycle route along the Wylam Waggonway.
Dogs: on leads in garden only.

Access for all: 🅿️🦽📷♿ 🅰️
Building 🦽 Garden 🦽

Getting here: 88:NZ126650. ½ mile east of Wylam in Tyne Riverside Country Park. **Foot**: circular walk from Wylam ½ mile on Wylam Waggonway or riverside footpath. **Cycle**: NCN72. **Bus**: Newcastle to Corbridge and Hexham, alight Wylam. **Train**: Wylam ½ mile, Tyne Valley line. **Road**: 8 miles west of Newcastle, 1½ miles south of A69. **Sat Nav**: NE41 8HP (car park). **Parking**: in village, ½ mile, pay and display (not National Trust).

Finding out more: 01661 853457 or georgestephensons@nationaltrust.org.uk

George Stephenson's Birthplace		M	T	W	T	F	S	S
Cottage, tea-room and tea garden								
1 Mar–29 Sep	11–5				T	F	S	S
3 Oct–3 Nov	11–3				T	F	S	S
Tea-room and tea garden								
5 Jan–24 Feb	11–3						S	S
9 Nov–29 Dec	11–3						S	S
Open Bank Holiday Mondays.								

Gibside

near Rowlands Gill, Gateshead, Tyne & Wear NE16 6BG

Map ⑥ H5

For a taste of the country on the edge of the city, escape to this stunning landscape park and nature reserve. Gibside is a forest garden created by one of the richest men in Georgian England, offering fantastic views, miles of walks, fascinating historic buildings and wide open spaces. It's also the setting of Mary Eleanor Bowes' true story of torture and escape from her ruthless husband, inspiration for a Stanley Kubrick film and best-selling biography, *Wedlock*. After centuries of neglect we're bringing Gibside to life by restoring the gardens for people and wildlife, so there's always something new to discover.

Eating and shopping: Potting Shed café and Renwick's coffee and bookshop. Gibside Larder shop selling food, plants and gifts. Friday evening beer garden.

Making the most of your day: events inspired by our stories, wildlife and food, from family outdoor adventures to guided walks. Twice-monthly farmers' markets. Open-air music. **Dogs**: welcome on leads.

Access for all: 🅿️🅿️🦽🦽🦽♿📷♿ 🅰️
Chapel 🦽🦽🦽 Stables 🦽🔼
Garden 🦽🦽➡️♿🦽

Getting here: 88:NZ172583. 6 miles south-west of Gateshead and Newcastle. **Foot**: ½ mile from Rowlands Gill. **Cycle**: NCN14, ¼ mile. Arrive by bike and get a free cake. **Bus**: from Newcastle (passing 🚇 and Metrocentre) to Consett, alight Rowlands Gill, ½ mile, new local shuttle bus service. **Train**: Metrocentre 5 miles; Newcastle 8 miles. **Road**: entrance on B6314 between Rowlands Gill and Burnopfield; follow brown signs from A1, taking exit onto A694 at north end of Metrocentre. **Parking**: free, 100 yards.

Relaxing near the chapel at Gibside, Tyne & Wear

Finding out more: 01207 541820 or
gibside@nationaltrust.org.uk

Gibside		M	T	W	T	F	S	S
Landscape gardens and woodlands								
1 Jan–28 Feb	10–4	M	T	W	T	F	S	S
1 Mar–3 Nov	10–6	M	T	W	T	F	S	S
4 Nov–31 Dec	10–4	M	T	W	T	F	S	S
Chapel								
5 Jan–24 Feb	10–4	·	·	·	·	·	S	S
1 Mar–3 Nov	10–5	M	T	W	T	F	S	S
9 Nov–29 Dec	10–4	·	·	·	·	·	S	S
Café, gift and food shop								
1 Jan–28 Feb	10–4	M	T	W	T	F	S	S
1 Mar–3 Nov	10–5	M	T	W	T	F	S	S
4 Nov–31 Dec	10–4	M	T	W	T	F	S	S
Beer garden and pub								
4 Jan–24 May	6–9	·	·	·	·	F	·	·
31 May–31 Aug	6–9	·	·	·	·	F	S	·
6 Sep–27 Dec	6–9	·	·	·	·	F	·	·

Estate closed 24 and 25 December. Last entry: winter 3:30,
summer 5.

Goddards

27 Tadcaster Road, York,
North Yorkshire YO24 1GG

Map ⑤ H5

Goddards was the home of Noel Terry, of
the Terry's of York chocolate firm. The house
opened last year for visitors to discover the
story of the famous family and life at the
chocolate factory. Designed in the Arts and
Crafts style, the house is complemented by
beautiful gardens. **Note**: selected rooms only
open (National Trust regional office).

Eating and shopping: new 1930s-style
tea-room. Small gift shop. Picnics welcome
in garden.

Making the most of your day: 1930s
newspapers available in the drawing
room, where you can reminisce and share
memories of the Terry's factory, the family
and a royal visit. Events and family activities.
Dogs: welcome on leads in garden.

Access for all: 🅿️🚻♿🛗🏠
House 🔼♿👨‍🦽
Grounds ♿➡️

Getting here: 105:SE589497. 1½ miles
from York. **Cycle**: close to city cycle
routes. **Bus**: frequent services from York 🚆.
Train: York 1½ miles. **Road**: on A1036. Take
A1237/A64 to A1036 Tadcaster Road (signed
York city centre). Turn right after St Edward's
Church, through brick gatehouse arch.
Parking: designated parking only.
Nearest visitor parking at city centre
car parks (1 to 2 miles).

Finding out more: 01904 771930 or
goddards@nationaltrust.org.uk

Goddards		M	T	W	T	F	S	S
1 Mar–3 Nov	11–5	·	·	W	T	F	S	S

Open Bank Holiday Mondays. On York race days,
please call for opening arrangements.

Hadrian's Wall and Housesteads Fort

Bardon Mill, Hexham,
Northumberland NE47 6NN

Map (6) F5

Running through a wild landscape with vast panoramic views, the wall was one of the Roman Empire's most northerly outposts. Visitors can gain an evocative picture of military life at Housesteads Fort. Built around AD122, the fort is one of the best preserved of 16 military bases along the wall. **Note**: fort is owned by the National Trust and maintained and managed by English Heritage.

Eating and shopping: small shop selling local and 'Roman' souvenirs. Refreshment kiosk.

Making the most of your day: family trail. Events at Housesteads. **Dogs**: welcome on leads.

Access for all: 🅿♿🚻🔍👁 Buildings 🦽

Getting here: 87:NY790688. 6 miles north-east of Haltwhistle. **Foot**: Hadrian's Wall Path and Pennine Way. **Cycle**: NCN72. **Bus**: Hadrian's Wall service, April to November daily, Newcastle 🚆 to Hexham 🚆 to Carlisle (passing Haltwhistle 🚆). **Train**: Hexham or Haltwhistle (bus connection). **Road**: car parks at Housesteads, Cawfields and Steel Rigg. **Parking**: pay and display (not National Trust), charge including members. Car and coach parks operated by National Park Authority at Housesteads (½-mile walk to fort), Steel Rigg and Cawfields.

Finding out more: 01434 344525 (visitor centre). 01434 344363 (English Heritage museum) or housesteads@nationaltrust.org.uk

Hadrian's Wall
Closed 1 January and 24 to 26 December. Call or visit website for opening arrangements.

Hadrian's Wall, Northumberland, snakes across a wild and open landscape – perfect for walking

Why not visit us on foot or by public transport? See pages 6 and 374

Hardcastle Crags

near Hebden Bridge, West Yorkshire

Map ⑤ E6

This beautiful wooded valley has deep ravines, tumbling streams and glorious waterfalls. There are miles of footpaths through woodland rich in wildlife, with ever-changing birdsong. The seasonal colours are simply stunning, with carpets of bluebells in spring and golden leaves in autumn. Nestling alongside the river, Gibson Mill, a former cotton mill and entertainment emporium, is now a visitor centre powered by sustainable energy. You can discover more about the valley's 200-year history here with exhibitions, tours and family fun. **Note**: steep paths and rough terrain.

Eating and shopping: Weaving Shed Café serving sandwiches, soup, cakes and ice-cream. Shop selling books, gifts, cards and sweets.

Making the most of your day: family activities, including dressing up. Events. Guided and themed walks. Circular walks (downloadable). **Dogs**: under close control at all times.

Access for all: ⓟ⃝ ⒹⒿ 🆆🄲 ⒷⓁ🄻 🅻🄾 ⬚ 🄹 :̈ •
Building 🄰🅻 ⬆️ Grounds 🄰🅻

Getting here: 103:SD988291. 1½ miles north-east of Hebden Bridge. **Foot**: via Walkers are Welcome trail from Hebden Bridge. Pennine Way passes nearby. **Cycle**: NCN68 passes nearby. Cycling restricted. **Bus**: local services. **Train**: Hebden Bridge. **Road**: at end of Midgehole Road, off A6033. **Sat Nav**: Midgehole car park: HX7 7AA. Clough Hole car park: HX7 7AZ. **Parking**: nearest 1 mile (pay and display). Disabled badge holders only allowed access to mill (book space). 25 spaces at Clough Hole car park, Widdop Road (steep walk).

Finding out more: 01422 844518 (weekdays). 01422 846236 (weekends) or hardcastlecrags@nationaltrust.org.uk. Hollin Hall, Crimsworth Dean, Hebden Bridge, West Yorkshire HX7 7AP

Hardcastle Crags		M	T	W	T	F	S	S
Countryside								
Open all year			M	T	W	T	F	S	S
Gibson Mill and Weaving Shed Café								
5 Jan–24 Feb	11–3		·	·	·	·	·	S	S
2 Mar–31 Oct	11–4		·	T	W	T	·	S	S
2 Nov–22 Dec	11–3		·	·	·	·	·	S	S

Weaving Shed Café open daily in local school holidays (16 to 24 February, 29 March to 14 April, 24 May to 2 June, 20 July to 1 September, 26 October to 3 November), Gibson Mill open Saturday to Thursday. Also open Good Friday, 26 December and all Bank Holiday Mondays. 1 May to 30 September: café open to 5 on Saturday and Sunday.

Holy Jesus Hospital

City Road, Newcastle upon Tyne,
Tyne & Wear NE1 2AS

Map ⑥ H5

Holy Jesus Hospital survives amid 1960s
city-centre developments, displaying features
from all periods of its 700-year existence.
The National Trust's Inner City Project is
based here, working to provide opportunities
for inner-city dwellers to gain access to and
enjoy the countryside on their doorstep.
Note: owned by Newcastle City Council but
managed by the National Trust.

Eating and shopping: tea, coffee and biscuits
available on Saturday open days.

Making the most of your day: exhibition
room. Guided tour. **Dogs**: assistance dogs only.

Access for all: ⬛⬛⬛⬛⬛
Building ⬛⬛⬛

Getting here: 88:NZ253642. In centre
of Newcastle upon Tyne. **Cycle**: close to
riverside routes. **Bus**: local services from
city centre. **Train**: Newcastle, ½ mile.
Underground: Monument Metro, ¼ mile.
Road: close to Tyne Bridge and A167.
Parking: in city centre, 30 yards.
Pay and display (not National Trust).

Finding out more: 0191 255 7610 or
holyjesushospital@nationaltrust.org.uk

Holy Jesus Hospital		M	T	W	T	F	S	S
15 Jan–27 Jun	12–4	·	T	W	T	·	·	·
1 Jul–30 Aug	12–4	M	T	W	T	F	·	·
3 Sep–12 Dec	12–4	·	T	W	T	·	·	·

Open for full guided tours on first Saturday of every month,
10 to 4 (not January), no booking required. Closed August
Bank Holiday Monday.

Lindisfarne Castle, Northumberland,
sits proud on its rocky outcrop and
can only be reached via a
tidal causeway

Lindisfarne Castle

Holy Island, Berwick-upon-Tweed,
Northumberland TD15 2SH

Map ⑥ G1

Location has always been the main attraction
for the owners and occupiers of Lindisfarne
Castle. From a former fort to the holiday home
of a wealthy Edwardian bachelor seeking a
quiet retreat from London, the idyllic location
of the castle has intrigued and inspired for
centuries. Arts and Crafts architect Edwin
Lutyens' renovation both hides and emphasises
the old fort, all the while overlooking leading
garden designer of her day Gertrude Jekyll's
enchanting walled summer garden. The
Lime Kilns have an unexpected grandeur, an
imposing and striking reminder of Lindisfarne's
industrial past. **Note**: limited toilet facilities.
Island accessed via tidal causeway
(check safe crossing times).

Eating and shopping: shop selling local
products and ice-cream. Picnics welcome.

Making the most of your day: family trails,
small charge (including members). Kites and
binoculars available to borrow. **Dogs**: welcome
on leads. Assistance dogs only in castle.

Access for all: ⬛⬛⬛
Castle ⬛⬛   Grounds ⬛

Getting here: 75:NU136417. Holy Island, off
Northumberland coast. **Foot**: from Holy Island
village. **Cycle**: NCN1. Coast and Castles cycle
route. **Train**: Berwick-upon-Tweed 10 miles
from causeway. **Road**: 5 miles east of A1
via tidal causeway (check crossing times in
advance). **Parking**: in the interests of village
residents please use main island car park,
1 mile (signposted before village). Pay and
display (not National Trust). Private transfer
available most days.

Finding out more: 01289 389244 or
lindisfarne@nationaltrust.org.uk

Lindisfarne Castle		M	T	W	T	F	S	S
16 Feb–3 Nov			T	W	T	F	S	S
9 Nov–10 Nov	10–3						S	S
23 Nov–24 Nov	10–3						S	S
7 Dec–8 Dec	10–3						S	S
21 Dec	10–3						S	

16 February to 3 November: opening times vary due to tides,
either 10 to 3 or 12 to 5. Check times on our website or call
before visiting. Open Bank Holiday Mondays and every day
in August. Some additional Monday openings.

Lindisfarne Castle: once a fort and later a holiday home

Maister House

160 High Street, Hull, East Yorkshire HU1 1NL

Map (5) J6

A merchant family's tale of fortune and tragedy
is intertwined with the intriguing history of
Maister House. **Note**: staircase and entrance
hall only on show. No toilet.

Finding out more: 01723 870423
or www.nationaltrust.org.uk.
c/o Peakside, Ravenscar, Scarborough,
North Yorkshire YO13 0NE

Malham Tarn Estate

Waterhouses, Settle, North Yorkshire BD24 9PT

Map ⑤ D4

Malham Tarn in the Dales, part of which is a National Nature Reserve, is the perfect place to enjoy the great outdoors. There are stunning views across limestone pavements and the tarn's rippling water. Popular with walkers and cyclists, it is wonderful for a stroll, picnic or family adventure. **Note**: nearest toilet Malham national park car park, or Orchid House exhibition (weekends only).

Eating and shopping: tea-rooms, pubs and facilities in Malham village (not National Trust).

Making the most of your day: guided walks, events and outdoor activities, including family fun (summer holidays). Upper Wharfedale nearby. **Dogs**: welcome on leads (livestock).

Access for all: Town Head Barn 🖼 Grounds 🖼

Getting here: 98:SD890660. Estate extends from Malham village, north past Malham Tarn. **Foot**: Pennine Way and Pennine Bridleway cross estate. **Bus**: Skipton to Malham (passing Skipton ▆), limited service, 1 mile. Shuttle bus (call to confirm running). **Train**: Settle 7 miles. **Parking**: in Malham village, pay and display (not National Trust). Free at Watersinks car park, south side of Malham Tarn.

Finding out more: 01729 830416 or malhamtarn@nationaltrust.org.uk

Malham Tarn Estate		M	T	W	T	F	S	S
Countryside								
Open all year		M	T	W	T	F	S	S
Town Head Barn								
16 Feb–31 Oct	10–4	M	T	W	T	F	S	S

Marsden Moor Estate

Marsden, Huddersfield, West Yorkshire

Map ⑤ E7

This wild uninterrupted moorland covers nearly 2,248 hectares (5,553 acres) and spans the South Pennines and Peak District National Park. A Site of Special Scientific Interest, the environment supports moorland birds and is important for carbon storage and water provision. **Note**: nearest refreshments and toilets in Marsden village.

Eating and shopping: tea-rooms, restaurants and shops in Marsden village (not National Trust).

Making the most of your day: events. Guided walks. Marsden Heritage Trail (leaflet available to use in conjunction with downloadable walk or OS map). **Dogs**: welcome on leads.

Access for all: Exhibition 🖼 Grounds 🖼

Walking on the Malham Tarn Estate, North Yorkshire, below left, and Marsden Moor Estate, West Yorkshire, below

Getting here: 109:SE025100. Surrounding Marsden village. **Foot**: Kirklees Way, Pennine Way, Huddersfield Narrow Canal towpath and Colne Valley Circular all run onto the estate. Pennine Bridleway crosses estate. **Bus**: services from Huddersfield and Oldham. **Train**: Marsden. **Road**: between A640 and A635. **Parking**: free – including Marsden village (not National Trust), Buckstones and Wessenden Head.

Finding out more: 01484 847016 or marsdenmoor@nationaltrust.org.uk. Estate Office, The Old Goods Yard, Station Road, Marsden, Huddersfield, West Yorkshire HD7 6DH

Marsden Moor Estate	Open every day all year

Middlethorpe Hall Hotel, Restaurant and Spa

Bishopthorpe Road, York,
North Yorkshire YO23 2GB

Map (5) H5

Built in 1699, this quintessentially William and Mary house next to York Racecourse was once the home of the 18th-century diarist Lady Mary Wortley Montagu. Furnished with antiques and fine paintings and set in eight hectares (20 acres) with manicured gardens and parkland beyond, Middlethorpe Hall's country-house character remains unspoilt.

The house and gardens are already accessible to the public as a hotel, and we welcome guests to stay, dine in the restaurant and have afternoon tea (booking strongly advised). Contact hotel direct for best available offers. **Note**: paying guests to the hotel only are able to walk in the garden and park. Children above the age of six are welcome.

Finding out more: 01904 641241. 01904 620176 (fax) or info@middlethorpe.com. www.middlethorpe.com

Moulton Hall

Moulton, Richmond,
North Yorkshire DL10 6QH

Map (5) F2

Elegant 17th-century tenanted manor house with a beautiful carved staircase. **Note**: no toilet. Visit by arrangement in advance with the tenant.

Finding out more: 01325 377227 or www.nationaltrust.org.uk

Mount Grace Priory

Staddle Bridge, Northallerton,
North Yorkshire DL6 3JG

Map (5) G3

England's most important Carthusian ruin, with individual cells reflecting the hermit-like isolation of the monks. **Note**: operated by English Heritage; members free, except on event days.

Finding out more: 01609 883494 or www.nationaltrust.org.uk

The stylish Middlethorpe Hall Hotel, North Yorkshire

Nostell Priory, West Yorkshire, was built by the very best craftsmen using only the finest materials

Nostell Priory and Parkland

Doncaster Road, Nostell, near Wakefield, West Yorkshire WF4 1QE

Map ⑤ G6 🏛➕🏠✂️🎐⚘🌳

Power, pleasure and prestige. Nostell Priory and Parkland has been the home of the Winn family for more than 300 years. The Georgian mansion was built to show off the family's wealth, using the best that money could buy. Inside the house, we have the largest fully documented collection of Chippendale furniture in the world, made specially for Nostell. There are also paintings by Brueghel, Hogarth and Kauffman, as well as a John Harrison (of *Longitude* fame) longcase clock and 18th-century doll's-house. Outside there are more than 121 hectares (300 acres) of garden and parkland, including lakeside walks.

Eating and shopping: Courtyard Café serving hot food. Snacks and ice-cream available from Bite to Eat. Shop selling gifts, souvenirs and plants. Picnics welcome.

The Top Hall at Nostell Priory, West Yorkshire

Exploring the extensive parkland at Nostell Priory

Nunnington Hall

Nunnington, near York,
North Yorkshire YO62 5UY

Map ⑤ H4

This cosy former family home sits nestled on the quiet banks of the River Rye. You can explore period rooms and find out what's been hiding under the floorboards, while our guides share tales of life in the Hall. In the attic you'll find one of the world's finest collections of miniature rooms, plus a year-round changing programme of art exhibitions. Outside, the informal atmosphere continues in the sheltered walled garden. There are also spring-flowering organic meadows, orchards and flamboyant resident peacocks.

Making the most of your day: family activities and adventure playground. Craft fairs. Theatre and concerts. Guided walks, trails, talks and tours, including 'Upstairs Downstairs' (booking essential). Geocaching in park. Extensive gardens, developing orchard and parkland. Collections featuring masterpieces by Chippendale, John Harrison, Brueghel and Kauffman. **Dogs**: on leads in park and exercise area at car park. Assistance dogs only in gardens.

Access for all: 🅿️ 🇩 🏬 🚾 🍴 🎫 🖼️ ♨️ •• 🅰️
House 🦽 ⬆️ 👇 Grounds 🦽 🦽 ➡️ 🏞️ 👇

Getting here: 111:SE407172. 5 miles south-east of Wakefield. **Foot**: via pedestrian entrance on the A638. **Cycle**: NCN67, 3 miles. **Bus**: services from Wakefield to Doncaster. **Train**: Fitzwilliam 1½ miles. **Road**: on A638 towards Doncaster. **Sat Nav**: use WF4 1QD. **Parking**: £2.50 for non-members.

Finding out more: 01924 863892 or nostellpriory@nationaltrust.org.uk

Nostell Priory and Parkland		M	T	W	T	F	S	S
House								
2 Mar–27 Oct*	1–5	·	·	W	T	F	S	S
30 Nov–15 Dec	11–4	·	·	·	·	·	S	S
Gardens**								
2 Jan–27 Oct	11–5:30	·	·	W	T	F	S	S
30 Oct–29 Dec	11–4	·	·	W	T	F	S	S
Shop and tea-room								
1 Jan–27 Oct	10–5:30	M	T	W	T	F	S	S
28 Oct–31 Dec	10–4:30	M	T	W	T	F	S	S
Parkland***								
Open all year	9–7	M	T	W	T	F	S	S

*Open 11 to 12:15 for guided tours, places limited and allocated on arrival (not bookable). Open Bank Holiday Mondays. **Rose Garden may close for private functions. Garden open daily: 16 to 24 February, 28 March to 14 April, 23 July to 1 September, 26 October to 3 November, 20 December to 31 December. ***Parkland closes dusk if earlier. Property closed 25 December.

Delicate fritillary at Nunnington Hall, North Yorkshire

Eating and shopping: licensed tea-room with waitress service. Picnic spots and tea-garden. Shop selling local ranges.

Making the most of your day: events, including exhibitions, family activities, food events. **Dogs**: welcome in car park only.

Access for all: ⓅⓌⒷⒹⓄ
Building ⒧ⒶⒷ Grounds ⒶⒷ

Getting here: 100:SE670795. 4½ miles south-east of Helmsley. **Bus**: from Hovingham to Helmsley. **Road**: A170 Helmsley to Pickering road; 11½ miles north of Malton to Helmsley road (B1257); 21 miles north of York, via B1363. **Parking**: free, 50 yards.

Finding out more: 01439 748283 or nunningtonhall@nationaltrust.org.uk

Nunnington Hall		M	T	W	T	F	S	S
16 Feb–3 Nov	11–5	·	T	W	T	F	S	S
9 Nov–15 Dec	11–4	·	·	·	·	·	S	S

Open Bank Holiday Mondays.

Nunnington Hall, North Yorkshire, seen from the orchard

The Old Coastguard Station

The Dock, Robin Hood's Bay, North Yorkshire YO22 4SJ

Map ⑤ I2

A visitor centre at the edge of the sea. Our hands-on exhibition shows how the power of the tides, waves and wind has shaped the coastline and tells the story of local life, from dinosaurs to the present day. You can come face to face with rock-pool inhabitants in our tank. **Note**: steep walk from car park.

Eating and shopping: wide range of gifts, books and local information available.

Making the most of your day: rock-pooling. Arts and crafts exhibitions. **Dogs**: allowed in building if carried.

Access for all: ⒹⒷⒹⒿ
Building ⒧Ⓐ⬍

Getting here: 94:NZ953049. On slipway at bottom of village. **Foot**: Cleveland Way passes alongside. Coast-to-Coast path finishes at building. **Cycle**: NCN1 nearby. **Bus**: from Middlesbrough, Guisborough, Whitby and Scarborough. **Train**: Whitby 5 miles. **Road**: off A171 Whitby to Scarborough, signposted Robin Hood's Bay. No access for cars down the steep hill to the old village. **Parking**: at top of hill, not National Trust (charge including members).

Finding out more: 01947 885900 or oldcoastguardstation@nationaltrust.org.uk

The Old Coastguard Station		M	T	W	T	F	S	S
1 Jan–6 Jan	10–4	·	T	W	T	F	S	S
12 Jan–3 Feb	10–4	·	·	·	·	·	S	S
9 Feb–24 Feb	10–4	M	T	W	T	F	S	S
2 Mar–17 Mar	10–4	·	·	·	·	·	S	S
23 Mar–3 Nov	10–5	M	T	W	T	F	S	S
9 Nov–22 Dec	10–4	·	·	·	·	·	S	S
27 Dec–31 Dec	10–4	M	T	·	·	F	S	S

The drawing room in the classic Georgian mansion of Ormesby Hall, Redcar & Cleveland, is stately yet homely

Ormesby Hall

Ladgate Lane, Ormesby, near Middlesbrough,
Redcar & Cleveland TS3 0SR

Map ⑤ G2

This classic Georgian mansion was home to the Pennyman family for nearly 400 years. The last of the Pennyman line was Colonel Jim Pennyman, who lived at the Hall with his arts-loving wife Ruth. While exploring the intimate period rooms, visitors will hear inspiring tales of their generosity and acts of kindness, and will also discover a stylish legacy of another family member, 'Wicked' Sir James – whose extravagant lifestyle led him to gamble with the family fortune. The Hall also provides lively resources for local schools and community groups and is a unique venue for weddings and corporate events.

Eating and shopping: tea served in servants' hall or on terrace. Souvenirs available from reception.

Making the most of your day: special interest activities and events, including lunchtime lectures and conservation tours. Model railway layouts (only one owned by the National Trust). **Dogs**: on leads in park only.

Access for all: 🅿️🅳♿🅦🅱️📷📷📷🅰️
Building 🏠♿ Grounds ➡️♿

Getting here: 93:NZ530167. 3 miles south-east of Middlesbrough. **Cycle**: NCN65, 2¼ miles. **Bus**: services from Middlesbrough (passing close Middlesbrough ☎). **Train**: Marton 1½ miles; Middlesbrough 3 miles. **Road**: west of A171. From A19 take A174 to A172. Follow signs for Ormesby Hall. Entrance on Ladgate Lane (B1380). **Parking**: free, 100 yards.

Finding out more: 01642 324188 or ormesbyhall@nationaltrust.org.uk. Church Lane, Ormesby, Middlesbrough TS7 9AS

Ormesby Hall		M	T	W	T	F	S	S
16 Mar–28 Jul	1:30–5	·	·	·	·	·	S	S
1 Aug–1 Sep	1:30–5	·	·	·	T	·	S	S
7 Sep–3 Nov	1:30–5	·	·	·	·	·	S	S

*Gardens open at 12:45. Open Bank Holiday Mondays and Good Friday. Hall open Thursdays in August for guided tours. Call for confirmation of opening arrangements.

Rievaulx Terrace

Rievaulx, Helmsley, North Yorkshire YO62 5LJ

Map (5) H3

This 18th-century landscape is one of Ryedale's true gems. Visitors can stroll through the woods and out onto the long grassed terrace for stunning views down over the Cistercian ruin of Rievaulx Abbey. Every season brings something new. In spring, the bank between the temples is awash with wild flowers, while in the summer the lawns are the perfect spot to enjoy a picnic while admiring the North Yorkshire countryside. An autumn walk through the beech woods, when the leaves have turned a mass of rich golden hues, is pure pleasure. **Note**: no access to Rievaulx Abbey from terrace.

Eating and shopping: ice-cream, takeaway drinks and sweet snacks available. Shop.

Making the most of your day: events, including family activities in school holidays and guided tours. **Dogs**: welcome on leads.

Access for all:

Visitor centre Temples
Grounds

Getting here: 100:SE579848. 2½ miles north-west of Helmsley. **Foot**: Cleveland Way within ¾ mile. **Bus**: from Helmsley. **Road**: on B1257. **Parking**: free, 100 yards.

Finding out more: 01439 798340 (summer). 01439 748283 (winter) or rievaulxterrace@nationaltrust.org.uk

Rievaulx Terrace		M	T	W	T	F	S	S
16 Feb–3 Nov	11–5	**M**	**T**	**W**	**T**	**F**	**S**	**S**

Last admission one hour before closing or dusk if earlier.

Roseberry Topping

Newton-under-Roseberry, North Yorkshire TS9 6QR

Map (5) G2

Layers of human and geological history have shaped this iconic landmark. **Note**: no toilet.

Finding out more: 01723 870423 or www.nationaltrust.org.uk. c/o Peakside, Ravenscar, Scarborough, North Yorkshire YO13 0NE

An autumnal scene at the Ionic Temple at Rievaulx Terrace, North Yorkshire

Designed by Sir John Vanbrugh, stately Seaton Delaval Hall in Northumberland is being brought back to life

Seaton Delaval Hall

The Avenue, Seaton Sluice,
Northumberland NE26 4QR

Map (6) H4 🏛️🏚️⛓️✳️🎭🔊🍵

Designed by Sir John Vanbrugh, this was the home of the Delavals, the most notorious Georgian family of party-goers, adulterers, actors and pranksters. They turned the estate into a stage for drama, revelry and romance, while the surrounding landscape fuelled the Industrial Revolution. The hall has survived terrible fires, military occupation and potential ruin. Now a work in progress, we are bringing the hall and its colourful gardens back to life. We welcome everyone to come and see the latest developments as we prepare the hall for its next 100 years. **Note**: ongoing building works (some areas may be inaccessible).

Eating and shopping: Stables café serving light lunch or snacks. Seaton Delaval ice-cream available in the West Pavilion and tea at the summerhouse. Souvenir shop in ticket hut.

Making the most of your day: events, including arts and crafts, outdoor fun and

lectures. Activity days and trails (most school holidays). **Dogs**: welcome on leads in designated areas only.

Access for all: 🅿️♿🚻👓📷🖼️
Hall 🏠 Stables 🏚️ Grounds ➡️🪑

Getting here: NZ321766. 2 miles from Whitley Bay. **Foot**: footpaths at Seaton Sluice (¾ mile), Seaton Delaval (1 mile), Blyth and North Tyneside. **Cycle**: NCN1. Cycle paths, old mining waggonways, coastal paths. **Ferry**: North Shields terminal 8 miles. **Bus**: frequent services from Newcastle to Blyth, alight Seaton Delaval Hall (services connect to Whitley Bay and North Tyneside). **Train**: West Monkseaton Metro 3 miles. **Road**: A190, linking to A193 coast road and A19; 5 miles from A1.

Finding out more: 0191 237 9100 or seatondelavalhall@nationaltrust.org.uk

Seaton Delaval Hall		M	T	W	T	F	S	S
23 Mar–29 Apr	11–5	M	·	·	·	F	S	S
2 May–30 Jun	11–5	M	T	·	T	F	S	S
1 Jul–31 Aug	11–5	M	T	W	T	F	S	S
1 Sep–30 Sep	11–5	M	T	·	T	F	S	S
4 Oct–30 Dec	11–3	M	·	·	·	F	S	S

Last entry 45 minutes before closing. Closed 23 December.
Our Conservation in Action programme may result in parts of the property being closed at short notice.

Souter Lighthouse and The Leas

Coast Road, Whitburn, Sunderland,
Tyne & Wear SR6 7NH

Map (6) l5

Souter is an iconic beacon standing proud
on the coastline midway between the Tyne
and the Wear. Hooped in red and white, it
was the first purpose-built lighthouse in the
world powered by electricity. Opened in 1871
and decommissioned in 1988, the machinery
remains in working order. Follow the coastline
to the north and discover The Leas. This
2½-mile stretch of magnesian limestone cliffs
has a wave-cut foreshore and coastal grassland,
perfect for walking. The nearby cliffs and rock
stacks of Marsden Bay are home to nesting
kittiwakes, fulmars, cormorants, shags and
guillemots. **Note**: steep stairs (ground-floor
CCTV shows views from the top for those
unable to climb).

Eating and shopping: tea-room and coffee
shop. Picnics welcome.

The Wherry, near Souter Lighthouse, Tyne & Wear

Souter Lighthouse, Tyne & Wear, opened in 1871

Making the most of your day: events and
family activities, including rock-pool rambles
and pirate days. Foghorn demos. Open-air play
area. Trails. **Dogs**: on leads outdoors only.

Access for all: 🅿️🅳♿🚻🦽📷🎦📖♿🅰️
Building 🅰️♿ Grounds 🅰️

Getting here: 88:NZ408641. North-east coast,
on River Tyne 2½ miles south of South Shields
and 5 miles north of Sunderland. **Foot**: South
Tyneside Heritage Trail. **Cycle**: NCN1, adjacent
to property. **Ferry**: Shields Ferry crosses River
Tyne from North Shields to South Shields twice
hourly. **Bus**: services from Sunderland to
South Shields (passes Sunderland 🚉 and South
Shields). One bus passes lighthouse, others
pass close by. **Train**: East Boldon and South
Shields (Tyne & Wear Metro) both 3 miles.
Road: on A183 coast road. **Parking**: free.

Finding out more: 0191 529 3161 or
souter@nationaltrust.org.uk

Souter Lighthouse and The Leas		M	T	W	T	F	S	S
16 Feb–24 Feb	11–5	M	T	W	T	F	S	S
2 Mar–10 Mar	11–5	·	·	·	·	·	S	S
16 Mar–30 Jun	11–5	M	T	W	T	·	S	S
1 Jul–31 Aug	11–5	M	T	W	T	F	S	S
1 Sep–3 Nov	11–5	M	T	W	T	·	S	S
9 Nov–15 Dec	11–4	·	·	·	·	·	S	S

Open Good Friday.

Treasurer's House, York

Minster Yard, York, North Yorkshire YO1 7JL

Map (5) H5

Treasurer's House was owned by Yorkshireman Frank Green from 1897 and was the first house given complete with its contents to the National Trust, in 1930. His love for antiques can be seen in his collection of furniture, ceramics, paintings and textiles that cover a 300-year period. Famed for threatening to haunt us if we ever move the furniture, his ghost is one of many said to haunt the house. The house has a history spanning 2,000 years, from the Roman road in the cellar to the Edwardian servants' quarters in the attics, accessible by daily tours. **Note**: cellar and attic tour charges (including members).

Eating and shopping: table service tea-room. Shop located in historic kitchen. Takeaway food and drinks available.

Making the most of your day: tours of Roman ghost cellar or Edwardian servants' attics. Themed house tours (February/November). Family trails and activities (school holidays). Events. **Dogs**: on lead in garden only.

Access for all: 🏷️🛋️🔊🖥️♿🔆📷
Building 🏛️♿ Grounds ♿➡️

Getting here: 105:SE604523. In city centre adjacent to minster (north side, at rear). **Cycle**: NCN65, ⅓ mile. Close to city cycle routes. **Bus**: from surrounding areas. **Train**: York ½ mile. **Parking**: nearest in Lord Mayor's Walk. Park and ride service from city outskirts.

Finding out more: 01904 624247 or treasurershouse@nationaltrust.org.uk

Treasurer's House		M	T	W	T	F	S	S
House, garden, tea-room and shop								
16 Feb–28 Feb	11–3	M	T	W	T	.	S	S
2 Mar–3 Nov	11–4:30	M	T	W	T	.	S	S
4 Nov–1 Dec	11–3	M	T	W	T	.	S	S
Tea-room and shop								
2 Dec–22 Dec	11–3	M	T	W	T	.	S	S

February and November: house entry by guided tour only, some of the collection covered.

Treasurer's House, York, in North Yorkshire

Upper Wharfedale

near Buckden, North Yorkshire

Map (5) E4

The spectacular landscapes in this part of the Yorkshire Dales are great for walking and cycling. The characteristic dry-stone walls and barns look striking in summer when surrounded by beautiful flowering hay meadows. Combined with river and valley-side woodland, this a wonderful place to relax and explore the great outdoors.

Eating and shopping: village tea-rooms, shops and pubs, farm shops (not National Trust).

Making the most of your day: guided walks, events and activities. Workshops, including family fun for the holidays. Also visit the nearby National Nature Reserve at Malham Tarn.

Dogs: on leads only (livestock).

Access for all: [P] [WC]
Town Head Barn [icon] Grounds [icon]

Getting here: 98:SD935765. Extends from Kettlewell village north to Beckermonds and Cray. **Foot**: Dales Way runs along River Wharfe. **Cycle**: Kettlewell on Yorkshire Dales Cycleway (Sustrans Regional Route 10). **Bus**: Skipton [icon] to Buckden. **Train**: Skipton, 12 miles. **Road**: B6160 runs along Upper Wharfedale through Cray, Buckden and Kettlewell. **Sat Nav**: use BD23 5JA. **Parking**: in Kettlewell and Buckden, not National Trust (pay and display).

Finding out more: 01729 830416 or upperwharfedale@nationaltrust.org.uk. Yorkshire Dales Estate Office, Waterhouses, Settle, North Yorkshire BD24 9PT

Upper Wharfedale		M	T	W	T	F	S	S
Countryside								
Open all year		M	T	W	T	F	S	S
Town Head Barn								
16 Feb–31 Oct	10–4	M	T	W	T	F	S	S

Wallington, Northumberland, above and below: an impressive yet friendly house, surrounded by lawns, lakes and park

Wallington

Cambo, near Morpeth,
Northumberland NE61 4AR

Map (6) G4 [icons]

Wallington, the much-loved home to generations of the unconventional Trevelyan family, is an impressive, yet friendly, house. It contains beautiful furniture, family paintings and treasured collections, and you can find out about the history of Northumberland through the huge Pre-Raphaelite paintings around the remarkable Central Hall. The Trevelyans loved being outdoors and close to nature, and the house is surrounded by an informal landscape of lawns, lakes, woodland, parkland and farmland. There is even a beautiful walled garden hidden in the woods, a colourful haven of tranquillity whatever the season.

Eating and shopping: shop selling gifts and treats. Clocktower Café serving brunch, lunch and afternoon tea. Refreshments available from potting shed kiosk in walled garden.

Making the most of your day: events for all ages, including themed weekends, talks, tours, guided walks, hands-on activities, food and craft festival and seasonal events. Woodland and riverside walks. Edwardian conservatory. Children's trail, family-friendly wildlife hide, adventure playground and new play train. Cabinet of curiosities and doll's-house collection. **Dogs**: welcome on leads in grounds and walled garden only.

Members may have to pay on special events days

Washington Old Hall

The Avenue, Washington Village,
Washington, Tyne & Wear NE38 7LE

Map ⑥ H5

Washington Old Hall stands as a testimony
to Anglo-American friendship. Due to be
demolished in 1933, this charming Hall is a
historic landmark with links to the first US
President, George Washington. The house
predominantly dates from the 17th century but
still incorporates a large portion of the original
12th-century building. It was once home to
George Washington's ancestors and it's from
here they took the family name. By 1860 the
house had slid down the social scale. It became
a tenement until 1933, when it was saved from
demolition by Frederick Hill.

Eating and shopping: tea-room
(run by Friends of Washington Old Hall).
Souvenirs available from reception. Friends'
bric-a-brac display. Picnic welcome in gardens.

Making the most of your day: croquet.
Seasonal garden trails, events and activities,
including Fourth of July Independence Day
ceremony. **Dogs**: on leads in garden only.

Access for all: ⊞ ⊞ ⊞ ⊞ ⊞ ⊞ ⊞ ⊞ ⊞
House ⊞ ⊞ ⊞ ⊞ Grounds ⊞ ⊞ ⊞ ➡ ⊞ ⊞

Getting here: 81:NZ030843. 6 miles
north-west of Belsay. **Bus**: infrequent services
from Morpeth. **Road**: A1 north to Newcastle,
then 20 miles north-west on A696
(airport/Ponteland road) and turn off on
B6342 to Cambo. A1 south to Morpeth,
through Morpeth on A192 then 12 miles west
on B6343. **Parking**: free, 200 yards.

Finding out more: 01670 773600 or
wallington@nationaltrust.org.uk

Wallington		M	T	W	T	F	S	S
House								
16 Feb–24 Feb*	12–3	M		W	T	F	S	S
2 Mar–3 Nov	12–5	M		W	T	F	S	S
Walled garden								
1 Jan–31 Mar	10–4	M	T	W	T	F	S	S
1 Apr–30 Sep	10–7	M	T	W	T	F	S	S
1 Oct–31 Dec	10–4	M	T	W	T	F	S	S
Gift shop and café								
2 Jan–15 Feb	10:30–4:30	M	T	W	T	F	S	S
16 Feb–3 Nov	10:30–5:30	M	T	W	T	F	S	S
4 Nov–23 Dec	10:30–4:30	M	T	W	T	F	S	S
27 Dec–30 Dec	10:30–4:30	M				F	S	S

Last admission to house one hour before closing. Garden
closes 6 in March and October, or dusk if earlier. Café last
orders 30 minutes before closing. *Ground floor only.

Washington Old Hall, Tyne & Wear, has historic US links

Access for all: 🅿️♿🚻♿📷♿📷📷

Building ♿♿♿ Grounds ♿♿♿➡️♿

Getting here: 88:NZ312566. Washington village, 7 miles south of Newcastle. **Cycle**: NCN7, 1 mile. **Bus**: services to Washington Galleries and Washington village. **Train**: Heworth (Metro) 4 miles; Newcastle 7 miles. **Road**: from A1 take J64 (A195), continue over Princess Anne Interchange roundabout. Left at Biddick Lane roundabout, follow brown signs. From A19/other routes follow 'Washington', join A1231, follow brown signs. **Parking**: free, small car park. Other parking on The Avenue.

Finding out more: 0191 416 6879 or washingtonoldhall@nationaltrust.org.uk

Washington Old Hall		M	T	W	T	F	S	S
House								
31 Mar–30 Oct	11–5	M	T	W	·	·	·	S
Gardens								
31 Mar–30 Oct	10–5	M	T	W	·	·	·	S
Tea-room								
31 Mar–30 Oct	10–4	M	T	W	·	·	·	S

Open Good Friday 29 March and Easter Saturday 30 March.

Yorkshire Coast

near Ravenscar, North Yorkshire

Map ⑤ I2   🏛️🚻🏊🏄🐾🛏️

Along the coastline from Saltburn to Filey there are many beautiful places where you can take in the sea air, enjoy stunning views, clifftop walks and sandy bays with excellent rock-pooling. Ravenscar Visitor Centre offers a warm and informative welcome. The Cleveland Way walking route runs all along the coast.

Eating and shopping: shop selling walking equipment, gifts and light refreshments. Picnic area (coastal views).

Making the most of your day: wildlife activities and guided walks (Ravenscar, Boggle Hole and Robin Hood's Bay). Geocaching. Exhibition at Ravenscar Visitor Centre. **Dogs**: allowed on leads.

Access for all: 🚻♿📷📷

Visitor centre ♿ Grounds ♿

Getting here: 94:NZ980016. On the North Yorkshire coast. **Foot**: Cleveland Way passes through property. **Cycle**: NCN1. **Bus**: regular local services. **Train**: Saltburn, Whitby, Scarborough, Filey for access to coast. **Road**: Saltburn to Whitby A174, Ravenscar signposted off Whitby to Scarborough A171. **Parking**: free on roadside at Ravenscar. Also at Saltburn and Runswick Bay (not National Trust).

Finding out more: 01723 870423 or yorkshirecoast@nationaltrust.org.uk. Peakside, Ravenscar, Scarborough, North Yorkshire YO13 0NE

Yorkshire Coast		M	T	W	T	F	S	S
Countryside								
Open all year		M	T	W	T	F	S	S
Ravenscar Visitor Centre								
23 Mar–3 Nov	10–4:30	M	T	W	T	F	S	S

Wildflower meadow on the Yorkshire Coast, North Yorkshire: just one of the many varied and beautiful places on this very special stretch of coastline

Wales

Sea, sand and a kite: just what's needed
for a perfect day on the beach.
Rhossili Bay, Gower

Map (4)

Outdoors in Wales

High mountains and deep valleys, rolling estates, spectacular beaches and a coastline that goes on for miles, Wales is rich in dramatic landscapes, many of which are cared for by the National Trust. These inspirational places offer relaxation and peace, as well as an opportunity for adventure that will provide happy memories for years to come.

Right:
**a patchwork
of fields at
St David's Head,
Pembrokeshire**

Nature and wildness in Pembrokeshire

Rugged, beautiful and geologically fascinating, 60 miles of Pembrokeshire's coastline is cared for by the Trust. Wales' patron saint, St David, was born here, on a Pembrokeshire clifftop.

The restoration of traditional cattle and sheep grazing has seen Pembrokeshire's coastal heaths and inland commons bloom again. But the real star of the Pembrokeshire coast is the chough; there are now more than 60 breeding pairs here. Other sights not to be missed are the seal pups on a number of beaches and the guillemots at Stackpole.

With hundreds of miles of footpaths on the coast and inland, walkers are spoilt for choice. Fine circular walks can be found at Stackpole (lakes and cliffs), Marloes, St David's Head, Dinas Island, near Fishguard, Little Milford and Lawrenny Woods on the secluded River Cleddau.

Ceredigion's timeless charm

There's an intimate charm to Ceredigion's unspoilt coastline. Gently rolling, it has striking rocky outcrops and steep wooded river valleys running inland.

Find secluded beaches and wooded valleys at Cwm Tydu. Head north from the car park and look out to sea for dolphins or the odd turtle in spring. The lovely, sandy beach at Penbryn is a popular destination for families with their buckets and spades, windbreaks and picnics. There's a timeless quality to Ceredigion, thanks to the relative lack of development. It is a quality that the Trust is working hard to preserve.

Majestic Snowdonia

A total of 11 of Snowdonia's majestic peaks and many hectares of upland in this land wreathed in myth and legend are cared for by the Trust. These include a wheelchair-accessible riverside path in the village of Beddgelert, home to the legendary heroic dog.

The walking choices at Craflwyn are limitless – from riverside strolls to a full-scale ascent of Snowdon. Nearby is Llyndy Isaf farm and estate, an unspoilt gem rich in wildlife, archaeology and history. The red dragon of Wales was born here too!

From towering Tryfan, to the dramatic Carneddau mountain range and the waters of Llyn Idwal, the peaks and valleys of Eryri offer a challenge to the adventurous, as well as relaxation and inspiration.

Mae'r wybodaeth sydd yn y llawlyfr hwn am feddiannau'r Ymddiriedolaeth Genedlaethol yng Nghymru ar gael yn Gymraeg o Swyddfa'r Ymddiriedolaeth Genedlaethol, Sgwar y Drindod, Llandudno LL30 2DE, ffôn 01492 860123.

Above:
one of the panoramic views from the Brecon Beacons, Powys

The power of nature is all too apparent at Llandanwg, where a medieval church lies half buried under the sandy beach. Above Barmouth is Dinas Oleu, which occupies a special place in our history. For this coastal hillside was the first place passed to the Trust, in 1895. Nearby, Egryn is also special. A home for more than 5,000 years, the medieval hall-house and outbuildings have been newly restored and the award-winning house is a truly unique place to stay. Visit **www.nationaltrustcottages.co.uk**

Anglesey's wildlife haven

Every year Cemlyn's lagoon, a haven for wildlife and nesting birds, witnesses the wonderful sight of migrating birds, with a colony of Arctic and common terns returning to nest in late spring. If you are looking for a day out at the beach, Porth Dafarch is a great destination – a sandy beach in a rocky cove.

Ancient Brecon Beacons

Every year about 250,000 pairs of walking boots climb and ramble through the distinctive landscape of deep valleys and flat-topped summits that makes up the Brecon Beacons. Some of the most popular summits of this ancient land – Pen y Fan, Sugar Loaf and Skirrid – are cared for by the Trust, and clues to its history are all around.

Hidden within the narrow steep-sided gorges at the heads of the Neath and Tawe rivers is a series of stunning waterfalls, including Henrhyd Falls, the highest in South Wales.

Walks at Dinefwr and Dolaucothi

The parkland at historic Dinefwr, a National Nature Reserve, is home to some of this area's oldest inhabitants. When you visit, you will be able to see fallow deer and White Park cattle, which have been in Dinefwr for more than 1,000 years.

The upland 1,000-hectare (2,500-acre) Dolaucothi Estate – which is home to a Roman gold mine – offers three walks, all with fabulous views across the Cothi Valley. It also has a caravan park.

Another vista that's hard to match is from Paxton's Tower – built in 1811 by Sir William Paxton as a memorial to Lord Nelson.

Follow in the steps of ancestors at Gower

Gower has few rivals when it comes to sandy bays, secluded coves, sand dunes, salt-marsh, grassy clifftops and commons.

There are miles of paths, so walking is a great way to explore the huge variety of habitats and wildlife here.

That the Old Rectory at Rhossili Bay is the most popular National Trust holiday cottage is hardly surprising, given its away-from-it-all situation and enviable view. If you walk to the top of Rhossili Down you can see for miles in every direction or, when the tide is out, you can cross the rocky causeway to the tidal island of Worm's Head, where grey seals laze on the rocks.

There has been farming on Gower since the Stone Age and this has continued to change its landscape ever since. Reminders of this tradition and our ancestors' lives are everywhere, especially in the archaeological features, including Neolithic burial chambers, Iron Age forts and the Vile at Rhossili (a medieval open-field strip system).

The jewel-like Llŷn Peninsula

The Llŷn Peninsula is a dazzling jewel of a place, with sparkling seas, sandy beaches and vast skies. Multicoloured beach huts create a vibrant backdrop to the long, sweeping beach at Llanbedrog, while in the sheltered bay at Porthoer the sand famously whistles underfoot. The fishing village of Porthdinllaen, huddled into the cliff in a sandy cove, is an unforgettable place. Look out for the pub on the beach, where you can enjoy a drink while the children build sandcastles.

If you stroll to the Coastguards' Hut on top of Mynydd Mawr, you will be rewarded, on a clear day, with one of the finest views in Wales – stretching all the way to Ireland. Rare choughs fly overhead, dolphins swim in the bay and seals bask in the sun at this special place. A coastal path now skirts the whole peninsula.

Below: **Llŷn Peninsula, Gwynedd**

Car parks in Wales

Ceredigion

Mwnt	SM 193 519
Penbryn	SM 296 520

Gower

Pennard	SS 553 872

Llŷn Peninsula

Aberdaron	SH 174 264
Llanbedrog	SH 331 335
Porthdinllaen	SH 284 408
Porthoer	SH 166 296
Uwchmynydd	SH 155 264

Pembrokeshire

Broadhaven	SR 977 938
Bosherston	SR 968 947
Marloes	SM 770 085
Martin's Haven	SM 758 091
Stackpole Quay	SR 992 958
Porthclais	SM 741 242
Stackpole Court	SR 976 962

Snowdonia

Craflwyn	SH 599 489
Cregennan	SH 660 140
Nantmor	SH 597 463

Below: **Traeth Llyfn Ynys Barri, St David's, Pembrokeshire**

Why not try...?

Riding a wave
Our glorious sandy beaches are perfect, whether you want to catch your own wave or watch others ride the surf. Still beside the sea, we have some of Britain's most important colonies of seabirds, while Worm's Head is a great place to see grey seals.

Dolphin watching
One of the best spots in the UK for dolphin watching is Mwnt Bay. In season families of bottlenose dolphins are a regular sight. If you like to be active, the lovely coastline is a great – and quiet – place to stretch your legs.

A family holiday at Llŷn
Llŷn is home to picture-postcard beaches, sparkling seas and campsites with a view, in fact it is the perfect place for a traditional family holiday. The sailing is great, too, and an excellent way to explore the coastline.

A Snowdonian adventure
The mountains of Snowdonia need little introduction for walkers and climbers. For bouldering fans, our ancient, glaciated boulders are the best place to train. Campsites come with splendid scenery attached, and while the cycling is strenuous, it's something to boast about afterwards!

Birding or climbing on Anglesey
For the best views of our choughs, puffins and porpoises, be sure to bring your binoculars. The other memorable sight to be seen on the 1,000-million-year-old sea cliffs are the rock climbers who flock here each summer. The inland lagoon at Cemlyn is a birdwatchers' paradise, with its colony of Arctic and common terns.

Volunteering in the Brecon Beacons
One of the best ways to explore the highest peaks in southern Britain and discover their history, is to take a working holiday. You can learn the ancient rural skills that keep these uplands in tip-top condition.

Wild activities in Pembrokeshire
The ultimate place to throw yourself off a cliff into the waves (while wearing a wetsuit) has to be Pembrokeshire. Or if you are a wildlife lover and prefer dry land to the thrills of coasteering, this is the place to watch birds and spot butterflies to your heart's content. Just want to chill out? We've miles of sandy beaches.

Aberconwy House

Castle Street, Conwy LL32 8AY

Map ④ E2

This is the only medieval merchant's house in Conwy to have survived the turbulent history of the walled town over nearly six centuries. Furnished rooms and an audio-visual presentation show daily life from different periods in its history. **Note**: nearest toilet 50 yards.

Eating and shopping: shop selling souvenirs.

Making the most of your day: live music. Ghost stories. Children's trail. Easter and Hallowe'en activities. Lace demonstrations. Guided tours. **Dogs**: assistance dogs only.

Access for all: ☐ 🔲 **Building** 🔲

Getting here: 115:SH781777. At junction of Castle Street and High Street. **Cycle**: NCN5. **Bus**: from surrounding areas. **Train**: Conwy 🚉 300 yards. **Parking**: no onsite parking.

Finding out more: 01492 592246 or aberconwyhouse@nationaltrust.org.uk

Aberconwy House, Conwy: medieval merchant's home

Aberconwy House		M	T	W	T	F	S	S
House								
9 Feb–17 Feb	11–5	M	T	W	T	F	S	S
16 Mar–30 Jun	11–5	M		W	T	F	S	S
1 Jul–31 Aug	11–5	M	T	W	T	F	S	S
1 Sep–3 Nov	11–5	M		W	T	F	S	S
9 Nov–22 Dec	12–3						S	S
Shop								
2 Jan–28 Feb	11–5		T	W	T	F	S	
1 Mar–3 Nov	11–5:30	M	T	W	T	F	S	S
4 Nov–31 Dec	11–5	M	T	W	T	F	S	S

Closed 25 December.

Aberdeunant

Taliaris, Llandeilo, Carmarthenshire SA19 6DL

Map ④ E8 🔲 🔲 🔲

Traditional Carmarthenshire farmhouse in an unspoilt setting. **Note**: administered by tenant. No toilet. Open once a month (booking essential).

Finding out more: 01558 650177 or www.nationaltrust.org.uk

Aberdulais Tin Works and Waterfall

Aberdulais, Neath, Neath Port Talbot SA10 8EU

Map ④ E9 🔲 🔲 🔲 🔲 🔲

Do you dig archaeology? If so you'll love what's been uncovered in one of Britain's oldest tin works – where industry and nature have worked side by side for centuries. Recent projects have made the ruins more accessible than ever before and your imagination will be sparked by the hundreds of stories that those walls could tell. The tea-room, in the Old Schoolhouse, re-lives its Victorian past, only the school dinners are so much nicer in 2013! A spectacular waterfall and Europe's largest generating waterwheel bring you back down to earth and close to nature. **Note**: waterwheel and turbine subject to water levels and conservation work.

Europe's largest generating waterwheel at Aberdulais Tin Works and Waterfall in Neath Port Talbot

Eating and shopping: shop and Schoolhouse tea-room.

Making the most of your day: activities, including Conservation in Action. Demonstrations and family Tracker Packs. Painting, photography and archaeology days. **Dogs**: welcome on leads.

Access for all: ♿🅿🅳♿🚻♿♿♿

Stable and Tin Exhibition ♿♿♿

Turbine House ♿♿♿♿♿

Grounds ♿♿♿➡♿

Getting here: 170:SS772995. 3 miles north-east of Neath. **Foot**: via Neath to Aberdulais Canal footpath. **Cycle**: NCN47 passes. Access near B&Q Neath to Neath Canal towpath and Aberdulais Canal Basin. **Bus**: services from Swansea to Brecon, Swansea to Aberdare and Banwen, Neath

to Aberdulais and Neath ⊠ to Aberdulais. **Train**: Neath 3 miles. **Road**: A4109, 3 miles north-east of Neath. Exit 43 off M4 (Llandarcy), take A465 signposted Vale of Neath. **Sat Nav**: follow brown signs, not Sat Nav. **Parking**: limited, 50 yards.

Finding out more: 01639 636674 or aberdulais@nationaltrust.org.uk

Aberdulais		M	T	W	T	F	S	S
5 Jan–23 Feb	11–4						S	S
24 Feb–28 Mar	11–4:30	M	T	W	T	F	S	S
29 Mar–14 Apr	10:30–5	M	T	W	T	F	S	S
15 Apr–24 May	11–4:30	M	T	W	T	F	S	S
25 May–1 Sep	10:30–5	M	T	W	T	F	S	S
2 Sep–3 Nov	11–4:30	M	T	W	T	F	S	S
9 Nov–22 Dec	11–4						S	S

Schoolhouse tea-room opening arrangements available on website.

Bodnant Garden

Tal-y-Cafn, Colwyn Bay, Conwy LL28 5RE

Map ④ F2   🏠 ❖ 🔔

Marvel at plants from all over the world grown from seed and cuttings collected over a century ago on plant-hunting expeditions. Created by five generations of one family, this 32-hectare (80-acre) garden is superbly located, with spectacular views across Snowdonia. With expansive lawns and intimate corners, grand ponds and impressive terraces, a steep wooded valley and stream, awe-inspiring plant collections and continually changing glorious displays of colour, there's always something to enjoy. Paths throughout allow you to explore and discover the garden's beauty, while enjoying the clean, fresh scents. **Note**: garden and tea-rooms managed on behalf of the National Trust by Michael McLaren.

Eating and shopping: two tea-rooms (Pavilion tea-room serving local wine and beer). Garden centre, craft shops (neither National Trust).

Making the most of your day: guided walks, family events and evening theatre. Adventure playground, family trails and Explorer backpacks. **Dogs**: assistance dogs only.

Access for all: 🅿️ ♿ 🚻 ♿ 🐕 📷 ♿
Grounds 🚶 ♿ ➡️ ♿

Getting here: 115/116:SH801723. 8 miles south of Llandudno and Colwyn Bay. **Bus**: from Llandudno. **Train**: Llandudno Junction. **Road**: off A470. Signposted from A55, junction 19. **Parking**: 150 yards.

Finding out more: 01492 650460 or bodnantgarden@nationaltrust.org.uk

Bodnant Garden		M	T	W	T	F	S	S
Garden*								
1 Jan–28 Feb	11–3	M	T	W	T	F	S	S
1 Mar–27 Oct	10–5	M	T	W	T	F	S	S
28 Oct–10 Nov	11–3	M	T	W	T	F	S	S
27 Dec–31 Dec	11–3	M	T			F	S	S
Tea-room								
1 Jan–28 Feb	11–3	M	T	W	T	F	S	S
1 Mar–27 Oct	10–5	M	T	W	T	F	S	S
28 Oct–24 Dec	11–3	M	T	W	T	F	S	S
27 Dec–31 Dec	11–3	M	T			F	S	S

*Garden open January, February and December, weather permitting.

Bodnant Garden, Conwy: the Lily Terrace and pool, with the pretty little Pin Mill beyond

Bodysgallen Hall Hotel, Conwy: a perfect retreat

Bodysgallen Hall Hotel, Restaurant and Spa

Llandudno, Conwy LL30 1RS

Map (4) F2

This Grade I-listed 17th-century house has the most spectacular views towards Conwy Castle and Snowdonia. It's set in 89 hectares (220 acres) of award-winning romantic gardens, highlights of which include a rare parterre – filled with sweet-smelling herbs – several follies, a cascade, walled garden and formal rose gardens. Beyond, the hotel's parkland offers miles of stunning walks.

The house and gardens are already accessible to the public as a hotel and welcome guests to stay, to dine in the restaurants and to have traditional afternoon tea (booking strongly advised). Contact hotel direct for best available offer. **Note**: all paying guests to the hotel are welcome to walk in the garden and park. Children above the age of six are welcome.

Finding out more: 01492 584466. 01492 582519 (fax) or info@bodysgallen.com. www.bodysgallen.com

Chirk Castle

Chirk, Wrexham LL14 5AF

Map (4) G3

Completed in 1310, Chirk is the last Welsh castle from the reign of Edward I still lived in today. Features from its 700 years include the medieval tower and dungeon, 17th-century Long Gallery, grand 18th-century state apartments, servants' hall and historic laundry. The newly refurbished east wing depicts the life of Lord Howard de Walden during the 1930s. The award-winning gardens contain clipped yews, herbaceous borders, shrub and rock gardens. A terrace with stunning views looks out over the Cheshire and Shropshire plains. The parkland provides a habitat for rare invertebrates, wild flowers and contains many mature trees. **Note**: all visitors, including members, need to obtain tickets before going to castle, tower or garden.

Eating and shopping: tea-room and coffee shop serving home-grown produce. Farm and gift shops, plant sales and second-hand books.

Making the most of your day: our new leaflets tell you all about the many places to explore (including the fortress, gardens and woods), plus fascinating stories about servants' lives and the Myddelton family home. **Dogs**: welcome on leads, assistance dogs only in formal gardens.

History comes to life at Chirk Castle, Wrexham

Access for all: P♿ D♿ 🚲 🎧 📷 🔍 🎫 ♿ 👓

State rooms ♿ 🚶 👶   Adam Tower ♿

Gardens 🏔 ♿ ➡ 👶

Getting here: 126:SJ275388. 2 miles west of Chirk village, 7 miles from Wrexham and Llangollen. **Foot**: permitted footpaths open April to September. 1½ miles from Llangollen Canal to moor near Chirk Tunnel. **Bus**: from Wrexham to Oswestry. **Train**: Chirk, 1½ miles. **Road**: signposted off A483. **Parking**: at home farm, 200 yards (via steep hill).

Finding out more: 01691 777701 or chirkcastle@nationaltrust.org.uk

Chirk Castle		M	T	W	T	F	S	S
Estate*								
Open all year	7–7	M	T	W	T	F	S	S
Garden, tower, shops and tea-rooms								
1 Feb–28 Feb	10–4	M	T	W	T	F	S	S
4 Nov–22 Dec	10–4	M	T	W	T	F	S	S
Whole property**								
1 Mar–31 Mar	10–4	M	T	W	T	F	S	S
1 Apr–30 Sep	10–5	M	T	W	T	F	S	S
1 Oct–3 Nov	10–4	M	T	W	T	F	S	S
State rooms								
9 Nov–1 Dec***	11–3	·	·	·	·	·	S	S
7 Dec–22 Dec	11–4	M	T	W	T	F	S	S

*Closes dusk if earlier and open until 9, June to August.
**State rooms by guided tour only, 11 to 12 (places limited), free-flow 12 to closing. ***Conservation guided tours only (places limited).

Cilgerran Castle

near Cardigan, Pembrokeshire SA43 2SF

Map ④ C7

Striking 13th-century castle in a stunning location, overlooking the Teifi Gorge. **Note**: in the guardianship of Cadw – Welsh Government's historic environment service. Dogs on leads allowed.

Finding out more: 01239 621339 or www.nationaltrust.org.uk

Admiring a sculpture at Colby Woodland Garden in Pembrokeshire

Colby Woodland Garden

near Amroth, Pembrokeshire SA67 8PP

Map ④ C8   🔼 ❄ 🍽 🛏 🔍

Set in a tranquil and secluded valley, this glorious informal woodland garden with its fascinating industrial past is always rich with colour and wildlife. Spring brings carpets of bluebells and a vivid display of camellias, rhododendrons and azaleas. In the summer the wildflower meadow and walled garden are bursting with colour, followed by marvellous autumnal hues. There are shady woodland walks and the meadow boasts a meandering stream and abundance of dragonflies, butterflies and other insects. To discover more about the garden's wildlife and history and to take a virtual tour of Pembrokeshire, visit the Bothy exhibition. **Note**: house not open.

A tempting path at Colby Woodland Garden

Eating and shopping: shop and plant sales. Bothy tea-room (Trust-approved concession). Gallery selling Pembrokeshire arts and crafts. Second-hand books. Summerhill farm shop (tenant-run).

Making the most of your day: rope swings, den-building, pond-dipping and games equipment. Easter trails, wildlife events and summer holiday activities. **Dogs**: under control in estate woodlands. On leads in garden and meadow.

Access for all: 🅿♿🚻♿🔊🔊🔊📷🚐📹 Grounds ♿➡♿

Getting here: 158:SN155080. 1½ miles inland from Amroth beside Carmarthen Bay. **Foot**: from beach via public footpath in Amroth (beside Amroth Arms). **Bus**: from Tenby (passing Kilgetty 🚆). **Train**: Kilgetty 2½ miles. **Road**: follow brown signs from A477 or off coast road at Amroth Castle caravan park. **Parking**: free, 50 yards. Pay and display from January to mid-February, plus November and December.

Finding out more: 01834 811885 or colby@nationaltrust.org.uk

Colby Woodland Garden		M	T	W	T	F	S	S
Woodland and walled gardens and bothy exhibition*								
2 Jan–8 Feb	10–3	M	T	W	T	F	S	S
4 Nov–31 Dec	10–3	M	T	W	T	F	S	S
Woodland and walled gardens, shop and bothy exhibition*								
9 Feb–3 Nov	10–5	M	T	W	T	F	S	S
Tea-room								
5 Jan–24 Mar	11–3						S	S
25 Mar–3 Nov	10–5	M	T	W	T	F	S	S
9 Nov–29 Dec	11–3						S	S
Gallery								
25 Mar–3 Nov	11–5	M	T	W	T	F	S	S

*Car park open as woodland and walled gardens. Closed 1 January, 25 and 26 December.

Conwy Suspension Bridge

Conwy LL32 8LD

Map ④ E2

Designed in the 1820s by Thomas Telford, this graceful bridge with its beautifully restored tiny toll-keeper's house has stunning views over the Conwy estuary. Kept open by a husband and wife at a time when trade and travel brought Conwy to life, it never closed, whatever the weather. **Note**: no toilet.

Eating and shopping: bring your own picnic to enjoy on the grassed area.

Making the most of your day: guided talks on Thomas Telford. **Dogs**: allowed.

Access for all: Building ♿ Grounds ♿

Getting here: 115:SH785775. 100 yards from town centre, adjacent to Conwy Castle. **Cycle**: NCN5. **Bus**: services from surrounding areas. **Train**: Conwy ¼ mile; Llandudno Junction ½ mile. **Parking**: no onsite parking.

Finding out more: 01492 573282 or conwybridge@nationaltrust.org.uk

Conwy Suspension Bridge		M	T	W	T	F	S	S
16 Mar–3 Nov	11–5	M	T	W	T	F	S	S

Conwy Suspension Bridge, Conwy: grace and strength

Dinefwr

Llandeilo, Carmarthenshire SA19 6RT

Map ④ E8

A place of power and influence for more than 2,000 years, Dinefwr holds an iconic position in Welsh history. The spirits of Welsh princes still inhabit this magical landscape, designed in the 18th century by the visionaries George and Cecil Rice. There are 323 hectares (800 acres) to explore – three-quarters of which is a National Nature Reserve – including a ruined castle, bogland walk, deer-park, woodlands, hay meadows and streams. Newton House is not your traditional dressed period house; instead the rooms tell the story of Dinefwr across the centuries, giving our visitors an atmospheric and hands-on experience. **Note**: castle owned by Wildlife Trust, in guardianship of Cadw, Welsh Government's historic environment service.

Eating and shopping: shop, tea-room and café (licensed).

Making the most of your day: daily tours of Newton House and White Park cattle. Seasonal tours of the National Nature Reserve and fallow deer herd. School holiday and family activities. Events. Holiday cottages. **Dogs**: welcome on leads, in outer park only.

Access for all: ▣▣▣▣▣▣▣▣▣ Building ▣▣▣ Grounds ▣

Getting here: 159:SN625225. 1 mile west of Llandeilo. **Bus**: Llandeilo, 1 mile. **Train**: Llandeilo, 1 mile. **Road**: from Carmarthen or Llandovery on A40(T); from Swansea M4 to Pont Abraham, then A48(T) to Cross Hands and A476 to Llandeilo. **Sat Nav**: do not use. **Parking**: 50 yards.

Finding out more: 01558 824512 or dinefwr@nationaltrust.org.uk

Dinefwr		M	T	W	T	F	S	S
Park and castle								
1 Jan–30 Apr	10–4	M	T	W	T	F	S	S
1 May–31 Aug	10–6	M	T	W	T	F	S	S
1 Sep–31 Dec	10–4	M	T	W	T	F	S	S
Newton House, grounds, café and shop								
1 Jan–30 Apr	11–4	M	T	W	T	F	S	S
1 May–31 Aug	11–6	M	T	W	T	F	S	S
1 Sep–31 Dec	11–4	M	T	W	T	F	S	S

Last admission to Newton House, grounds, café and shop is 1 hour before closing. Property closed 24 and 25 December. Cadw manage Dinefwr Castle and may alter opening times.

Newton House sits surrounded by the magical landscape park at Dinefwr in Carmarthenshire

A family pans for gold at Dolaucothi Gold Mines in Carmarthenshire, which were first worked by the Romans

Dolaucothi Gold Mines

Pumsaint, Llanwrda, Carmarthenshire SA19 8US

Map (4) E7

The story of Welsh gold starts at Dolaucothi Gold Mines, set amid the wooded hillsides overlooking the beautiful Cothi Valley. More than 2,000 years ago the Romans mined for gold here, and mining continued in the 19th and 20th centuries. The mine yard is preserved as it was in the 1930s, when gold mining ceased. Underground tours bring the harsh working conditions to life, and you can see the 1930s mine machinery, have a go at gold panning and learn about Welsh gold. For a relaxing break, stay on at our caravan site opposite the gold mines. **Note**: steep slopes, stout footwear essential. Underground tours.

Eating and shopping: tea-room and gift shop selling Welsh gold jewellery.

Making the most of your day: daily underground tours (please note younger children may not be carried). Overground tours of Roman adits. Regular school holiday and family activities. Self-guided walks around estate. **Dogs**: on leads only.

Access for all: ⟦symbols⟧
Building ⟦symbols⟧

Getting here: 146:SN662403. Between Lampeter and Llanwrda. **Bus**: from Lampeter. **Train**: Llanwrda, 8 miles. **Road**: on A482. **Parking**: free. Overflow car park opposite main entrance.

Finding out more: 01558 650177 or dolaucothi@nationaltrust.org.uk

Dolaucothi Gold Mines		M	T	W	T	F	S	S
Estate and walks								
Open all year		M	T	W	T	F	S	S
Mines, shop and tea-room								
22 Mar–30 Jun	11–5	M	T	W	T	F	S	S
1 Jul–31 Aug	10–6	M	T	W	T	F	S	S
1 Sep–3 Nov	11–5	M	T	W	T	F	S	S
Caravan site								
22 Mar–31 Oct		M	T	W	T	F	S	S
Christmas shop (Coach House Pumsaint)								
22 Nov–20 Dec	11–4	·	·	·	T	F	S	·

Dyffryn Gardens, Vale of Glamorgan, features intimate garden rooms, formal lawns and an extensive arboretum

Dyffryn Gardens

St Nicholas, Vale of Glamorgan CF5 6SU

Map ④ G10

One of our latest additions in Wales, these Grade I gardens cover 22 hectares (55 acres) and feature a stunning collection of intimate garden rooms, formal lawns and an extensive arboretum. Designed by eminent landscape architect Thomas Mawson, the gardens are the early 20th-century vision of industrialist John Cory and his son Reginald Cory. The spectacular symmetry of Mawson's lawn is best appreciated from the terrace of the Grade II* late Victorian house, reminiscent of a French château. The tiered garden rooms are overlooked by a reinstated glasshouse that houses an impressive collection of cacti and orchids.

Note: Dyffryn House is undergoing restoration, with some rooms to be opened in 2013.

Eating and shopping: tea-rooms and shop selling gifts and books. Seasonal plant sales.

Access for all: 🅿️♿🚻♿♿
Grounds 🚶♿➡️♿♿

Getting here: 171:ST09657217. 7 miles from Cardiff city centre. **Train**: Cardiff Central. **Road**: from M4 take junction 33 onto A4232 (to Barry). Exit second slip road, at roundabout take the fourth exit A48 (to Cowbridge). In St Nicholas village follow signs for Dyffryn. **Sat Nav**: do not use. **Parking**: on site.

Finding out more: 02920 593328 or dyffryn@nationaltrust.org.uk. www.nationaltrust.org.uk/wales

Dyffryn Gardens
Visit website for opening arrangements.

Erddig

Wrexham LL13 0YT

Map ④ H3　🏛➕🏚⛴✴️⚑

Described as 'the jewel in the crown of Welsh country houses', Erddig is a fascinating yet unpretentious early 18th-century country house which reflects a gentry family's 250 years of upstairs-downstairs life. The extensive downstairs area contains Erddig's unique collection of servants' portraits, while the upstairs rooms are an amazing treasure trove of fine furniture, textiles and wallpapers. Outside, an impressive range of outbuildings includes stables, a smithy, joiners' shop and sawmill. It's set within a superb 18th-century formal garden and romantic landscape park – which are the starting points for walks, bicycle and carriage rides through the estate.

Eating and shopping: gift shop. Plant sales. Restaurant, tea-room and Coachman's Tea Garden.

Face to face with a garden carving at Erddig

Making the most of your day: events, including open-air theatre, festivals, craft fairs, Christmas markets and family fun days. Guided walks, tree trails and discovery tours. **Dogs**: welcome on leads in country park only.

Access for all: ♿🅿️♿🔤🅱️🎞️🖼️📷👓

Building 🅱️♿　Grounds 🅱️♿♿♿

Getting here: 117:SJ326482. 2 miles from Wrexham. **Bus**: from Wrexham, alight Felin Puleston, 1 mile through country park. **Train**: Wrexham Central 2½ miles; Wrexham General 3½ miles via Erddig Road and footpath. **Road**: signposted A525 Whitchurch road. A483 exit 3. **Parking**: free, 200 yards.

Finding out more: 01978 355314 or erddig@nationaltrust.org.uk

Erddig		M	T	W	T	F	S	S
House								
1 Jan–8 Mar*	11:30–3:30	M	T	W	T	F	S	S
9 Mar–3 Nov	12:30–4:30	M	T	W	T	F	S	S
4 Nov–31 Dec*	11:30–3:30	M	T	W	T	F	S	S
Garden, restaurant and shop								
1 Jan–8 Mar	11–4	M	T	W	T	F	S	S
9 Mar–3 Nov	11–5	M	T	W	T	F	S	S
4 Nov–31 Dec	11–4	M	T	W	T	F	S	S

Open every day except Christmas Day. Last admission to house one hour before closing. 9 March to 3 November: house themed tours 11:30 and 12, free-flow from 12:30. No electric light in the house, for close study of pictures avoid dull days. *Below stairs only, by guided tours running throughout the day.

Enjoying a carriage ride at Erddig in Wrexham

The magnificent, curving sandy Rhossili Beach, with Rhossili Down behind, on the Gower

Gower: Rhossili Shop and Visitor Centre

Coastguard Cottages, Rhossili, Gower, Swansea SA3 1PR

Map (4) D9

Perched on the clifftop, and overlooking the spectacular Rhossili Bay, the shop and visitor centre offers everything you need to enjoy fully this beautiful area of outstanding, historical natural beauty. Local information, advice and a wide range of gifts and tempting treats to take home afterwards. **Note**: car park charges (including members).

Eating and shopping: refreshments and Joe's Ice Cream available. Goods for sale, ranging from camping equipment to laverbread.

Making the most of your day: free Tracker Packs and GPS units (geocaching). Events and guided walks. **Dogs**: welcome, on leads near livestock.

Access for all: 🅿♿🚹👫🅿 Visitor Centre 👣
Grounds 👣➡

Getting here: 159:SS414881. South-west tip of Gower Peninsula. **Bus**: services from Swansea to Rhossili. **Road**: from Swansea take A4118, then B4247. **Parking**: 50 yards (not National Trust), charge including members.

Finding out more: 01792 390707 or rhossili.shop@nationaltrust.org.uk

Rhossili Visitor Centre		M	T	W	T	F	S	S
4 Jan–10 Feb	11–4					F	S	S
11 Feb–23 Mar	10:30–4	M	T	W	T	F	S	S
24 Mar–3 May	10:30–4:30	M	T	W	T	F	S	S
4 May–2 Sep	10:30–5	M	T	W	T	F	S	S
3 Sep–3 Nov	10:30–4:30	M	T	W	T	F	S	S
4 Nov–22 Dec	10:30–4	M	T	W	T	F	S	S
27 Dec–29 Dec	11–4					F	S	S

The Visitor Centre closes 15 minutes before the shop.
Open until 6 on Saturdays and Sundays during August.

The Kymin

The Round House, The Kymin, Monmouth, Monmouthshire NP25 3SF

Map (4) H8

Georgian banqueting house and temple set among woods and pleasure grounds.

Finding out more: 01600 719241 or www.nationaltrust.org.uk

Llanerchaeron

Ciliau Aeron, near Aberaeron,
Ceredigion SA48 8DG

Map ④ D6

A totally self-sufficient 18th-century Welsh minor gentry estate. The villa, designed in the 1790s, is the most complete example of the early work of John Nash. It has its own service courtyard with dairy, laundry, brewery and salting house, giving a full upstairs-downstairs experience. The walled kitchen gardens, pleasure grounds, ornamental lake and parkland offer peaceful walks, while the Home Farm complex has an impressive range of traditional, atmospheric outbuildings. A working farm, there are Welsh Black cattle, Llanwenog sheep and rare Welsh pigs.

Eating and shopping: café serving light meals and cakes. Picnic site. Fresh garden produce and plants, farm meat, local crafts, art, gifts and books for sale. Second-hand bookshop.

Making the most of your day: activities during local school holidays, including crafts, gardening, nature activities and self-led trails. Special events days. Cycle hire.
Dogs: welcome in the parkland only on leads.

Access for all: ⬛⬛⬛⬛⬛⬛⬛⬛⬛⬛
Visitor building ⬛⬛ Villa ⬛⬛ Grounds ⬛➡

Getting here: 146:SN480602. 2½ miles east of Aberaeron. **Foot**: 2½ miles foot/cycle track from Aberaeron to property along old railway line. **Bus**: service from Aberystwyth ➡ to Carmarthen ➡, alight New Inn Forge, about ½ mile. **Road**: off A482. **Parking**: free, 50 yards.

Finding out more: 01545 570200 or llanerchaeron@nationaltrust.org.uk

Llanerchaeron		M	T	W	T	F	S	S
Farm, garden, woodland walks and shop only								
1 Jan–8 Feb	11:30–3:30	M	T	W	T	F	S	S
18 Feb–17 Mar	11:30–3:30	M	T	W	T	F	S	S
4 Nov–31 Dec*	11:30–3:30	M	T	W	T	F	S	S
Entire property								
9 Feb–17 Feb	11:30–3:30	M	T	W	T	F	S	S
18 Mar–3 Nov**	10:30–5	M	T	W	T	F	S	S
Christmas Fair								
7 Dec–8 Dec	11–4	·	·	·	·	·	S	S

First entry to villa 11:30, last entry one hour before closing. Full café open 9 February to 3 November. *Entire property closed 21 to 25 December. **Geler Jones Collection open Wednesday and Friday 12 to 4. Bad weather can cause access problems (telephone for information before visiting between November and March). Parkland accessible daily.

A proud mother keeps a watchful eye over her litter of piglets at Llanerchaeron in Ceredigion

Penrhyn Castle

Bangor, Gwynedd LL57 4HN

Map ④ E2

An imposing fortress built to create a lasting impression, this 19th-century castle commands its position in the landscape, nestled between the mountains of Snowdonia and the Menai Strait. There are many grand spaces to explore, which capture the height of Victorian opulence, and North Wales' premier art collection to discover. You can get a feel for life 'downstairs' in the Victorian kitchens, or climb aboard an engine in the Railway Museum. A visit to the grounds, where you can enjoy the tranquillity of the gardens and the breathtaking views, is the perfect way to finish your day.

Eating and shopping: shop and tea-room.

Making the most of your day: exhibitions and events, including summer fun days. Railway Museum in the old stables. Cathedral-like interiors housing an opulent art collection. Hidden parts of garden to discover.
Dogs: on leads in grounds only.

Drawing room, top, and kitchen, above, at Penrhyn

Getting here: 115:SH602720. 1 mile east of Bangor. **Cycle**: NCN5, 1¼ miles. **Bus**: services from Bangor to Caernarfon and Llandudno, alight castle driveway (1 mile long). **Train**: Bangor 3 miles. **Road**: on A5122 (Llandygai). Signposted from junction 11 of A55 and A5. **Sat Nav**: use LL57 4HT. **Parking**: free, 500 yards.

Access for all: 🅿️ ♿ 🏪 ⛪ 🚽 💺 📷 🏠 🚶 ∷ Ⓐ
Mansion ♿ 🏠 🦽   Stable block 🏠 ⬍
Grounds ♿ 🏠

Finding out more: 01248 363219 (Infoline). 01248 353084 or penrhyncastle@nationaltrust.org.uk

Penrhyn Castle		M	T	W	T	F	S	S
Castle and Victorian kitchens*								
1 Mar–30 Jun	12–5	M	·	W	T	F	S	S
1 Jul–31 Aug	11–5	M	T	W	T	F	S	S
1 Sep–3 Nov	12–5	M	·	W	T	F	S	S
Grounds and tea-room								
1 Mar–30 Jun	11–5	M	T	W	T	F	S	S
1 Jul–31 Aug	10–5	M	T	W	T	F	S	S
1 Sep–3 Nov	11–5	M	T	W	T	F	S	S
Railway Museum, grounds and café								
1 Jan–28 Feb	12–3	M	T	W	T	F	S	S
1 Mar–3 Nov	11–5	M	T	W	T	F	S	S
4 Nov–31 Dec	12–3	M	T	W	T	F	S	S

*Limited booked guided tours available on Tuesdays (March to June and September to October). Last entry to castle 4:30. Closed 25 December.

The imposing keep at Penrhyn Castle, Gwynedd

Plas Newydd Country House and Gardens

Llanfairpwll, Anglesey LL61 6DQ

Map (4) D2

Plas Newydd, the ancestral home of the Marquess of Anglesey, bears witness to a turbulent history: noble beginnings during Henry VIII's reign, triumphant success at Waterloo, bankruptcy at the turn of the 20th century and the revival of the family fortunes in the 1930s. The house is famous for its association with Rex Whistler, and contains his exquisite romantic mural and the largest exhibition of his works. Located on the Menai Strait, with glorious views across Snowdonia, you can stroll through an Australasian arboretum, Italianate summer terrace or follow a woodland path leading to the marine walk along the strait.

Eating and shopping: Old Dairy Tea-room. Coffee shop. Two gift shops. Second-hand bookshop.

Making the most of your day: events, including summer fair, 1930s weekend and Christmas Craft and Food Fair. House taster tours. Specialist garden 'Walks and Talks'. Exhibitions. Summer night music. Wet and Wild activities. **Dogs**: in the car park only.

Access for all:
Building **Grounds**

Getting here: 114/115:SH521696. 2 miles south-west of Llanfairpwll. **Cycle**: NCN8, ¼ mile. **Bus**: Bangor to Llangefni (passing Bangor and close Llanfairpwll). **Train**: Llanfairpwll 1¾ miles. **Road**: from A55 take junctions 7 and 8a, then A4080 to Brynsiencyn; from A5 at west end of Britannia Bridge.

Finding out more: 01248 715272 (Infoline). 01248 714795 or plasnewydd@nationaltrust.org.uk

Plas Newydd		M	T	W	T	F	S	S
House								
2 Mar–10 Mar*	11–4	·	·	·	·	·	**S**	**S**
16 Mar–6 Nov**	12–4:30	**M**	**T**	**W**	·	·	**S**	**S**
Garden								
1 Jan–13 Mar	11–4	**M**	**T**	**W**	·	·	**S**	**S**
16 Mar–6 Nov	10–5:30	**M**	**T**	**W**	·	·	**S**	**S**
9 Nov–31 Dec	11–4	**M**	**T**	**W**	·	·	**S**	**S**
Shop, tea-room, playground and frisbee golf course								
1 Jan–15 Mar	11–4	**M**	**T**	**W**	**T**	**F**	**S**	**S**
16 Mar–6 Nov	10–5:30	**M**	**T**	**W**	**T**	**F**	**S**	**S**
7 Nov–31 Dec	11–4	**M**	**T**	**W**	**T**	**F**	**S**	**S**
Coffee shop and second-hand bookshop								
16 Mar–6 Nov	11:30–5	**M**	**T**	**W**	·	·	**S**	**S**

*Taster tours only, no free-flow. **Specialist tours 11 to 12. Rhododendron garden at its best April to June. Property closed 25 December.

The new tree-house at Plas Newydd, Anglesey, is irresistible to the young and not-so-young alike

Plas yn Rhiw

Rhiw, Pwllheli, Gwynedd LL53 8AB

Map ④ C4 🏠❋🐾🛏

The house was rescued from neglect and lovingly restored by the three Keating sisters, who bought it in 1938. The views from the grounds and gardens across Cardigan Bay are among the most spectacular in Britain. The house is 16th-century with Georgian additions, and the garden contains many beautiful flowering trees and shrubs, with beds framed by box hedges and grass paths. It is stunning whatever the season.

Eating and shopping: shop selling gifts, hot or cold drinks and ice-cream. Plant sales.

Rambling roses in Plas yn Rhiw's lovely garden

Making the most of your day: events, including plant sales and Easter Egg hunt. Guided tours (by arrangement). **Dogs**: on woodland walk below car park only (on leads).

Access for all: 🅿️🏢♿🔦📷🎵👓
Building 🔦♿
Grounds 🔦♿

Getting here: 123:SH237282. 12 miles south-west of Pwllheli. **Foot**: easily accessed from Llyn coastal path. **Bus**: Pwllheli to Aberdaron (passing Pwllheli ≋), alight at gate. **Train**: Pwllheli 10 miles. **Road**: B4413 to Aberdaron (drive gates at bottom Rhiw Hill). **Parking**: small car park, 80 yards. Not suitable for large vehicles. Narrow lanes.

Finding out more: 01758 780219 or plasynrhiw@nationaltrust.org.uk

Plas yn Rhiw		M	T	W	T	F	S	S
21 Mar–27 May	12–5	M	·	·	T	F	S	S
29 May–2 Sep	12–5	M	·	W	T	F	S	S
5 Sep–30 Sep	12–5	M	·	·	T	F	S	S
3 Oct–3 Nov	12–4	·	·	·	T	F	S	S

Open Bank Holidays. Garden only open 1, 3, 10 and 17 March, 12 to 3. Garden and snowdrop wood open occasionally at weekends in January and February.

The library at Plas yn Rhiw, Gwynedd

Powis Castle and Garden

Welshpool, Powys SY21 8RF

Map (4) G5

On the terrace at Powis Castle and Garden, Powys

The world-famous garden, overhung with clipped yews, shelters rare and tender plants. Laid out under the influence of Italian and French styles, it retains its original lead statues and an orangery on the terraces. High on a rock above the terraces, the castle, originally built *circa* 1200, began life as a medieval fortress. Remodelled and embellished over more than 400 years, it reflects the changing needs and ambitions of the Herbert family – each generation adding to the magnificent collection of paintings, sculpture, furniture and tapestries. A superb collection of treasures from India is displayed in the Clive Museum. **Note**: all visitors (including members) need a ticket from reception.

Eating and shopping: restaurant. Plant sales. Shop.

Making the most of your day: castle and garden family fun trails, children's activities during school holidays. Gardening demonstrations and themed castle tours on selected days of the week. **Dogs**: assistance dogs only.

Access for all: ⊞⊡⊞⊞⊞⊞⊞⊞⊞⊞⊞
Building 🔾 Grounds 🔾🔾➡️🔾

Getting here: 126:SJ216064. 1 mile south of Welshpool. **Foot**: 1-mile walk from Park Lane, off Broad Street in Welshpool. Access from High Street (A490). **Bus**: services from Oswestry and Shrewsbury. Alight High Street, 1 mile. **Train**: Welshpool, 1¼ miles on footpath. **Road**: signed from main road to Newtown (A483); enter by first drive gate on right. **Parking**: free.

Finding out more: 01938 551944 (Infoline). 01938 551929 or powiscastle@nationaltrust.org.uk

Powis Castle and Garden		M	T	W	T	F	S	S
Castle								
5 Jan–24 Feb*	12:30–3:30						S	S
9 Nov–29 Dec	12:30–3:30						S	S
Castle and Clive Museum								
1 Mar–31 Mar	12:30–4	M	T	W	T	F	S	S
1 Apr–30 Sep	12:30–5	M	T	W	T	F	S	S
1 Oct–3 Nov	12:30–4	M	T	W	T	F	S	S
Garden, restaurant and shop								
1 Jan–28 Feb	11–3:30	M	T	W	T	F	S	S
1 Mar–31 Mar	11–4:30	M	T	W	T	F	S	S
1 Apr–30 Sep	11–5:30	M	T	W	T	F	S	S
1 Oct–3 Nov	11–4:30	M	T	W	T	F	S	S
4 Nov–31 Dec	11–3:30	M	T	W	T	F	S	S

*By guided tour only, last tour at 2:30, booking essential. Limited number of state rooms open from 5 January to 24 February and 9 November to 29 December. From 1 March, last admission to castle 45 minutes before closing. Clive Museum closed on 10 March. Property closed on 25 December.

A patchwork of fields at St David's Head, as seen from Penberry in Pembrokeshire

St David's Visitor Centre and Shop

Captain's House, High Street, St David's, Pembrokeshire SA62 6SD

Map ④ A8

Opposite The Cross in the centre of St David's, Wales's smallest historic city, the visitor centre and well-stocked shop is open all year. For a complete guide to the National Trust in Pembrokeshire, visitors can take a tour of our special places, beaches and walks using interactive technology. **Note**: no toilet.

Eating and shopping: books, cards, maps, wide range of gifts and local produce. New walks leaflets available.

Making the most of your day: guided walks, evening talks and events.

Access for all: Building [symbol]

Getting here: 115:SM753253. In the centre of St David's. **Foot**: Pembrokeshire Coast Path

within 1 mile. **Bus**: from Haverfordwest [symbol]. Additional services during main holiday season. **Parking**: no onsite parking.

Finding out more: 01437 720385 or stdavids@nationaltrust.org.uk

St David's Visitor Centre		M	T	W	T	F	S	S
2 Jan–16 Mar	10–4	**M**	**T**	**W**	**T**	**F**	**S**	
17 Mar–31 Dec	10–5	**M**	**T**	**W**	**T**	**F**	**S**	**S**

Closes 4 on Sunday. Closed 1 January, 25 and 26 December.

Segontium

Caernarfon, Gwynedd

Map ④ D2

Fort built to defend the Roman Empire against rebellious tribes. **Note**: in the guardianship of Cadw – Welsh Government's historic environment service. Museum not National Trust.

Finding out more: 01286 675625 or www.nationaltrust.org.uk

Skenfrith Castle

Skenfrith, near Abergavenny,
Monmouthshire NP7 8UH

Map (4) H8

Remains of early 13th-century castle, built
beside the River Monnow to command one
of the main routes from England.
Note: in the guardianship of Cadw – Welsh
Government's historic environment service.

Finding out more: 01874 625515
or www.nationaltrust.org.uk

Stackpole

Stackpole, near Pembroke, Pembrokeshire

Map (4) B9

A former grand estate stretching down to some
of the most beautiful coastline in the world,
including Broadhaven South and Barafundle.
Today Bosherston Lakes and the dramatic
cliffs of Stackpole Head are a National Nature
Reserve, and the former site of Stackpole Court
gives the historical background to the estate.

Eating and shopping: Boathouse at Stackpole
Quay serving lunch and tea. Estate-grown
produce for sale at Mencap walled garden.

Making the most of your day: guided kayak
and coasteering trips. Guided walks. Beach
activity days. Coarse fishing. Theatre and music
concerts. Wild camping with Rangers. Stay
at holiday cottages or the Outdoor Learning
Centre. **Dogs**: under control on estate.

Access for all:
Building   Grounds

Getting here: 158:SR992958. 6 miles south of
Pembroke. **Foot**: Pembrokeshire Coast Path.
Bus: Pembroke to Angle. **Train**: Pembroke
6 miles. **Road**: B4319 from Pembroke to
Stackpole and Bosherston. **Parking**: pay and
display at Stackpole Quay, Broadhaven South,
Bosherston Lakes and Stackpole Court site.

Finding out more: 01646 661359 or
stackpole@nationaltrust.org.uk.
Old Home Farm Yard, Stackpole, near
Pembroke, Pembrokeshire SA71 5DQ

Stackpole		M	T	W	T	F	S	S
Estate								
Open all year	Dawn–dusk	M	T	W	T	F	S	S
Boathouse tea-room								
8 Feb–17 Feb	10:30–5	M	T	W	T	F	S	S
22 Feb–24 Mar	11–4	·	·	·	·	F	S	S
29 Mar–3 Nov	10:30–5	M	T	W	T	F	S	S
8 Nov–15 Dec	11–4	·	·	·	·	F.	S	S
20 Dec–31 Dec	11–4	M	T	·	T	F	S	S

Boathouse tea-room closed 24 and 25 December.

Glorious golden sands at Broadhaven South at Stackpole in Pembrokeshire

Stackpole Outdoor Learning Centre

Old Home Farm Yard, Stackpole,
near Pembroke, Pembrokeshire SA71 5DQ

Map ④ B9

Our platinum eco award-winning centre is perfectly located to enjoy the Stackpole Estate. The recently upgraded residential centre with theatre, meeting and classroom facilities can accommodate up to 140 guests and is ideal for educational groups, corporate clients, private group hire and family holidays. **Note**: contact the centre for activity programmes, prices and availability.

Eating and shopping: self-catering or chef-catered options. Full entertainment licence for events with bar. Residents' barbecue area. Shop and information hub.

Making the most of your day: events, including rock-pool rambles, guided walks, open-air theatre, music festivals and concerts. Kayaking or coasteering. Otter-spotting. **Dogs**: assistance dogs only.

Access for all:

Getting here: 158:SR9795. 6 miles south of Pembroke. **Foot**: via Pembrokeshire Coast Path. **Bus**: Pembroke ᕎ to Angle. **Train**: Pembroke 6 miles. **Road**: B4319 from Pembroke (follow brown signs for Stackpole Centre). **Sat Nav**: ignore and follow brown signs for Stackpole Centre. **Parking**: free.

Finding out more: 01646 661425 (reception). 01646 661359 (estate office) or stackpoleoutdoorlearning@ nationaltrust.org.uk

Stackpole Outdoor Centre	Open every day all year

Please contact the centre for more information on residential group bookings, courses and activities.

Tredegar House

Newport, Newport NP10 8YW

Map ④ G9

For more than four centuries this country estate, with its fine Grade I 17th-century restoration house, was the home of the flamboyant Morgan family. Their fascinating narrative is told throughout the house, with everything from ancestral portraits adorning the walls to the cosmopolitan craftsmanship of the state rooms adding to the story. The Morgans' enthusiasm for racing and hunting is reflected by the impressive Grade I stables flanking the courtyard. It is surrounded by 36 hectares (90 acres) of parkland, along with the great lake, three walled gardens, an orangery and outbuildings.

Eating and shopping: Brewhouse tea-room (licensed) serving morning coffee, hot and cold lunches or afternoon tea and cakes. Lakeside picnics welcome. Shop at park entrance.

Making the most of your day: events, including folk festival, vintage car rally and pirates' day. Parkland and woodland walks. Traditional games in the parlour and formal gardens. We're continuing to review our offer (details on website). **Dogs**: welcome in parkland and on leads in garden.

Access for all: ⓟ 🏬 ♿ ♿ 🔲 🎧 ♿
House 🏠 Grounds 🏠 ♿

Getting here: 171:ST287849. 2 miles west of Newport (south-east Wales). **Train**: Newport. **Road**: from M4 take junction 28, then exit roundabout A48 (to St Mellons). **Parking**: onsite pay and display.

The richly decorated Gilt Room, left, and north-west front, above, of Tredegar House in Newport: home to the flamboyant Morgan family

Finding out more: 01633 815880 or tredegar@nationaltrust.org.uk

Tredegar House		M	T	W	T	F	S	S
House and garden								
9 Feb–28 Feb*	11–4:30	M	T	W	T	F	S	S
1 Mar–3 Nov**	11–5	M	T	W	T	F	S	S
Tea-room and shop								
2 Jan–8 Feb	10:30–4:30			W	T	F	S	S
9 Feb–28 Feb	10:30–4:30	M	T	W	T	F	S	S
1 Mar–3 Nov	10:30–5:30	M	T	W	T	F	S	S
6 Nov–29 Dec***	10:30–4			W	T	F	S	S
Park								
Open all year	Dawn–dusk	M	T	W	T	F	S	S

Last admission to house one hour before closing. 4 November to 21 December bookable tours and Christmas events in the house. *Below stairs only. **Gardens open 10:30. ***Tea-room and shop closed 24 to 26 December.

Tudor Merchant's House

Quay Hill, Tenby, Pembrokeshire SA70 7BX

Map (**4**) C9

Imagine yourself back in 1500, as you step into the world lived in by a successful merchant and his family when this fine three-storey house was built. The merchant's shop, kitchen and first-floor hall have all been transformed by colourful wall-hangings, painted cloths and finely crafted replica Tudor furniture.
Note: no toilet.

Eating and shopping: merchant's shop selling Tudor pottery, based on finds at the house, pewterware, horn cups, glass, beeswax candles and books about the Tudors.

Making the most of your day: Tudor Family Fortunes game, costumes to try on and replica toys. Easter, Hallowe'en and Tudor-themed family events. **Dogs**: assistance dogs only.

Access for all: 🖼️📷♿👁️ Building 🐾

Getting here: 158:SN135004. In the centre of Tenby, between Tudor Square and Tenby harbour. **Foot**: finger posts direct from Tudor Square by Lifeboat Tavern, from Bridge Street and Crackwell Street. **Bus**: services from surrounding areas, drop off at town walls, ¼ mile. **Train**: Tenby ½ mile. **Parking**: very limited on-street parking within town walls. July to August: pay and display car parks only or park and ride (charge including members).

Finding out more: 01834 842279 or tudormerchantshouse@nationaltrust.org.uk

Tudor Merchant's House		M	T	W	T	F	S	S
9 Feb–17 Feb	11–3	M	T	W	T	F	S	S
23 Feb–24 Mar	11–3	·	·	·	·	·	S	S
25 Mar–21 Jul	11–5	M	·	W	T	F	S	S
22 Jul–1 Sep	11–5	M	T	W	T	F	S	S
2 Sep–3 Nov	11–5	M	·	W	T	F	S	S
9 Nov–29 Dec	11–3	·	·	·	·	·	S	S

Open Tuesdays of Bank Holiday weeks, 11 to 5. Open to 7 on Tuesdays and Wednesdays 23 July to 28 August.

Tŷ Mawr Wybrnant

Penmachno, Betws-y-Coed, Conwy LL25 0HJ

Map (**4**) E3

Set in the heart of the beautiful Conwy Valley, this traditional stone-built upland farmhouse is one of the most important houses in the history of the Welsh language, and was once the home of Bishop William Morgan. A gem definitely worthy of a visit.

Eating and shopping: picnics welcome.

Making the most of your day: introductory talks. Tudor kitchen garden and woodland walks. Exhibition room. Children's art packs, family activity sheets and woodland animal puzzle trail. **Dogs**: under close control.

Access for all: 🅿️📷♿ Building 🐾♿ Grounds ♿

Getting here: 115:SH770524. 2½ miles north-west of Penmachno, at head of the Wybrnant Valley. **Bus**: Llanrwst to Cwm Penmachno (passing Betws-y-Coed 🚌), alight Penmachno, 2 miles. **Train**: Pont-y-Pant 2½ miles. **Road**: from A5 6 miles south of Betws-y-Coed, take B4406 to Penmachno, then take forest road. **Parking**: free, 500 yards.

Finding out more: 01690 760213 or tymawrwybrnant@nationaltrust.org.uk

Tŷ Mawr Wybrnant		M	T	W	T	F	S	S
21 Mar–27 Oct	12–5	·	·	·	·	T	F	S	S

Open Bank Holiday Mondays.

Tŷ Mawr Wybrnant, Conwy: birthplace of Bishop Morgan

Northern Ireland

Enjoying the tranquil pleasures of
shimmering Lough Erne at Crom,
County Fermanagh

Outdoors in Northern Ireland

Above: cattle on White Park Bay, County Antrim

Famed for its outstanding natural beauty, Northern Ireland's landscape is remarkably diverse. The dramatic scenery ranges from the peaceful Fermanagh lakeland and drumlin landscape of Strangford Lough, to the bizarrely shaped basalt columns of the Giant's Causeway and the wild granite peaks of the Mourne Mountains. With many miles of beautiful coastline, huge stretches of countryside and panoramic views, we have a wealth of treasures for all to enjoy.

Wildly beautiful Down
Visit the wildly beautiful Strangford Lough, Britain's largest sea inlet and one of Europe's key wildlife habitats, and discover its tidal treasures. The rock pools brim with marine life and there is some of the best birdwatching in the British Isles. Or take a bracing coastal walk and spot delicate wild flowers as well as numerous varieties of butterflies.

Explore Slieve Donard and neighbouring Slieve Commedagh in the Mourne Mountains, and follow the intriguingly named Brandy Pad – an ancient smugglers' route which runs from the shore deep into the heart of the mountains.

Enjoy the circular walk to Port Kelly, Barhall Bay and Barhall Hill at Ballyquintin on the southern tip of the Ards Peninsula. Here you will find yourself surrounded by the Irish Sea, with views in every direction.

On the Irish Sea coast of the Ards Peninsula, a long narrow road runs through green drumlins to the sandy beach of Knockinelder and the charming village of Kearney, where a choice of attractive walks start at the little cluster of 14 cottages. Meanwhile the wilder Ballymacormick Point, with its gorse scrub, shingle beaches, rocky islets and coves, offers an escape from the crowds.

Glorious Antrim coast

For quiet relaxation, stroll along the spectacular sandy beach at White Park Bay. A beautiful white arc running between two headlands, this idyllic beach is backed by ancient dunes, which provide a range of rich habitats for birds, mammals and plants.

Set on a wonderful stretch of coastline on the Islandmagee Peninsula, Portmuck and Skernaghan Point offer spectacular views over Muck Island towards Scotland. This is a Site of Special Scientific Interest and has some of Northern Ireland's largest colonies of cliff-nesting seabirds.

Look out for the impressive 30-foot waterfall in a deep gorge in the small village of Glenoe. Or visit Cushendun, a charming historic village of immense character which has numerous folk tales associated with it. There is also a circular walking trail which boasts the most breathtaking scenery.

Above: **Murlough Bay, County Antrim**
Below: **Downhill Demesne, County Londonderry**

Murlough Bay and Fair Head is an idyllic corner of County Antrim. The sheer cliffs of Fair Head rise 600 feet above sea level (in fact it is Northern Ireland's tallest cliff face) and contrast strongly with the lush green slopes of Murlough Bay.

Rathlin is a peaceful and beautiful island with a distinctive landscape and way of life. The land at Ballyconagan is a mosaic of heaths, grasslands, mires and ponds, and offers fabulous walks and birdwatching.

City and country side by side
Close to the city yet at the same time in the heart of the
country – that's the paradox of Minnowburn. Riverbank,
meadow and woodland walks link the landmarks of Shaw's
Bridge and the Giant's Ring, while the Terrace Hill rose garden
has glorious views across the Lagan Valley.

Cregagh Glen and Lisnabreeny is an easily overlooked
haven in the heart of Belfast. Climb up alongside a tumbling
stream through mixed woodland and farmland, and you will
find magnificent views across Belfast Lough, Lagan Valley,
Strangford Lough and the Ards Peninsula.

Meanwhile, tucked away in the heart of West Belfast, between
Collin Hill and Black Mountain, is the wonderful Collin Glen.
Look out for the impressive carpets of bluebells in spring.

The mystery of mid-Ulster
The mixed woodland of Ballymoyer has the atmosphere and
mystery of a fairy glen. Surrounded by the wild and dramatic
scenery of the Fews Mountains, it was once the haunt of
robbers and highwaymen.

Tiny Coney Island in Lough Neagh is only 2.8 hectares (seven
acres) and it is believed there have been people here since
8000BC. Originally connected to the mainland by a causeway,
which can be easily seen in summer when it is under less than
two feet of water, the island is notable for its variety of bats.

Further information
Euro notes are accepted
by the Trust's Northern
Ireland places.

Under the Ulster Gardens
Scheme, a number of
private gardens are
generously opened to
the public to provide
income for Trust gardens
in Northern Ireland. For
the 2013 programme
telephone 028 9751 0721.

To find out what is
happening in Northern
Ireland this year, see our
2013 *Events Guide*.

Below: **strolling
in the grounds
of Castle Ward,
County Down**

Right: the view towards Portstewart, County Londonderry
Below: limpets and barnacles on the rocks at Portstewart Strand

Why not try...?

Exploring our great open spaces
With more than 120 miles of coastline and 40 square miles of scenic countryside in our care in Northern Ireland, we've got a world of outdoors waiting to be explored and enjoyed.

Walking or hiking
You don't have to be an expert to go walking, and we cater for a wide range of abilities and experience, offering everything from short circular routes to more challenging hill walks. With more than 35 accredited 'Quality Walks' across Northern Ireland (assessed by the Countryside Access and Activities Network, Northern Ireland Tourist Board and Northern Ireland Environment Agency), there's a walking trail to suit everyone.

For more information visit **www.walkni.com**

A two-wheel adventure
Hire a bike at Castle Ward and see parts of this lovely place that you would probably never venture to on foot. The cycle trails – which are about 12 miles long – run through atmospheric woodlands and around the boundary walls of Castle Ward demesne.

A wide range of bicycles is available for hire, including tandems and wheelchair tandem bicycles – unique in Northern Ireland.

Camping or caravanning
Our camping and touring sites are located in some of the most beautiful areas of Northern Ireland and are a great base from which to explore nearby Trust coast and countryside or built places. The camping and caravan park at Castle Ward, for example, is in a secluded location on the shores of Strangford Lough, while the breathtaking Crom demesne is set amid the romantic and tranquil landscape of Upper Lough Erne. Alternatively, experience the charming spirit of Springhill, with its walled garden and parklands, full of tempting paths and trails. So what are you waiting for – let's go outdoors!

In the farmyard at Ardress House, County Armagh

Ardress House

64 Ardress Road, Annaghmore, Portadown,
County Armagh BT62 1SQ

Map ⑦ D7

This charming 17th-century farmhouse,
elegantly remodelled in Georgian times, offers
fun and relaxation for all the family. Set in 40
hectares (100 acres) of countryside, there are
apple orchards, beautiful woodland and walks.
The atmosphere of a working farmyard has
been rekindled with the return of small animals.

Eating and shopping: drinks and ice-cream
available. Picnic in the garden or woodlands.

Making the most of your day: miniature
Shetland ponies, pygmy goats, Soay sheep,
ducks and chickens. Children's play area.
Events, including 'Keep it Country' and Apple
Press Day. **Dogs**: on leads in garden only.

Access for all: 🚾 ♿ Building 🏠 ♿
Grounds ♿ ➡

Getting here: H914561. Portadown 7 miles.
Bus: Portadown to Tullyroan Bridge (passing
close Portadown 🚆), to within ¼ mile.
Train: Portadown 7 miles. **Parking**: free,
10 yards.

Finding out more: 028 8778 4753 or
ardress@nationaltrust.org.uk

Ardress House		M	T	W	T	F	S	S
Farmyard and house								
16 Feb–19 Feb	12–5	M	T				S	S
16 Mar–30 Jun	1–6						S	S
29 Mar–7 Apr	1–6	M	T	W	T	F	S	S
4 Jul–31 Aug	1–6				T	F	S	S
1 Sep–29 Sep	1–6						S	S
Lady's Mile Walk								
Open all year	Dawn–dusk	M	T	W	T	F	S	S

House: admission by guided tour (last admission one hour
before closing). Open Bank Holiday Mondays and all other
public holidays in Northern Ireland.

The Argory

144 Derrycaw Road, Moy, Dungannon,
County Armagh BT71 6NA

Map (7) C7 ⊞✿♨▲⊤

Built in the 1820s, this handsome Irish gentry
house is surrounded by its 130-hectare
(320-acre) wooded riverside estate. The former
home of the MacGeough Bond family, a tour
of this Neo-classical masterpiece reveals it is
unchanged since 1900 – the eclectic interior
still evoking the family's tastes and interests.
Outside there are sweeping views, superb
spring bulbs, scenic walks, playground and
fascinating courtyard displays and exhibitions.

Eating and shopping: Courtyard Coffee Shop
serving light lunches and snacks. Gift shop and
second-hand bookshop, Blackwater Books.

In the garden, top, and looking at pictures in the
Organ Lobby, above, at The Argory

Making the most of your day: events, Including
children's, musical and general – such as craft
fairs. **Dogs**: on leads in grounds and garden only.

Access for all: ⊓♿⌷wc☺⦂⦂ Grounds ⌷♿⟶

Getting here: H871577. 4 miles from
Charlemont. **Cycle**: NCN95, 7 miles.
Bus: Portadown to Dungannon (passing close
Portadown ➔), alight Charlemont, 2½-mile
walk. **Road**: 3 miles from M1, exit 13 or 14.
Parking: 100 yards.

Finding out more: 028 8778 4753 or
argory@nationaltrust.org.uk

The Argory		M	T	W	T	F	S	S
Courtyard, coffee shop and shop								
2 Feb–24 Feb	12–5	·	·	·	·	·	S	S
18 Feb–19 Feb	12–5	M	T	·	·	·	·	·
House, courtyard, coffee shop and shop								
16 Mar–30 Jun	12–5	·	·	·	T	F	S	S
29 Mar–7 Apr	12–5	M	T	W	T	F	S	S
1 Jul–31 Aug	12–5	M	T	W	T	F	S	S
1 Sep–29 Sep	12–5	·	·	·	T	F	S	S
5 Oct–27 Oct	12–4	·	·	·	·	·	S	S
Grounds								
Open all year	10–5	M	T	W	T	F	S	S

Admission to house by guided tour (last tour one hour
before closing). Grounds open at 12 on event days.
Open Bank Holiday Mondays and all other public holidays
in Northern Ireland. Closed 25 and 26 December.

The Argory, County Armagh: the shimmering West Hall

www.nationaltrust.org.uk

Carrick-a-Rede

119a Whitepark Road, Ballintoy,
County Antrim BT54 6LS

Map (7) D3 🏖️⚓📷

Take the rope bridge to Carrick-a-Rede island
for a unique clifftop experience. This 30-metre
deep and 20-metre wide chasm is traversed by
a rope bridge traditionally erected by salmon
fishermen. Visitors bold enough to cross to
the rocky island, a Site of Special Scientific
Interest, are rewarded with fantastic views.
Note: maximum of eight people on bridge.

Eating and shopping: Weighbridge tea-room
and gift shop offering light lunches, snacks,
sweets, gifts and souvenirs.

Making the most of your day: coastal
path – part of the Causeway Coast Way from
Portstewart to Ballycastle and the Ulster Way.
Birdwatching and unrivalled coastal scenery,
plus unique flora and fauna. Guided tours
(by prior arrangement). Carrick-a-Rede holiday
cottage for a longer stay. **Dogs**: on leads
(not permitted to cross bridge).

Access for all: 🅿️♿🚻♿📷🔵
Grounds ♿♿➡️

Getting here: D049446. 5 miles from
Ballycastle, ½ mile from Ballintoy village.
Foot: North Antrim Coastal Path and road.
Cycle: NCN93. **Bus**: services from Coleraine
and Belfast. **Road**: on B15, 7 miles from
Bushmills and Giant's Causeway. **Parking**: free.

Finding out more: 028 2076 9839 or
carrickarede@nationaltrust.org.uk

Carrick-a-Rede		M	T	W	T	F	S	S
Bridge								
1 Jan–24 Feb	10:30–3:30	M	T	W	T	F	S	S
25 Feb–26 May	10–6	M	T	W	T	F	S	S
27 May–1 Sep	10–7	M	T	W	T	F	S	S
2 Sep–27 Oct	10–6	M	T	W	T	F	S	S
28 Oct–31 Dec	10:30–3:30	M	T	W	T	F	S	S

Last entry to rope bridge 45 minutes before closing. Car park
and North Antrim Coastal Path open all year. Bridge open
weather permitting. Closed 25 and 26 December.

Carrick-a-Rede, County Antrim: on the rope bridge

Two rocky islands off the coastline near Carrick-a-Rede on a calm, clear day

We welcome dogs assisting visitors with disabilities

Castle Coole

Enniskillen, County Fermanagh BT74 6JY

Map (7) A7

Stunning 18th-century mansion set in a beautiful wooded landscape park – which is ideal for family walks. Castle Coole is one of Ireland's finest Neo-classical houses: the sumptuous Regency interior and the State Bedroom prepared for George IV provide a rare treat for visitors, allowing them to glimpse what life was like in the home of the Earls of Belmore. The stories of the people who lived and worked below stairs are revealed as you explore the extensive basement.

Eating and shopping: Tallow tea-room and shop selling souvenirs and gifts.

Making the most of your day: musical events throughout year. Guided tours of historic basement. **Dogs**: on leads in grounds only.

Access for all: ⊞
Building ⊞ Grounds ⊞

Getting here: H245431. 1½ miles south-east of Enniskillen. **Cycle**: NCN91. **Bus**: Enniskillen to Clones (connections from Belfast).
Road: on Belfast to Enniskillen road (A4).
Parking: walkers' car park.
Main car park, 150 yards.

The sumptuous oval-shaped Saloon at Castle Coole, County Fermanagh

Finding out more: 028 6632 2690 or castlecoole@nationaltrust.org.uk

Castle Coole		M	T	W	T	F	S	S
Grounds								
1 Jan–28 Feb	10–4	M	T	W	T	F	S	S
1 Mar–31 Oct	10–7	M	T	W	T	F	S	S
1 Nov–31 Dec	10–4	M	T	W	T	F	S	S
House, tea-room and shop								
16 Mar–26 May	11–5						S	S
29 Mar–7 Apr	11–5	M	T	W	T	F	S	S
1 Jun–31 Aug	11–5	M	T	W	T	F	S	S
1 Sep–29 Sep	11–5						S	S

House: admission by guided tour (last tour one hour before closing). Open Bank Holiday Mondays and all other public holidays in Northern Ireland.

Castle Coole, Enniskillen: a fine Neo-classical house

www.nationaltrust.org.uk

Castle Ward, County Down: the classical side

Castle Ward

Strangford, Downpatrick,
County Down BT30 7LS

Map (7) F7

Sitting boldly on a rolling hillside overlooking Strangford Lough, the magnificent, eccentric 18th-century house oozes personality, boasting two very different styles of façade – one classical and the other Gothic. History meets re-creation throughout the 332-hectare (820-acre) walled demesne. A 16th-century tower-house stands firmly in the farmyard, while the working cornmill is a fine example of Irish industrial heritage, and the exotic garden and 21 miles of walking, cycling and equestrian trails through woodlands and along the shoreline are exceptional. An impressive laundry, tack room, children's Victorian play centre and adventure playground complete the picture.
Note: 1 March to 30 November visitor access to livestock grazing areas may be restricted.

Eating and shopping: Coach House café. Gift shop selling local produce and souvenirs. Second-hand bookshop.

Making the most of your day: bicycles for hire. Guided house tours. Farmyard with animals. Children's activities and Tracker Packs. Events, including Pirates' Picnic, Pumpkinfest, Book Fair and Santa's House. Caravan park and pods. **Dogs**: on leads in grounds only (livestock grazing areas out of bounds).

Access for all: ⬚⬚⬚⬚⬚⬚⬚⬚ ⬚⬚
Building ⬚⬚⬚ Grounds ⬚⬚➡

Getting here: J573484. 7 miles north-east of Downpatrick. **Foot**: on Lecale Way. **Ferry**: from Portaferry. **Bus**: Downpatrick to Strangford, bus stop at gates. Summer bus service weekends only. **Road**: 1 mile from Strangford on A25. **Sat Nav**: follow signs for Castle Ward only. **Parking**: free.

Finding out more: 028 4488 1204 or castleward@nationaltrust.org.uk

Castle Ward	M	T	W	T	F	S	S
Parkland, woodland and garden							
1 Jan–31 Mar	10–4	M	T	W	T	F	S	S
1 Apr–30 Sep	10–8	M	T	W	T	F	S	S
1 Oct–31 Oct	10–5	M	T	W	T	F	S	S
1 Nov–31 Dec	10–4	M	T	W	T	F	S	S
House, laundry and pastimes centre							
16 Mar–7 Apr	12–5	M	T	W	T	F	S	S
10 Apr–30 Jun	12–5			W	T	F	S	S
1 Jul–31 Aug	12–5	M	T	W	T	F	S	S
1 Sep–27 Oct	12–5						S	S
Coach House café, shop and second-hand bookshop							
5 Jan–10 Mar	12–4						S	S
16 Mar–7 Apr	12–5	M	T	W	T	F	S	S
10 Apr–30 Jun	12–5			W	T	F	S	S
1 Jul–31 Aug	12–5	M	T	W	T	F	S	S
1 Sep–22 Dec	12–4			W	T	F	S	S
Trailhead and refreshments							
1 Jul–1 Sep	12–5	M	T	W	T	F	S	S

Last admission to house is one hour before closing. Timed tickets apply to guided house tours. Open Bank Holiday Mondays and all other public holidays in Northern Ireland. The Barn is open throughout the year when primary schools are closed. The cornmill operates on Sundays from Easter to September, 2 to 5.

Why not visit us on foot or by public transport? See pages 6 and 374

Walking down an avenue at Castle Ward

Crom

Upper Lough Erne, Newtownbutler,
County Fermanagh BT92 8AP

Map ⑦ A8

Breathtaking 810-hectare (2,000-acre) demesne, set amid the romantic and tranquil landscape of Upper Lough Erne. One of Ireland's most important nature conservation areas, Crom's ancient woodland and picturesque islands are home to many rare species. Stay for longer at one of our holiday cottages or campsite. **Note**: castle not open to public.

Eating and shopping: afternoon tea, gifts and souvenirs available in visitor centre.

Making the most of your day: regular guided walks. Historic castle ruins. Cot trips (Bank Holiday Mondays). **Dogs**: on leads only.

Access for all: 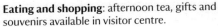 Building 🏠🚶
Grounds 🏞️➡️🚲

Getting here: H380255. 3 miles west of Newtownbutler. **Cycle**: NCN91. **Ferry**: from Derryvore church (must be booked 24 hours in advance). Crom is next to the Shannon to Erne waterway. Public jetty at visitor centre. **Bus**: Enniskillen to Clones (connections from Belfast), alight Newtownbutler, 3 miles. **Road**: on Newtownbutler to Crom road, or follow signs from Lisnaskea (7 miles). **Parking**: 100 yards.

Finding out more: 028 6773 8118 or crom@nationaltrust.org.uk

Crom		M	T	W	T	F	S	S
Grounds								
16 Mar–31 May	10–6	M	T	W	T	F	S	S
1 Jun–31 Aug	10–7	M	T	W	T	F	S	S
1 Sep–31 Oct	10–6	M	T	W	T	F	S	S
Visitor centre								
16 Mar–30 Sep	11–5	M	T	W	T	F	S	S
5 Oct–27 Oct	11–5	·	·	·	·	·	S	S

Open Bank Holiday Mondays and all other public holidays in Northern Ireland. Last admission one hour before closing. Tea-room open as visitor centre (closed October).

The Crown Bar

46 Great Victoria Street, Belfast, County Antrim BT2 7BA

Map ⑦ E6 🏠🍽️

Wonderfully ornate interior of brightly coloured tiles, carvings and glass, with period gas lighting and cosy snugs. **Note**: run by Mitchells and Butlers.

Finding out more: 028 9024 3187 or www.nationaltrust.org.uk

Lough Erne at Crom in County Fermanagh

Derrymore House

Bessbrook, Newry, County Armagh BT35 7EF

Map (7) D8

Elegant 18th-century thatched cottage with a peculiar gentrified vernacular style.
Note: no toilet.

Finding out more: 028 8778 4753 or www.nationaltrust.org.uk

Divis and the Black Mountain

Divis Road, Hannahstown, near Belfast, County Antrim BT17 0NG

Map (7) E6

The mountains rest in the heart of the Belfast Hills, which provide the backdrop to the city's skyline, while the rich, varied archaeological landscape is home to a host of wildlife. There are walking trails along a variety of terrain – through heath, on stone tracks, along boardwalks and road surface.
Note: cattle roam freely during summer months.

Eating and shopping: tea and coffee available in the Long Barn.

Making the most of your day: guided walks – themes are biodiversity and archaeology.
Dogs: welcome but please note cattle roam freely during summer.

Access for all: 🅿♿🚾♿🎵 Visitor centre ♿ Mountain ♿

Getting here: J266741. 1 mile west of Belfast.
Bus: alight Divis Road. **Road**: minor road west of A55. **Parking**: free.

Finding out more: 028 9082 5434 or divis@nationaltrust.org.uk

Divis and the Black Mountain	Open every day all year
Car park open 9 to 8.	

Wonderfully wild countryside at Divis and the Black Mountain, County Antrim, above and below

Downhill Demesne and Hezlett House

Mussenden Road, Castlerock,
County Londonderry BT51 4RP

Map (7) C3

Downhill Demesne has beautiful gardens and magnificent clifftop walks, affording rugged headland views across the awe-inspiring north coast. The striking 18th-century mansion of the eccentric Earl Bishop now lies in ruin, while Mussenden Temple sits perched on a cliff edge. As an extra treat visitors can learn about the reality of life in the rural 17th-century cottage of Hezlett House, one of Northern Ireland's oldest surviving buildings.

Eating and shopping: tea and coffee facilities. Picnics welcome in gardens.

Making the most of your day: events throughout year. Guided tours (booking essential). **Dogs**: on leads only.

Access for all: **Building** **Grounds**

Getting here: C757357. 1 mile west of Castlerock. **Cycle**: NCN93. **Ferry**: Magilligan to Greencastle ferry (8 miles). **Bus**: Coleraine to Londonderry. **Train**: Castlerock ½ mile. **Road**: 1 mile from Castlerock and 5 miles from Coleraine (A2). **Parking**: at Lion's Gate.

Finding out more: 028 7084 8728 or downhilldemesne@nationaltrust.org.uk. 107 Sea Road, Castlerock, County Londonderry BT51 4TW

Downhill and Hezlett		M	T	W	T	F	S	S
Hezlett House and facilities								
16 Mar–18 Mar	10–5	M	·	·	·	·	S	S
29 Mar–14 Apr	10–5	M	T	W	T	F	S	S
27 Apr–28 Apr	10–5	·	·	·	·	·	S	S
4 May–8 Sep	10–5	M	T	W	T	F	S	S
14 Sep–29 Sep	10–5	·	·	·	·	·	S	S
Downhill Demesne grounds								
Open all year	Dawn–dusk	M	T	W	T	F	S	S

Open Bank Holiday Mondays and all other public holidays in Northern Ireland. Closed 25 and 26 December.

Downhill Demesne and Hezlett House, County Londonderry: two views of Mussenden Temple, top and middle, and Hezlett House, above

Florence Court

Enniskillen, County Fermanagh BT92 1DB

Map ⑦ A7   🏠 ❀ 🎣 🛏 🔔 🍵 .

There is something for all the family at this warm and welcoming 18th-century property, the former home of the Earls of Enniskillen. The house enjoys a peaceful setting in West Fermanagh, with a dramatic backdrop of mountains and forests. This classical Irish house is brought to life on fascinating guided tours. Outside there are glorious walks to enjoy in the estate and numerous places to explore, including the ice house, sawmill and charming walled garden. Don't miss the Rock Hound Room, where children can enjoy activities based around the 3rd Earl's fossil collection.

Eating and shopping: Stables restaurant. Coach House gift shop.

Making the most of your day: events throughout year. Children's Tracker Packs. **Dogs**: on leads in garden and grounds only.

Access for all: 🅿️ 📷 ♿ 🚻 🔊 📷 ∶ 🏞️
Building 🔊♿🔊 Grounds ♿➡️🚃

Getting here: H176349. 8 miles south-west of Enniskillen. **Cycle**: NCN91. Entrance on Kingfisher Trail. **Bus**: Enniskillen to Swanlinbar, alight Creamery Cross, 2 miles. **Road**: by A4 Sligo road and A32 Swanlinbar road, 4 miles from Marble Arch Caves. **Parking**: 200 yards.

Finding out more: 028 6634 8249 or florencecourt@nationaltrust.org.uk

Florence Court		M	T	W	T	F	S	S
Gardens and park								
1 Jan–28 Feb	10–4	M	T	W	T	F	S	S
1 Mar–31 Oct	10–7	M	T	W	T	F	S	S
1 Nov–31 Dec	10–4	M	T	W	T	F	S	S
House, tea-room and shop								
16 Mar–28 Apr	11–5						S	S
29 Mar–7 Apr	11–5	M	T	W	T	F	S	S
1 May–30 May	11–5	M	T	W	T		S	S
1 Jun–31 Aug	11–5	M	T	W	T	F	S	S
1 Sep–30 Sep	11–5	M	T	W	T		S	S
5 Oct–27 Oct	11–5						S	S

House: admission by guided tour (last admission one hour before closing). Open Bank Holiday Mondays and all other public holidays in Northern Ireland. Open Irish Bank Holiday 28 October. Gardens and park, Colonel's Room, tea-room and gift shop also open 27 to 31 December.

Warm and welcoming Florence Court in County Fermanagh, offers something of interest to all the family

Giant's Causeway

44 Causeway Road, Bushmills,
County Antrim BT57 8SU

Map (7) D3

Northern Ireland's iconic World Heritage
Site and Area of Outstanding Natural Beauty
is home to a wealth of local history and
legend. The basalt stone columns were left by
volcanic eruptions 60 million years ago and
include distinctive stone formations fancifully
named the Camel, Harp and Organ. With the
development of a new world-class visitor centre
and upgraded walking trails, the site offers an
innovative and enhanced visitor experience.

The new world-class visitor facility at Giant's Causeway

Eating and shopping: light lunches and snacks
available. Gift shop.

Making the most of your day: interactive
exhibition brings the science and stories to
life. Outdoor audio guides unlock the secrets
of the landscape. Walks, including the coastal
path, which extends 11 miles to Carrick-a-Rede
Rope Bridge, and Runkerry Head two-mile
walk. Geology, flora and fauna of international
importance. **Dogs**: on leads only.

Access for all: 🅿️ 🚻 ♿ 🐕 📷 🅰️ 🔆 ♿

Grounds ♿ ♿ ➡️

Getting here: C944439. 2 miles from Bushmills.
Foot: Causeway Coast Way. **Cycle**: NCN93.
Bus: services from Coleraine and Belfast.
Train: from Belfast and Londonderry to
Coleraine or Portrush (onward via bus).
Road: on B146. **Parking**: three car parks
on site, plus park and ride at Bushmills.

Finding out more: 028 2073 1855 or
giantscauseway@nationaltrust.org.uk

Giant's Causeway		M	T	W	T	F	S	S
Stones and coastal path								
Open all year	Dawn–dusk	M	T	W	T	F	S	S
Visitor centre								
1 Jan–31 Jan	9–5	M	T	W	T	F	S	S
1 Feb–31 Mar	9–6	M	T	W	T	F	S	S
1 Apr–30 Jun	9–7	M	T	W	T	F	S	S
1 Jul–31 Aug	9–9	M	T	W	T	F	S	S
1 Sep–30 Sep	9–7	M	T	W	T	F	S	S
1 Oct–31 Oct	9–6	M	T	W	T	F	S	S
1 Nov–31 Dec	9–5	M	T	W	T	F	S	S

Last admission to visitor centre is one hour before closing.
Closed 24, 25 and 26 December.

The iconic Giant's Causeway, County Antrim

Gray's Printing Press

49 Main Street, Strabane,
County Tyrone BT82 8AU

Map (7) B5 🏠🚻

A treasure trove of galleys, ink and presses
hidden behind an 18th-century shop front
in the heart of Strabane.

Finding out more: 028 8674 8210
or www.nationaltrust.org.uk

Minnowburn

Edenderry Road, Belfast,
County Down BT8 8LD

Map (7) E6 🏛️🅿️♣️👪🚶

Minnowburn is a paradox, set in beautiful
countryside and yet just a couple of miles from
Belfast city centre. Nestled in the heart of
Lagan Valley Regional Park, it offers magnificent
woodland walks, one of the finest viewpoints
in South Belfast and tranquil riverbank trails
leading to the Giant's Ring. **Note**: no toilets.
Trails are uneven and steep in places.

Tranquil Minnowburn is close to Belfast's centre

Eating and shopping: Lock Keepers' Inn tea-
room (not National Trust) serving lunch and
tea. Terrace Hill Garden is perfect for picnics.

Making the most of your day: guided walks,
including heritage, history and woodlands.
Waymarked walks, including the Giant's Ring
Trail. Sculpture trail. **Dogs**: on leads only.

Getting here: NW445242. 3 miles from city
centre, south Belfast. **Foot**: Lagan Towpath
from Stramillis. **Cycle**: NCN9. **Bus**: services
from Europa bus centre, Belfast. **Road**: A55
ring road. At Shaw's Bridge, follow brown signs
to Minnowburn car park. **Parking**: free.

Finding out more: 028 9064 7787.
minnowburn@nationaltrust.org.uk or .
Minnowburn Wardens' Office, Ballynahatty
Road, Belfast, County Down BT8 8LE

Enjoying a picnic at Minnowburn, County Down

Minnowburn	M	T	W	T	F	S	S
Open every day all year	Dawn–dusk						

Mount Stewart House, Garden and Temple of the Winds

Portaferry Road, Newtownards,
County Down BT22 2AD

Map ⑦ F6 🏠✦🔔🗙

Mount Stewart is one of the most unique and unusual gardens that the Trust owns. It contains a rich tapestry of design and the great planting artistry that was the hallmark of Edith, Lady Londonderry. The mild climate of Strangford Lough allows astonishing levels of planting experimentation. The formal areas exude a strong Mediterranean feel and resemble an Italian villa landscape, while the wooded areas support a range of plants from all corners of the world – ensuring something to see whatever the season. Engaging tours of the opulent house reveal its fascinating heritage and historic world-famous artefacts and artwork. **Note**: house open during major conservation project.

Eating and shopping: shop selling local craft products. Plant shop. Award-winning Bay Restaurant. Mount Stewart ice-cream.

Making the most of your day: numerous events, including music in the garden, garden fête and Vehicles of Yesteryear. Guided walks and garden tours – gardens being re-created using diaries of Edith, Lady Londonderry. Children's events and Santa's grotto. Family activity packs.

The Shamrock Garden, top, and glorious colours on the lake, above, at Mount Stewart

Dogs: on leads in grounds and garden only.

Access for all: 🅿♿♿♿♿♿♿🏠♿
Building 🚻♿♿ Grounds 🚻♿➡♿♿

Getting here: J555694. 5 miles south-east of Newtownards. **Bus**: Belfast to Portaferry, alight at gates. **Train**: Bangor 10 miles. **Road**: on Newtownards to Portaferry road, A20, 15 miles south-east of Belfast. **Parking**: free, 100 yards.

Finding out more: 028 4278 8387 or mountstewart@nationaltrust.org.uk

Mount Stewart		M	T	W	T	F	S	S
Formal and lakeside gardens								
1 Jan–15 Mar	10–4	M	T	W	T	F	S	S
16 Mar–3 Nov	10–6	M	T	W	T	F	S	S
4 Nov–31 Dec	10–4	M	T	W	T	F	S	S
House								
16 Mar–3 Nov	12–5	M	T	W	T	F	S	S
Temple of the Winds								
17 Mar–3 Nov	2–5	·	·	·	·	·	·	S

House: admission by guided tour (timed tickets only) and free-flow on Bank and public holidays. Last admission to house and gardens one hour before closing. Open Bank Holiday Mondays and all other public holidays in Northern Ireland. Formal and lakeside gardens closed 25 and 26 December. Call for shop and restaurant opening times.

Octagonal hall at Mount Stewart House, County Down

Murlough National Nature Reserve

Keel Point, Dundrum, County Down BT33 0NQ

Map (7) E8

Murlough is an extraordinarily beautiful dune landscape, fringing one of Northern Ireland's most popular beaches and overlooked by the rounded peaks of the Mourne Mountains. The fragile 6,000-year-old sand dunes, Northern Ireland's first nature reserve, are an excellent area for walking and wildlife. **Note**: limited toilet facilities.

Finding out more: 028 4375 1467 or murlough@nationaltrust.org.uk

Murlough		M	T	W	T	F	S	S
Nature reserve								
Open all year		M	T	W	T	F	S	S
Facilities								
16 Mar–26 May	10–6	·	·	·	·	·	S	S
29 Mar–7 Apr	10–6	M	T	W	T	F	S	S
1 Jun–29 Sep	10–6	M	T	W	T	F	S	S
5 Oct–27 Oct	10–6	·	·	·	·	·	S	S

Open Bank Holiday Mondays and all other public holidays in Northern Ireland.

Murlough, County Down, with the Mourne Mountains

Eating and shopping: beach café. Picnics welcome on beach or in car park.

Making the most of your day: self-guided nature walk, series of guided walks, volunteer events and family activities throughout year. **Dogs**: welcome on leads, restrictions apply when ground-nesting birds are breeding or cattle are grazing.

Access for all:

Getting here: J401350. 1 mile south of Dundrum, 10 miles east of Downpatrick. **Foot**: from Dundrum, 1 mile, or Newcastle, 2-mile beach walk. **Cycle**: NCN99 passes entrance. **Bus**: Belfast to Newcastle, alight Lazy BJ Caravan Park (main entrance to reserve). **Road**: signposted off A2, between Dundrum and Newcastle. **Parking**: open all year.

Patterson's Spade Mill

751 Antrim Road, Templepatrick, County Antrim BT39 0AP

Map (7) E6

Visitors can hear the hammers, smell the forge and feel the heat of traditional spade-making in the last working water-driven spade mill in the British Isles. Guided tours vividly capture life during the Industrial Revolution and dig up the history and culture of the humble spade.

Eating and shopping: handcrafted spades on sale and made to specification. Tea and coffee available from drinks machine.

Hard at work at Patterson's Spade Mill, County Antrim

Making the most of your day: guided tours and demonstrations for all the family. **Dogs**: on leads only.

Access for all: 🅿️📱🚽📋 Building 🏛️♿

Grounds 🏛️

Getting here: J261854. 2 miles east of Templepatrick. **Bus**: services from Belfast to Cookstown, bus stop at gates. **Train**: Antrim 8 miles. **Road**: on Antrim to Belfast road, A6; M2 exit 4. **Parking**: free, 50 yards.

Finding out more: 028 9443 3619 or pattersons@nationaltrust.org.uk

Patterson's Spade Mill		M	T	W	T	F	S	S
29 Mar–7 Apr	12–4	M	T	W	T	F	S	S
13 Apr–26 May	12–4	·	·	·	·	·	S	S
1 Jun–31 Aug	12–4	M	T	W	·	·	S	S
1 Sep–29 Sep	12–4	·	·	·	·	·	S	S

Admission by guided tour (last admission one hour before closing). Open Bank Holiday Mondays and all other public holidays in Northern Ireland from 29 March to 30 September.

Portstewart Strand

118 Strand Road, Portstewart, County Londonderry BT55 7PG

Map ⑦ C3

This magnificent two-mile strand of glistening golden sand is one of Northern Ireland's finest and most popular beaches with all ages. It is the perfect spot to spend lazy summer days and take long walks exploring the sand dunes, which are a haven for wild flowers and butterflies.

Eating and shopping: beach toys and light refreshments available in visitor centre.

Making the most of your day: waymarked nature trail. Barmouth estuary bird hide. **Dogs**: on leads only.

Access for all: 🚽♿ Visitor centre 🏛️ Beach ➡️

Getting here: C811366. Just outside the centre of Portstewart. **Cycle**: NCN93 runs nearby. **Bus**: service from Coleraine (connections from Belfast route 218). **Train**: Coleraine. **Parking**: on beach.

Finding out more: 028 7083 6396 or portstewart@nationaltrust.org.uk

Portstewart Strand		M	T	W	T	F	S	S
Facilities								
29 Mar–5 May	10–5	M	T	W	T	F	S	S
6 May–31 May	10–6	M	T	W	T	F	S	S
1 Jun–1 Sep	10–7	M	T	W	T	F	S	S
2 Sep–29 Sep	10–6	M	T	W	T	F	S	S
Beach								
Open all year	Dawn–dusk	M	T	W	T	F	S	S

Barrier closes two hours after facilities close. Open Bank Holiday Mondays and all other public holidays in Northern Ireland. Closed 25 and 26 December. Facilities may be open at other times, weather permitting.

Tackling a climbing challenge at the popular beach of Portstewart Strand in County Londonderry

Rowallane Garden

Saintfield, County Down BT24 7LH

Map ⑦ E7 ❖ 🔔

Rowallane contains a treasure trove of exotic plants from around the world, intriguingly mixed into County Down's drumlins. It was created by Reverend John Moore in the mid-1860s, planting woodland and using interesting stone ornamentation to sculpt this informal landscape. His nephew, Hugh Armytage Moore, continued his work from 1903, mingling exotic species with native plants – giving the garden a dramatic atmosphere. All types of plant groups are represented. Trees, shrubs, herbaceous perennials and bulbs abound throughout the 21 hectares (52 acres), which includes a walled garden, rock garden, woodland and wildflower meadows.

Eating and shopping: new garden café. Second-hand bookshop. New garden shop.

Making the most of your day: events, including spring and autumn plant fair, Ghosts and Gourds and Yuletide market. Children's activity sheets. **Dogs**: on leads in garden only.

Getting here: J412581. 1 mile south of Saintfield, 11 miles south-east of Belfast. **Bus**: Belfast to Downpatrick (passing Belfast Great Victoria Street ▤). **Road**: on Downpatrick road (A7). **Parking**: free.

Finding out more: 028 9751 0131 or rowallane@nationaltrust.org.uk

Rowallane Garden		M	T	W	T	F	S	S
Garden								
1 Jan–28 Feb	10–4	M	T	W	T	F	S	S
1 Mar–30 Apr	10–6	M	T	W	T	F	S	S
1 May–31 Aug	10–8	M	T	W	T	F	S	S
1 Sep–31 Oct	10–6	M	T	W	T	F	S	S
1 Nov–31 Dec	10–4	M	T	W	T	F	S	S
Café and shop								
5 Jan–24 Feb	12–3	·	·	·	·	·	S	S
1 Mar–28 Mar	11–4	·	·	·	T	F	S	S
29 Mar–7 Apr	11–4	M	T	W	T	F	S	S
11 Apr–28 Apr	11–4	·	·	·	T	F	S	S
1 May–31 Aug	11–5	M	T	W	T	F	S	S
1 Sep–31 Oct	11–4	·	·	·	T	F	S	S
2 Nov–29 Dec	12–3	·	·	·	·	·	S	S

Café and shop open all Sundays from 12. Open Bank Holiday Mondays and all other public holidays in Northern Ireland. Closed 25 and 26 December.

Perfect autumn day at Rowallane Garden, County Down

Springhill

20 Springhill Road, Moneymore, Magherafelt, County Londonderry BT45 7NQ

Map ⑦ C6 🏛❖♿▲🔔☂

Charming 17th-century 'Plantation' home, with walled gardens and parkland, full of tempting waymarked paths. Informative tours breathe life into the fascinating past of this welcoming family home. There are ten generations of Lenox-Conyngham family tales to enthrall you, an intriguing link with the *Titanic* through a letter written on board, not forgetting the stories of one of Ireland's most-documented ghosts, Olivia. The old laundry houses the celebrated Costume Collection, which features some fine 18th- to 20th-century pieces that highlight its great appeal and enthralling past.

Springhill, County Londonderry: a 'Plantation' home

Eating and shopping: tea-room serving cream teas. Gift shop. Second-hand bookshop. Picnics welcome in garden.

Making the most of your day: guided tours and links with the world-famous ship, the *Titanic*. **Dogs**: on leads in grounds only.

Access for all: ⬚⬚⬚⬚⬚⬚
Building ⬚⬚

Getting here: H866828. 1 mile from Moneymore village. **Foot**: from Moneymore village, 1 mile. **Cycle**: NCN94/95, 5 miles. **Bus**: services from Belfast to Cookstown, alight Moneymore village, 1 mile. **Road**: on Moneymore to Coagh road, B18. **Parking**: 50 yards.

Finding out more: 028 8674 8210 or springhill@nationaltrust.org.uk

Springhill		M	T	W	T	F	S	S
Costume collection, tea-room and shop								
3 Feb–24 Feb	1–5	·	·	·	·	·	·	S
16 Feb–19 Feb	12–5	M	T	·	·	·	S	S
House, costume collection, tea-room and shop								
16 Mar–26 May	12–5	·	·	·	·	·	S	S
29 Mar–7 Apr	12–5	M	T	W	T	F	S	S
1 Jun–30 Jun	12–5	·	·	·	T	F	S	S
1 Jul–31 Aug	12–5	M	T	W	T	F	S	S
1 Sep–29 Sep	12–5	·	·	·	·	·	S	S
Grounds								
Open all year	10–5	M	T	W	T	F	S	S

House admission by guided tour (last admission one hour before closing). Grounds open at 1 on event days. Open Bank Holiday Mondays and all other public holidays in Northern Ireland. Closed 25 and 26 December.

Wellbrook Beetling Mill

20 Wellbrook Road, Corkhill, Cookstown, County Tyrone BT80 9RY

Map ⑦ C6

Set in an idyllic wooded glen with lovely walks and picnic spots, this, the last working water-powered linen beetling mill, offers a unique experience for all the family. You can try scutching, hackling and weaving as part of the hands-on demonstrations, set against the thundering cacophony of beetling engines.

Eating and shopping: tea and coffee available on request. Small cottage shop. Picnic tables near river.

Making the most of your day: mill tours cover history and linen-making processes. Walks up to the head-race. **Dogs**: on leads in grounds only.

Access for all: ⬚⬚⬚⬚ Building ⬚⬚
Grounds ⬚⬚

Getting here: H750792. 4 miles west of Cookstown. **Cycle**: NCN95. **Bus**: from Cookstown, with connections from Belfast, ½ mile. **Road**: ½ mile off Cookstown to Omagh road (A505): from Cookstown turn right at Kildress Church or follow Orritor Road (A53) to avoid the town. **Parking**: free, 10 yards.

Finding out more: 028 8675 1735 or wellbrook@nationaltrust.org.uk

Wellbrook Beetling Mill		M	T	W	T	F	S	S
16 Mar–30 Jun	2–5	·	·	·	·	·	S	S
29 Mar–7 Apr	2–5	M	T	W	T	F	S	S
4 Jul–31 Aug	2–5	·	·	·	T	F	S	S
1 Sep–29 Sep	2–5	·	·	·	·	·	S	S

Admission by guided tour. Open Bank Holiday Mondays and all other public holidays in Northern Ireland. Last admission one hour before closing.

Your visit

Welcoming families

Most places have baby-changing and baby-feeding areas – some also have parent and baby rooms. Restaurants and cafés have highchairs, children's menus and colouring sheets. Unfortunately it is usually difficult to accommodate prams and pushchairs inside historic houses, as they can impede other visitors and cause accidental damage, so you may be asked to leave them at the entrance.

Front-carrying slings for smaller babies and hip-seat carriers or reins for toddlers are often available to borrow. We welcome baby back-carriers wherever we can, although where space is limited (and at very busy times) it may not be possible to admit them.

Many places have guides, trails or quizzes for children and families, and some have special activity kits, such as Tracker Packs (bags packed with activities to do as you explore). These are free to borrow, although a deposit may be required. Many sites have discovery rooms and play areas. Obviously everyone is welcome to play in our gardens and parkland, although there may be restrictions due to conservation reasons or the time of year, such as the nesting season. Staff are happy to advise on the best areas to go to. Throughout the year there are things to get involved with, from spring lambing to autumn harvests. Visit **www. nationaltrust.org.uk/visit/ families/family-activities**

Eating and shopping

Every time you buy something in our shops, restaurants, tea-rooms and coffee shops, your purchase helps our work.

Shops: our many property-based shops offer a wide range of merchandise, much of which is exclusive to the National Trust. You can buy many Trust gifts online at **www.shop. nationaltrust.org.uk**

Restaurants and tea-rooms: we open about 150 tea-rooms and cafés – often in very special buildings, such as stable blocks or hothouses. Many offer special winter and Christmas food events.

Dogs

We always try to provide facilities such as water, areas where dogs can be exercised and shady spaces in car parks (though dogs should not be left in cars). Dogs are welcome at most countryside places, where they should be kept under close control at all times. Please observe local notices on the need to keep dogs on leads, particularly at sensitive times of year. Dogs should be kept on a short lead on access land between 1 March and 31 July, and always when near livestock.

In some areas, particularly on beaches, there may be restrictions, usually seasonal. Where access for dogs is restricted, we try to identify suitable alternative locations nearby.

Please clear up dog mess and dispose of it responsibly. Where dog-waste bins are not provided, please take the waste away with you.

Learning

We welcome visitors from across the educational sector and from special interest groups. We recommend that teachers make a preliminary visit, which can be arranged free of charge. Frequent visitors should consider Educational Group Membership. Visit **www.nationaltrust.org.uk/ membership/educational-group-memberships**

Doggy fun at Woolacombe, Devon

Events

We offer a variety of events throughout the year, from wildflower walks to family fun at Easter and Hallowe'en. There are live summer concerts, living history events, countryside open days and open-air theatre productions. Our lecture lunches and 'behind-the-scenes' tours explain the work of our gardeners and house staff, while our 'Conservation in Action' events provide opportunities for you to see conservation specialists at work and talk to them about their techniques. The year ends with Christmas craft fairs, carol concerts and winter walks.

For details visit **www. nationaltrust.org.uk/events**

Weddings and private functions

The bell and glass symbols at the top of entries indicate that the place is licensed for civil weddings (bell symbol) and/or available for private functions (glass symbol), such as wedding receptions and family celebrations.

Contact the place for more information or visit **www. nationaltrust.org.uk/hiring**

See our website or call supporter services on 0844 800 1895 for more information.

A wedding at Mount Stewart House and Garden, County Down

National Trust Holiday Collection

Want to holiday independently, with family and friends, or travel with like-minded people? The National Trust Holiday Collection has holidays to suit all tastes – from our own holiday cottages set in stunning locations (such as Nanceglos House, right, in Cornwall) and our hands-on working holidays, to a programme of cruises, escorted tours, activity holidays and short breaks operated by carefully selected tour operators. We also offer historic house hotels, bed and breakfasts run by our tenants and superbly situated camping and caravanning sites. Visit **www.nationaltrust.org.uk/ holidays**

Walk, cycle or drive

Walking

Long-distance walking routes, including 13 National Trails, link many Trust places, on top of a scenic web of local paths and access land.

- Hundreds of guided walks take place at our sites each year. Many places also offer waymarked trails, leaflets and maps.

- Hundreds of walks sheets are available free on the Trust website to download, print and take on your day out.

- Before setting out visit **www.nationaltrust.org.uk/walks** for a route map and description of our interesting walks.

Handbook entries give information on pedestrian access from the nearest town or railway station and details of routes passing through or nearby.

Opposite: **visitors at Ilam Park, White Peak Estate, Derbyshire** Below: **cycling fun at Clumber Park, Nottinghamshire**

Cycle hire venues

Onsite:
Blickling Estate, Norfolk (01263 738015)

Castle Ward, County Down, Northern Ireland (028 4372 3933)

Clumber Park, Nottinghamshire (01909 544911)

Dunstable Downs, Chilterns Gateway Centre and Whipsnade Estate, Bedfordshire (01582 500920)

Ickworth, Suffolk (01284 735350)

Llanerchaeron, Ceredigion, Wales (01545 573022)

Wicken Fen National Nature Reserve, Cambridgeshire (01353 720274)

Nearby:
Long Mynd, Shropshire (01694 720133)

Lydford Gorge, Devon (01837 861141)

Car-free days out

In support of car-free travel, many places offer incentives for visitors arriving without a car, such as a tea-room voucher. Visit **www.nationaltrust.org. uk/carfreedaysout**

Car parks

Visitors use car parks at Trust places entirely at their own risk. You are advised to secure your car and not to leave any valuable items. When walking in the car park, be aware of moving traffic. Parking in Trust car parks is free for members displaying current stickers, although a valid membership card should always be shown to a member of staff on request. Individual members' stickers cannot be used to gain free parking for coaches.

Car-parking sticker

Your car-parking sticker can be found on the inside front cover of this *Handbook*, lightly glued to a bookmark which can also be easily removed.

If you need a replacement or additional sticker, please ask a member of staff at the visitor reception on your next visit.

You will need to show your current membership card, which should continue to be shown to staff on request whenever you enter Trust places and pay and display car parks.

The sticker is not a substitute or alternative to a current membership card – it's just for use in pay and display car parks.

Your questions answered

Where can I take photographs? We welcome amateur photography out of doors at our places and – without flash (for visitor comfort, not conservation reasons) or tripods – indoors when houses are open, at the discretion of the Property/General Manager and where owners of loan items have granted permission.

The use of mobile phones with built-in cameras is similarly permitted indoors (again, no flash please). At most places special arrangements can be made for interested amateurs (as well as voluntary National Trust speakers, research students and academics) to take interior photographs by appointment outside normal opening hours. Requests to arrange a mutually convenient appointment must be made in writing to the place concerned, giving your address. This facility isn't offered everywhere and we may make an admission charge (including National Trust members).

All requests for commercial, non-editorial filming and photography need to go through the Broadcast and Media Manager (020 7799 4547).

Is there somewhere to leave large or bulky bags? You will be asked to leave large items of hand luggage at the house entrance. This is standard practice at museums and galleries worldwide to prevent accidental damage and to improve security.

The restriction includes rucksacks, large handbags, carrier (including open-topped) bags, bulky shoulder bags and camera/camcorder bags.

What types of footwear are restricted? Any heel which covers an area smaller than a postage stamp can cause irreparable damage to floors, carpets and rush matting. So sharp-heeled shoes aren't allowed. Overshoes may be provided and boot-scrapers and brushes are available for ridged-sole shoes, as well as plastic slippers for visitors with unsuitable, wet or muddy footwear.

What may I touch? We'd love you to be able to touch as much as possible, but many objects and surfaces are simply too fragile to be handled.

Volunteer room guides and staff will guide you on what can be touched. At some places you are welcome to play a piano or even try your hand at snooker.

Why is it dark inside some historic rooms? This is to slow down the deterioration of light-sensitive contents, especially textiles and watercolour paintings. We recommend that you allow time for your eyes to adapt to these darker conditions.

What happens during winter? Many historic houses offer special tours during the winter months, when house staff share the secrets of their traditional housekeeping practices and explain why we have to close many of our houses during at least part of the winter.

Why is it so cold inside some houses in winter? The heating systems in National Trust houses were not designed for the levels of domestic heating that we have become used to in our own homes.

We suggest that you dress warmly – just like our hardy staff and volunteers! – when you visit during the winter.

May I use my mobile? We'd be really grateful if you could turn off your mobile or put it on silent before going into one of our houses. Just as in a theatre, mobiles can really disrupt the atmosphere and detract from other people's experience.

Where may I sit down? We want you to be able to rest and relax, so we are increasing the seating in our houses and gardens. Room guides will be happy to show you where it is safe to sit.

Joining in with the Trust

As a charity we rely greatly upon additional support, beyond membership fees, to help us to protect and manage the coastline, countryside, historic buildings and gardens in our care. You can help us in several ways, such as making a donation or leaving a gift to us in your will, or by volunteering.

Volunteer with us

During 2011 we enjoyed the support of more than 62,000 volunteers, who together contributed a truly remarkable 3.6 million hours of combined effort in a hugely diverse range of roles – such as bringing our historic houses to life through room guiding and storytelling, tackling vital countryside conservation tasks, running workshops in schools and welcoming visitors of all ages to special events throughout the year. Volunteers are involved behind the scenes at our places too, working alongside staff on strategic projects and managing and training other volunteers. You could also enjoy a working holiday, join a supporter group (see below) or take part in our voluntary internship programme. We even have roles which families can take on together. By volunteering you could make new friends, gain work experience, use and develop your skills and see behind the scenes at our beautiful places. And with your help we'll make a real difference to those places, and to the people who love to visit them. Whatever your interests and motivations there's bound to be something to suit you – so if you'd like to get involved we'd love to hear from you. Contact your local place or visit **www.nationaltrust.org.uk/volunteering** or **www.nationaltrustjobs.org.uk/other_ways_in/internships**

Voluntary talks service

Enthusiastic and knowledgeable volunteer speakers are available to give illustrated talks to groups of all sizes. Subjects range from the Neptune Coastline Campaign to garden history, conservation, individual places and regional round-ups. Telephone 01793 817632.

Your local Trust supporter group

Getting together with people who feel passionate about the same things as you do is priceless. Sharing experiences and finding out more about the places you visit is just part of the pleasure of joining a local National Trust supporter group. You'll also enjoy learning from expert speakers, going on behind-the-scenes tours and taking holidays. Our supporter groups promote the National Trust within their local area and raise money through all kinds of events.

You could also join one of our local friends or advisory groups and develop a unique relationship with the place which is most special to you.

If you can see yourself in the great outdoors, a National Trust Volunteer Group could be the perfect choice for you. You might be constructing a footpath, building a fence or helping to restore natural coastal habitats, and you'll be in the company of a great bunch of like-minded people.

Supporter groups play a vital role in bringing our places to life for everyone to enjoy. To find out more visit **www.nationaltrust.org.uk/supportergroups**

Work, rest and play with a group of like-minded people

How you can support us

Gift Aid on Entry
The Gift Aid on Entry scheme gives non-members a choice between paying the standard admission price or paying the Gift Aid Admission, which includes a voluntary donation of at least 10 per cent.
Gift Aid Admissions enable the Trust to reclaim tax on the whole amount – currently an extra 25 per cent.

Gift Aid donations must be supported by a valid Gift Aid declaration, which can only cover donations made by an individual for themselves or for themselves and members of their family.

Admission prices are shown on our website, and are available from our Supporter Services Centre. Both the standard admission price and the Gift Aid Admission are displayed onsite and on our website. Telephone 0844 800 1895 for more information.

Donations and gifts
You can help us protect the special places in our care by donating to appeals, such as the work to reveal the fascinating industrial heritage at Quarry Bank Mill. Or perhaps you would like to give to the Lake District, or the coastline – the Neptune Coastline Campaign. Visit **www.nationaltrust.org.uk/donations**

Supporting the National Trust is an ideal way to remember someone you've loved, or to celebrate a special occasion. To find out more about our Commemorative

Giving Programme visit **www.nationaltrust.org.uk/tributegiving**

We also organise special programmes to enable donors to see at first hand the work they support, such as the Guardian, Benefactor, Patron and Quercus Supporter Programmes. Email enquiries@nationaltrust.org.uk or telephone 0844 800 1895.

Legacies
By leaving a gift for the National Trust in your Will you can look after the places you love, as well as the people, and provide a lasting gift for future generations. Every gift, whatever the size, will help us to safeguard permanently the places in our care across England, Wales and Northern Ireland. Legacy gifts are only spent on vital projects, endowments or acquisitions – never on overheads or administration. You can choose where you would like your gift to be directed – a place, region, or long-term campaign which means the most to you.

Find out more by requesting our legacies guide or attending a legacy event. Visit **www.nationaltrust.org.uk/legacies** or telephone our Supporter Services Centre on 0844 800 1895.

National Gardens Scheme
Each year many of the National Trust's gardens are opened in support of the National Gardens Scheme. If this is on a day when the garden is not usually open, National Trust members pay for entry.

All money raised goes to support nurses', caring and garden charities, including the National Trust Academy training scheme for gardeners. The Trust acknowledges with gratitude the generous and continuing support of the National Gardens Scheme Charitable Trust.

The Royal Oak Foundation
The Royal Oak Foundation inspires Americans to learn about, experience and support places of historic and natural significance in the UK in partnership with the National Trust. Through the generous, tax-deductible support of its members and donors across the US, Royal Oak makes grants that advance the Trust's mission. Royal Oak members receive free entry and parking at all properties, the Trust's magazine and Royal Oak's newsletter.

Royal Oak sponsors a national lecture series in the US that informs Americans about the Trust and related topics. Email general@royal-oak.org or see our website **www.royal-oak.org**

Art Fund
The National Trust is grateful to the Art Fund (**www.artfund.org**) for its continuing generous support in the acquisition of historic contents (a Brueghel painting for Nostell Priory and Seaton Delaval Hall are recent examples). We warmly welcome Art Fund members, who may visit places which have benefited directly, free of charge.

Have your say

Governance

A guide to the Trust's governance arrangements is available on our website **www.nationaltrust.org.uk/about-us** and on request from The Secretary.

Our Annual Report and Accounts are available online at **www.nationaltrust.org.uk/annualreport** or by email.

Please send the request to annualreport@nationaltrust.org.uk

Annual General Meeting

Every autumn we hold our Annual General Meeting (AGM). This event is for our members and gives you the opportunity to meet our Trustees and staff, and to help steer the organisation through contributing to debates and voting on resolutions.

The AGM is also a great opportunity for us to talk to you about the ways we work, to show you what's been happening over the past year and update you on our recent campaigns and appeals.

We send the formal papers for our AGM – including voting papers – with the autumn magazine. We hope you will consider attending this year's AGM. However, you don't need to come to the meeting to join in. You can follow the event and share your views with us by watching the live webcast (see **www.nationaltrust.org.uk/agm**). You can also let us know your views by returning your voting papers – or voting online – ahead of the meeting.

In addition, you have the opportunity to elect members of our Council. The Council is made up of 52 members, 26 elected by you and 26 appointed by organisations whose interests coincide in some way with those of the National Trust.

This mix of elected and appointed members appoints our Trustees and ensures that the Trust takes full account of the wider interests of the nation, for whose benefit it exists. The breadth of experience and perspective which this brings also enables the Council to act as the Trust's conscience in delivering its statutory purposes.

Privacy Policy

The National Trust's Privacy Policy sets out the ways in which we process personal data. The full Privacy Policy is available on our website **www.nationaltrust.org.uk** The National Trust makes every effort to comply with the principles of the Data Protection Act 1998.

Use made of personal information

Personal information provided to the National Trust via our website, membership forms, fundraising responses, emails and telephone calls will be used for the purposes outlined at the time of collection or registration in accordance with the preferences you express.

By providing personal data to the National Trust you consent to the processing of such data by the National Trust as described in the full Privacy Policy. You can alter your preferences as explained in the following paragraph.

Verifying, updating and amending your personal information

If, at any time, you want to verify, update or amend your personal data or preferences please write to:

National Trust,
Supporter Services Centre,
PO Box 574,
Manvers,
Rotherham,
S63 3FH.

Verification, updating or amendment of personal data will take place within 28 days of receipt of your request.

If subsequently you make a data protection instruction to the National Trust which contradicts a previous instruction (or instructions), then the Trust will follow your most recent instruction.

Subject access requests

You have the right to ask the National Trust, in writing, for a copy of all the personal data held about you (a 'subject access request') upon payment of a fee of £10.

To access your personal data held by the National Trust, please apply in writing to:

The Data Protection Officer,
National Trust,
Heelis, Kemble Drive,
Swindon,
Wiltshire,
SN2 2NA.

Your membership

Through your membership of the National Trust you not only have free access to visit more than 400 places listed in this *Handbook*, as many times as you like all year, and the right to park free of charge in Trust car parks on coast and countryside sites, but reassurance that your subscription forms a significant part of the financial bedrock of the Trust. As an independent registered charity this support is absolutely vital to us – thank you very much indeed.

Here are some important messages about your membership; please take a moment to read them.

– Membership of the National Trust allows you free parking in Trust car parks and free entry to most Trust places open to the public during normal opening times and under normal opening arrangements, provided you can present a current valid membership card.

– **Remember to display your current car-parking sticker.**

– **Please check that you have your card with you before you set out on your journey. Without it, we regret that you may not be admitted free of charge, nor will we subsequently be able to refund any admission charges.**

– Membership cards are **not transferable**.

– If your card is lost or stolen, please contact the Supporter Services Centre (address opposite) or telephone 0844 800 1895.

– A temporary card can be sent quickly to a holiday address or emailed to you.

– Members wishing to change from one category of life membership to another, or requiring information on pensioner membership, should contact the Supporter Services Centre for the scale of charges.

– In some instances an entry fee may apply. Additional charges may be made:

• when a special event is in progress;

• when we open specially for a National Gardens Scheme open day;

• where the management of a place is not under the National Trust's direct control, for example Tatton Park, Cheshire;

• where special attractions are additional and/or separate elements of the property, for example Steam Yacht Gondola in Cumbria, Dunster Watermill in Somerset, and the model farm and museum at Shugborough in Staffordshire;

• where special access conditions apply, for example The Beatles' Childhood Homes in Liverpool, where access is only by minibus from Speke Hall and Liverpool city centre, and all visitors (including Trust members) pay a fare for the minibus journey.

Reciprocal visiting

National Trust members enjoy reciprocal visiting arrangements with certain overseas National Trusts, including Australia, New Zealand, Barbados, Bermuda, Canada, Italy and – closer to home – Jersey and Guernsey. A similar arrangement is in place with the Manx Museum and National Trust on the Isle of Man (your current membership card is always needed). A full list is on our website and may be obtained from the Supporter Services Centre.

Entry to places owned by the Trust but maintained and administered by English Heritage or Cadw (Welsh Historic Monuments) is free to members of the Trust, English Heritage and Cadw.

National Trust for Scotland (NTS)

Members of the National Trust are also admitted free of charge to properties of the NTS, a separate charity with similar responsibilities. NTS places include the famous Inverewe Garden, Bannockburn, Culloden and Robert Adam's masterpiece, Culzean Castle. Full details are contained in *The National Trust for Scotland Guide to Properties* (£5, including post and packaging), obtained by contacting the NTS Customer Service Centre (0844 493 2100). Information is also available at **www.nts.org.uk**

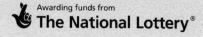
Tourist areas

For information on the properties below, please visit **www.nationaltrust.org.uk** and follow links to the new website.

North Devon
Arlington Court and the National Trust Carriage Museum
Bideford Bay and Hartland
Croyde, Woolacombe and Mortenhoe
Dunsland
Heddon Valley
Lundy
Watersmeet

Somerset Countryside
Brean Down
Cheddar Gorge
Fyne Court
Glastonbury Tor
Holnicote Estate
King John's Hunting Lodge
Mendip Hills

South Downs
Birling Gap and the Seven Sisters
Black Cap
Black Down
Cissbury Ring
Ditchling Beacon
Uppark House and Garden
Woolbeding Gardens

Isle of Wight
Bembridge and Culver Downs
Bembridge Windmill
Borthwood Copse
Chillerton Down
Compton Bay and Downs
Mottistone Estate
Mottistone Manor Garden
Newtown National Nature Reserve
St Catherine's Down and Knowles Farm
St Helens Duver
The Needles Headland and Tennyson Down
The Needles Old Battery and New Battery
Ventnor Downs

The Lake District
Acorn Bank Garden and Watermill
Arnside and Silverdale
Beatrix Potter Gallery
Borrowdale
Bridge House
Buttermere and Ennerdale
Cartmel Priory Gatehouse
Coniston and Tarn Hows
Dalton Castle
Fell Foot Park
Steam Yacht Gondola
Grasmere
Great Langdale
Hawkshead and Claife
Hill Top
Little Langdale

Isle of Wight — Sandscale Haws
Sizergh
Stagshaw Garden
Townend
Ullswater and Aira Force
Wasdale, Eskdale and Duddon
Windermere and Ambleside
Wordsworth House and Garden

Brecon Beacons
Abergwesyn Common
Central Beacons
Lanlay
Sugarloaf and Usk Valley
The Kymin

Snowdonia
Carneddau and Glyderau
Craflwyn and Beddgelert
Eifionydd
South Snowdonia
Tŷ Mawr Wybrnant
Ysbyty Ifan

Pembrokeshire
Abereiddi to Abermawr
Cilgerran Castle
Cleddau Woodlands
Colby Woodland Garden
Marloes Peninsula
Solva Coast
St David's Peninsula
Stackpole
Strumble Head to Cardigan
Tudor Merchant's House

Area maps

For clarity, the nine regions covered in this *Handbook* have been broken down into 12 areas on the maps (please see the key on the right). The seven maps show those places which have individual entries as well as many additional coast and countryside sites in the care of the National Trust.

In order to help with general orientation, the maps show main roads and population centres. However, the plotting of each site serves only as a guide to its location. Please note that some countryside places, for example those in the Lake District, cover many thousands of hectares. In such cases the symbol is placed centrally as an indication of general location.

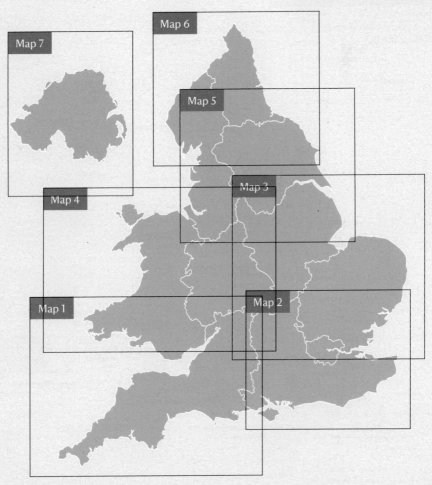

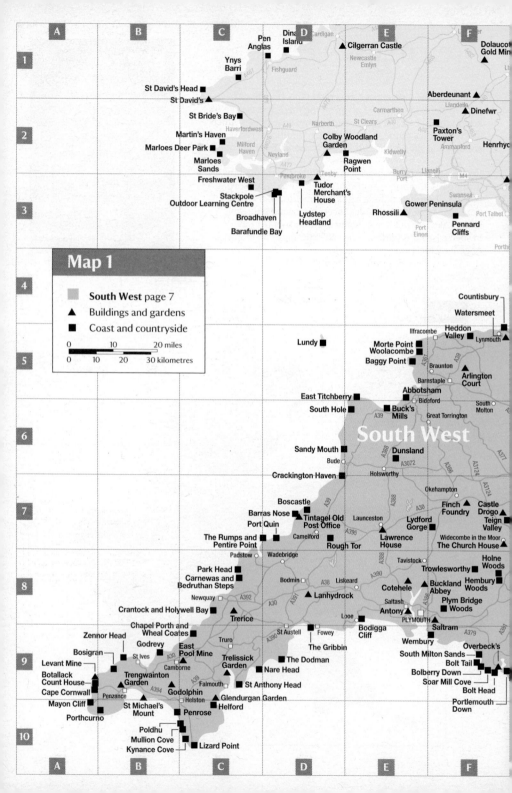

Map 1

South West page 7

▲ Buildings and gardens

■ Coast and countryside

0	10	20 miles
0	10	20	30 kilometres

South West

Grid labels: A B C D E F across top and bottom; 1–10 down left side

Pen Anglas
Dinas Island
Cardigan
▲ Cilgerran Castle
Newcastle Emlyn
Dolaucothi Gold Mine ▲

Ynys Barri ■
Fishguard

St David's Head ■
St David's ▲
Llandeilo
Aberdeunant ▲
▲ Dinefwr

St Bride's Bay ■
Haverfordwest
Narberth
St Clears
Carmarthen
Paxton's Tower ▲
Henrhyd

Martin's Haven ■
Milford Haven
Colby Woodland Garden ■
Kidwelly
Ammanford

Marloes Deer Park ■
Neyland

Marloes Sands ■
Ragwen Point ■

Freshwater West ■
Pembroke
Tenby
Tudor Merchant's House ▲
Burry Port
Llanelli
M4

Stackpole Outdoor Learning Centre ■
Lydstep Headland ■
Rhossili ▲
Gower Peninsula ■
Swansea
Port Talbot

Broadhaven ■
Pennard Cliffs ■
Port Einon

Barafundle Bay ■
Porthcawl

Countisbury ■
Watersmeet ■

Ilfracombe
Heddon Valley ■
Lynmouth ■

Lundy ■
Morte Point ■
Woolacombe ■
Baggy Point ■
Braunton
Arlington Court ▲

Barnstaple

East Titchberry ■
Abbotsham ■
Bideford
South Molton

South Hole ■
Buck's Mills ■
Great Torrington

Sandy Mouth ■
Dunsland ■
Bude
Holsworthy

Crackington Haven ■

Okehampton

Boscastle ■
Finch Foundry ▲
Castle Drogo ▲

Barras Nose ■
Tintagel Old Post Office ▲
Launceston
Lydford Gorge ■
Teign Valley

Port Quin ■

The Rumps and Pentire Point ■
Camelford
Rough Tor ■
Lawrence House ▲
Widecombe in the Moor
The Church House ▲

Padstow
Wadebridge

Park Head ■
Trowlesworthy ■
Holne Woods ■

Carnewas and Bedruthan Steps ■
Bodmin
Liskeard
Cotehele ▲
Buckland Abbey ▲
Hembury Woods ■

Newquay
Lanhydrock ▲
Saltash
Plym Bridge Woods ■

Crantock and Holywell Bay ■
Antony ▲
PLYMOUTH

Trerice ▲
Looe
Bodigga Cliff
Saltram ▲

Chapel Porth and Wheal Coates ■
Truro
St Austell
Fowey
Wembury ■
Overbeck's ▲

Zennor Head ■
Godrevy ■
The Gribbin ■
South Milton Sands ■
Bolt Tail ■

Bosigran ■
St Ives
East Pool Mine ▲
The Dodman ■
Bolberry Down ■

Levant Mine ■
Camborne
Trelissick Garden ▲
Nare Head ■
Soar Mill Cove ■
Bolt Head ■

Botallack Count House ■
Trengwainton Garden ▲
St Anthony Head ■
Portlemouth Down ■

Cape Cornwall ■
Penzance
Godolphin ▲
Falmouth

Mayon Cliff ■
St Michael's Mount ▲
Helston
Glendurgan Garden ▲
Helford

Porthcurno ■
Penrose ■

Poldhu ■
Mullion Cove ■
Kynance Cove ■
Lizard Point ■

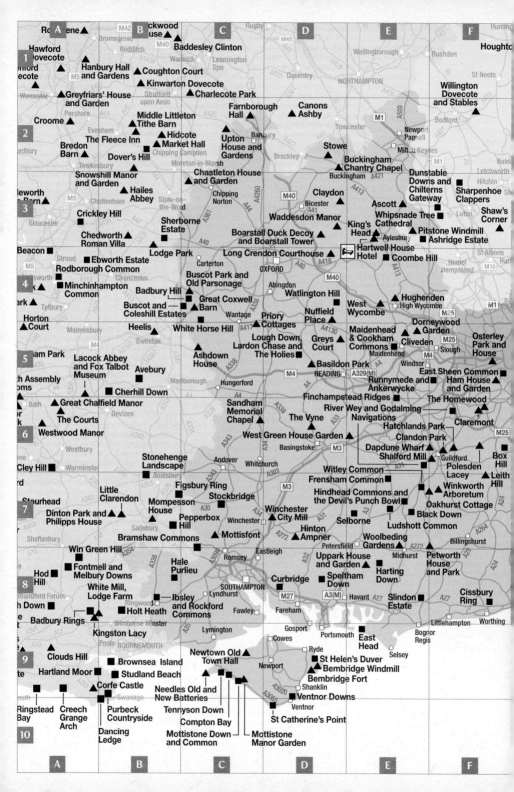

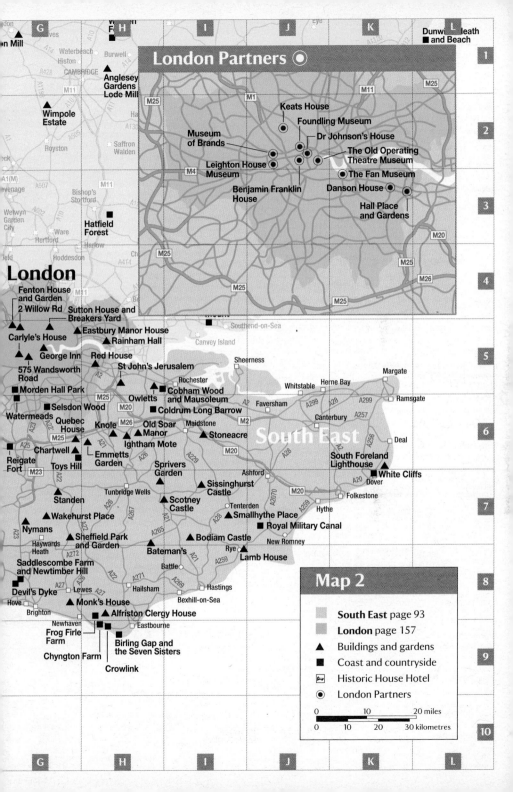

London Partners ⊙

Dunwich Heath and Beach ■

G
F
H
I
J
K
L

1

Waterbeach
Histon
Burwell
CAMBRIDGE
A14
A10
A14
M25
M11
M25

M11
M428
Anglesey Gardens Lode Mill ▲

Wimpole Estate ▲

M11

M25

Ha...
A130

Keats House ●
Foundling Museum ●

2

Royston
Saffron Walden

Museum of Brands ●
Dr Johnson's House ●

A1(M)
Stevenage
A507
Bishop's Stortford
M11
M4
Leighton House Museum ●
The Old Operating Theatre Museum ●

The Fan Museum ●

Welwyn Garden City
Ware
Hertford
Hatfield Forest ■
Harlow
Benjamin Franklin House
Danson House ●

3

Hall Place and Gardens

M20

field
Hoddesdon
A414
M25
M25

M25
M26

4

M25

M25

London

Fenton House and Garden
2 Willow Rd
Sutton House and Breakers Yard
Southend-on-Sea ■

5

Carlyle's House
Eastbury Manor House ▲
Rainham Hall ▲
Canvey Island

George Inn
Red House ▲
Sheerness

575 Wandsworth Road
St John's Jerusalem ▲
Margate

Morden Hall Park ■
Rochester
Whitstable
Herne Bay
Ramsgate

Selsdon Wood ■
Owletts ■
Cobham Wood and Mausoleum ■
Faversham
A299
A28
A299

Watermeads ■
Quebec House ■
M25
M26
Coldrum Long Barrow ▲
A2
Canterbury
A257
Deal

6

Knole ■
Old Soar Manor ▲
Maidstone
M2
A256

Chartwell ▲
Ightham Mote ▲
Stoneacre ▲
South East

Reigate Fort ■
M23
Toys Hill ■
Emmetts Garden ▲
Sprivers Garden ▲
Ashford
M20
Dover
South Foreland Lighthouse ■
White Cliffs ■

Standen ■
Sissinghurst Castle ▲
Folkestone

7

Wakehurst Place ▲
Tunbridge Wells
Scotney Castle ▲
Tenterden
Smallhythe Place ▲
Hythe

Nymans ▲
Haywards Heath
A272
Sheffield Park and Garden ▲
A28
Royal Military Canal ■

Saddlescombe Farm and Newtimber Hill ■
Bateman's ▲
Battle
New Romney
Lamb House ▲
Rye

8

Devil's Dyke ■
A27
Lewes
Hailsham
Hastings
Bexhill-on-Sea

Hove
Monk's House ■
Alfriston Clergy House ▲

Brighton
Newhaven
Eastbourne

Frog Firle Farm
Birling Gap and the Seven Sisters ■

Chyngton Farm

Crowlink

Map 2

■ **South East** page 93

■ **London** page 157

▲ Buildings and gardens

■ Coast and countryside

⌂ Historic House Hotel

⊙ London Partners

0 ——— 10 ——— 20 miles

0 —— 10 —— 20 —— 30 kilometres

9

10

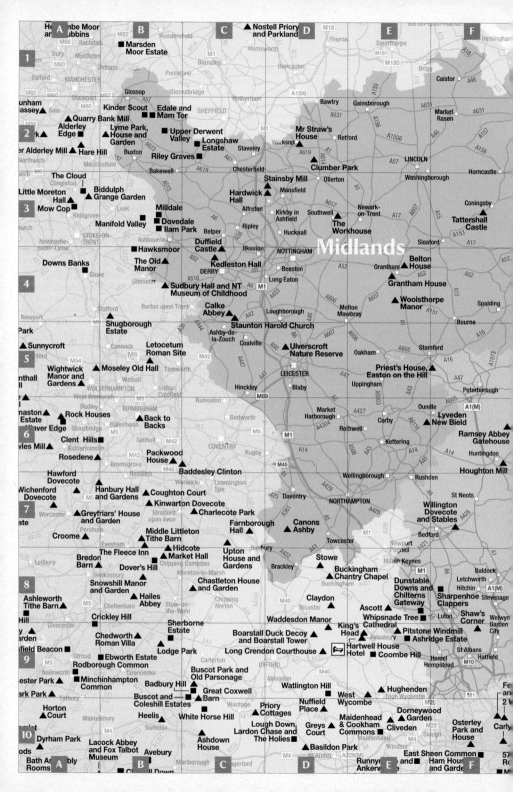

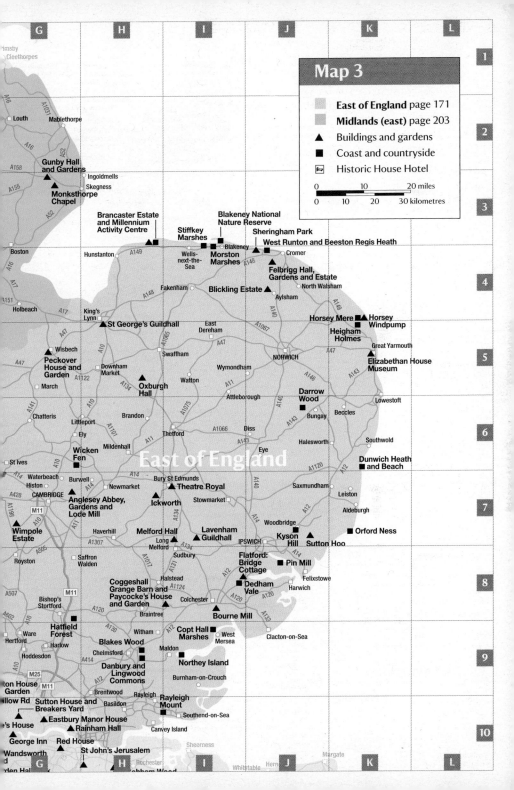

Map 3

- **East of England** page 171
- **Midlands (east)** page 203
- ▲ Buildings and gardens
- ■ Coast and countryside
- ⌂ Historic House Hotel

0   10   20 miles
0   10   20   30 kilometres

East of England

Grimsby
Cleethorpes
Louth
Mablethorpe
Ingoldmells
Skegness
Gunby Hall and Gardens
Monksthorpe Chapel
Boston
Holbeach
Hunstanton
Brancaster Estate and Millennium Activity Centre
Stiffkey Marshes
Wells-next-the-Sea
Morston Marshes
Blakeney
Blakeney National Nature Reserve
Sheringham Park
West Runton and Beeston Regis Heath
Cromer
Felbrigg Hall, Gardens and Estate
North Walsham
Aylsham
Blickling Estate
Fakenham
King's Lynn
St George's Guildhall
East Dereham
NORWICH
Horsey Mere ■▲ **Horsey Windpump**
Heigham Holmes
Great Yarmouth
Elizabethan House Museum
Wisbech
Peckover House and Garden
Downham Market
March
Swaffham
Watton
Wymondham
Attleborough
Oxburgh Hall
Darrow Wood
Lowestoft
Chatteris
Littleport
Ely
Brandon
Thetford
Diss
Bungay
Beccles
Mildenhall
Wicken Fen
Halesworth
Southwold
St Ives
Waterbeach
Burwell
Newmarket
Bury St Edmunds
Theatre Royal
Stowmarket
Saxmundham
Dunwich Heath and Beach
Histon
CAMBRIDGE
Anglesey Abbey, Gardens and Lode Mill
Ickworth
Leiston
Aldeburgh
Woodbridge
Wimpole Estate
Haverhill
Melford Hall
Long Melford
Lavenham Guildhall
IPSWICH
Kyson Hill
Sutton Hoo
■ **Orford Ness**
Royston
Saffron Walden
Sudbury
Flatford: Bridge Cottage
■ **Pin Mill**
Felixstowe
Halstead
Dedham Vale
Harwich
Coggeshall Grange Barn and Paycocke's House and Garden
Colchester
Bishop's Stortford
Braintree
Bourne Mill
Ware
Hertford
Hatfield Forest
Witham
Copt Hall Marshes
West Mersea
Clacton-on-Sea
Harlow
Blakes Wood
Chelmsford
Maldon
Hoddesdon
Danbury and Lingwood Commons
Northey Island
Burnham-on-Crouch
Brentwood
Rayleigh
Rayleigh Mount
Sutton House and Breakers Yard
Basildon
Southend-on-Sea
Eastbury Manor House
Rainham Hall
Canvey Island
George Inn
Red House
St John's Jerusalem
Wandsworth
Sheerness
Margate
Rochester
Whitstable

Map 4

Midlands (west) page 203

Wales page 325

▲ Buildings and gardens

■ Coast and countryside

⌂ Historic House Hotel

0   10   20 miles
0   10   20   30 kilometres

Wales

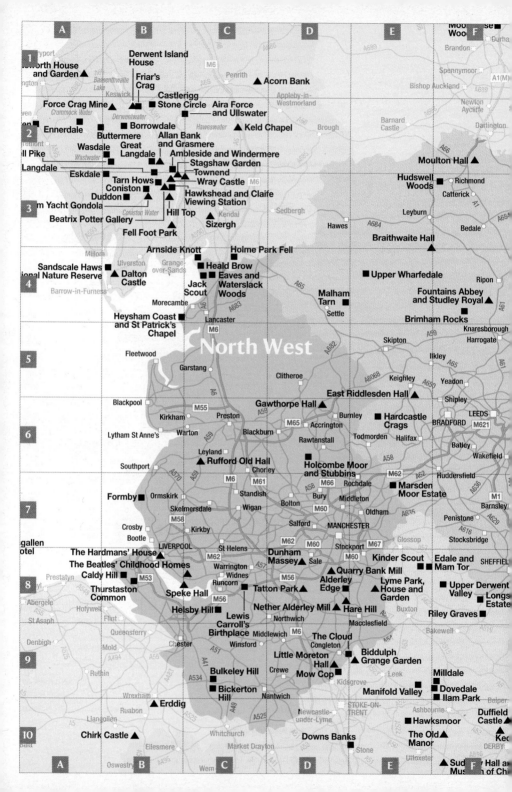

North West

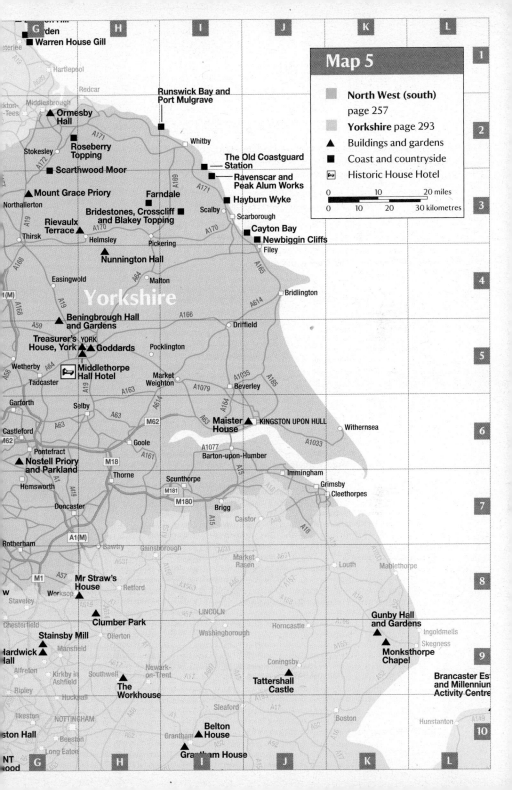

Map 5

North West (south)
page 257

Yorkshire page 293

▲ Buildings and gardens

■ Coast and countryside

⇦ Historic House Hotel

0   10   20 miles

0   10   20   30 kilometres

G H I J K L

1

2

3

4

5

6

7

8

9

10

den
■ Warren House Gill

eterlee

Hartlepool

kton-   Middlesbrough
-Tees   ▲ Ormesby
         Hall

Redcar

Runswick Bay and
Port Mulgrave

Stokesley   ■ Roseberry
            Topping

Whitby

The Old Coastguard
— Station

■ Scarthwood Moor

— Ravenscar and
   Peak Alum Works

▲ Mount Grace Priory

Northallerton

Farndale

■ Hayburn Wyke

Rievaulx
Terrace ▲

Bridestones, Crosscliff ■
and Blakey Topping

Scalby

Scarborough

Thirsk

Helmsley

Pickering

Cayton Bay
■ Newbiggin Cliffs

▲ Nunnington Hall

Filey

Easingwold

Malton

Bridlington

1(M)

Yorkshire

▲ Beningbrough Hall
   and Gardens

Driffield

Treasurer's   YORK
House, York ▲ ▲ Goddards

Pocklington

Wetherby

⇦ Middlethorpe
   Hall Hotel

Tadcaster

Market
Weighton

Beverley

Garforth

Selby

Castleford

Goole

Maister ▲
House

KINGSTON UPON HULL

Withernsea

Pontefract

Barton-upon-Humber

▲ Nostell Priory
   and Parkland

Thorne

Scunthorpe

Immingham

Grimsby

Hemsworth

Cleethorpes

Doncaster

Brigg

Caistor

Rotherham

A1(M)

Bawtry

Gainsborough

Market
Rasen

Louth

Mablethorpe

Mr Straw's
House

Retford

w   Worksop

Staveley

LINCOLN

Gunby Hall
and Gardens

Chesterfield

▲ Clumber Park

Washingborough

Horncastle

Ingoldmells

Skegness

Stainsby Mill

Ollerton

Monksthorpe
Chapel

Hardwick ▲
Hall

Mansfield

Coningsby

Brancaster Es
and Millenniun
Activity Centre

Kirkby in
Ashfield

Southwell

Newark-
on-Trent

The
Workhouse

Tattershall
Castle

Sleaford

Boston

Hunstanton

ilkeston   NOTTINGHAM

Belton ▲
House

ston Hall

Grantham

NT
ood

Grantham House

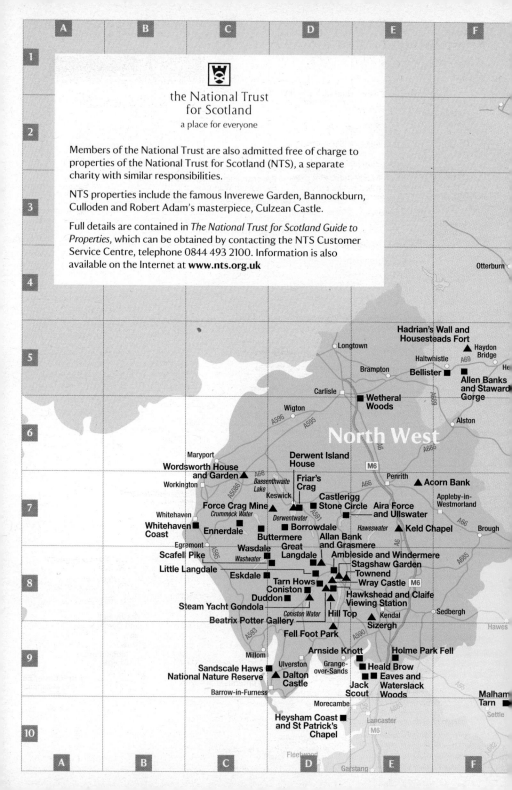

the National Trust for Scotland
a place for everyone

Members of the National Trust are also admitted free of charge to properties of the National Trust for Scotland (NTS), a separate charity with similar responsibilities.

NTS properties include the famous Inverewe Garden, Bannockburn, Culloden and Robert Adam's masterpiece, Culzean Castle.

Full details are contained in *The National Trust for Scotland Guide to Properties*, which can be obtained by contacting the NTS Customer Service Centre, telephone 0844 493 2100. Information is also available on the Internet at **www.nts.org.uk**

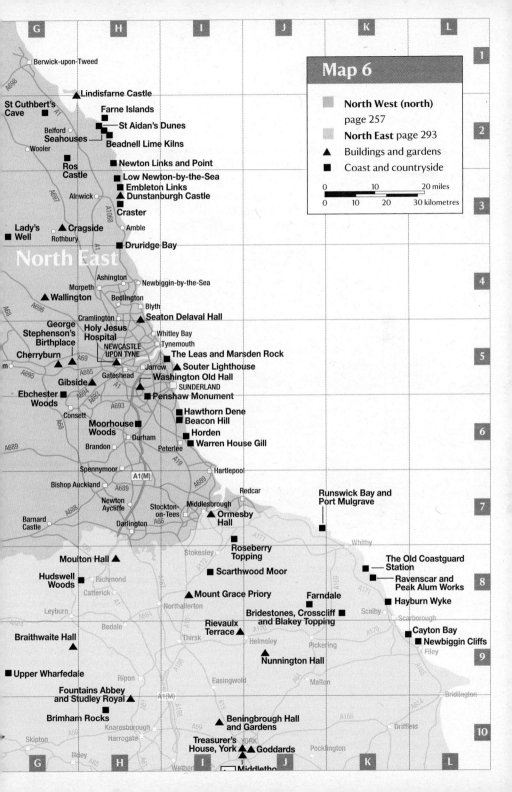

Map 6

North West (north)
page 257

North East page 293

▲ Buildings and gardens

■ Coast and countryside

0   10   20 miles
0 10 20 30 kilometres

Berwick-upon-Tweed

▲ Lindisfarne Castle

St Cuthbert's Cave ■

Farne Islands ■

Belford
Seahouses — ▲ St Aidan's Dunes

Wooler
■ Beadnell Lime Kilns

Ros Castle
■ Newton Links and Point

Alnwick
■ Low Newton-by-the-Sea
▲ Embleton Links
▲ Dunstanburgh Castle
■ Craster

Lady's ▲ Cragside
■ Well
Rothbury
Amble

■ Druridge Bay

North East

Ashington
Newbiggin-by-the-Sea

Morpeth
▲ Wallington

Bedlington
■ Blyth

Cramlington
▲ Seaton Delaval Hall

George Stephenson's Birthplace
Holy Jesus Hospital
Whitley Bay
Tynemouth

NEWCASTLE UPON TYNE

Cherryburn
▲ The Leas and Marsden Rock

Jarrow
▲ Souter Lighthouse

Gibside ▲
Gateshead
Washington Old Hall

Ebchester Woods
SUNDERLAND

Consett
■ Penshaw Monument

Moorhouse Woods ■
■ Hawthorn Dene
■ Beacon Hill

Brandon
Durham
■ Horden

Peterlee
■ Warren House Gill

Spennymoor
Hartlepool

Bishop Auckland
A1(M)

Newton Aycliffe
Redcar

Barnard Castle
Stockton-on-Tees
Middlesbrough
▲ Ormesby Hall

Darlington

Runswick Bay and Port Mulgrave ■

Moulton Hall ▲

Stokesley
■ Roseberry Topping

Whitby

Hudswell Woods
Richmond
■ Scarthwood Moor

The Old Coastguard Station ■
■ Ravenscar and Peak Alum Works

Catterick

▲ Mount Grace Priory
Farndale
■ Hayburn Wyke

Leyburn
Northallerton
Bridestones, Crosscliff ■
and Blakey Topping
Scalby

Bedale
Rievaulx Terrace ▲
Scarborough

Braithwaite Hall ▲
Thirsk
Helmsley
Pickering
■ Cayton Bay
■ Newbiggin Cliffs
Filey

■ Upper Wharfedale

Fountains Abbey and Studley Royal ▲
Ripon
Easingwold
Malton
Bridlington

Brimham Rocks ■

Knaresborough
A1(M)
▲ Beningbrough Hall and Gardens

Skipton
Harrogate
Driffield

Treasurer's House, York ▲▲ Goddards

Ilkley
YORK
Pocklington

Wether...
Middleth...

Map 7

Northern Ireland
page 351

▲ Buildings and gardens
■ Coast and countryside

0	10	20 miles
0	10 20	30 kilometres

Carrick-a-Rede and Larrybane

White Park Bay

Ballyconagan
Rathlin Island
■ The Manor House

North Antrim Cliff Path

Dunseverick Castle

Giant's Causeway

Portstewart Strand Portrush

Downhill Demesne ▲ ■■ Barmouth and
and Hezlett House   Grangemore Dunes Ballycastle

■ Fair Head and
Murlough Bay

■ Cushleake Mountain

Coleraine

■ Cushendun

A44

A2

A37 Ballymoney A26 Cushendall

Limavady

LONDONDERRY

Northern Ireland

Dungiven

A6

M2 A42

A43

Gray's
▲ Printing Press
Strabane

Maghera

Ballymena

A42 A26

A36 A2 Larne

Skernaghan
Point
■ Portmuck
Islandmagee

Newtownstewart

Magherafelt

Randalstown

Ballyclare

Glenoe ■ Whitehead

■ The Gobbins
■ Mullaghdoo
and Ballykeel

Castlederg

A5

A505

Moneymore

Wellbrook ▲
Beetling Mill

▲ Springhill

Cookstown

M22

Antrim

Patterson's
▲ Spade Mill Carrickfergus
M2 Newtownabbey
Holywood Bangor

■ Lighthouse
Island ■

Omagh

Coalisland

Divis and the
Black Mountain ▲
Crumlin

■ Ballymacormick Point
and Orlock Point
Newtownards

Dungannon

Coney Island ■

Collin Glen
Minnowburn
Lisburn

The Crown Bar ▲ BELFAST
■■■
Lisnabreeny

Comber

▲ Mount Stewart
House and Garden

The Argory ▲
Ardress House ▲

M1

Lurgan
Craigavon
Portadown
Tandragee

Carryduff

Rowallane ▲
Garden

■ Strangford
Lough

Enniskillen

▲ Castle Coole

A28

A3

Armagh

Dromore

Ballynahinch

Castle Ward
▲

■ Kearney and
Knockinelder

Lisnaskea

A34

Keady

Banbridge

Castlewellan A25

Ballyquintin
Farm

Florence
Court ▲

■ Crom

Ballymoyer ■

Rathfriland

A25

Downpatrick

Derrymore House ▲

Newcastle

■ Murlough Nature
Reserve

Newry

■ Slieve Donard

Warrenpoint Rostrevor

■ Mourne
Coastal Path

Crossmaglen

Kilkeel

■ Blockhouse and
Green Islands

Index

Places not in italics have an individual entry.
* Denotes properties shown only on maps.

Index   **395**

Getting in touch

The National Trust supports the National
Code of Practice for Visitor Attractions. We
are very willing to answer questions and
keen to receive comments. Many National
Trust places provide their own comment
cards and boxes. All your comments will be
read, considered and action taken where
necessary, but it is not possible to answer
every comment or suggestion individually.

Enquiries by telephone, email or in writing
should be made to the Trust's Supporter
Services Centre (see opposite), open seven days
a week (9 to 5:30 weekdays, 9 to 4 weekends
and Bank Holidays). (Our 0844 numbers are
charged at 5p per minute from BT landlines,
charges from mobiles and other operators may
vary.) You can also obtain information from our
website **www.nationaltrust.org.uk**

National Trust Supporter Services Centre
PO Box 574, Manvers, Rotherham S63 3FH.
0844 800 1895, 0844 800 4410 (minicom)

Email **enquiries@nationaltrust.org.uk** for all
general enquiries, including membership.

Central Office
The National Trust and National Trust
(Enterprises) Ltd, Heelis, Kemble Drive,
Swindon, Wiltshire SN2 2NA.
01793 817400, 01793 817401 (fax)

National Trust Holiday Cottages
0844 800 2072 (brochures)
0844 800 2070 (reservations)

To contact the Editor email
lucy.peel@nationaltrust.org.uk